Palgrave Studies in Prisons and Penology

This is a unique and innovative series, the first of its kind dedicated entirely to prison scholarship. At a historical point in which the prison population has reached an all-time high, the series seeks to analyse the form, nature and consequences of incarceration and related forms of punishment. Palgrave Studies in Prisons and Penology provides an important forum for burgeoning prison research across the world. 

More information about this series at
http://www.springer.com/series/14596

Tom Daems • Luc Robert
Editors

# Europe in Prisons

## Assessing the Impact of European Institutions on National Prison Systems

palgrave
macmillan

*Editors*
Tom Daems
Leuven Institute of Criminology (LINC)
KU Leuven
Leuven, Belgium

Luc Robert
National Institute of Forensic Sciences and Criminology (NICC)
Brussels, Belgium

Palgrave Studies in Prisons and Penology
ISBN 978-3-319-62249-1 ISBN 978-3-319-62250-7 (eBook)
DOI 10.1007/978-3-319-62250-7

Library of Congress Control Number: 2017947193



Cover illustration: OJO Images Ltd / Alamy Stock Photo

Printed on acid-free paper

This Palgrave Macmillan imprint is published by Springer Nature
The registered company is Springer International Publishing AG
The registered company address is: Gewerbestrasse 11, 6330 Cham, Switzerland

# Preface

This book grew out of a two-day workshop 'Europe in Prisons' which was organized in December 2015 at the Leuven Institute of Criminology (LINC), KU Leuven, Belgium. This workshop formed part of a two-year research project 'Degradation, civilization and denial: a European and comparative perspective on punishment' which was funded by the Research Council of KU Leuven. In this project we aimed to explore inter alia what kind of responses state authorities formulate to the judgments of the European Court of Human Rights and recommendations of the European Committee for the Prevention of Torture and Inhuman or Degrading Treatment or Punishment in relation to matters of prison policy and how such responses vary across European jurisdictions, more particularly in Belgium, Norway, Poland and Spain. In order to widen the geographical scope of the book, we decided to include additional chapters on Albania, Austria and Ireland.

We are grateful to the Research Council of KU Leuven for having provided financial support to organize the workshop. We also would like to thank the editors of *Palgrave Studies in Prisons and Penology* for welcoming this volume to the series and the editorial team at Palgrave (Stephanie Carey, Josie Taylor and Julia Willan) for their help and support. Finally, we wish to thank our contributing authors and the participants in the workshop for stimulating discussions and for helping us to produce this book at this particularly challenging moment in European history. Most of all, we are both grateful to our families, especially Eva (Tom's wife) and Lieve (Luc's wife), because of their patience and support when their partners were working late evenings and nights on this edited volume.

Tom Daems
Luc Robert

# Editorial Note

Throughout the edited volume, references to judgments by the European Court of Human Rights are mentioned in footnotes, not in the literature list at the end of each chapter. The same is done for domestic judgments and for judgments by the European Union Court of Justice. References to reports from the European Committee for the Prevention of Torture and Inhuman or Degrading Treatment or Punishment (CPT) and government responses are consistently referred to only in the text of each chapter in the format used by the CPT (e.g. CPT/Inf(2016)6). These reports are easily retrievable on the CPT website: http://www.coe.int/en/web/cpt/home.

Tom Daems and Luc Robert

# Contents

# List of Figures

# List of Tables

# Introduction: From Prisons in Europe to Europe in Prisons

Tom Daems and Luc Robert

European prison systems and the uses (and abuses) of pre-trial detention and deprivation of liberty as punishment have been given a great deal of attention in recent years. The study of imprisonment in Europe usually takes a more or less comparative approach, that is, the principal objective often is to document and analyse similarities and differences in terms of law, policy, penal rationalities, prison conditions, and so on. Typically a country-specific approach is being applied whereby (native) authors with a great deal of expertise about their respective prison system report and reflect upon the key characteristics and developments and, if possible, on how this national system fits within a broader penal system and relates to wider developments in society. One could call this a 'prisons in Europe' approach.

T. Daems (✉)
Leuven Institute of Criminology (LINC), KU Leuven, Leuven, Belgium

L. Robert
National Institute of Forensic Sciences and Criminology (NICC), Brussels, Belgium



T. Daems, L. Robert (eds.), *Europe in Prisons*, Palgrave Studies in Prisons and Penology, DOI 10.1007/978-3-319-62250-7_1

Such studies are very useful and we can learn a lot from them. Indeed, they often offer insight into the peculiar historical trajectories and contemporary challenges of prison systems throughout (and beyond) Europe (see e.g. Weiss and South 1998; van Zyl Smit and Dünkel 2001; Dünkel and Snacken 2005; Dünkel et al. 2010; Ruggiero and Ryan 2013). In this book, however, we adopt a somewhat different though ultimately complementary approach, that is, a 'Europe in prisons' perspective. Such an approach shifts scholarly attention to a different set of research questions: the focus moves from comparing prison systems to an exploration of the multiple ways in which 'Europe' penetrates prison systems. What has been the impact—if any—of major European institutions on prison policymaking and daily life in prisons throughout Europe? How have ideas been transferred from key European judicial and policymaking institutions and expert networks into local prison systems?

Most of the chapters in this book focus on one or both of the following European institutions: the European Court of Human Rights (ECtHR) and the European Committee for the Prevention of Torture and Inhuman or Degrading Treatment or Punishment (CPT). First, from a judicial perspective the ECtHR has come to set boundaries to what is acceptable in terms of inflicting punishment on offenders and the physical and social conditions in which sentences are executed. The ECtHR took up this role in particular in the wake of its landmark decision of *Golder v. UK* on 21 February 1975, where the Court rejected the up till that moment taken-for-granted theory of inherent limitations.[1] From then onwards limitations of prisoners' rights needed to be justified on the basis of the grounds that are listed in the European Convention itself; it could therefore no longer be assumed that inmates enjoy automatically—that is, because of the deprivation of their liberty—less protection than citizens who are not imprisoned (Smaers 1994). Over the past four decades judicial litigation by or on behalf of (ex-)prisoners before the European Court has grown exponentially (see e.g. van Zyl Smit and Snacken 2009, 2013; Tulkens 2014). In particular Articles 2 (right to life), 3 (prohibition of torture), 5 (right to liberty and security), 6 (right to a fair trial), and 8 (right to respect for private and family life) of the European Convention on Human Rights (ECHR) have been regularly invoked before the Court in Strasbourg. As a result, the Court now deals with a wide variety of issues, ranging from writing letters and family visits to strip searches, prison overcrowding, and failing health care for mentally ill offenders. The Court's judgments are obviously of direct interest for the parties involved in the case but they also affect all other inmates who fall within its jurisdiction, that is, on a daily basis, about 2 million detainees.

Second, from a preventive perspective, the CPT has become utterly important over the past quarter of a century. The CPT visits places of detention (prisons, police stations, centres for asylum seekers, etc.) in member states of the Council of Europe in order to monitor the treatment of persons who are deprived of their liberty. After each visit the CPT writes a report detailing its findings, recommendations, and requests for information which is then transmitted to the authorities of the visited member state. Every visit report is accompanied by an invitation for the state concerned to provide a detailed response to the findings and recommendations of the CPT. According to Article 10 of the Convention, every States Party is obliged to fully cooperate with the CPT. When a state fails to cooperate or refuses to improve the situation in the light of the CPT's recommendations, the Committee can pronounce a public statement in order to bring this failure to the attention of the international community. The CPT was, at the time when it became operational (in November 1989), a unique institution and it has, in many ways, been perceived as an example and forerunner for similar institutions across the globe, in particular for the United Nations Subcommittee on Prevention of Torture (SPT) which became operational in 2007 (Evans and Haenni-Dale 2004; Murray et al. 2011). As a monitoring body that is engaged in a continuing dialogue with European member states, the CPT has developed into a key player on the human rights scene (Evans and Morgan 1998; Morgan and Evans 1999; Murdoch 2006; De Lange 2008) as well as offering advice to and cooperating with the SPT, its United Nations sister committee which was created by the 2002 Optional Protocol to the UN Convention Against Torture (OPCAT) (Murray et al. 2011; Daems 2013). Like with the European Court also here the potential impact of its activities is not limited to the parties who are directly involved. Indeed, over the years, the CPT has developed (and continues to develop) a set of standards which are intended 'to give a clear advance indication to national authorities of its views regarding the manner in which persons deprived of their liberty ought to be treated and, more generally, to stimulate discussion on such matters' (CPT/Inf/E(2002)1-Rev. 2015: 5).

What has been the impact of such processes of Europeanization on prison policy in member states? Do judgments of the ECtHR and recommendations of the CPT trickle down to local prison systems? In recent years, interest in the role of European judicial and monitoring bodies—as well as related discussions on policy transfer, globalization, and cosmopolitanism—has grown slowly but steadily and sparked further debate about the distinctiveness of penology in Europe (Daems et al. 2013). These developments are particularly interesting because the *ius puniendi* has been for centuries a defining feature of the nation state. As Europe increasingly becomes a 'partner in punishment' such newer developments have invited scholars to reflect upon their 'methodological nationalism' (Beck 2005). In addition, there has been a great deal of normative reflection on what is happening in this field. From this angle the European inroad in the nation state's right to punish has come to be seen as a humanizing or civilizing force that embodies a mission to eradicate inhuman and degrading penal practices from the continent's penal institutions and practices. Europe, then, is understood as a normative power and instrumental in creating a regional human rights regime that brings penal enlightenment to all corners of Europe and that can be mobilized to resist punitive tendencies in member states' policies (Snacken 2010; Karstedt 2013).

The chapters in *Europe in Prisons* share a similar interest in the transnational and European influences on policymaking. However, it is striking how little we know about the impact of European institutions on prison systems. Notwithstanding such significant developments at a European level responsibility for prison policy is, ultimately, a domestic responsibility. It is up to national and local institutions and actors to comply with and translate European norms into practice or, alternatively, to contest, challenge, or ignore treaty obligations or recommendations (Daems 2017). But how does this process of implementation take place in practice? Are there variations in terms of compliance across Europe and, if so, how can we account for them?

These and related questions have inspired the authors writing for this book. In the first chapter, Christine Bicknell and Malcolm Evans tackle the increasingly complex institutional landscape of monitoring prisons. Already subject to regular monitoring visits by the CPT, the majority of Council of Europe Member States are now also States Parties to the UN OPCAT, which came into force in 2006. Accordingly, these States Parties may be subject to periodic visits by both the CPT and the UN SPT. Under OPCAT, States Parties must also designate or establish their own independent National Preventive Mechanisms, which undertake regular visits to all places of detention across the state. The result is that prisons in the majority of Council of Europe States now receive three levels of external scrutiny. The present chapter provides the background context, explaining the European Convention for the Prevention of Torture and OPCAT frameworks before exploring in greater detail the practical implications of this more complex area and in particular the relationships between the different monitoring bodies.

The second chapter deals with another key institution, that is, the ECtHR. Dia Anagnostou and Dimitris Skleparis explore the domestic implementation of the ECtHR judgments related to overcrowding and poor material conditions in European prisons. Their chapter provides an overview of the kind of claims reviewed by the ECtHR. First, they describe processes and mechanisms of domestic implementation of ECtHR's judgments, their supervision and monitoring by the Committee of Ministers, and the extent and the ways in which they can influence domestic reform of the penitentiary system. Next, based on a self-compiled data set of 165 adverse judgments by the ECtHR, an overview of the relevant ECtHR's judgments is provided, including the issues that those judgments raise, the states most frequently implicated, and the nature and range of measures that national authorities institute in response to Strasbourg Court's judgments that find violations of the Convention. Finally, the chapter describes and discusses the kind of reforms and measures that national authorities undertake by way of implementing the general measures that are called for by the relevant ECtHR judgments.

Next, Tom Vander Beken brings in an original view on monitoring. His chapter draws from a study of the role of prisons in Europe for which the research was undertaken by visiting prisons in six countries, as well as by reading, by observing, and by listening to those who could say something about those prisons. The aim of his chapter is twofold. On the one hand, the chapter comments on the methodological choices and consequences of a so-called prison tourism design. It is argued that, in spite of ethical challenges and intrinsic epistemological deficiencies, studying prisons and prison systems from a prison tourist perspective has the potential to provide unique and special information and can shed light on questions and themes that are not on the agenda of international monitoring bodies. On the other hand, the chapter summarizes some of the findings about the countries that have been visited and draws general conclusions about the study as a whole and reflects on the differences between prison tourist findings and what official international monitoring bodies report on.

From then on, chapters are included that zoom in on one or several countries. A first country-specific chapter deals with monitoring prisons in Albania. Brunilda Pali and Xhilda Vocaj first present descriptive information about Albania which has been awarded the status of EU candidate in 2014. They sketch the institutional situation of prison monitoring in Albania, with a specific focus on the CPT. Next, Pali and Vocaj set out to map the role of the CPT in relation to three core themes for Albania, beginning with ill-treatment and human rights violations, to then zoom in on overcrowding, pre-trial detention and other poor material conditions, and finally they focus on health-related concerns. Next to the CPT's influence, amidst national monitoring instances, their chapter also illustrates how countries that are not part of the EU may be influenced by EU policies generally and views on prisons and human rights specifically.

A second country-specific chapter deals with the CPT in Austria, one of the first countries visited by the CPT. Ursula Kriebaum provides a detailed description and analysis of the topics on which the CPT has focused during its six visits to Austria. The CPT's recommendations that relate to prison institutions as well as the Austrian government's reactions towards the recommendations are discussed. Furthermore, the chapter describes the creation and operation of the Human Rights Advisory Board which was competent among other subjects to deal with institutions under the jurisdiction of the ministry of the interior where human beings were deprived of their liberty. In the context of the Human Rights Advisory Board, six independent commissions had been created which were modelled after the CPT and which monitored the implementation of HR standards in all of these institutions. The current system which continues this model in an adapted form under the responsibility of the Austrian Ombudsman office is also being described. Kriebaum then concludes her chapter by discussing the impact of the CPT.

In the next chapter Tom Daems and Luc Robert assess how the CPT and the ECtHR have impacted upon prisons in Belgium. The chapter begins with an in-depth description of the CPT's visits to Belgium, with a particular focus on the most pressing issues the CPT has addressed in its reports and the reaction of the Belgian government to those observations and recommendations. Three areas are singled out: physical conditions in prisons, social conditions (including (the consequences of) industrial actions by prison officers), and safeguards against ill-treatment. Secondly, the focus is on the ECHR and the ECtHR. The chapter describes relevant judgments by the ECtHR involving mentally ill prisoners (internees) in Belgium. The evolutive case law of the ECtHR also serves as a reference for domestic courts when dealing with cases involving interned prisoners, which is discussed as well. In the last part of the chapter, the impact of both the CPT and the ECtHR on Belgian prisons are assessed. The picture that emerges is one of complexity and wide diversity in impact.

Next, Claire Hamilton broaches the question of Europe in Irish prisons. She sketches how the incorporation of the ECHR has been met with some complacency in Ireland, with tangible influence of European human rights norms and standards on some issues, including prisoner voting. According to Hamilton, Ireland can be regarded as more willing than its closest neighbour, the UK, to engage in a process of 'controlled liberalization' or tactical concession to forestall potential criticisms. Other areas of penal policy, such as the law and policy on parole, continue to highlight Ireland's resistance to European human rights norms. Her chapter shows how, somewhat counterintuitively, Ireland as a small jurisdiction has not always taken its cue in matters of penal policy from the European model.

Thomas Horn and Thomas Ugelvik then shed light on how Europe has entered prisons in Norway. Interestingly, they start by sketching the Norwegian self-perception and attitudes towards human rights and penal policy, with Norway as a 'self-styled humanitarian superpower'. This self-perceived status provides an interesting starting point when it comes to European human rights-based criticisms. They then go on to describe the influence of the ECHR which has become 'cemented' into the

Norwegian Constitution in 2014. Horn and Ugelvik discuss part of the philosophy behind prisons in Norway, which is in and by itself strongly linked to principles also important in European standards (such as normalization). Although there are as of yet no ECtHR cases of prisoners in Norway where violations have been found, Horn and Ugelvik raise doubts about whether this should be seen as proof for Norway's perfect respect of ECHR and other European standards. They also zoom in on the influence of CPT visits in Norway and focus on two particular cases in greater detail, the case of pre-trial solitary confinement and the country's single high-security immigration detention centre.

In the last country-specific chapter, José Cid and Ariadna Andreu focus on Spain. In their chapter, European prison policies serve as a yardstick for Spanish prison policies and practices over several time periods, beginning with Spain's transition to democracy after the death of Franco in 1975. They observe a 'radical transformation' of Spain's prison-related legislation and practices, including the introduction of alternatives to imprisonment, changes in the standards of prisoners' rights and quality of life in Spanish institutions and opportunities given to prisoners for rehabilitation and resettlement. Cid and Andreu explore to what extent these changes can be linked to the CPT's visits to Spain and to judgments of the ECtHR. Next, they also identify other aspects of Spanish penal practices that are less adapted to European policies, such as the increasing length of prison terms, that go against Recommendations of the Council of Europe, and explore a number of explanations for the remaining mismatch or gap between European prison policies and Spanish penal practices.

Jonas Visschers and Tom Daems then present the results of a comparative study that focuses on three countries: Norway, Poland, and Spain. The CPT, which celebrated its 25th anniversary in 2015, has become a major player on the European human rights scene. However, in recent years, the CPT has repeatedly complained about a lack of follow-up of its recommendations. In their chapter, Visschers and Daems zoom in on the CPT observations and recommendations related to the prison regime in Norway, Poland, and Spain and excavate the interplay (or lack thereof) between CPT comments and the authorities of these three countries in response to CPT remarks. The CPT has been critical of prison regime issues in all three countries and these have been followed by diverging governmental responses. Visschers and Daems use this comparative analysis to explore wider issues about the implementation gap with respect to the CPT's recommendations.

Finally, in a short concluding chapter, Tom Daems and Luc Robert raise a number of issues that emerge in this book. This includes, inter alia, the complexity to measure the impact of European institutions on domestic prison policy. Furthermore, while most of the chapters in the book have focused on the CPT and the ECtHR, they also draw attention to the growing importance of the European Union, and illustrate this by referring to a recent judgment by the European Union Court of Justice. Finally, Daems and Robert raise the open question about the future of Europe in prisons, especially given the recent events of the Brexit and elections that are planned in several major European countries.

## Notes

1. *Golder v. UK*, App. No. 4451/70 of 21 February 1975.

## Literature

Beck, U. 2005. *Power in the Global Age*. Cambridge: Polity Press.

Daems, T. 2013. Punishment and the Question of Europe. In *European Penology?* ed. T. Daems, D. van Zyl Smit, and S. Snacken. Oxford: Hart Publishing.

———. 2017. Slaves and Statues: Torture Prevention in Contemporary Europe. *British Journal of Criminology* 57 (3): 627–643.

Daems, T., D. van Zyl Smit, and S. Snacken, eds. 2013. *European Penology?* Oxford: Hart Publishing.

De Lange, J. 2008. *Detentie genormeerd*. Nijmegen: Wolf Legal Publishers.

Dünkel, F., T. Lappi-Seppälä, C. Morgenstern, and D. van Zyl Smit, eds. 2010. *Kriminalität, Kriminalpolitik, strafrechtliche Sanktionspraxis und Gefangenenraten im europäischen Vergleich*. Mönchengladbach: Forum Verlag.

Dünkel, F., and S. Snacken. 2005. *Les prisons en Europe*. Paris: L'Harmattan.

Evans, M.D., and C. Haenni-Dale. 2004. Preventing Torture? The Development of the Optional Protocol to the UN Convention Against Torture. *Human Rights Law Review* 4 (1): 19–55.

Evans, M.D., and R. Morgan. 1998. *Preventing Torture*. Oxford: Oxford University Press.
Karstedt, S. 2013. State Crime: The European Experience. In *The Routledge Handbook of European Criminology*, ed. S. Body-Gendrot, M. Hough, K. Kerezsi, R. Lévy, and S. Snacken. London: Routledge.
Morgan, R., and M.D. Evans, eds. 1999. *Protecting Prisoners*. Oxford: Oxford University Press.
Murdoch, J. 2006. *The Treatment of Prisoners. European Standards*. Strasbourg: Council of Europe Publishing.
Murray, R., E. Steinerte, M. Evans, and A. Hallo de Wolf. 2011. *The Optional Protocol to the UN Convention Against Torture*. Oxford: Oxford University Press.
Ruggiero, V., and M. Ryan, eds. 2013. *Punishment in Europe: A Critical Anatomy of Penal Systems*. Basingstoke: Palgrave Macmillan.
Smaers, G. 1994. *Gedetineerden en mensenrechten*. Antwerpen: Maklu.
Snacken, S. 2010. Resisting Punitiveness in Europe? *Theoretical Criminology* 14 (3): 273–292.
Tulkens, F. 2014. Les prisons en Europe. Les développements récents de la jurisprudence de la Cour européenne des droits de l'homme. *Déviance et société* 38 (4): 425–448.
Van Zyl Smit, D., and F. Dünkel, eds. 2001. *Imprisonment Today and Tomorrow: International Perspectives on Prisoners' Rights and Prison Conditions*. Leiden: Martinus Nijhoff.
Van Zyl Smit, D., and S. Snacken. 2009. *Principles of European Prison Law and Policy: Penology and Human Rights*. Oxford: Oxford University Press.
Van Zyl Smit, D., and S. Snacken. 2013. Distinctive Features of European Penology and Penal Policy-Making. In *European Penology?* ed. T. Daems, D. van Zyl Smit, and S. Snacken. Oxford: Hart Publishing.
Weiss, R.P., and N. South, eds. 1998. *Comparing Prison Systems: Toward a Comparative and International Penology*. Amsterdam: Gordon & Breach.

**Tom Daems** is Associate Professor of Criminology at the Leuven Institute of Criminology (LINC), KU Leuven, Belgium.

**Luc Robert** is a research fellow at the National Institute of Forensic Sciences and Criminology (NICC), Brussels, Belgium.

# Monitoring Prisons: The Increasingly Complex Relationship Between International and Domestic Frameworks

Christine Bicknell and Malcolm Evans

## 1 Introduction

The institutional landscape relating to the monitoring of prisons within Europe has become increasingly complex. The purpose of this chapter is to chart and consider some of the practical implications of the increased complexity of the international monitoring frameworks and the relationship(s) between them. The focus will be on the work of the Committee for the Prevention of Torture (CPT) established under the European Convention for the Prevention of Torture (ECPT) and of the bodies established within the framework of the Optional Protocol to the UN Convention against Torture (OPCAT), these being the UN Sub-Committee for the Prevention of Torture (SPT) and the National Preventive Mechanisms (NPMs), all of which will be briefly introduced

C. Bicknell (✉)
University of Exeter, Exeter, UK

M. Evans
University of Bristol, Bristol, UK



T. Daems, L. Robert (eds.), *Europe in Prisons*, Palgrave Studies in Prisons and Penology, DOI 10.1007/978-3-319-62250-7_2

below. There are, of course, a great number of other international bodies and agencies undertaking important work in this field.[1] However, the CPT, the SPT and the NPMs are unique conduits for the transmission of international standards into the domestic sphere and so provide an essential point of departure when considering the influence of European and international approaches on domestic practice within European states.

Moreover, the CPT, SPT and the NPMs work in a distinctive fashion: rather than focus on compliance with agreed standards or on regulatory processes, they are concerned with the *prevention* of ill-treatment in detention. Thus their work is centred on human rights issues rather than on compliance with more general operational and institutional issues relating to the functioning of penal institutions. Moreover, the work of these bodies is also unusual even from within a human rights-focused approach. Rather than being primarily concerned with compliance or accountability for breaches of human rights obligations, they are focused on measures that might be taken in order to ensure that ill-treatment does not occur, in the sense of detainees being treated in an inhuman or degrading fashion. As a result, these bodies are operating within a different paradigm than that traditionally employed by monitoring and inspectoral regimes, and as a result the mechanisms for securing compliance with the outcomes of their work ought also to be of a different nature. It is beyond the scope of this chapter to consider this aspect in any detail since its primary purpose is to outline the contours of the system which has been put in place by these international instruments and to consider how they reach into the domestic systems. The experience of their doing so will be considered in subsequent contributions to this volume which focus on the experience of particular States. What does need to be said at the outset, however, is that one of the litmus tests of the success of these mechanisms must surely be the extent to which they have been able to inculcate a similarly human rights-focused approach within domestic practice—and if the experience of the NPMs currently operating within Europe is anything to go by, there is still quite some way to go before this can be said to have been achieved.

## 2 The ECPT and the OPCAT Frameworks[2]

The ECPT was adopted in June 1987 in the midst of a welter of international institution-building relating to the prevention of torture and ill-treatment.[3] When it entered into force on 1 February 1989, the CPT was unique in having a mandate to undertake visits to all places of detention within States Parties without the need for prior consent. The OPCAT was adopted by the UN General Assembly in December 2002 and entered into force on 22 June 2006, and so for the last 10 years, the CPT has exercised its visiting mandate alongside that of the SPT at the international level and, increasingly, the NPMs established within the OPCAT framework at the national level. As a result, there is a much more complex operational environment in Europe for the CPT as an international body than when the ECPT was adopted almost 30 years ago.

The idea underpinning both instruments is that the risk of torture and ill-treatment can be lessened by visits of a preventive nature being undertaken by independent bodies to places where persons may be deprived of their liberty by, or with the acquiescence of, the public authorities.[4] As a result, States Parties are required to allow the CPT (under the ECPT, art. 2), the SPT (under the OPCAT, art. 4) and their designated NPM (also under the OPCAT, Part V, arts. 17–23) to visit any such place and have free access to them, and to those held there. Following their visits, the bodies are to produce reports containing appropriate recommendations which form the basis of an 'on-going dialogue' between the state and the Committee or NPM on their implementation (OPCAT, art. 16(1); ECPT, art. 10(1)). The reports of the CPT and SPT (but in most cases, not of the NPM) are confidential, but may be made public if the states to which they are addressed give their consent (OPCAT, art. 16(2); ECPT, art. 10(2)). In addition, the SPT has the specific mandate to advise and assist States Parties on the establishment of their NPM and to advise and assist both the state party and the NPM itself on the conduct of the NPM's work (OPCAT, art. 11(b)).[5] This is a very broad-brush description of the essential features of the two systems, but it is sufficient for the purpose of this chapter.[6]

When the ECPT was adopted in 1987, few would have foreseen how its reach would so rapidly extend across Europe. When it entered into force, the Convention bound only 8 of the then 23 member states of the Council of Europe, but a year later, in December 1990, it had been ratified by 19 of the Council's then 25 member states.[7] The political changes ushered in by the collapse of communism in Central and Eastern Europe and the Soviet Union opened up the prospect of further expansion,[8] and 10 years later the Council had already grown to 43 members, of which 41 were already parties to the ECPT.[9] Today the Council has 47 members, all of whom are also States Parties to the ECPT.

Turning to the OPCAT, although the precise numbers have fluctuated somewhat, European states have from the outset comprised approximately half of all States Parties. For example, at the end of 2015 there were 80 States Parties, of which 38 were from Europe—all of which were parties to the ECPT—18 from Africa, 15 from the Americas and 9 from Asia-Pacific (see SPT Ninth annual report, CAT/C/57/4, 22 March 2016: 3). Whilst this proportional predominance of ECPT States Parties within the OPCAT system will inevitably decline—at the time of writing (April 2016) only 9 such states are yet to ratify the OPCAT[10]—it remains highly likely that there will be many more States Parties from Europe than from any other single region for many years to come.

As has been mentioned, the OPCAT requires that all States Parties shall 'set up, designate or maintain at the domestic level one or several visiting bodies for the prevention of torture and other cruel, inhuman or degrading treatment or punishment' (OPCAT, art. 3). The NPM is to be established within 1 year of the OPCAT's entry into force.[11] By the end of 2015, 57 of the 76 States Parties which should have established their NPM by that date had officially notified the SPT of the designation of their NPM, whilst the establishment of 19 NPMs was officially overdue (see SPT Ninth annual report, CAT/C/57/4, 22 March 2016: 5). However, it is known that over 64 NPMs are currently in existence worldwide, and within the European region all OPCAT state parties have now established an NPM, with the exception of Bosnia-Herzegovina, although many did not do so within the stipulated timeframe.

NPMs are, of course, to be established and operate in accordance with the principles set out in the OPCAT but no one standard model or approach is suggested or used. Most European countries have adopted what has been termed the 'Ombudsman Plus' model, in which the NPM function has been given to an existing ombudsman's office, whose powers have been enlarged in order to invest it with the appropriate legal capacities to undertake the NPM mandate.[12] Not all have followed this path, however: some have designated an existing National Human Rights Institution as the NPM (e.g. Turkey), some have established new bodies to undertake the NPM functions (e.g. France and Switzerland), whilst others have assigned it to existing mechanisms and bodies, either with or without an overarching coordinating body (e.g. Malta (without a coordinating body) and the United Kingdom (with a coordinating body)).

Moreover, even as between NPMs which, at first sight, appear to be of a common nature there are in fact many points of difference. Within the dominant model of the 'Ombudsman Plus', there are many variations: in some the NPM function is assigned to a discrete internal office with its own independent leadership (e.g. Georgia and Serbia), in some the NPM forms a separate unit but functions under the direct managerial control of the Ombudsman (e.g. Sweden and Ukraine), whilst in others the NPM function is dispersed across the Office of the Ombudsman as a whole (e.g. Finland and Portugal). Some NPMs utilise civil society in their work, either directly (e.g. Denmark and Slovenia) or in the form of an advisory panel (e.g. Hungary). States with federal structures may have bodies operating at both a Federal and regional level in tandem (e.g. Austria and Germany), whereas states with a politically devolved structure may have separate bodies working in each (e.g. the United Kingdom), and so on. Once again, this adds considerably to the complexity of the interactions between the international and the domestic bodies, as each set of relationships depends on the nature of the domestic arrangements which have been put in place by the States Parties to the OPCAT. Naturally, these can—and do—vary considerably, as do the various foci of their work, and hence of their contribution to prevention of ill-treatment in prisons. Those who owe their origins to inspectorates are, perhaps, more adept at grasping the nature of a preventive visit and preventive mandate than some of those which are grounded in the investigative and complaints-based methodologies of Ombudsman's offices.

# 3 The 'Triangular Relationship' Between the CPT, the SPT and NPMs

The relationship between the CPT, the SPT and the NPMs has aptly been described as 'triangular', linking as it does three mechanisms engaged in preventive visiting across the regional, international and national divides.[13] Whilst this provides a useful framework for analytical purposes, and will be used here to illustrate the nature of the relationships, it has to be remembered that there is in fact no such thing as 'an' NPM: each NPM is a distinct entity in its own right and with its own complexities. As a result, it is difficult to be prescriptive about the nature of the relationship between these bodies and how they can (or might) cohere in the abstract: there are, in fact, a web of relationships of greater or lesser intensity between the CPT, SPT and some 37 European NPMs.[14] An exploration of all of these relationships is well beyond the scope of this chapter. Nevertheless, the essential contours of the relationship between these preventive bodies can be traced and will be considered below. To that end, the following sections will sketch the formal relationship that exists based on the texts of the legal instruments and briefly consider a range of practical issues concerning key issues, including visits, guidance to NPMs, standards, working methodologies and the overarching issue of how to achieve cooperation whilst working confidentially.

## 3.1 The CPT and the SPT

When the ECPT was drafted there was no other international human rights body with a preventive visiting mandate. It is, then, perhaps unsurprising that there is little in the text concerning engagement with others working in the field of torture and torture prevention.[15] Inevitably, the OPCAT is very different, given that the ECPT was not only in existence when it was adopted but that during its drafting the very need for its applicability, and relevance, to those states which were already party to the ECPT was called into question.[16] As a result, OPCAT art. 31 addresses the relationship in a direct fashion, providing that:

> The provisions of this present Protocol shall not affect the obligations of States Parties under any regional convention instituting a system of visits to

> places of detention. The Subcommittee on Prevention and the bodies established under such regional conventions are encouraged to consult and cooperate with a view to avoiding duplication and promoting effectively the objectives of the present Protocol.[17]

There is, then, an express recognition of the desirability of not duplicating each other's work. Given that by the time the OPCAT entered into force the CPT was already actively engaged in visiting many of its States Parties, what does this mean in practice?

At one level, it could mean that the SPT ought to step back from visiting those states which are routinely visited by the CPT and not visit them *at all.* In its early years, this was the position in practice. With the exception of a visit to Sweden in its first year of operation (2007), and which was determined on the basis of drawing lots, the SPT did not formally undertake a visit to any European country until 2011, when it visited Ukraine. Since then, it has undertaken visits to Council of Europe countries more frequently each year, but so far these have all been focused on the work of the NPMs, rather than on visiting places of detention as such. So whilst the SPT has not refrained from visiting, it has clearly chosen to focus its visits on elements of its mandate which reduce the scope for duplication of activities by concentrating on work relating to NPMs. Even this, however, requires a degree of coordination to avoid both the SPT and CPT undertaking visits, albeit of different natures, more or less simultaneously within the same country.[18]

It is doubtful where more could usefully be done to reduce the risk of duplication. It must be remembered that a visit from a UN mechanism produces outcomes which can feed into the work of other UN mechanisms and processes in a way which material generated by a regional body cannot. It is also important that international mechanisms work in a truly international context, both to avoid questions of partiality and bias and, more positively, in order to ensure that there is proper learning from the experience and practice in all parts of the world. Rather more prosaically, an SPT which ignored half of its States Parties in order to focus its efforts on the other half would simply lack credibility within the global community. Total abstention from such 'duplication' is not a realistic long-term option.

It is more helpful, therefore, to think in terms of achieving a degree of coordination so as to avoid 'getting in each other's way'.[19] It is fairly obvious that it would be unhelpful for both the SPT and the CPT to be visiting the same country at the same time. What is not so obvious is that it may be equally unhelpful for one body to be visiting at a time when the state may have just received a report from the other, and is considering its response. Confusing matters in this way would be best avoided. Yet the process of dialogue arising out of a visit is lengthy[20] and, in the case of the CPT, will blur into the conduct of a subsequent visit within a few years.[21] It is impossible to avoid the problem of parallel dialogues arising from visits, even when some considerable time has elapsed between those visits. As a result, the best that can be done is to avoid visits taking place in too close a proximity to each other; though even this can be more difficult than it sounds. Both the SPT and CPT make their decisions within complex factual and practical matrices and which must also reflect the work of other bodies operating within their respective international organisations. Against that background, ensuring that the CPT and SPT 'keep out of each other's way' may not be a particularly compelling factor.[22] Moreover, the deliberations of each are confidential and the timings of decision making may mean that the relevant information is just not yet there to share.[23] Nevertheless, these considerations tend to support, not undermine, the case for the CPT and SPT engaging with each other, whilst, of course, respecting the principles of confidentiality. But how is this to be done?

This question must not be approached in an overly theoretical fashion. In the early years following the establishment of the SPT, this was easy enough since four of the ten original SPT members were either serving or former members of the CPT[24] and the first Chair of the SPT had until her election been President of the CPT.[25] From the outset, then, there was a high degree of interconnection between the CPT and SPT. This was not only at the level of the members. In its formative years a member of the CPT secretariat was seconded to the SPT secretariat and experts who accompanied some of the first SPT visits had also worked in various capacities with and for the CPT.[26] At the time of writing, one member of the CPT is also a member of the SPT, another is a former member, some have considerable experience as experts on CPT visits whilst others have long academic and practical knowledge of both systems. There is, then, a wealth of common knowledge and practical connection.

At the same time, the impact of this must not be overstated. Each body works within its own organisational structures which have their own practical dynamics and consequences. Although the CPT and SPT do invite representatives to each other's meetings from time to time,[27] these are largely formal encounters which, whilst valuable, do not really provide an opportunity to probe substantive and practical issues.[28] More useful, in practice, are the frequent informal meetings which take place in the context of the many conferences and seminars on torture and torture prevention which members and secretariat of both bodies routinely attend.

Nevertheless, the rather loose relationship means that there is the potential for disjuncture regarding the ways in which the CPT and SPT work. Much more importantly, however, is that there is also the potential for disjuncture between the standards which they advance and the particular recommendations which they make. These issues were discussed at length at a major conference in Strasbourg in 2009[29]—tellingly, convened by the CPT, with SPT members attending as invitees—and it is instructive to quote from the Foreword to the Conference Proceedings, in which the conveners observed:

> With more actors on the stage, there is a greater need for coordination and to share information about what each body is doing, how they are going about their tasks and what they are finding. It is also important that preventive bodies do not develop contradictory and diverging standards but instead ensure a degree of coherence. (Thomson and Stevens 2010: 7–8)

The very point of a preventive approach is to suggest to states what they ought to do in order to try to reduce the likelihood of a breach of the substantive standard occurring, and it is easy to see that suggesting different preventive strategies or priorities might be problematic. Alternatively this could be viewed as an opportunity, an advantage even. When faced with the same problem, there may be two or more possible solutions and having these set out in recommendations would arguably present the state with more options and ways of addressing whatever the matter.

Nevertheless, this is not the dominant view. As is well known, the CPT has set out its standards in some detail and over a considerable period of time.[30] The question is whether this could be undermined by the SPT setting out different standards.

In practice, the SPT has gone a long way to mitigate this risk by consciously deciding not to set out formal statements of standards in the same way. Rather, it has taken the view that '…there is no logical limit to the range of issues that, if explored, might have a preventive impact'[31] and, as a result, there is no need to be limited to the application of a given set of 'standards' as such.[32] As a result, the guiding principle behind the SPT's approach is that:

> …there is more to the prevention of torture and ill-treatment than compliance with legal commitments. In this sense, the prevention of torture and ill-treatment embraces—or should embrace—as many as possible of those things which in a given situation can contribute towards the lessening of the likelihood or risk of torture or ill-treatment occurring. Such an approach requires not only that there be compliance with relevant international obligations and standards in both form and substance but that attention also be paid to the whole range of other factors relevant to the experience and treatment of persons deprived of their liberty and which by their very nature will be context specific.[33]

By taking this approach, it has been possible to avoid becoming ensnared in discussion of applicable standards and to focus on crafting recommendations which are relevant to the particular situation in hand, inspired by as many sets of standards as it seems appropriate to consult and draw inspiration from. Thus the SPT has not gone down the road of setting out formal statements of standards.

Rather, it has said that '…it is appropriate to focus on those issues which, in the light both of its visit to the State party in question and its more general experience, appear to it to be most pressing, relevant and realizable'.[34] It has to be admitted that there is a degree of disingenuousness about this since, at the end of the day, there has to be some reference back to what might be thought to be the most appropriate response to a situation, and it cannot all be context driven, not least because the international framework provides an element of that context.

Nevertheless, at a formal level, and since there is no shortage of standards, the SPT's approach is not to endorse or replicate the standards articulated by others but to focus on what using such standards in a preventive fashion might mean in practice. For current purposes, this means that there is, at least in the near future, no need for the CPT to be concerned about the SPT propagating 'rival' standards to its own. That said, it ought to be alert to the nature and focus of SPT recommendations as these will certainly convey a flavour of its thinking as regards what it believes to be of significance. Moreover, the SPT has gone so far as setting out in its Annual Reports its 'approach' to a variety of substantive issues.[35] Whilst not statements of standards per se, these serve a not dissimilar function insofar as they are a guide to the way in which the SPT may respond to situations it encounters and as to how it might expect to see others—such as NPMs—responding to similar situations.

## 3.2 The SPT and the NPMs

Turning now to the NPMs, the OPCAT obliges the SPT to undertake a broad range of tasks in relation both to their establishment by the States Parties and, once established, to their day-to-day operational activities. Indeed, the OPCAT envisages something of another 'triangular' relationship, this time between the SPT, NPM and State party. NPMs have '… the right to have contacts with the Subcommittee on Prevention, to send it information and to meet with it' (OPCAT art. 20(d)). This is the counterpart to art. 11(b)(ii) of the OPCAT which mandates the Subcommittee to '…maintain direct, if necessary confidential, contact with the national preventive mechanisms'. The web of relationships is then completed by art. 12 (c), under which the States Parties undertake to '…encourage and facilitate contacts between the Subcommittee on Prevention and the national preventive mechanisms'. There should, therefore, be a fluid and on-going set of relationships between them. .

To this end, the SPT has issued *Guidelines on National Preventive Mechanisms* which concern both the process by which the NPM is to be identified and established, how it is to be supported and engaged with by the State and how the NPM ought to operate in order to fulfil its OPCAT obligations (SPT fourth Annual Report, CAT/C/46/2, 3 February 2011, paras 63–102). In addition, the SPT has produced various other tools to assist NPMs in their work.[36] Perhaps most importantly, in 2012 the SPT inaugurated the concept of 'NPM advisory Visits', these being short visits focused on the work of the NPM in the country visited, exploring how it undertakes its functions and any difficulties faced.[37] At the end of such visits the SPT currently issues two confidential reports, one to the NPM itself, the other to the State Party, concerning the work and functioning of the NPM. In 2015 the SPT further developed this idea by inaugurating short visits to countries which were yet to establish an effective operational NPM.[38]

It is a matter of record that the decision to establish NPM Advisory visits was based on the experience gained under a project established by the Council of Europe and European Union, the 'European NPM Project' which ran from 2009–2011 and which included short visits to a number of NPMs within the Council of Europe area. NPM Advisory visits enable the SPT to undertake visits within the European area which do not directly overlap with those undertaken by the CPT and which also focus on matters—the establishment and operation of the NPMs—which formally speaking are clearly within its mandate rather than within that of the CPT. The SPT has further developed its work with NPMs by establishing Regional Teams[39] which focus on the work of the NPMs at each SPT session, meeting with them as often as possible and issuing guidance to them in response to questions which they might ask the SPT in order to assist them in their work.

The relationship between the SPT and NPMs is not, however, limited to one of oversight and support. Naturally, NPMs are a major source of information which can inform the visiting programme of the SPT, and the SPT takes time to meet with the NPM (if established) during all of its official visits, irrespective of whether or not it has an NPM focus. The reports produced by the SPT after its visit, like those of the CPT, are confidential and can only be made public with the consent of the State concerned. However, OPCAT art. 16(1) permits the SPT to '…communicate its recommendations and observations' to the NPM on a confidential basis, 'if relevant'. It has done so on a number of occasions. The purpose is to permit the NPM to assist the SPT in the follow-up to its reports and this highlights the extent to which the NPM, whilst a 'national' mechanism, is also recognised as having a distinct role within the international system established by OPCAT.

## 3.3 The CPT and the NPMs

There are, then, strong links between the SPT and the NPMs which are growing ever stronger. Moreover, the NPMs are, legally speaking, bodies operating within the OPCAT system, not under the ECPT. Nevertheless, the CPT can hardly be expected to be indifferent to the establishment of national bodies focused on preventive visits to places of detention. This, then, raises the question of the nature of the relationship between the CPT and the NPMs established within the OPCAT framework.

It seems fair to say that the CPT initially responded with caution to the establishment of NPMs. The 2009 seminar on 'New Partnerships for Prevention in Europe' marked an important development, seeing the NPMs as a part of the context in which the CPT was working and focusing on how to maximise that relationship. It has to be said, however, that that vision was still something of a one-way street. In the words of the Background Document prepared for the Conference, '…it is true to say that, to date, CPT delegations visiting States Parties will meet with NPMs and that, although there will be an exchange of views on particular topics, the flow of information will tend to be in one direction—towards the CPT' (Council of Europe and Association for the Prevention of Torture 2010: 133). The chief reason for this concerned confidentiality and will be briefly considered in the next section. To that extent, then, the approach of the CPT appeared to be not dissimilar from its approach to domestic civil society—a potentially valuable source of information to inform its work and an additional voice to assist in the implementation of recommendations contained in published CPT reports, but little more. Reflecting this cautious approach, CPT reports tended to limit themselves to fairly general statements of support for the establishment and work of NPMs.

A significant change came about in 2012 when, in its 22nd General Report, the CPT included a section on 'Relations between the CPT and

NPMs' (CPT/Inf (2012)25, paras 27–52). This re-set the nature of the relationship in much more positive terms, arguing that '…from the outset of its activities…the CPT has been recommending the establishment of independent national structures' (CPT/Inf (2012)25, para 29). Whilst recognising the significance of the relationship between the CPT and SPT, it says that establishment of NPMs is '…arguably even more significant' than the establishment of the SPT itself, noting that '…the NPMs are natural partners for the CPT' and the effectiveness of its work 'will in future depend to a large extent on the quality of the interaction between the Committee and these mechanisms' (CPT/Inf (2012)25, para 29).

This marks a major shift in perception of the relationship between the CPT and NPMs. The CPT sets out a series of 'provisional thoughts' on those future relations. What is striking is that the CPT carves out for itself an 'oversight' role in relation to the NPMs and the OPCAT, saying that when it (the CPT) 'encounters situations' in which the NPM does not appear to fulfil the OPCAT criteria or conform to the SPT's NPM guidelines 'it will raise matters with the national authorities' (CPT/Inf (2012)25, para 34). The intention is clearly to assist NPMs to fulfil their OPCAT mandate, but it is also striking that the CPT says nothing about liaising with the SPT concerning the raising of such issues, which the SPT may of course already be doing itself.

The CPT then stresses the importance of knowledge exchange, noting the involvement of its members in the European NPM project and other initiatives and says that, in order to promote synergy, it envisages '…the organisation of regular exchanges of views on topical issues with representatives of established and operational NPMs' (CPT/Inf (2012)25, para 37). The issue of divergent standards is, however, still in view, with the CPT noting that, as the work of the NPMs develops, so does '…the risk of diverging approaches and interpretations vis a vis given situations' (CPT/Inf (2012)25, para 38). Whilst accepting that 'it may not be possible to arrive at common standards in all areas', the CPT embraces the language used in the 2009 seminar when it calls for 'coherence' of the actions proposed (CPT/Inf (2012)25, para 38; see also Council of Europe and Association for the Prevention of Torture 2010: 69–71). Interestingly, the CPT then raises the importance of 'common methodologies' for conducting visits, and suggesting that the CPT might share 'available internal tools' with NPMs to assist them (CPT/Inf (2012)25, para 39). It is difficult to resist the conclusion that, despite what is said, the overall aim of 'knowledge exchange' is to ensure that NPMs reflect the working methods and substantive standards of the CPT as far as possible.

The CPT then proceeds to a series of suggestions concerning the practical liaison between the CPT and NPMs in the context of the preparation for, and execution of, CPT visits (CPT/Inf (2012)25, paras 42–43).[40] Interestingly, and importantly, the CPT says that the presence of the NPM at its final talks with the authorities 'is particularly useful' (CPT/Inf (2012)25, para 44).[41] This would make the NPM privy to comments which hitherto have been confidential, and seems to mark a significant change in the CPT's approach to confidentiality. The CPT clearly considers its actual report to remain confidential but believes that the state might consider transmitting it to the NPM on a confidential basis, even when it is not yet published (CPT/Inf (2012)25, para 45). This reflects an enhanced understanding of the role which the NPM can play in follow-up discussions and the CPT suggests that, once an NPM 'is in possession of the full visit report', the CPT 'intends to consult with the mechanism on how it can best help the Committee take forward its recommendations' (CPT/Inf (2012)25, para 46).[42] There are, however, limits to what might be done, and the CPT makes it clear that it does not consider joint visits conducted by the NPM and CPT to be appropriate (CPT/Inf (2012)25, para 52).[43]

One reason for this enhanced level of interaction might be that an increasing number of CPT members are also members of their own state's NPM. As a result, the work of the CPT is, de facto, known to at least some within the NPM and it is implausible to expect this knowledge to be held in limbo. Once again, there is a sense in which the approach of the CPT, as set out in its General Report, is as much about controlling the way in which its output is used as it is about releasing the potential of the NPM as a partner in prevention. This assessment may, however, be unduly negative as there is currently little in the public domain on which the extent and experience of such enhanced level of interaction can be assessed. What is clear is that the CPT now recognises the NPMs as a significant force in torture prevention in the Council of Europe area and is seeking to develop its practical engagement with the NPMs to a degree which now far outstrips the levels of its engagement with the SPT, and the capacity of the SPT to engage with the NPMs. This is a source of challenge for the coherence of the triangular relationship, as NPMs find themselves increasingly under pressure to engage with both the SPT and CPT. It is likely to be an increasingly important element of the operational landscape in the near future.

### 3.4 Cooperation and Confidentiality

The work of the CPT, like that of the SPT, is subject to an obligation of confidentiality which can only be lifted by the state itself or if, as a result of a lack of cooperation, it is decided to issue a Public Statement: something which the CPT has done very rarely and the SPT not at all. This flows from concerns relating to state sovereignty in permitting international mechanisms to visit places of detention as a matter of right. The same concerns do not (or ought not) apply to national mechanisms and so NPMs are not bound by such an obligation. Indeed, openness and transparency ought to be the hallmarks of their work. This has practical implications for the manner and extent to which the CPT, SPT and NPMs can cooperate and support each other. Whilst confidentiality may help cooperation between the international bodies and states, it impedes cooperation between those bodies. Ultimately, however, it is a question of confidence building between the various bodies concerned whilst recognising that there are some clear lines which are not to be crossed. Where those lines are to be found is, however, itself becoming increasingly blurred as more and more NPM members become members of the CPT, the SPT or, indeed, both.

## 4 Conclusion

In the light of this complex background, what is to be done? It is of course important that the various international and national bodies work in harmony—though it is important to stress that harmony does not necessarily imply a harmonisation of practice or process. Rather, it is more about finding ways of working which respect and reflect the various institutional and other parameters which bear upon their functioning in such a way as to maximise their respective practical impacts.

Even at the most basic levels, the degree of procedural coherence that can be achieved between the work of the mechanisms operating within different institutional frameworks is severely limited. If this is so as regards the CPT and the SPT, it must be even more so as regards the NPMs. There is little likelihood of the international bodies taking account of the visiting work of the NPMs when constructing their programmes, let alone vice versa. The entire point of unannounced visiting is that it is unpredictable and if this creates a degree of incoherence and duplication, it may be just an inevitable by-product of the system itself. Rather than trying to address this as a problem, perhaps it is best seen as a reinforcement of the system, or, at the very least, something that one just has to learn to live with it. From the perspective of the mechanisms themselves, such incoherence need only become a problem when it impacts upon the levels of cooperation received from states who are at the 'receiving end' of such multiple attentions.

Finally, and perhaps most importantly for the work of 'domesticating' international standards, it is important to remember that in many ways it is strange to be concerned about the lack of substantive coordination between independent international mechanisms. It is hardly unusual for international human rights bodies to take different views on similar questions. As regards the CPT and SPT, whilst each is doubtless aware of the work of the other and draws on that work to help inform its own activities—and to reinforce the work of the other when it is possible and appropriate to do so[44]—each works within its own context and responds to the situations which it encounters in the light of the substantive obligations in the manner which it considers most appropriate. What else ought they to do? What is really at issue is not so much the coordination of 'outputs' but of ensuring that there are no significant differences of approach in their understanding of essentially similar substantive norms and applicable concepts. This is a very real concern, since such variance has occurred in other contexts and resulted in unhelpful 'forum shopping'. The problem is exacerbated when the norm or concept is of a relatively undefined or inchoate nature. There is, then, a clear need to strive for a degree of consistency if the work of the various bodies is to have credibility, let alone coherence. Yet once again, this is not necessarily easy to achieve and, to the extent that this has been achieved by the SPT and CPT it has largely been the result of the SPT abstaining from producing documentation in a form which might have such an effect.

It may well be that the context of prevention is different from other contexts: the very point of a preventive approach is to suggest to states what they ought to do in order to try to reduce the likelihood of a breach of the substantive standard occurring, and it is easy to see that whilst suggesting different preventive strategies or priorities might be problematic, it may be considerably less problematic than one body finding something to be a breach of an international obligation when another does not. Indeed, constructive alternatives might even be helpful. Ultimately, what is most important is that there is a common vision to which all participants in the increasingly complex landscape subscribe and which they are all attempting to realise, albeit that this may sometimes be in rather different ways and perhaps along different trajectories.

## Notes

1. Within the Council of Europe itself the CPT is now one of a number of bodies tasked with the monitoring of human rights obligations at a national level. Whilst the nature of its treaty-based visiting mandate is still unique within the Council of Europe, it now takes its place among bodies such as the European Commission against Racism and Intolerance (ECRI) and the European Advisory Committee on the Framework Convention for the Protection of National Minorities (ACFC), which also undertake country visits as an element of their oversight activities. The establishment of the Council of Europe Commissioner for Human Rights in 1999 has also given rise to a complementary means of addressing both thematic and in-country human rights issues. The CPT is also operating in a very much changed European landscape from that which existed at the time of its creation, including the growth in European Union (EU) competence in relation to criminal justice issues, and in particular the introduction of the European Arrest Warrant and the Prisoner Transfers Directive which reflect increasing activism in its work

relating to prisons and policing. The establishment of FRONTEX and of the European External Action Service (EEAS) following the Lisbon Treaty is not only important in its own right but has also increased the significance of instruments such as the EU Torture Guidelines.

2. For a general comparison, see de Beco (2011: 257).
3. The United Nations Convention Against Torture and Other Cruel, Inhuman or Degrading Treatment or Punishment (UNCAT) had been adopted by the UN General Assembly in 1984 and entered into force on 26th June 1987, the very day on which the Committee of Ministers of the Council of Europe adopted the text of the ECPT. In 1985, the United Nations Commission on Human Rights had also established the position of UN Special Rapporteur on Torture (the SRT), whose first report was presented to the Commission on Human Rights in 1986.
4. Indeed, the original idea was even bolder in its claims, being publically launched in a pamphlet entitled *Torture: How to Make the International Convention Effective* (International Commission of Jurists and Swiss Committee against Torture 1979).
5. For a recent examination of the work of the SPT relative to NPMs, see Steinerte (2014).
6. For detailed overviews, see Evans and Morgan (1998), Murray et al. (2011) and Kicker (2012).
7. For a list of ratification dates, see http://www.coe.int/en/web/conventions/full-list/-/conventions/treaty/126/signatures.
8. In 1993 the Committee of Ministers of the Council of Europe adopted the First Protocol to the ECPT which was intended to permit non-member states of the Council to become, by invitation, parties to the Convention. By the time the First Protocol entered into force on 1 March 2002 it had already become a dead letter.
9. The two member states not parties to the ECPT at that point were Armenia and Azerbaijan which had only become members of the Council in January 2001 and both had ratified the ECPT by the end of 2002.
10. These being Andorra, Belgium, Iceland, Ireland, Latvia, Monaco, Russia, San Marino and Slovakia. All these states are currently parties to the Convention against Torture and so in a position to become a party to the OPCAT.
11. Under OPCAT art. 24, a state may, at the time of ratification or accession, make a declaration permitting it to delay doing so for up to 3 years, and it also permits it to request a further postponement of up to 2 years.

Within Europe, Bosnia-Herzegovina, Germany, Hungary and Romania all made such Declarations, though Germany established its NPM well within 3 years, whilst Romania requested an extension—the only country so far to have done so.

12. For an overview of each model, see the NPM Directory maintained by the Human Rights Implementation Centre, Bristol Law School at http://www.bristol.ac.uk/law/research/centres-themes/hric/resourcesreferences/npmdirectory/.
13. See, for example, the conference organised by the Netherlands Inspectorate of Justice and the VU University of Amsterdam, June 2012, entitled 'the triangular working relationship between the SPT, CPT and NPM: inspection in the field of detention on a global, regional and domestic level'.
14. Indeed, given that numerous NPMs are themselves comprised of multiple bodies with their own internal sets of relationships, the resulting picture is even more complex again.
15. All there is, is a fairly standard stipulation that it should not prejudice international agreements providing for greater protection of persons deprived of their liberty (ECPT, art. 17(1)).
16. For more on the OPCAT's drafting history, see Murray et al. (2011: chapters 1–3). Indeed, even following its entry into force, such questions continued to be posed. See, for example, Nowak and McArthur (2008: 1154), who ask '…for states party to both instruments…what added value will the Protocol have'.
17. This is further supported by OPCAT art. 11(c) which mandates the SPT to 'Co-operate, for the prevention of torture in general, with the relevant United Nations organs and mechanisms as well as with the international, regional and national institutions or organisations working towards the strengthening of the protection of all persons against torture and other cruel. Inhuman or degrading treatment or punishment.' This, again, clearly embraces the ECPT and CPT.
18. This was, until recently, hampered by both the CPT and SPT only announcing their visiting programme in November for the forthcoming year. This has now been alleviated by the CPT announcing its visiting plans significantly earlier, in March/April, which means that when the SPT decides on its programme, in June, the CPT's regular programme is already known.
19. For an endorsement of this fairly minimal ambition, see Kicker and Möstl (2012: 88).

20. On average, a CPT visit report is transmitted about eight or nine months after the visit takes place, and a response is requested within six months. Thus the state is likely to be most engaged substantively about a year after the actual visit has taken place. Although the SPT tends to transmit its reports four or five months after a visit, the period of response is similar.
21. The may also undertake 'follow-up visits' and at the time of writing (April 2016) has done so on four occasions: to Paraguay in 2010, following up on a visit undertaken in 2009; to Cambodia in 2013, following up on a visit undertaken in 2009; to Maldives in 2014, following up on a visit undertaken in 2007; to Benin in 2015 following a visit undertaken in 2008. Since the SPT has more recently begun to visit previously visited countries within its more general programme of work, the need for 'follow-up visits' of this nature may well decline.
22. Thus in its third Annual Report (CAT/C/44/2, 25 March 2010, para 19) the SPT said that it took account, inter alia, of the date of ratification, establishment of an NPM, geographical distribution, size and complexity of a state, regional preventive monitoring and urgent issues reported. These are by no means the only factors; others include the work of other UN mechanisms, discussed in the following section, and practical, technical and logistical issues.
23. Thus, whilst the decision making of the SPT takes place in June of the preceding year, that of the CPT now takes places earlier and is made public in time for it to be taken into consideration. Obviously, the CPT will not be aware of the SPT's as yet undecided plans. This reverses the situation before 2014, when the decision-making of the SPT was made in ignorance of the CPT's plans, though it must be said that there is a degree of predictability to the CPT's cycle of regular visits. The CPT's ad hoc visits are of course entirely unpredictable and cannot be factored into any planning process. It seems unlikely that the CPT takes much account of the SPT's visiting programme when considering whether to undertake an ad hoc visit, but given their differing natures and backgrounds, that is reasonable.
24. Silvia Casale (CPT member from 1997–2009; SPT member from 2006–2009); Zdenek Hayek (CPT member from 1996–2008; SPT member from 2007–2014); Leopoldo Torres-Boursault (CPT member from 1993–2000; SPT member from 2007–2009) and Marija Definis-Gojanovic (CPT member from 2002–2013; SPT member from 2007–2012 and from 2014).

25. See 17th General Report (CPT/Inf (2007)39, para 31), recording the resignation of Silvia Casale as President of the CPT following her election as Chair of the SPT in March 2007.
26. One such expert, Mark Kelly, was a former member of the CPT secretariat, and is now an elected member of the CPT.
27. See, for example, 17th General Report (CPT/inf (2007)39, para 19), 18th General Report (CPT/Inf (2008)25, para 22) and 23rd General Report (CPT/inf (2013)29, para 28).
28. This is not to say that the desirability of making such meetings more meaningful is not accepted. For example, in its 22nd General Report the CPT says that '…it is incumbent on the CPT and SPT to seize all opportunities to cooperation and the sharing of know-how, and in this regard there are regular exchanges of views between the two bodies and their respective secretariats' (CPT/inf (2012)25, para 28). Regretfully, 'regular' does not necessary imply 'frequent'.
29. See the Conference Proceedings published as *New partnerships for torture prevention in Europe* (Council of Europe and Association for the Prevention of Torture 2010).
30. These tend to be included as substantive comments in the General Reports, and are then replicated in the CPT's 'CPT Standards' document, CPT/Inf/E (2002)1 Rev. 2015, available at http://www.cpt.coe.int/en/documents/eng-standards.pdf.
31. See *The approach of the Subcommittee on Prevention of Torture to the concept of prevention of torture and other cruel, inhuman or degrading treatment or punishment under the Optional Protocol to the Convention against Torture and Other Cruel, Inhuman or Degrading Treatment or Punishment,* CAT/OP/12/6 (30 December 2010), para 5(f).
32. This contrasts with the CPT which does issue statements of standards on a periodic basis. Interestingly, former CPT member Renate Kicker now distinguished between the normative standards applicable to states and the 'implementation standards' which guide the work of expert bodies: see generally Kicker and Möstl (2012).
33. See *The approach of the Subcommittee on Prevention of Torture to the concept of prevention of torture and other cruel, inhuman or degrading treatment or punishment under the Optional Protocol to the Convention against Torture and Other Cruel, Inhuman or Degrading Treatment or Punishment,* CAT/OP/12/6 (30 December 2010), para 3.
34. Ibid, para 5 (f).

35. Section V of each SPT Annual Report from the fourth (CAT/C/46/2, 3 February 2011) onwards addresses 'Substantive Issues' which '...may be taken to reflect the current approach of the SPT to the issues that it addresses' (ibid, para 4). Recent examples include: prevention of torture and lesbian, gay, bisexual, transsexual and intersex persons para (ninth Annual Report, CAT/OP/C/57/4, 22 March 2016, paras 48–82) pre-trial detention (eight Annual Report, CAT/C/54/2, 26 March 2015, paras 73–96); corruption and the prevention of torture (seventh Annual Report, CAT/C/52/2, 19 March 2014, paras 72–100); indigenous justice and the prevention of torture (sixth Annual Report, CAT/C/50/2, 23 April 2013, paras 69–94).
36. For example the Analytical Assessment Tool for National Preventive Mechanisms (25 January 2016), available at http://www.ohchr.org/Documents/HRBodies/OPCAT/AnalyticalTtoolsNPM_en.pdf.
37. By the end of 2015, the SPT has undertaken NPM advisory visits to Honduras, Senegal, Moldova, Germany, Armenia, Ecuador, Malta, The Netherlands and Turkey.
38. By the end of 2015 the SPT had undertaken two such visits, to Nigeria and to Nauru.
39. The SPT Regional Teams are not based on the five UN regional groupings but on four functional regions, which includes a single European Regional Team covering the Council of Europe area. Details are on the SPT website at http://www.ohchr.org/EN/HRBodies/OPCAT/Pages/ContactRegionalTeams.aspx.
40. See also the CPT's 24th General Report '...the CPT delegations have had consultations with [national preventive] mechanisms during many visits' (CPT/Inf (2015)1, para 32).
41. This is in addition to its 'welcoming the presence of representatives of the mechanisms at its meetings' during the course of the visit.
42. This might include a meeting in the country concerned and which might also involve 'other relevant actors' (para 46).
43. This contrasts with the practice of the SPT which *does* visit places of detention with NPMs in the context of its NPM Advisory Visits.
44. Thus the CPT now routinely raises issues concerning the establishment of NPMs under the OPCAT. When planning its own visits the SPT will also regularly have regard to the published reports of the CPT and the recommendations which they contain.

## Literature

Council of Europe and Association for the Prevention of Torture, eds. 2010. *New Partnerships for Torture Prevention in Europe. Proceedings of the Conference. Strasbourg, 6 November 2009*. Council of Europe, Strasbourg.

De Beco, G. 2011. The Optional Protocol to the Convention Against Torture and Other Cruel, Inhuman or Degrading Treatment or Punishment (the OPCAT) in Europe: Duplication or Reinforcement? *Maastricht Journal of European and Comparative Law* 18 (3): 257–274.

Evans, M., and R. Morgan. 1998. *Preventing Torture. A Study of the European Convention for the Prevention of Torture and Inhuman or Degrading Treatment or Punishment*. Oxford: Oxford University Press.

International Commission of Jurists and Swiss Committee against Torture, eds. 1979. *Torture: How to Make the International Convention Effective*. Geneva: International Commission of Jurists and Swiss Committee against Torture.

Kicker, R. 2012. The European Committee for the Prevention of Torture and Inhuman and Degrading Treatment. In *Human Rights Monitoring Mechanisms of the Council of Europe*, ed. G. de Beco, 43–70. London: Routledge.

Kicker, R., and M. Möstl. 2012. *Standard Setting Through Monitoring? The Role of Council of Europe Expert Bodies in the Development of Human Rights*. Strasbourg: Council of Europe.

Murray, R., E. Steinerte, M. Evans, and A. Hallo de Wolf. 2011. *The Optional Protocol to the UN Convention Against Torture*. Oxford: Oxford University Press.

Nowak, M., and E. McArthur. 2008. *The United Nations Convention Against Torture. A Commentary*. Oxford: Oxford University Press.

Steinerte, E. 2014. The Jewel in the Crown and its Three Guardians: Independence of National Preventive Mechanisms Under the Optional Protocol to the UN Torture Convention. *Human Rights Law Review* 14 (1): 1–29.

Thomson, M., and T. Stevens. 2010. Foreword. In *New partnerships for torture prevention in Europe. Proceedings of the Conference. Strasbourg, 6 November 2009*, ed. Council of Europe and Association for the Prevention of Torture, 5–8. Strasbourg: Council of Europe.

**Christine Bicknell** is Lecturer in Law at the University of Exeter, United Kingdom.

**Malcolm Evans** is Professor of Public International Law at the University of Bristol, United Kingdom.

# Human Rights in European Prisons: Can the Implementation of Strasbourg Court Judgments Influence Penitentiary Reform Domestically?

Dia Anagnostou and Dimitris Skleparis

## 1 Introduction

The state of prisons in European states has over the past 20 years increasingly come under the purview of the European Court of Human Rights (ECtHR). In hundreds of judgments, the Strasbourg Court has applied fundamental human rights principles, pre-eminently the prohibition of torture and ill-treatment (art. 3 of the European Convention of Human Rights [ECHR]), to review complaints of detainees. Such complaints are

D. Anagnostou (✉)
Panteion University of Social and Political Sciences, Athens, Greece

ELIAMEP (Hellenic Foundation for European & Foreign Policy), Athens, Greece

D. Skleparis
ELIAMEP (Hellenic Foundation for European & Foreign Policy), Athens, Greece



T. Daems, L. Robert (eds.), *Europe in Prisons*, Palgrave Studies in Prisons and Penology, DOI 10.1007/978-3-319-62250-7_3

related to deficient conditions of imprisonment, such as overcrowding, poor hygiene and sanitation, and lack of access to adequate health, among others. Until the 1990s, the European Commission of Human Rights (ECommHR) and the ECtHR applied a high threshold for detecting breaches of human rights.[1] The ECtHR though took a more scrutinizing approach since the late 1990s and 2000s, gradually recognizing that particular kinds of conditions and practices of incarceration cross the acceptable threshold of severity and violate the human rights of inmates. At the same time, European institutions and bodies, such as the European Committee for the Prevention of Torture and Inhuman and Degrading Treatment or Punishment (CPT), the European Commissioner for Human Rights of the Council of Europe (CoE), and more recently the EU, have over the past 15 years engaged in standard setting in regard to persons deprived of their liberty and in closer monitoring of European prisons.

On the basis of reviewing complaints by persons deprived of their liberty, the ECtHR issues judgments that states that have ratified the ECHR are obliged to implement (art. 46 of the ECHR). Through the domestic implementation of those judgments, a process closely supervised by the Committee of Ministers (CoM) of the CoE, the ECtHR's case law can exert a significant influence over prison reform in European states. National authorities are obliged to provide an individual remedy if they are found to have violated the ECHR, but also to institute general measures aimed at preventing similar human rights infringements from recurring. General measures can take the form of legal reform, change in domestic courts' jurisprudence, or change in administrative practices, and it can amount to broader policy change. To be sure, the ability of human rights judgments to influence, let alone instigate, reform of national laws and policies is highly contingent, and it is rarely direct or straightforward. Yet, studies show that under certain conditions and/or in certain issue areas, the reform and policy impact of the ECtHR's judgments can be significant (Anagnostou 2013; Hillebrecht 2012; Helfer and Voeten 2014).

This chapter provides an overview of ECtHR judgments related to the state of European prisons and explores broad patterns of their implementation across different states. In particular, it reviews the kinds of claims raised in petitions before the ECtHR, the main issues that emerge as salient and the states that are most frequently implicated in prison-related infringements. It also discusses the measures that states tend to take to redress the respective violations, as well as the apparent obstacles to implementation. On the basis of the empirical data that we present, we provide a general appraisal rather than a systematic investigation of state implementation. In view of the large number of states reviewed, this study does not engage in any in-depth analysis of the domestic factors that impact upon implementation of prison-related judgments or of the influence of these judgments upon domestic prison reform—tasks which far exceed the size and scope of our chapter.

In this study, we are primarily concerned with the human rights review of cases that pertain to 'passive' ill-treatment of inmates, in large part a result of deficient material conditions and organization, as well as of unacceptable penitentiary practices of a state's prison system. We do not examine cases pertaining to deliberate or 'active' infliction of ill-treatment of inmates by prison and police authorities. While the latter is also a part and characteristic of a country's penitentiary system and culture, we focus on the former aspect of ill-treatment because it is more directly connected to the concrete and structural conditions of imprisonment, as well as to penal law and policy.[2] The material infrastructure and organizational arrangements shape the general environment and the physical conditions in which persons are detained, but also the specific circumstances of the prisoner (Marochini 2009: 1113).

For the purpose of this study, we have compiled a data set of 165 adverse judgments of the ECtHR issued in 1990–2015, which find violations of the Convention. Many of these judgments pertain to prison overcrowding, and to poor material conditions more broadly, as well as to inhuman or degrading conditions that are specifically experienced by inmates with a variety of health problems (mental, psychological, and physical). Individuals with health problems, often severe ones that occasionally lead to suicidal tendencies or suicide, are often more vulnerable and less able to withstand the general prison conditions. Many inmates also develop health problems while being held in prison or placed in disciplinary cells and other kinds of solitary confinement. Although the Convention does not guarantee the right to prisoners' health care, the

ECtHR in its case law has conceded that prison authorities are under a positive obligation to protect the health of persons deprived of their liberty. The lack of appropriate medical care or delay in providing medical help to inmates may constitute a violation of art. 3.[3]

A major sub-category of judgments related to detention conditions originates from immigrants and asylum seekers, who are lawfully or unlawfully detained in facilities that are unacceptable by human rights standards. While we cover human rights judgments that pertain to detention conditions experienced by migrants and asylum seekers, we do not consider how states respond to violations regarding the lawfulness of migrants' detention per se; the latter issue exclusively falls within the remit of migration policy rather than of prison conditions and penal reform. Furthermore, in this study, we do not include cases that concern hunger strikes in detention, a special category of cases that is not directly linked to overall conditions of detention. We also do not include a rich and highly controversial strand of case law that pertains to the interference of prison authorities with prisoners' correspondence, and therefore with their right to privacy, as well as the body of case law in which the political rights of prisoners are at stake. We exclude these bodies of case law, which, albeit highly significant, are also not directly related to prison conditions as such.

The supervision mechanism of the ECHR system is centred on the CoM. This supervisory mechanism has been in a process of rapid change and radical overhaul over the past 10 years. It has placed an emphasis on the systemic causes of human rights violations and has had a major impact on the execution of judgments related to prison conditions and penal reform. The large number of repetitive human rights violations has rendered this issue area a typical one for the application of the pilot procedure.[4] The first part of the chapter describes the processes and mechanisms of domestic implementation of ECtHR's judgments and their supervision and monitoring by the CoM. The second part provides an overview of the relevant ECtHR's judgments and the issues that they raise, and the violations detected by the Court. The third part of the chapter describes and discusses the kind of reforms and measures that national authorities undertake by way of implementing the general measures that are called for by the relevant ECtHR judgments.

## 2 The ECHR System and Other Bodies Monitoring Prison Conditions

Since the 1990s, the overall prison population across Europe and the CoE states has been rising. Nonetheless, substantial variation remains both in the evolution of the total population of inmates over time and in the prison population rate (PPR) across countries.[5] Persons from marginalized groups and ethnic minorities tend to be over-represented among the prison population, while the proportion of non-nationals among inmates has also been rising in European countries (Coyle 2006: 129).[6] The large discrepancies observed in the prison population of the different European states are arguably related to differences in prevalent views about imprisonment as the most severe form of punishment in contemporary Europe (since the death penalty and corporal punishment have been abolished) and what is intended to achieve (Coyle 2006: 107) or to low levels of social trust and political legitimacy that may render policies in some countries more punitive than others (Lappi-Seppälä 2011). The causes of this rising trend are complex, and they cannot be seen to be a direct reflection of increased levels of criminality. Instead, it is significantly linked to factors such as the introduction of more punitive criminal justice legislation with prison sentences for crimes that would not have previously received such sentences (e.g. for drug abuse) or lengthier periods of incarceration. Prevailing stances among politicians and the media, which encourage judicial authorities to send more people to prison for longer periods of time, have arguably also contributed to the overall rise in prison population.

Regardless of the actual causes of increased levels of incarceration, the available prison places in many CoE member states have not kept up with the rising number of prisoners. This has led to a significant and generalized problem of prison overcrowding, which is often more pronounced in pre-trial detention facilities. Besides overcrowding, a variety of other conditions, rules, and practices that define detention regimes have come under fire from international organizations and NGOs for constituting a living situation for inmates that does not meet basic human rights standards (Coyle 2006: 104). The CoE Commissioner for Human

Rights has recently characterized prison conditions in several European countries as 'appalling', referring to prison overcrowding, lack of privacy, unacceptable disciplinary procedures to deal with violence and other types of misconduct by inmates, solitary confinement, inadequate provision of and access to medical care, education and job training, as well as a particularly harsh regime for those serving life sentences (so-called lifers) (Hammarberg 2011: 241–246).

Already in the early 1970s, the CoE, prompted by the UN Standard Minimum Rules for the Treatment of Prisoners (1957), adopted its first set of prison standards (the European Standard Minimum Rules for the Treatment of Prisoners 1973). These were later revised and published in 1987 as European Prison Rules, and they were subsequently amended in 2006.[7] At the same time, the CPT was set up under the CoE's European Convention for the Prevention of Torture and Inhuman or Degrading Treatment or Punishment, which came into force in 1989 and which has been ratified by all the 47 member states of the CoE. The CPT's main activity is practical and pre-emptive action through non-judicial intervention by means of on-site visits to assess existing conditions and practices in places of detention in the contracting states. Through its reports, it communicates its findings to the state concerned and seeks to engage in constructive dialogue and cooperation with the national authorities. Its main goal is to improve respect for and compliance with human rights standards for detainees.

The application of human rights principles in relation to prison conditions by the ECtHR, and by courts more broadly, is constrained by a number of aspects. Lawful imprisonment is intended to be a form of punishment. In this context, practices, such as social isolation, which may be considered harsh or inhuman in general, are accepted to inhere in the nature of incarceration as a punitive institution. Therefore, they are less likely to be regarded as contrary to the prohibition of degrading and inhuman treatment, unless there is indication or proof that a particular kind of mistreatment was deliberately inflicted upon an inmate. This may be even more so when an offender is considered to pose a danger to public safety. In this case, more stringent disciplinary measures may be considered necessary for the sake of maintaining prison order, re-evaluating accordingly the standards of humane treatment in reference to what is otherwise an absolute prohibition of inhuman and degrading treatment (art. 3 of the ECHR). All of these aspects weaken the potential of judicial bodies' review to uphold robust human rights standards in prisons.

An additional factor constraining the effectiveness of judicial review in relation to prisons is the fact that the provision of decent detention conditions requires substantial economic resources. Courts, however, are often reluctant to interfere with matters dependent on policy decisions about how to allocate a finite amount of resources (for a discussion of these factors, see Foster 2015: 383). Still, the ECtHR observes that the lack of resources cannot justify prison conditions which are so poor as to reach the threshold of treatment contrary to art. 3 of the Convention, even as it recognizes that a country's socio-economic hardships may hamper attempts to improve such conditions.[8]

Through its standard-setting and fact-finding activities, the CPT complements the judicial work of the ECtHR (Murdoch 2006: 164). Applicants to the ECtHR often rely on the CPT's findings to establish the factual background to conditions of detention in a particular country, as well as to construct the normative arguments that condemn a particular kind of treatment of detainees, largely in reference to art. 3 ECHR. The ECtHR (and formerly the ECommHR) has also regularly drawn on CPT reports in assessing the impact of detention conditions on the applicant (Marochini 2009: 1120). Some of the standards that the CPT has developed concern living accommodation and basic needs; staff selection, training and management; provision of an adequate regime of activities; and provision of health care in prisons. As regards living accommodation and basic needs, the CPT has established some rough guidelines, especially concerning the size of cell space (Marochini 2009: 1119). Developments in the protection of prisoners resulting from the cumulative work of the ECtHR and the CPT have created new standards for the treatment of prisoners and their detention conditions (Marochini 2009: 1109). While the standards promoted by the CPT were more detailed and rigorous in comparison to the ECtHR—in part, a difference stemming from the fundamentally different nature of each body's work and intervention—the Strasbourg Court has increasingly aligned the norms it applies in its case law with the CPT standards and assumed a more proactive approach (Murdoch 2006: 166–167).

National authorities must choose the individual and general measures whereby they will implement the final judgments. The Court cannot annul, repeal, or modify statutory provisions or decisions taken by administrative, judicial, or other national authorities. While it is not empowered to indicate or suggest which specific individual or general measures the national authorities in a case should undertake, the Court has, in certain types of cases, which involve structural and systemic problems, become more willing and forthcoming in indicating appropriate general measures (Forst 2013: 4; Sicilianos 2014). General measures in response to the ECtHR's judgments may include legislative amendments and administrative or executive measures (i.e. ministerial circulars or regulations) in areas of state laws and policies that directly or indirectly come under the Court's purview in the context of examining individual cases (Sundberg 2001: 573–574). They may also include other actions, such as translation and dissemination of the ECtHR's judgments to national judges, as well as educational activities and other practical measures. Under the new working methods introduced as of January 2011, respondent states have to submit action plans/reports for the implementation of judgments within six months from the time a judgment becomes final. This prompts governments to react quickly to a finding of a violation by the Court.

In its periodic but regular meetings, the CoM, with the assistance of the Directorate General of Human Rights, reviews the information about the individual and general measures, which is communicated to it by national authorities. When these are considered to be sufficient to remedy the underlying violation, as well as to prevent its recurrence, the CoM terminates its supervision of a case by adopting a final resolution (Anagnostou and Mungiu-Pippidi 2014: 210–211).[9] For a long time, the supervisory role of the CoM was viewed as highly deferential to national authorities (Martens 1996: 77). Since 2000, however, despite the political constraints that underpin the CoM as a body, its role has become more transparent and scrutinizing in order to determine the efficacy of state actions (see CoM 2013: 21–27). Following the introduction of new rules in 2001 and subsequently in 2006, the agenda and content of the CoM meetings are no longer confidential (Bates 2005). Instead, detailed and timely publication of all relevant documents examined by the CoM has provided greater visibility to the process of judgments' execution by states. The CoM is now entitled to receive information pertaining to execution of the ECtHR's judgments from national human rights institutions, from other states, civil society, as well as from international organizations and other CoE organs such as the Parliamentary Assembly of the Council of Europe (PACE) and the CPT (Sitaropoulos 2008: 530–532).

The new rules of procedure and the new tools that the CoM possesses to exercise its supervisory role significantly dwell upon judgments detecting human rights violations of a systemic nature. The first explicit attempt by the ECtHR to specifically deal with the challenges of breaches stemming from structural problems was the introduction of a 'pilot judgment' procedure.[10] Through this process, the Court selects a particular case as characteristic of a structural problem, which has led to violations in a large number of cases brought before the Court. It asks the respondent state to identify the dysfunction(s) that is at the root of repetitive violations, and it gives some indication about the measures that should be instituted with the goal of eliminating those violations. The cases processed under a pilot procedure are given priority by the Court, which may adjourn the examination of all similar applications pending the adoption of the remedial measures in the pilot judgment.[11] In this way, the pilot-judgment procedure induces the respondent state to also take retroactive measures to address infringements in all similar cases arising from the same structural problem at the domestic level (Forst 2013: 19). The CoM now (following the adoption of Protocol No. 14, June 2010) adopts the enhanced procedure (as opposed to the 'standard procedure') for pilot judgments and judgments raising structural and/or complex problems as identified by the Court or by the CoM (see Department for the Execution of Judgments of the ECtHR (DG-HL), CM/Inf/DH(2010) 37, 6 September 2010: 2).

In view of this more rigorous kind of supervision exercised by the CoM over the past couple of years, states are likely to be under enhanced pressure to address human rights problems related to unacceptable prison conditions. Nonetheless, in its latest report on the implementation of the ECtHR judgments, the PACE expressed concern about the large number of non-implemented judgments pending before the CoM (nearly 11,000 cases), many of which reflect complex, structural problems. It also identified poor prison conditions among the most persisting structural causes of human rights violations, as well as among the outstanding human rights issues in the seven states with the highest number of non-implemented cases (Italy, Russia, Ukraine, Romania, Greece, Poland, and Bulgaria) (Committee on Legal Affairs and Human Rights 2015). At the end of 2014, poor detention conditions made up 14% of all cases under enhanced supervision by the CoM (based on the number of leading cases, i.e. cases that reveal complex and systemic problems in a state and which are often sources of recurrent infringements) (Committee on Legal Affairs and Human Rights 2015: 11).[12] We now turn to review the kinds of issues and problems related to places of detention, which give rise to numerous human rights violations.

## 3 Strasbourg Court Judgments Pertaining to Prison Conditions in Europe

While there were a few petitions related to prisoners' claims and rights in the 1970s and in the 1980s (mainly from the UK), the ECtHR did not find a violation related to detention conditions until much later—according to our sample, until 1998 in the case of *Ilhan v. Turkey*—[13]which was not primarily about conditions of detention but about the mistreatment that a Kurdish applicant had suffered by prison authorities in the north-eastern parts of Turkey, which were then under a state of emergency. Earlier, ECtHR judgments implicating countries such as Belgium and Switzerland occasionally found a violation,[14] but they often found no violation[15] or ended with a friendly settlement.[16] Our data set comprises 165 adverse judgments, namely cases in which the ECtHR found at least one violation of the ECHR in relation to prisons and imprisonment conditions. We selected these judgments by searching through the official database of the ECtHR (HUDOC), the Court's factsheets, other reports, and secondary literature. While we have no way of ensuring or verifying its representativeness, our close perusal of the Strasbourg Court's case law makes us confident that the studied sample contains most of the important judgments issued by the ECtHR. We also believe that it provides a fairly accurate picture of the European countries and issue areas, where human rights violations occur.

Spread across 21 countries, the violations recorded in our data set can be subdivided into six issue areas. In the first place, unacceptable *conditions of detention in pre-trial/remand centres* is a major source of human rights violations. Such conditions are characterized by overcrowding, substandard material infrastructure, limited or no outdoor access or out-of-cell activities,[17] limited or no family visits, extended periods of pre-trial detention,[18] interference with a detainee's communication with his/her lawyer, and lack of or no health provisions for prisoners suffering from serious illnesses.[19] Lack of space in pre-trial centres is particularly pronounced. Applicants referred to cells, where each detainee had between 1 and 2 $m^2$,[20] or even less than 1 $m^2$ available.[21] Moreover, they referred to situations where they had to sleep in turns due to the fact that there were not enough beds available.[22] Lack of windows or ventilation,[23] no proper heating, poor food quality, disrupted water and electricity provision,[24] and cockroaches, ants, and rats infestation[25] were some of the characteristics of deficient conditions in pre-trial detention facilities. Poor or no sanitary facilities were common in pre-trial/remand centres.[26] Detainees described situations where they were allowed limited short visits a day to the sanitary facilities, and in order to relieve themselves outside the time earmarked for toilet visits, detainees had to use a bucket.[27] Applicants also complained about obstacles in the communication with their lawyers, such as rooms where they were separated by a glass partition, with no space for exchanging documents, across which they claimed they had to shout to hear each other.[28]

Cases involving *health-related issues in prison* were about the following: (a) inadequate medical care given the applicant's health record; (b) negligence in prescribing appropriate medical treatment and subsequent deterioration of applicant's health due to the lack of medical treatment; and (c) detention conditions that were unsuitable for the therapeutic needs of the applicant or for his/her disability. A large number of cases concerned the failure to provide due medical care to an applicant suffering from a serious disease.[29] In one case, for instance, despite the fact that the competent authorities had been informed that the applicant was suffering from cirrhosis and that his condition necessitated appropriate treatment, it was not until measures had been indicated by the ECtHR that the applicant began to receive regular check-ups.[30] Moreover, in a number of cases, negligence in failing to prescribe adequate medical treatment and subsequent deterioration of the applicant's health due to the lack of medical treatment were reported.[31] For instance, in one case, the Court concluded that the applicant had developed tuberculosis between the time he had been taken into police custody and the date on which the disease had been detected, on account of the poor conditions of his detention.[32] Furthermore, detention conditions that were inappropriate for the therapeutic needs of the applicant were at stake in other cases.[33]

The vulnerability of mentally ill people and persons with disability[34] calls for special protection and was at stake in a number of cases. In one case, for instance, the Court stated that the authorities had failed to comply with their obligation to protect the applicant's right to life, as the applicant's placement in a punishment cell deprived him of visits and all activities, and subsequently aggravated the existing risk of suicide.[35] In another case, the Court concluded that inadequate medical care forced a prisoner suffering from severe epilepsy to rely for assistance and emergency medical care on his cellmates.[36] In its judgment of *Vincent v. France*, the Court found that the detention facility was particularly unsuited to the imprisonment of persons with a physical handicap who could move about only in a wheelchair.[37]

Judgments related to the *material conditions of prison facilities* detected violations stemming from (a) overcrowding and (b) poor material conditions (e.g. ill-lit, poorly ventilated cells, insanitary conditions, and inadequate outdoor exercise). A large number of violations concerned overcrowded cells.[38] The Court observed that for substantial periods of time, applicants' cells had been overcrowded, leaving them with less than the statutory minimum 'humanitarian' amount of space. In one case, for instance, the Hungarian government had acknowledged overcrowding in the Hungarian prisons and that there had been 50% more prisoners in the Budapest prison than existing places. In this regard, the Court further noted that the Hungarian authorities had to rapidly take the necessary administrative and practical measures in order to improve the conditions in which detainees were kept in Hungarian prisons.[39] In yet another case, the Italian government had acknowledged that there was a structural problem of overcrowding in Italian prisons. The Court decided to apply the pilot-judgment procedure in view of the growing number of persons potentially concerned in Italy. It called on the authorities to put in place, within one year, a remedy or combination of remedies providing redress in respect of violations of the Convention resulting from overcrowding in prison.[40]

Overall, poor material conditions were a common violation in a number of cases.[41] With specific regard to such cases, the Court stated that lack of space had been made worse by aggravating factors, such as the lack of exercise, particularly outdoor exercise, lack of privacy, and insalubrious conditions. In one case, for instance, the Court observed that the applicant had been held in ill-lit and poorly ventilated cells for almost four years and had had to endure cramped and insanitary conditions and a total lack of privacy when using the toilet facilities.[42] In another case, the Court observed that the problems arising from prison overcrowding in Belgium, and the problems of unhygienic and dilapidated prison institutions, were structural in nature. In this regard, it recommended that Belgium envisage adopting general measures guaranteeing prisoners conditions of detention compatible with art. 3 of the Convention.[43] Similarly, in another case, the Court identified a systemic problem within the Bulgarian prison system because of the serious and persistent nature of the problems on account of overcrowding and lack of privacy and personal dignity when going to the toilet.[44] A pilot-judgment procedure was adopted in regard to Bulgaria. Overcrowding and poor material conditions often lead to deterioration of an applicant's already fragile health condition.[45]

Violations related to *inhuman treatment while in detention* pertain to solitary confinement, strip searches, and generally behaviour towards inmates that amounts to degrading treatment. A large number of cases concerned violations with respect to solitary confinement.[46] In those cases, the Court generally criticized the conditions and length of solitary confinement, and emphasized that solitary confinement was only appropriate as an exceptional and temporary measure. In one case, for instance, the Court found that the conditions of the applicant's detention in solitary confinement had been such as to cause him both mental and physical suffering and a strong feeling of being stripped of his dignity.[47] In the same case, the Court further found that the main reason for the applicant's solitary confinement had not been his protection but rather his sexual orientation, which constituted discriminatory treatment. In another case, the applicant had spent almost his entire time in prison under a special security regime, alone in his cell, seeing almost no other people, being constantly handcuffed when outside his cell, and having to endure daily body cavity searches as a security measure.[48]

Additionally, a large number of cases also concerned strip searches, which the Court found that they resulted in human rights violations.[49] The Court reiterated that strip searches and even full body searches could be necessary on occasion to ensure prison security—including the prisoner's own safety—or to prevent disorder or crime. However, they also had to be conducted in an 'appropriate manner' so that the prisoner's distress or humiliation did not exceed the level which such searches inevitably entail. In one case, for instance, the applicant alleged that he had been obliged to strip naked in the presence of a woman prison officer with the intention of humiliating him; he had been then ordered to squat, and his sexual organs and the food he had received from the visitor had been examined by guards who had worn no gloves.[50] Finally, degrading treatment was another main issue related to inhuman detention violations.[51] In one case, for instance, prison authorities had deliberately withheld a drug-addict prisoner's medication and locked her in her cell as a punishment for her difficult behaviour; they had administered her medication irregularly, and they had left her lying in her own vomit.[52] The Court reiterated that it was incumbent on states to organize their prison systems in such a way as to ensure respect for prisoners' dignity, regardless of logistical or financial difficulties.

In relation to *conditions of detention under special prison regimes*, there were 11 violations in our sample (5 of them from Ukraine). In the cases against Ukraine, the Court observed that the applicants' complaints raised serious issues of a general nature affecting the application of art. 3 of the Convention in relation to the conditions of detention of death-row prisoners. Moreover, the Court noted that where the death penalty was imposed, the personal circumstances of the condemned person, the conditions of detention awaiting execution, and the length of detention prior to execution were examples of factors capable of resulting to a treatment or punishment that infringes art. 3 of the ECHR. While bearing in mind Ukraine's socio-economic problems and the prison authorities' difficulties with the implementation of new legislation and regulations, the Court nonetheless concluded that a lack of resources could not in principle justify prison conditions so poor as to constitute inhuman and degrading treatment.[53]

A significant number of cases also concerned the conditions and duration of detention in special prison regimes.[54] The Court held that keeping detainees under the 'dangerous detainee' regime for several years, in isolation, without sufficient mental and physical stimulation, and without examining if there were concrete reasons for the prolonged application of that regime, was not necessary in order to ensure safety in prison. In two cases against Poland, the Court acknowledged that in order to ensure safety in prison, prisoners could be subjected to tighter security controls, involving constant supervision of their movements within and outside the cell, monitoring via close-circuit television, limitations on their contact and communication with the outside world, and some form of segregation from the prison community. However, the Court concluded that the duration and severity of the measures exceeded the requirements of prison security and that they were not in their entirety necessary.[55]

Finally, 13 violations in our sample related to *violence, ill-treatment, or suicide in prison*, specifically in regard to the failure of the authorities to guarantee the protection of a prisoner's life,[56] as well as a prisoner's physical and psychological integrity.[57] In one of these cases, for instance, the Court found that the Turkish authorities had not only been indifferent to the applicant's son's grave psychological problems, even threatening him with disciplinary sanctions for previous suicide attempts. They had also been responsible for a deterioration of his state of mind by detaining him in a prison with adults without providing any medical or specialist care, which eventually led to his suicide.[58] In another case, the facility's authorities had failed to guarantee the protection of a prisoner's physical and psychological integrity. The Court noted that the administration had not attempted to regularly monitor the conduct of inmates prone to being violent or take any disciplinary measures against the offenders. It was only after the last incident, which was described as the culmination of the applicant's ill-treatment, that the authorities removed him from his cell.

Still no meaningful attempts had been made to provide the applicant with psychological rehabilitation in the aftermath of the events.[59]

In identifying the countries with the largest numbers of human rights violations related to prisons and imprisonment, Table 1 must be read in conjunction with Table 2.

As we discussed in the previous section though, since 2010, the pilot procedure and the new rules of the CoM supervisory mechanism have enabled the Court and the Committee to group large numbers of cases together when it is recognized that certain kinds of violations in a country are repetitive and have systemic causes. While several CoE states have petitions and violations related to unacceptable detention conditions, as our sample shows, there are a number of states where the problem of prison overcrowding and poor detention conditions is particularly severe and widespread and from which dozens of repetitive petitions are pending before the Court. Our data confirm the findings of the latest report of the PACE of the Committee on Legal Affairs and Human Rights on the implementation of judgments, which identifies the following eight countries: Russia, Ukraine, Romania, Italy, Bulgaria, Greece, Hungary, and Poland (see Committee on Legal Affairs and Human Rights 2015: addendum). These eight countries assemble a much larger number of prison-related cases than Table 1 shows. In five of these countries, the ECtHR has applied the pilot-judgment procedure at least once (Russia, Italy, Hungary, Bulgaria, Romania) or it has grouped a larger number of cases under leading judgments (Greece, Bulgaria, Ukraine, Poland). While Bulgaria in Table 1 shows only 4 violations, Table 2 shows that 24 cases are grouped under the leading judgment of *Kehayov v Bulgaria*, 2005. In 2015, the ECtHR adopted the pilot judgment of *Neshkov and others v. Bulgaria* in view of the deteriorating situation of the penitentiary system in the country, despite earlier leading judgments and recommendations by the CPT, in response to which Bulgaria had pursued reforms. The vast majority of judgments involve violation of art. 3 of the ECHR.

Altogether, both Tables 1 and 2 depict the countries with the most serious prison-related human rights problems: Russia, Romania, Greece, Hungary, Bulgaria, and Ukraine, secondarily followed by France, Poland, Italy, and, less so, Belgium. The countries with the highest number of violations manifest problems across most issue

**Table 1** Prison-related judgments by country and by issue area

| Country against which complaint is lodged | Issue Area 1: Conditions of detention in pre-trial/ remand centres | Issue Area 2: Health-related issues (inmates with special health/mental problems, access to health care) | Issue Area 3: Inhuman detention (i.e. solitary confinement, degrading treatment, strip searches) | Issue Area 4: Overcrowding and poor material conditions overall | Issue Area 5: Special prison regime (high security or death-row inmates) | Issue Area 6: Violence, ill-treatment or suicide while in prison | Grand Total |
|---|---|---|---|---|---|---|---|
| Albania | | 2 | | | | | 2 |
| Armenia | | 1 | 1 | | | | 2 |
| Belgium | | 4 | | 1 | | 1 | 6 |
| Bulgaria | 1 | | 1 | 1 | 1 | | 4 |
| Croatia | | 1 | | 3 | | | 4 |
| Estonia | | | | 1 | | 1 | 2 |
| France | | 7 | 3 | 1 | 2 | 1 | 14 |
| Georgia | 1 | 6 | | | | | 7 |
| Greece | 3 | 2 | | 11 | | | 16 |
| Hungary | 2 | 2 | 1 | 3 | | | 8 |
| Italy | | 1 | 2 | 2 | | 1 | 6 |
| Latvia | 1 | 1 | | | | 1 | 3 |
| Lithuania | | | 1 | | | | 1 |
| Moldova | 1 | | | 1 | 1 | | 3 |
| Netherlands | | | 1 | 1 | | | 2 |
| Poland | | 2 | 1 | 2 | 2 | 1 | 8 |
| Romania | 1 | 6 | 2 | 24 | | | 33 |
| Russia | 6 | 6 | | 8 | | 2 | 22 |
| Turkey | 2 | 1 | 2 | | | 3 | 8 |
| Ukraine | | 3 | 1 | | 5 | 1 | 10 |
| The United Kingdom | | 2 | 1 | | | 1 | 4 |
| Total | 18 (10.9%) | 47 (28.5%) | 17 (10.3%) | 59 (35.7%) | 11 (6.6%) | 13 (7.8%) | 165 |

**Table 2** Pilot and leading judgments related to overcrowding and poor material conditions in prisons

| Countries | Pilot procedure (yes/no) | Pilot judgment(s) | Number of cases grouped with pilot judgment(s) | Leading cases grouped together under enhanced supervision | Number of cases grouped together | Number of additional cases pending before the ECtHR |
|---|---|---|---|---|---|---|
| Russia | Yes | *Kalashnikov v. Russia* (2002); *Ananyev and Others v. Russia* (2012) | 83 | | | 250 +[a] |
| Ukraine | No | | | *Yakovenko v. Ukraine* (2014); *Nevmerzhitsky v. Ukraine* (2005); *Logvinenko v. Ukraine* (2011); *Isayev v. Ukraine* (2009) | 15 cases grouped together with the leading cases | |
| Poland | No | | | *Orchowski v. Poland* (2009); *Norbert Sikorski v. Poland* (2009); *Kaprykowski v. Poland* (2009) | Eight cases with *Orchowski and Sikorski*; Nine cases with *Kaprykowski* | |
| Italy | Yes | *Torreggiani and Others v. Italy* (2013) | 7 | *Sulejmanovic v. Italy* (2009) | | |
| Greece | | | | *Nisiotis v. Greece* (2011) | 10 cases grouped under *Nisiotis*; | of the *Nisiotis* group of cases, *Taggatidis and others v. Greece* involves 47 petitions |

(*continued*)

**Table 2** (continued)

| Countries | Pilot procedure (yes/no) | Pilot judgment(s) | Number of cases grouped with pilot judgment(s) | Leading cases grouped together under enhanced supervision | Number of cases grouped together | Number of additional cases pending before the ECtHR |
|---|---|---|---|---|---|---|
| Hungary | Yes | *Varga and Others v. Hungary* (2015) | | *István Gábor Kovács* | Six cases grouped under the *István Gábor Kovács* | 450[a] |
| Bulgaria | Yes | *Neshkov and Others v. Bulgaria* (2015) | | *Kehayov v. Bulgaria* (2005) | 24 cases grouped under the *Kehayov* | 40 more applications related to detention conditions are currently pending before the ECtHR |
| Romania | Yes | *Bragadireanu v. Romania* (2008) | 44 | | | 93 cases altogether concerning prison conditions are pending for execution before the CoM as of February 2015; in 2014, the ECtHR communicated 64 new applications concerning prison conditions |

[a]Data from ECtHR factsheet on pilot judgments, July 2015

areas (Russia, Hungary, Ukraine, Greece, France, Poland). At the same time, some countries reveal a particularly problematic issue area that has given rise to a large number of violations, such as prisoners' health-related issues in France, prison overcrowding in Russia, Romania, and Greece, and violations related to special prison regimes in Ukraine. In France, studies have shown that people with mental health problems are over-represented in French prisons—an outcome of a variety of organizational and penal law changes since the 1980s—where appropriate and adequate care is woefully insufficient (Chantraine 2015: 38–39).

Across countries, the most problematic issue area is by far prison overcrowding and poor material conditions overall (with 35.7% of our sample of violations), with health-related violations—evidenced as much in long-standing members such as France and Belgium as in more recent CoE members from the ex-communist world such as Georgia, Romania, and Russia—coming second (28.5%). Prison overcrowding directly connected with issues such as personal privacy, hygiene, recreation space and time, and so on make up the material preconditions that shape the experience of incarceration; they both reflect and in turn reinforce the enhanced or conversely reduced ability of a penitentiary system to ensure basic human rights standards for detainees. Substandard conditions of detention in pre-trial or remand centres (issue area 1) can be considered as a subset of overcrowding and poor material conditions (issue area 4). Together, they show that the decrepit physical infrastructure that falls below minimum human rights standards is a widespread feature of European prisons where persons are detained for short or longer periods of time.

## 4 Domestic Implementation of Human Rights Judgments Related to Prison

This section provides an overview of how different states fare in implementing the ECtHR's judgments related to prison conditions and detention more broadly. We take a specific measure as a yardstick for assessing state implementation, namely, length of time in months. Anagnostou and Mungiu-Pippidi (2014) have used time to implementation as a measure of state performance in conjunction with the percentage of the respective ECtHR judgments that have been implemented by each state. The assumption is that the length of time that it takes states to give practical effect to an unfavourable judgment in tandem with the number of adverse judgments a state has implemented at each point in time captures a key parameter of human rights implementation—namely, foot-dragging. Reluctance to comply often takes the form of procrastination or purposeful neglect on the part of national authorities. Lengthy periods of implementation in the meantime lead to recurrence of similar violations, and thus of adverse judgments. As a measure, length of time to implementation is also used offhand by PACE and the CoM to distinguish states that are better implementers from those that are more problematic. According to Voeten (2014), though, time to implementation is directly connected to the complexity of the remedial measures and the difficulty of the implementation tasks required to redress particular human rights violations.

On the basis of time to implementation and percentage of executed cases, Table 3 provides a summary of state implementation of prison-related judgments. Length of time is counted in number of months from the delivery of a judgment by the ECtHR until the CoM terminates its supervision over it by issuing a final resolution (for closed cases), or number of months that a case is pending (for open, until March 2016). We see in the last three columns of Table 3 that prison-related violations are largely repetitive violations (45.5%). Another 31.5% are leading judgments, and a 3.6% are pilot judgments and are under enhanced supervision by the CoM (the remaining 19.4% of our sample is not classified because they were issued before the latest changes in the rules of the CoM that introduced this distinction).

Overall, Table 3 shows that state implementation of prison-related judgments is highly problematic: only in 23.6% of the judgments has the CoM terminated its supervision by March 2016, while implementation was still pending in the remaining 76.4% of the judgments. Average time to implementation for closed cases is a bit more than five years, while in open cases, state compliance is on average pending for nearly six years. There are apparently significant differences across states. However, in

**Table 3** Status of execution of prison-related judgments across countries (closed vs. open; time to implementation, leading, repetitive, pilot judgments)

| Country against which complaint is lodged | Closed | open | Grand total | Average of time for which implementation has been pending (in months, until March 2016), if case is open | Average of time to implementation (in months) if case is closed | Percentage of cases that have been closed (%) | Leading case | Repetitive case | Pilot judgments |
|---|---|---|---|---|---|---|---|---|---|
| Albania | | 2 | 2 | 85.5 | | 0 | 2 | | |
| Armenia | 1 | 1 | 2 | 66 | 78 | 50 | 1 | | |
| Belgium | 1 | 5 | 6 | 34.5 | 82 | 16.6 | 4 | 2 | |
| Bulgaria | 1 | 3 | 4 | 52.7 | 71 | 25 | 2 | | 1 |
| Croatia | | 4 | 4 | 86.8 | | 0 | 2 | 2 | |
| Estonia | 1 | 1 | 2 | 23 | 14 | 50 | | 1 | |
| France | 12 | 2 | 14 | 21 | 48.5 | 85.7 | 5 | 1 | |
| Georgia | 7 | | 7 | | 36.3 | 100 | 1 | 6 | |
| Greece | 2 | 14 | 16 | 39.7 | 101.5 | 12.5 | 2 | 11 | |
| Hungary | | 8 | 8 | 41.8 | | 0 | 2 | 5 | 1 |
| Italy | 4 | 2 | 6 | 109 | 79 | 66.7 | 3 | | 1 |
| Latvia | 1 | 2 | 3 | 69.5 | 22 | 33.3 | 1 | 1 | |
| Lithuania | 1 | | 1 | | 33 | 100 | | | |
| Moldova | 2 | 1 | 3 | 103 | 68.5 | 66.7 | | 1 | |
| Netherlands | 1 | 1 | 2 | 121 | 79 | 50 | 1 | | |

(*continued*)

**Table 3** (continued)

| Country against which complaint is lodged | Closed | open | Grand total | Average of time for which implementation has been pending (in months, until March 2016), if case is open | Average of time to implementation (in months) if case is closed | Percentage of cases that have been closed (%) | Leading case | Repetitive case | Pilot judgments |
|---|---|---|---|---|---|---|---|---|---|
| Poland | 2 | 6 | 8 | 66.5 | 104.5 | 25 | 3 | 3 | |
| Romania | | 33 | 33 | 67 | | 0 | 4 | 27 | 1 |
| Russia | | 22 | 22 | 89.9 | | 0 | 7 | 10 | 2 |
| Turkey | | 8 | 8 | 74.9 | | 0 | 6 | 2 | |
| Ukraine | | 10 | 10 | 123.3 | | 0 | 7 | 3 | |
| United Kingdom | 5 | | 5 | | 67.6 | 100 | | | |
| GRAND TOTAL | 39 (23.6%) | 126 (76.4%) | 165 (100%) | 70.8 (Average) | 61.8 (Average) | 39.3% | 52 | 75 | 6 |

view of the highly unbalanced distribution of judgments (a couple of countries have less than a handful), we do not rely on these values for a statistical analysis. Still, failure to implement clearly stands out in some states, especially those with a high number of violations: Poland, Romania, Russia, Turkey, and Ukraine have not implemented any prison-related judgment against them and implementation is pending for more than five years (Poland, Romania) or more than six years (Turkey) or more than seven years (Russia, Ukraine).

Similarly, Hungary has not implemented any of the violating judgments against it in our sample, which, however, have been pending for 3.5 years. Greece also displays poor performance with only 12.5% of adverse judgments against it, and this after more than eight years. In most of the remaining judgments of our sample against Greece, which are more recent (mostly about prison overcrowding), implementation is pending for a little over three years. Similarly, Italy implemented some of the adverse judgments against it extremely slowly (after more than six years), while the remaining two are pending for more than eight years. By contrast, France and Georgia have a high percentage of judgments, in which execution was completed in a relatively shorter period of time (48.5 and 36.28 months, respectively) on average.

Time to implementation and percentage of closed cases by issue area complement cross-national variation and reveal some interesting and potentially significant patterns (Table 4).

What stands out is the very small portion of implemented judgments related to overcrowding and poor prison conditions (issue 4, only 7.27% closed) and those related to conditions of detention in remand centres (issue 1, 16.6% closed). It is not accidental that all six pilot judgments of our sample are related to these two issues, from which the most grave prison-related human rights problems stem. By contrast, a substantially larger percentage of adverse judgments are implemented in relation to violence, ill-treatment or suicide while in prison (issue 6), inhuman treatment while in detention (issue 3), and somewhat less judgments related to special prison regimes (issue 5) and health-related violations (issue 2). Generally, the open judgments in all issue areas are pending for implementation for at least five years (on average for 78.9 months, see Table 4). Violations related to special prison regimes are on average pending for an

**Table 4** Status of execution of prison-related judgments across issue areas (leading, repetitive, pilot; open, closed; time to implementation)

| Main issue area | Leading | Not categorized | Pilot | Repetitive | Total violations | Open cases | Average time for which implementation has been pending (for open cases, until March 2016) | Closed cases | Average time to implementation (for closed cases, in months) | Percentage of cases that have been closed (%) |
|---|---|---|---|---|---|---|---|---|---|---|
| Issue 1: Conditions of detention in pre-trial/ remand centres | 8 | 4 | 2 | 4 | 18 (10.9%) | 15 | 78.4 | 3 | 84 | 16.6 |
| Issue 2: Health-related issues (inmates with special health/ mental problems, or access to health care) | 20 | 7 | | 20 | 47 (28.5%) | 32 | 71.1 | 15 | 47.5 | 31.9 |
| Issue 3: Inhuman detention (i.e. solitary confinement, degrading treatment, strip searches) | 6 | 9 | | 2 | 17 (10.3%) | 8 | 81 | 9 | 73 | 52.9 |

(*continued*)

**Table 4** (continued)

| Main issue area | Leading | Not categorized | Pilot | Repetitive | Total violations | Open cases | Average time for which implementation has been pending (for open cases, until March 2016) | Closed cases | Average time to implementation (for closed cases, in months) | Percentage of cases that have been closed (%) |
|---|---|---|---|---|---|---|---|---|---|---|
| Issue 4: Overcrowding and poor material conditions overall | 10 | 4 | 4 | 41 | 59 (35.8%) | 54 | 61 | 5 | 36.3 | 8.5 |
| Issue 5: Special prison regime (high security, dangerous, or death-row inmates) | 3 | 4 | | 4 | 11 (6.7%) | 7 | 122 | 4 | 60.5 | 36.4 |
| Issue 6: Violence, ill-treatment, or suicide while in prison | 5 | 4 | | 4 | 13 (7.9%) | 9 | 60 | 4 | 75.8 | 30.7 |
| Total | 52 | 32 | 6 | 75 | 165 | 126 | 78.9 | 39 | 62.8 | 31.8% |

excessively long time (122 months), which, however, partly reflects the dismal implementation record of Ukraine, from which nearly half of these violations originate (see Table 1).

The tiny proportion of judgments related to overcrowded and dilapidated conditions in prisons and remand centres (issues 1 and 4) that have been implemented by states possibly reflects the complexity of the necessary remedial measures and the amount of financial resources that the construction of new prisons or the revamping of old ones requires. Most of these judgments have been pending for implementation for at least five years on average. By contrast, a large percentage of violations related to inhuman detention, such as solitary confinement and strip searches (issues 3), have been implemented. These often require primarily individualized remedial measures or limited legal reform or internal disciplinary measures (if stemming from administrative practices), which are easier—at least if the political will exists—to apply. This finding appears to concur with the point raised by Voeten (2014), and which is mentioned earlier, namely, that the more complex, demanding and financially exigent the general measures, the slower and more reluctant national authorities are in implementing them.

In order to redress overcrowding, far-reaching, organizationally complex, and fiscally burdensome reforms are required, which take a long time to complete. In response to the detected violations related to poor prison conditions and overcrowding, governments in the above-mentioned eight states have pursued four sets of measures and reforms: (a) the building of new prison facilities or the creation of additional space in existing ones with the goal of improving cell space per inmate, (b) administrative and organizational changes in prison units, (c) legislative and policy changes in criminal law aimed at reducing the number of prisoners, the use and length of pre-trial detention, as well as the use of alternative punitive measures not involving physical deprivation of liberty for persons sentenced by a court, and (d) the establishment of bodies or offices to continuously monitor prison space and population. In the frame of judgment execution, these sets of measures are almost always accompanied by the dissemination—translated in national language—of the respective judgment(s) to the competent authorities, as well as some efforts to provide information and training to the prison staff and other administrative staff involved.

The construction of new prison facilities, or the reconstruction of existing facilities available in the penitentiary system into prisons, is among the reforms states initiate to address prison overcrowding. For example, already in the first decade of the 2000s (*Kalashnikov* group of cases), the Russian Ministry of Justice adopted a federal programme for reforming the country's penitentiary system. It included the building of new remand prisons and the reconstruction of existing ones. As a result of this, by 2010, the number of spaces available had increased by 13,100. Notwithstanding a perceptible trend of improvement, the Court found, in 2012, in the pilot judgment of *Ananyev and others v. Russia* that the problem persisted. The latest 2012 action plan of the Russian government contains numerous planned measures to improve the material conditions of detention, to establish effective domestic preventive and compensatory remedies, and to ensure a more balanced approach towards the choice of preventive measures for suspects and the accused.[60]

In the context of implementing the ECtHR judgment of *István Gábor Kovács*, the Hungarian government estimated that the capacity of the Hungarian penal institutions would have to be increased by 70% in order to meet the CPT standards for personal space per inmate, and stated its intent to complete the construction of new facilities by 2018. The actual increase of new places that was accomplished in 2013, though, was only 160.[61] The target of expanding prison facilities is to increase the average space per inmate in line with existing standards in domestic law and in European Prison Rules and the CPT reports. In response to the recent *Neshkov v. Bulgaria* pilot judgment, Bulgarian authorities have recently advanced legislative proposals for a more flexible initial allocation of prisoners, which are under consideration in order to place prisoners in facilities that are less rather than more crowded, with the ultimate goal of reaching the target of 4 $m^2$ per detainee.[62] Such measures, however, are viewed by the CPT and the CoM as largely ineffective because they tend to generate new problems for prison management, as well as to disregard other vital issues, such as proximity of prison to one's family.[63]

Together with the ECtHR, the CoM and the CPT have all underlined that the problem of unacceptable detention conditions is not solely or even mainly likely to be addressed through the construction of new prison facilities. Indeed, in its report on Hungary, the CPT stated that '…providing additional accommodation cannot on its own offer a lasting solution. The only viable way to control overcrowding is to adopt policies designed to limit or moderate the number of persons sent to prison' (CPT/Inf (2014)13, para 39). In this direction, the Court and the CoM strongly urge national authorities in countries with structural problems to pursue reform of criminal law and policy. Detention (whether at the pre-trial or the postconviction phase) must be a measure of last resort, and there should be greater use of alternative non-custodial sanctions. Adopted in response to the pilot judgment of *Bragadireanu v. Romania*, the new 2014 Criminal Code of Romania introduces new alternatives to detention on remand (house arrest and release under judicial supervision, extending the scope of pecuniary sentences). It also modifies the conditions for applying measures alternative to imprisonment and it strengthens the role of the probation service—all these with the aim of redressing one of the worst problems of prison overcrowding in Europe.[64] Romania witnessed a steady increase in its prison population in 2007–2013, while the small decrease that was recorded in 2014 was not considered sufficient or sustainable by the CoM.[65]

A main cause of prison overcrowding is the all too facile resort to pre-trial custody, including for persons suspected for economic crimes (as in Russia) as well as to imprisonment, even for persons committing petty offences (as in Hungary). In the past few years, in Greece, measures to decrease prison overcrowding have focused primarily on limiting the number of persons sent to prison to execute a sentence (alternatives to imprisonment) and on ensuring a reduction of the population of convicted inmates by means of suspension of prison terms or early release schemes.[66] In Italy, legislative reforms of criminal law and policy in 2013 aimed at reducing the prison entry flows have redefined the seriousness of a variety of offences and the conditions under which incarceration is necessary. They have also provided for early release in less serious cases, made possible home arrest for some vulnerable individuals, and made it possible to release offenders whose crime is less serious (i.e. drug addicts). Additional measures prepared by the Italian government to reduce prison overcrowding aim at reducing recourse to imprisonment through extending the use of alternative measures such as probation, social services, and the use of electronic monitoring.[67]

A third important kind of reform promoted by the ECtHR and the CoM is the provision of an effective domestic remedy, which prisoners, whose human rights were violated, can use to seek redress and compensation. The issue arose as central in the pilot judgments of *Ananyev and others v. Russia* and *Torreggiani and others v. Italy*. In 2013, the Russian government presented a draft law that would empower domestic courts to order specific remedial measures, to set limits for enforcement of the orders, and to define the authority responsible for enforcement. In response to the *Torreggiani* judgments, Italy also established in 2013 a remedy allowing inmates to complain about violations of their rights to a supervisory judge and introduced the legal means to enforce a relevant judicial order. Another Italian law that came into force in 2014 also provided the possibility for compensation of an inmate whose rights were violated due to prison conditions, in the form of pecuniary and non-pecuniary (i.e. reduction of his/her sentence) compensation.[68]

The CoM is particularly scrutinizing how and the extent to which such a domestic remedy is effective in practice. The Court has indicated that to be efficient, a remedial system must ensure a prompt and diligent handling of prisoners' complaints, secure their effective participation in the examination of grievances, and dispose of a wide range of legal tools for the purpose of eradicating the identified breach of the Convention. Taking the input contained in the submission of the NGO 'Public Verdict Foundation' on board,[69] the CoM urged the Russian government to further consider various aspects of the draft law to ensure that the burden of proof shifts to the prison authorities once the claimant has established a prima facie case that s/he has suffered ill-treatment due to unacceptable prison conditions, as well as to ensure that court fees and other costs for the complainants do not have a dissuasive effect.[70] In Romania, the CoM was critical of the compensatory aspect of the adopted remedy because it can succeed only if the applicant (prisoner) can prove the defendant's (the prison) fault; overcrowding may very well be linked to penal law and policy rather than stem from the prison system itself.[71] Last but not least, the adoption of a domestic remedy compliant with the ECHR and the Court's case law involves not only legal reform and procedural rules, but it also requires substantial changes in judicial approach and practice.

## 5 Discussion and Conclusion

The preceding broad review of state implementation of ECtHR judgments pertaining to prison conditions shows that their impact is limited, albeit far from insignificant. Prison-related human rights violations arose as early as the 1970s and 1980s in countries like the UK, Austria, Belgium, and Germany. The Strasbourg Court's judgments prompted significant reforms through the reluctant yet progressive recognition of prisoners' rights, in matters such as release procedures, communication of prisoners with the outside world, and formal discipline proceedings (Livingstone 2000: 321). Yet, the structural problem of prison overpopulation and debased material conditions has emerged as far more pronounced and extensive in the new post-communist member states that acceded to the ECHR and the CoE in the 1990s. In both parts of Europe, the rising numbers of incarcerated persons have been related to a distinctive trend in penal law to impose stricter and longer sentences intended to establish crime control and to remove seemingly dangerous individuals from the society at large (Snacken 2015).

Tackling prison overcrowding and inhumane conditions of imprisonment is an exceedingly complex, time-consuming, and demanding process, which cannot be carried out by legislative reform alone. Besides the (re)construction of prisons in order to create more spaces, redressing the problem at its root further requires fundamental reform towards more moderate penal policies—politically and socially a highly controversial issue. It also requires the establishment of effective domestic remedies, which in turn presupposes some level of acceptance of prisoners' rights, as well as a change in national judicial approach and culture. Where substantial or even dramatic reductions in imprisonment rates have been achieved (as in Finland since the 1970s and 1980s), it has been the result of deliberate and long-term policy change based on firm political will and consensus to bring down the number of inmates (Coyle 2006: 106).

Besides the complexity of reforming Europe's penitentiary systems, time to implementation is further prolonged by the more scrutinizing approach and demanding supervision exercised by the CoM, especially in regard to violations considered to be of structural and systemic nature. At least in relation to such violations, which form the bulk of prison-related judgments in the former communist countries but also in countries like Greece and Italy, the observation that the Court takes a highly individualized approach (Foster 2015: 395) does not hold. In fact, the states, which the ECtHR has identified as the ones plagued by systemic problems of prison overcrowding and inhumane detention conditions more broadly, are under enhanced pressure to engage in reforms in different areas, in order to mount an effective response. The action plans that the national governments submit to the CoM, in which they outline and describe the various measures, are often thorough and detailed. They include projections about the effects that the planned reforms are going to have on prison populations. This is the case even for reluctant states like Russia, which has nonetheless introduced significant even if insufficient measures to reform the country's prisons (Parrott 2015). Still, these action plans may contain proposed or intended reforms that are subsequently not legislated or are not put into practice.

The ECtHR judgments that find European prison conditions and practices to infringe basic human rights standards do not—cannot—bring about fundamental reform of the penitentiary systems of states. It would be unrealistic to expect judicial decisions to have such an effect; they are only one factor among many that affect policy making in such a controversial and multi-actor field as penal law and penitentiary institutions. Yet, what Strasbourg judgments have over time managed to do is to enhance judicial oversight over imprisonment standards and conditions, an area of largely administrative regulation, in which prison authorities had far-reaching (and still maintain considerable) discretion. By doing so, these judgments provide ample leverage to domestic prison reformers, among political elites but also state administrators, to pursue changes for improved conditions of incarceration.

The ECtHR judgments have also helped open up the closed nature of penitentiary institutions to independent supervisory bodies, such as ombudsman institutions. For example, the Bulgarian authorities reported that since 2012, the ombudsman is allowed to perform visits and inspections in detention facilities and to give recommendations on the treatment of detained persons. Along with civil society organizations, such as the Bulgarian Helsinki Committee and the Centre for the Study of Democracy as well as the NGO Bulgarian Lawyers for Human Rights, the ombudsman also takes part in the working group for the execution of the judgment *Neshkov and Others*, and in the drawing up of plans for improvement of conditions of detention in Bulgarian detention facilities.[72]

With the new rules and the greater transparency established in the supervision process by the CoM, NGOs are now actively engaged in following the ECtHR judgments and in drawing from them in the domestic contestation over penitentiary reform. The new role of NGOs in the process of execution of judgments appears to be highly significant. It tends to present a different and critical picture of the government's proposed and actual measures, substantiated by official data or by documentation obtained from NGO monitoring of prisons. For example, the report of the Association for the Defense of Human Rights in Romania—the Helsinki Committee (APADOR-CH) in the context of CoM supervision of execution in the pilot judgment of *Bragadireanu* was clearly influential in disputing the government's claim of improvement. On the basis of official data, APADOR-CH showed that the measures adopted to ameliorate poor detention conditions were thoroughly insufficient to change the state of dilapidation in Romanian prisons, the degrading treatment of vulnerable prisoners such as minors, and the lack of appropriate health care, which falls well below ECHR and CPT standards.[73]

In sum, despite the fact that the ECtHR judgments have not influenced any evident shift in penal policy in European states, they have triggered a variety of reforms that do show some, even if limited, positive change. The slow decline of prison overcrowding that is recorded over the past few years is possibly one visible consequence of the domestically implemented measures (Aebi and Delgrande 2015).

## Notes

1. On the significant prisoners' rights case law of the ECommHR and the ECtHR until the late 1990s, as well as their restrictive approach in this area, see Livingstone (2000).
2. The CPT draws this distinction between 'active' infliction of ill-treatment and 'passive' ill-treatment. See Murdoch (2006: 171).
3. *Ilhan v. Turkey*, App. No.22277/93, 27 June 2000; *Yakovenko v. Ukraine*, App. No. 15825/06, 25 January 2008.
4. Other kinds of violations of structural nature are the excessive length of proceedings and lack of domestic remedy, prolonged non-enforcement of court decisions and lack of domestic remedy, violations of the right to the protection of property, and exclusion of convicted prisoners from voting.
5. PPR is the rate of the registered prison population per 100,000 inhabitants in each country. For detailed data on prison population, see Walmsley (2013); Aebi and Delgrande (2015).
6. On the numbers and percentages of foreigners among inmates in the CoE states, see Aebi and Delgrande (2015: 90–91).
7. Rec(2006)2 of the CoM to member states on the European Prison Rules.
8. *Poltoratskiy v. Ukraine*, App. No. 38812/97, 29 April 2003; see Marochini (2009: 1115).
9. In some cases, when specific obstacles hamper implementation, the CoM may adopt as a form of pressure an interim resolution criticizing a state's failure to abide by a judgment and urging it to take further action.
10. The pilot procedure was first introduced in the case of *Broniowski v. Poland*, App. No. 31443/96, 22 June 2004.
11. The relevant procedure was codified in the Rules of Court in 2011 (Rule 61).
12. Other cardinal issues under enhanced supervision were actions by security forces (20%), excessive length of judicial proceedings (11%), and non-enforcement of domestic judicial decisions (7%), among others.

13. *Ilhan v. Turkey*, App. No. 22277/93, 27 June 2000.
14. *Aerts v. Belgium*, App. No. 25357/94, 30 June 1998.
15. *Kröcher and Möller v. Switzerland*, No. 8463/78, 9 July 1981.
16. *Hurtado v. Switzerland*, App. No. 17549/90, 28 January 1994.
17. *Kehayov v. Bulgaria*, App. No. 41035/98, 18 April 2005.
18. See *Moisejevs v. Latvia*, App. No. 64846/01, 23 October 2006.
19. See *Gülay Çetin v. Turkey*, App. No. 44084/10, 5 June 2013.
20. See *Fehér v. Hungary*, App. No. 69095/10, 2 October 2013; *Modârcă v. Moldova*, App. No. 14437/05, 10 August 2007.
21. See *Kalashnikov v. Russia*, App. No. 47095/99, 15 October 2002.
22. See *Kalashnikov v. Russia*, App. No. 47095/99, 15 October 2002.
23. See *Kehayov v. Bulgaria*, App. No. 41035/98, 18 April 2005; *Ramishvili and Kokhreidze v. Georgia*, App. No. 1704/06, 27 April 2009.
24. See *Modârcă v. Moldova*, App. No. 14437/05, 10 August 2007.
25. See *Kalashnikov v. Russia*, App. No. 47095/99, 15 October 2002.
26. See *Kehayov v. Bulgaria*, App. No. 41035/98, 18 April 2005; *Ramishvili and Kokhreidze v. Georgia*, App. No. 1704/06, 27 April 2009; *Ahmade v. Greece*, App. No. 50520/09, 25 December 2012; *Modârcă v. Moldova*, App. No. 14437/05, 10 August 2007; *Kalashnikov v. Russia*, App. No. 47095/99, 15 October 2002.
27. See *Kehayov v. Bulgaria*, App. No. 41035/98, 18 April 2005.
28. See *Modârcă v. Moldova*, App. No. 14437/05, 10 August 2007.
29. See *Ashot Harutyunyan v. Armenia*, App. No. 34334/04, 15 September 2010; *Yoh-Ekale Mwanje v. Belgium*, App. No. 10486/10, 20 March 2012; *Lankester v. Belgium*, App. No. 22283/10, 9 April 2014; *Claes v. Belgium*, App. No. 43418/09, 10 April 2013; *Poghossian v. Georgia*, App. No. 9870/07, 24 May 2009; *Kotsaftis v. Greece*, App. No. 39780/06, 12 September 2008; *Cirillo v. Italy*, App. No. 36276/10, 29 April 2013; *Kucheruk v. Ukraine*, App. No. 2570/04, 6 December 2007; *Melnik v. Ukraine*, App. No. 72286/01, 28 June 2006; *Grori v. Albania*, App. No. 7 October 2009; *V.D. v. Romania*, App. No. 7078/02, 28 June 2010.
30. See *Kotsaftis v. Greece*, App. No. 39780/06, 12 September 2008.
31. See *Dybeku v. Albania*, App. No. 41153/06, 2 June 2008; *Dobri v. Romania*, App. No. 25153/04, 20 June 2011.
32. See *Dobri v. Romania*, App. No. 25153/04, 20 June 2011.
33. See *L.B. v. Belgium*, App. No. 22831/08, 2 January 2013; *Riviere v. France*, App. No. 33834/03, 11 October 2006; *Mouisel v. France*, App. No. 67263/01, 21 May 2003; *Renolde v. France*, App. No. 5608/05, 16 January 2009.

34. See *Vincent v. France*, App. No. 6253/03, 26 March 2007; *Helhal v. France*, App. No. 10401/12, 19 May 2015; *Raffray Taddei v. France*, App. No. 36435/07, 21 March 2011; *Z.H. v. Hungary*, App. No. 28973/11, 8 February 2013; *Kaprykowski v. Poland*, App. No. 23052/05, 3 May 2009; *Flamînzeanu v. Romania*, App. No. 56664/08, 12 July 2011; *Price v. UK*, App. No. 33394/96, 10 October 2001.
35. See *Renolde v. France*, App. No. 5608/05, 16 January 2009.
36. See *Kaprykowski v. Poland*, App. No. 23052/05, 3 May 2009.
37. See *Vincent v. France*, App. No. 6253/03, 26 March 2007.
38. See *Orchowski v. Poland*, App. No. 17885/04, 22 January 2010; *Norbert Sikorski v. Poland*, App.No. 17599/05, 22 January 2010; *Szel v. Hungary*, App. No. 30221/06, 7 September 2011; *Nisiotis v. Greece*, App. No. 34704/08, 20 June 2011.
39. See *Szel v. Hungary*, App. No. 30221/06, 7 September 2011.
40. See *Torreggiani and others v. Italy*, App. No. 43517/09, 35315/10, 37818/10, 46882/09, 55400/09, 57875/09, 61535/09, 27 May 2013.
41. See *Moiseyev v. Russia*, App. No. 62936/00, 6 April 2009; *Alver v. Estonia*, App. No. 64812/01, 8 February 2006; *Sulejmanovic v. Italy*, App. No. 22635/03, 6 November 2009; *Vasilescu v. Belgium*, App. No. 64682/12, 20 April 2015; *Neshkov and others v. Bulgaria*, App. No. 36925/10, 21487/12, 72893/12, 73196/12, 77718/12, 9717/13, 1 June 2015; *Brânduşe v. Romania*, App. No. 6586/03, 7 July 2009.
42. See *Moiseyev v. Russia*, App. No. 62936/00, 6 April 2009.
43. See *Vasilescu v. Belgium*, App. No. 64682/12, 20 April 2015.
44. See *Neshkov and others v. Bulgaria*, App. No. 36925/10, 21487/12, 72893/12, 73196/12, 77718/12, 9717/13, 1 June 2015.
45. See *Bragadireanu v. Romania*, App. No. 22088/04, 6 March 2008; *Canali v. France*, App. No. 40119/09, 25 July 2013; *Martzaklis and Others v. Greece*, 20378/13, 9 October 2015; *Ţicu v. Romania*, App. No. 24575/10, 1 January 2014.
46. See *Plathey v. France*, App. No. 48337/09, 10 February 2012; *Csüllög v. Hungary*, App. No. 30042/08, 7 September 2011; *X v. Turkey*, App. No. 24626/09, 27 May 2013; *Nevmerzhitsky v. Ukraine*, App. No. 54825/00, 12 October 2005.
47. See *X v. Turkey*, App. No. 24626/09, 27 May 2013.
48. See *Csüllög v. Hungary*, App. No. 30042/08, 7 September 2011.
49. See *El Shennawy v. France*, App. No. 51246/08, 20 April 2011; *Frerot v. France*, App. No. 70204/01, 12 September 2007; *Valasinas v. Lithuania*,

App. No. 44558/98, 24 October 2001; *Lorsé And Others v. the Netherlands*, App. No. 52750/99, 4 May 2003; *Iwańczuk v. Poland*, App. No. 25196/94, 15 February 2002.

50. See *Valasinas v. Lithuania*, App. No. 44558/98, 24 October 2001.
51. See *Elefteriadis v. Romania*, App. No. 38427/05, 25 April 2011; *Öcalan v. Turkey (no. 2)*, App. No. 24069/03, 197/04, 6201/06, 10464/07, 13 October 2014; *Nevmerzhitsky v. Ukraine*, App. No. 54825/00, 12 October 2005; *McGlinchey and Others v. the United Kingdom*, App. No. 50390/99, 29 July 2003.
52. See *McGlinchey and Others v. the United Kingdom*, App. No. 50390/99, 29 July 2003.
53. See *Nazarenko v. Ukraine*, App. No. 39483/98, 29 July 2003; *Dankevich v. Ukraine*, App. No. 40679/98, 29 July 2003; *Kuznetsov v. Ukraine*, App. No. 39042/97, 29 April 2003; *Poltoratskiy v. Ukraine*, App. No. 38812/97, 29 April 2003; *Iorgov v. Bulgaria*, App. No. 40653/98, 7 July 2004.
54. See *Piechowicz v. Poland*, App. No. 20071/07, 17 July 2012; *Horych v. Poland*, App. No. 13621/08, 17 July 2012; *Payet v. France*, App. No. 19606/08, 20 April 2011; *Khider v. France*, App. No. 39364/05, 9 October 2009.
55. See *Piechowicz v. Poland*, App. No. 20071/07, 17 July 2012; *Horych v. Poland*, App. No. 13621/08, 17 July 2012.
56. See *Tarariyeva v. Russia*, App. No. 4353/03, 14 March 2007; *Jasinska v. Poland*, App. No. 28326/05, 1 September 2010; *Ketreb v. France*, App. No. 38447/09, 19 October 2012; *De Donder and De Clippel v. Belgium*, App. No. 8595/06, 6 March 2012; *Keenan v. the United Kingdom*, App. No. 27229/95, 2 April 2001; *Kilavuz v. Turkey*, App. No. 8327/03, 21 January 2009; *Coselav v. Turkey*, App. No. 1413/07, 18 March 2013; *Yuriy Illarionovich Shchokin v. Ukraine*, App. No. 4299/03, 3 January 2014.
57. See *Premininy v. Russia*, App. No. 44973/04, 20 June 2011; *D.F. v. Latvia*, App. No. 11160/07, 29 January 2014; *Indelicato v. Italy*, App. No. 31143/96, 18 January 2002.
58. See *Coselav v. Turkey*, App. No. 1413/07, 18 March 2013.
59. *Premininy v. Russia*, App. No. 44973/04, 20 June 2011.
60. Action plan on execution of the pilot judgment of the ECHR on application nos. 42525/07 and 60800/08 *Ananyev and Others v. Russia*, distributed by the Secretariat of the CoM, DH-DD(2012)1009, 29 October 2012.

61. See status of execution of *István Gábor Kovács*, CoM, last examined at its 1236th meeting (22–24 September 2015).
62. See Action Plan, communication from Bulgaria concerning the case of *Neshkov and Others* and the *Kehayov* group of cases against Bulgaria (Applications No. 36925/10, 41035/98), DH-DD(2015)755 rev, submitted on 8 August 2015, p. 6.
63. See status of execution of *István Gábor Kovács*, CoM, last examined at its 1236th meeting (22–24 September 2015).
64. Memorandum prepared by the Department for the Execution of Judgments of the ECtHR, H/Exec(2015)7, group of cases *Bragadireanu v. Romania*, 12 February 2015, p. 4. On the basis of data supplied by Romania's National Prison Administration, the NGO APADOR-CH indicates that the average living space available is a little over 2 $m^2$ per prisoner.
65. Memorandum prepared by the Department for the Execution of Judgments of the ECtHR, H/Exec(2015)7, Group of cases *Bragadireanu v. Romania*, 12 February 2015, pp. 5–6.
66. CoM, status of execution, *Nisiotis v. Greece* (App. No. 34704/08, 20 June 2011), last examined by the CoM at its 1230th meeting (9–11 June 2015).
67. CoM, communication from Italy concerning the case of *Torreggiani and others against Italy* (App. No. 43517/09), 27 May 2013, Action Plan presented by the Italian government, 27 November 2013.
68. CoM, status of execution of the *Torreggiani v. Italy* pilot judgment, last examined at the CoM 1214th meeting (2–4 December 2014).
69. Communication from an NGO (Public Verdict Foundation) in the *Ananyev and Others v. Russia*, 7 October 2013, CoM, considered at its 1193 meeting (4–6 March 2014), DH-DD(2014)44.
70. CoM, status of execution of the *Ananyev and Others v. Russia* judgment, last examined at the CoM 1201st meeting (3–5 June 2014).
71. Memorandum prepared by the Department for the Execution of Judgments of the ECtHR, H/Exec(2015)7, group of cases *Bragadireanu v. Romania*, 12 February 2015, p. 11.
72. See Action Plan, communication from Bulgaria concerning the case of *Neshkov and Others* and the *Kehayov* group of cases against Bulgaria, submitted on 8 August 2015, p. 13.
73. Communication from an NGO (APADOR-CH) in the *Bragadireanu* group of cases against Romania, 26 May 2014, CoM, DH-DD(2014)752.

## Literature

Aebi, M.F., and N. Delgrande. 2015. *SPACE I—Council of Europe Annual Penal Statistics: Prison populations. Survey 2013*. Strasbourg: Council of Europe.

Anagnostou, D., ed. 2013. *The European Court of Human Rights: Implementing Strasbourg's Judgments on Domestic Policy*. Edinburgh: Edinburgh University Press.

Anagnostou, D., and A. Mungiu-Pippidi. 2014. Domestic Implementation of Human Rights Judgments in Europe: Legal Infrastructure and Government Effectiveness Matter. *European Journal of International Law* 25 (1): 205–227.

Bates, E. 2005. Supervising the Execution of Judgments Delivered by the European Court of Human Rights: The Challenges Facing the Committee of Ministers. In *European Court of Human Rights: Remedies and Execution of Judgments*, ed. T. Christou and J.-P. Raymond, 49–106. London: British Institute of International and Comparative Law.

Chantraine, G. 2015. French Prisons of Yesteryear and Today. *Punishment and Society.* 12 (1): 27–46.

Committee of Ministers. 2013. *Supervision of the Execution of Judgments and Decisions of the European Court of Human Rights. 6th Annual Report of the Committee of Ministers. 2012*. Strasbourg: Council of Europe.

Committee on Legal Affairs and Human Rights. 2015. *Implementation of Judgments of the European Court of Human Rights*. 8th report. Doc.13864, September 9.

Coyle, A. 2006. Revision of the European Prison Rules, a Contextual Report. In *European Prison Rules*, 101–132. Strasbourg: Council of Europe.

Department for the Execution of Judgments of the European Court of Human Rights. 2010. Supervision of the Execution of Judgments and Decisions of the European Court of Human Rights: Implementation of the Interlaken Action Plan—Modalities for a Twin-Track Supervision System. CM/Inf/DH(2010) 37, 6 September 2010.

Forst, D. 2013. The Execution of Judgments of the European Court of Human Rights. Limits and Ways Ahead. *Vienna Journal on International Constitutional Law* 7 (3): 1–51.

Foster, S. 2015. The Effective Supervision of Prison Conditions. In *Protecting Vulnerable Groups—The European Human Rights Framework*, ed. F. Ippolito and S.I. Sánchez, 381–400. Oxford: Hart Publishing.

Hammarberg, T. 2011. *European Rights in Europe: No Grounds for Complacency. Viewpoints by Thomas Hammarberg*. Strasbourg: Council of Europe Commissioner for Human Rights.

Helfer, L.R., and E. Voeten. 2014. International Courts as Agents of Legal Change: Evidence from LGBT Rights in Europe. *International Organization* 68 (1): 77–110.
Hillebrecht, C. 2012. Implementing International Human Rights Law at Home: Domestic Politics and the European Court of Human Rights. *Human Rights Review* 13 (3): 279–301.
Lappi-Seppälä, T. 2011. Explaining Imprisonment in Europe. *European Journal of Criminology* 8 (4): 303–328.
Livingstone, S. 2000. Prisoners' Rights in the Context of the ECHR. *Punishment and Society* 2 (3): 309–324.
Marochini, M. 2009. The Ill-treatment of Prisoners in Europe: A Disease Diagnosed but not cured? *Zb. Prav. Fak. Sveuč. Rij.* 30 (2): 1108–1128.
Martens, S.K. 1996. Commentary. In *Compliance with Judgments of International Courts*, ed. M.K. Bulterman and M. Kuijer, 71–80. Leiden: Martinus Nijhoff.
Murdoch, J. 2006. The Impact of the Council of Europe's 'Torture Committee' and the Evolution of Standard-Setting in Relation to Places of Detention. *European Human Rights Law Review* 2: 159–179.
Parrott, L. 2015. Tools of Persuasion: the Efforts of the Council of Europe and the European Court of Human Rights to Reform the Russian Pre-trial Detention System. *Post-Soviet Affairs* 31 (2): 136–175.
Sicilianos, L.-A. 2014. The Involvement of the European Court of Human Rights in the Implementation of its Judgments: Recent Developments under Article 46. *Netherlands Quarterly of. Human Rights* 32 (3): 235–262.
Sitaropoulos, N. 2008. Supervising Execution of ECtHR Judgments Concerning Minorities—The Committee of Ministers' Potentials and Constraints. *Annuaire International des Droits de. L'Homme* 3: 523–550.
Snacken, S. 2015. Punishment, Legitimate Policies and Values: Penal Moderation, Dignity and Human Rights. *Punishment and Society* 17 (3): 397–423.
Sundberg, F.G.E. 2001. Control of Execution of Decisions under the ECHR. Some Remarks on the Committee of Ministers' Control of the Proper Implementation of Decisions Finding Violations of the Convention. In *International Human Rights Monitoring Mechanisms*, ed. G. Alfredsson, J. Grimheden, B. Ramchara, and A. de Zayas, 561–585. The Hague: Kluwer Law International.
Voeten, E. 2014. Domestic Implementation of European Court of Human Rights Judgments: Legal Infrastructure and Government Effectiveness

Matter: A Reply to Dia Anagnostou and Alina Mungiu-Pippidi. *European Journal of International Law* 25 (1): 229–238.

**Dia Anagnostou** is an assistant professor at the Panteion University of Social and Political Sciences and a senior research fellow at Hellenic Foundation for European & Foreign Policy (ELIAMEP), Athens, Greece.

**Dimitris Skleparis** is a postdoctoral research fellow at ELIAMEP, Athens, Greece.

# Learning from Carceral Tours: Reflections After a Howard Tour Across Europe

Tom Vander Beken

## 1 Introduction

This chapter draws upon a study on the role of prisons in Europe. The study was carried out by visiting prisons in six countries, as well as by reading, by observing and by listening to those who could say something about those prisons.[1] The study was inspired by the approach and work of John Howard (1726–1790) more than two centuries ago.

The aim of the chapter is twofold. On the one hand, we comment on how and for what purpose Howard visited prisons in his days and how this relates to contemporary methodological choices and consequences of a so-called carceral tour design. We pay special attention to carceral tours carried out by inspection and monitoring bodies today. On the other hand, the chapter summarises some of the findings about the countries that have been visited and draws general conclusions about the study as a whole. The ambition is not to make strong comparative statements on prisons in Europe but to reflect on what a carceral tour design can

T. Vander Beken (✉)
Ghent University, Ghent, Belgium



T. Daems, L. Robert (eds.), *Europe in Prisons*, Palgrave Studies in Prisons and Penology, DOI 10.1007/978-3-319-62250-7_4

contribute to studies in contemporary penology and penal policy. In particular, given the focus of this book, it is argued that a carceral tour design helps us clarify some of the inherent limitations of the approach and modus operandi of contemporary monitoring bodies, such as the European Committee for the Prevention of Torture (CPT).

## 2 In John Howard's Footsteps

Anyone interested in prisons ought to know who John Howard was. His countless visits to institutions of correction and of confinement all over Europe, and his books describing with exacting precision what he found, were an eye-opener for eighteenth-century society and set people thinking about what prisons were like and what they should (or should not) be. Although he was a man of rather limited personal ambition or skill in terms of policymaking, his activities and publications had a great impact, which often ended up placing him in the foreground as a major philanthropist and prison reformer. The content of his books remains highly relevant and readable to this day, especially his iconic *State of the prisons in England and Wales: with preliminary observations, and an account of some foreign prisons and hospitals* (first published in 1777) (Howard 1792) and *Prisons and lazarettos. An account of the principal lazarettos in Europe of 1789* (Howard 1791).

John Howard's mission in the late eighteenth century was to enter prisons in order to determine for himself what these institutions looked like and how they functioned. It is clear from his writings that he was mainly concerned about the organisation of prison life and how prisoners were treated. What prompted his flood of prison visits and his European tours was his appointment as High Sheriff of Bedfordshire in 1773, as a result of which he had an official visit to make to the county town jail. The things he witnessed there struck him dumb with revulsion. It is doubtful, however, whether that experience directly and solely caused Howard to spend the rest of his life visiting prisons and writing up his visits. The cause of his wanderlust should be sought more in his character and the course of his life than it should in some particular question in his mind that he needed to resolve (West 2011).

Our study had a somewhat different focus. Rather than starting from the question of what prisons are, what they look like or how prisons work, the basic premise has been to investigate what prisons in contemporary Europe are for and what functions they have in and for our society. Moreover, Europe's prisons have changed beyond all recognition since Howard's day. Hardly anything remains of the jailhouses that he visited; following literally in his footsteps, then, to see what has become of each site would not have been a sensible project. Besides, even if a good deal of relevant physical connections to what Howard visited had remained in situ, it would still have been an impracticably daunting task to have replicated his journeys. Between 1773 and his death in 1790, John Howard visited an immense number of prisons and other institutions, often making several repeat visits in a whole clutch of countries across the breadth of Europe.

What has directly informed the study is Howard's methodology. As a man of his time, he was resolute in his conviction that views and conclusions must be based upon empirical observation. Though he was anything but a man of science, and very far from being a man of letters or a rhetorician either, he had an abiding passion in all his undertakings for observations and measurements in all their forms. For instance, in the years of his life before the prison bug bit, Howard was interested in temperature, even having some of his measurements—with no accompanying rubric—published in an academic journal (Howard 1764, 1767, 1771). This was a bent that was still in evidence in his prison visiting years: on his travels, he was keen to see prisons before forming a judgement on them. Above all, he insisted on drawing his own conclusions on the spot and not just going by what the regulations or other documents asserted. For example, he would personally weigh the daily bread ration doled out to the inmates in the prisons he called in at. In addition, Howard was the kind of traveller who believed that seeing prisons in a range of contexts would set him in good stead to reflect intelligently on them. There is therefore no doubt that he was a comparatist, one who used his gargantuan stock of knowledge of prison systems to make authoritative pronouncements as to how they differed and how they were alike. That said, Howard was not just an observer; he also described at length what it felt like to witness what he saw (physically discomforting, disgusting or satisfying as the case may be) and did not shrink from airing his own views about what he had experienced. This included giving his unvarnished opinions to policymakers and very senior people, including the Tsarina of All the Russias (West 2011: 243), and he was unhesitant to flag up shortcomings or urge best practices upon them as informed by his research.

While it was the ambition to apply the essence of the Howard method, there is no avoiding that the modern-day practicalities of prison visits are more complicated. There is probably not a single prison left nowadays where one can show up unannounced, knock on the gate and expect to be let in for a look around. The prison visits for the study needed a great deal of dedicated preparation, eating up a large chunk of time in acquiring the requisite papers—and even with the permissions in place, things sometimes went wrong. Like Howard before, a number of French prisons closed their doors to me in the end; in my case, it was because the governor cancelled our visit at the last minute, citing operational exigencies. I ended up visiting 15 prisons in 6 countries between May 2013 and November 2014. The countries were visited in the order in which they appear in this chapter, apart from the Azerbaijan trip, which was not the last but the first of my journeys (May 2013). This turned out to be a good moment for me to travel there; it was most likely a narrow window of opportunity that would not have recurred. I visited Britain in February and again in November 2014; Norway in March of that year; France in April and June; and Italy in November.

Unlike Howard—unless he did so and preferred to conceal the fact—I did make my travels or call at prisons with the assistance of local guides. Prison researchers and academic colleagues from the various countries on my itinerary helped me, at my request, to get my permissions and to select the institutions to be visited. They often even joined me during the actual prison visits and on occasion acted as interpreters for me. Not the least of the ways in which they kindly helped me was by acting as a sounding board for my many questions and by reading initial drafts of my chapters. A final way in which my approach differed from Howard's is that I had far more opportunities than he did to consult existing written sources about the prisons and the country in question.

The approach that we have adopted is obviously not a method that will yield representative knowledge: one can only say something about what one has seen, heard, experienced and read first-hand. For that reason, the study is much more about my experiences as a prison *visitor* than it is about the prison *system* of this or that European country. What is seen, and the judgement formed on the basis of what is seen, is not representative of the whole; it is filtered through the layers of perspective of one's own background, character and the choices one has made. Undoubtedly, chance, too, plays an important role in these impressions. However, I am convinced that travelling and visiting prisons allowed me to gain insights that could not have been reached in any other way. That is why, in my opinion, carceral tours and what has come to be known as 'prison tourism' certainly can have a legitimate place in academic research.

## 3 Carceral Tours and Prison Inspection and Monitoring

Since Loïc Wacquant concluded in 2002 that prison researchers (in the United States) were making too few forays 'in and out the belly of the beast' (Wacquant 2002: 381), carceral tours have become a real bone of contention. Some argued that Wacquant was underestimating the limitations and disadvantages of visiting prisons: there is hardly a prison tour that is not essentially scripted so that the visitor only gets to see what the prison administration wants him to see (Dey 2009; Huckelbury 2009; Minogue 2009; Nagelsen and Huckelbury 2009; Piché and Walby 2009, 2010, 2012). The argument has therefore been made that carceral tours can offer highly misleading experiences and leave an impression that is very different from what is really going on. Nor should the many ethical dilemmas that surround prison visiting be disregarded. In the field notes he made on the first day of his visit to the Men's Central Jail in Los Angeles in 1998, Wacquant seemed to struggle with the emotions he felt during his visit: 'A sentiment of embarrassment, of "dirtiness", to have infringed on the dignity of human beings by the mere fact of having been there and seen that place, and thus to have treated its denizens as one might the occupants of a zoo' (Wacquant 2002: 381). According to Minogue (2009: 132), these bad feelings are largely a result of Wacquant's own attitude: 'Perhaps things would have been different if, when Loïc Wacquant felt this horror and this infringement of the dignity of others, he had stopped, squatted down on his haunches and stuck his hand through the bars to a man on his bunk and said: Hello, I am Loïc Wacquant, an academic doing research about prison, how are you doing?'

There are also advocates of carceral tours who insist that much can be learnt from ethically decent prison visiting (Pakes 2015; Wilson et al. 2011). In support of their claim on the added value of carceral tours, they tend to refer to famous 'prison tourists' such as John Howard, David Downes (1988), John Pratt (2008a, b) and Sharon Shalev (2013). Francis Pakes (2015: 267), for example, argues that prison visits, if conducted ethically, can '…be a useful tool for the comparative researcher and inform the visitor on the immediately discernible conditions in prison: the sights, the smells, the space'. They can, so he adds, '…shed light on the official stance on prisons and issues of punishment, rehabilitation, diversity and culture, and how these ideologies are reproduced on the ground'. In his view, '…during visits, informal interactions can at least lift the veil, to an extent, on climate and relations between staff and prisoners. In addition, valuable glimpses can be gained in situations where non-scripted events occur'. I share his conviction that, even during relatively brief and one-off visits, the prison visitor can form impressions and collate information that would be difficult to obtain in any other way. Visitors can use their own five senses to understand the world of the prison. Moreover, they are often able to see through the scene setting that has taken place before their arrival and they often are aware about aspects that have been hidden from view. Even matters such as how visitors enter or leave the institution and what security measures are applied (or not) can help them in the process of understanding what a prison is and what it is for. Even though such perceptions are often fleeting and cannot in quality or profundity be compared to findings of ethnographic research (Piché and Walby 2010: 576), I do agree with Pakes that prison visits can be very useful, in particular as a tool for the comparative analysis of prisons and prison systems.

Against this background one could argue that the work undertaken by national and international inspection and monitoring bodies can also be seen as studies that use such a carceral tour design. While there seems to be hardly any concern about the ethical dilemmas of prison visits in such a context, the epistemological challenges are very similar to those researchers face in their work. Even though the visiting methodology of bodies like the CPT is being described as a '…careful and objective documentation, by triangulation of information from various sources' (Casale 2009: 7), it is also conceded that the authorities in charge of the institutions that are being visited often tend to put their best foot forward and try to script the visit and the information provided in a way that fits that purpose. Unlike other carceral tour studies, the work of inspection and monitoring bodies is often framed in an evaluation approach or grid that points their attention to specific facts and evidence. Their core business is to look to prison conditions and standards without a need to be reflexive about questions that go beyond standards, rules, rights and practices. Issues related to the purpose of punishment and prisons and legitimacy of the system at stake very seldom get a solid place in most monitoring mechanisms. In the same line, some believe that monitors and inspectors should look better and further than what is presented in the prisons themselves. It would allow them to be more relevant and help to overcome the sometimes scripted and biased character of the information they have to work with: 'One of the factors inhibiting a rigorous empirical approach may be the reluctance on the part of some members of visiting bodies to step out their comfort zone. It is much easier to view a prison from the cosy vantage point of the director's office than to enter the sometimes bleak, malodorous, noisy and dilapidated areas where prisoners may be held. …Equally, it takes determination to go to those parts of the institution that are omitted on the "official" tour of the facilities and that management attempts to conceal from visiting delegations' (Casale 2009: 12).

In fact, the work of John Howard carries the embryo of a contemporary carceral tour design. He was one of the first to do on-site visits of prison facilities to report about how prisons were organised and prisoners treated. Unlike contemporary monitoring and inspection bodies, he had no other instrument or methodological tool than his own experience and moral standards to draw conclusions about what he observed. His comments and conclusions did not serve a direct preventive purpose. Though his findings did inspire policymakers, he himself used them on his multiple return visits to prisons to check if they had followed up on his recommendations and had changed for the better.

In the following sections we present and discuss some impressions and findings of our study. The aim is not to provide a solid picture of prisons in a given country but to illustrate what sort of data and conclusions such prison tourism design can produce and to what extent they can be compared to data and conclusions provided by inspection and monitoring bodies.

## 4 Impressions from Six Countries

### 4.1 The Jailer's Salary

In England I visited Bedford prison—mimicking John Howard's first prison visit in 1773—and Oakwood near Wolverhampton. Through these visits, I was able to collect and compare data and impressions from an older, local prison on the one hand and a newer, privately managed and large training prison on the other hand. In general, I was struck by the risk calculation, rankings and tax payers' discourse in discussions about prisons in England. Back then, Howard started his prison travels to find a precedent where jail keepers get an official salary and, as he had witnessed in Bedford prison, were not dependent on what they got or could take from the prisoners. Today, issues about the costs of detention still seem to be high on the English policy agenda.

Further, prisons rather look like instruments to punish (places to inflict pain as retribution) than as a punishment in itself (places for deprivation of liberty). From my Belgian perspective, life in English prisons is tough. I did not hear much about prisoner's rights. I was surprised by the incentives and earned privilege (IEP) system that creates different classes of prisoners, providing additional facilities and rights to those who seem to deserve it. Vulnerable prisoners are separated from the rest and seem to live in their own niche. Foreign national prisoners sometimes follow different tracks with a view to being deported. I experience these prisons as places where people are being locked up with very little to do. To me, the offer of so-called purposeful activities is very limited. This invites the question whether this prepares people for a life after prison or whether this merely keeps them busy, out of bed and quiet during detention. Oakwood was the first private prison I ever visited. What I had read about this prison before my visit (inter alia in inspectors' reports) was horrible and I was prepared for the worst. However, it was not as bad as I had expected. Would I immediately see or feel the difference between this institution and a public prison? More light, maybe. Staff younger, less institutional, less of them. Where was everybody? I am used to seeing prison officers standing, sitting and chatting everywhere.

## 4.2 The Northern Star

While travelling to Sweden, John Howard had high expectations about the quality of its prisons:

> In travelling through the country of Sweden, I observed the houses to be much cleaner than those in Denmark and this led me to hope I should find the same differences in prisons; especially as I was told they were visited every Saturday by an officer from the chancery. But I was disappointed, for I found them as dirty and offensive as those in Denmark. (Howard 1792: 82)

Today still, prisons in Nordic countries are generally believed to be exceptional because of the excellent prison conditions and low incarceration rates. Norway, a country that Howard had never visited, has the reputation of being the brightest star in the prison firmament. I visited prisons in Horten (Bastøy, a low-security facility situated on an island that is considered to be an ecological prison), Kroksrud, Ullersmo, Eidsberg and Trøgstadt. Prison facilities in Norway are excellent, and (mostly small-sized) prisons detain people in a variety of security levels, including open prison regimes. I was impressed by the investments made in meaningful prison activities, labour and reintegration tracks. But I do not believe that Norway is immune to what happens elsewhere in Europe. Norway's culture of *likhet* (equality) seems to be under pressure. Immigration and social evolutions change and sometimes divide Norwegian society. Prisons now detain much more foreigners than ever before. These prisoners face deportation after having served their prison sentence. What kind of re-socialisation can be offered to prisoners with no future in Norwegian society? Norway now looks for additional capacity in Sweden and the Netherlands.

## 4.3 The Paradox of Control

The Netherlands was Howard's favourite country, especially because he found the prisons there so clean. I visited prisons in Vught, Nieuwersluis and Dordrecht and saw very organised and well-managed prisons (procedures, plans, managerial discourse, etc.), good living conditions (clean!), many special units for special (dangerous) prisoners and evidence-based interventions. But there seems to be uncertainty about their impact: imprisonment rates are characterised by steep rises and falls. In recent years the Dutch prison population has again dropped dramatically but nobody seems to know why this is the case.

I have also seen a strong emphasis on the individual responsibility of prisoners to change themselves. The system invests in and rewards those who perform well in prison and who seem to deserve it (somewhat similar to the English IEP). But what about those (up to 80 %) who lag behind?

## 4.4 Words Ring Hollow

I visited the French prisons of Lille Sequedin and Paris Fresnes. To me, life in French prisons is tough, even compared to what I saw in England. I have observed a strong emphasis on security in the organisation of these institutions. I could barely interact with the prisoners (not even just shaking hands or having a chat). An inmate in Lille who wanted to talk to me—to tell me about what really happens in prisons—was forcefully removed (and got a disciplinary sanction for it). It sometimes seemed as if prisoners are a part of the prison itself. Very often, the staff just ignored the presence of an inmate as if there was nobody else in the room.

It struck me how complacent the French were in accepting bad living conditions in their prisons. I have seen old, dilapidated and dirty prisons. Prison officers seem to find that normal and just carry on. The conditions of the *parloir* (for visits) in Fresnes are one of the worst I have ever seen but there was no shame in showing that to me: 'It is not ideal and needs some refurbishment'. To me, France looks like a lawyer's paradise. There are rules and procedures for everything and the discussion of prisoners' rights is routine. But the implementation and translation of these typical French values about human rights and the rule of law into practice seem to fall short.

## 4.5 Dreams of Cesare Beccaria

In Italy I visited Tolmezzo and Bollate prisons. Tolmezzo is mainly a high-security prison near the Slovenian border that also houses those who have been convicted or suspected of Mafia-related crimes. Bollate prison in Milan is a training institution with 1200 inmates. While prisons in Italy are notorious for overcrowding, I saw a prison system that still seems to believe in the ideals of Cesare Beccaria (1738–1794): the ultimate goal of a prison sentence is to change a prisoner—even in high-security environments. Bollate prison had labour facilities for inmates that were comparable to what I have seen in Norway. Prisoners seem to be taken seriously as people and as partners in a detention trajectory that is oriented towards a future outside prison. It is significant to note that only in Italy, I was accompanied by prisoners—not prison staff—during my visit.

## 4.6 Eurovision Europrisons

John Howard died in Kherson (Ukraine) on 20 January 1790 during his longest journey east. By that time, his focus had shifted towards the plague, quarantine and hospitals. As it was not possible for me to go to Ukraine, I travelled to Azerbaijan where I had the opportunity to visit two prisons in the Baku region. On a map of the member states of the Council of Europe, Azerbaijan is the furthest east. I saw prisons in a semi-authoritarian state with lots of oil money. The visit taught me that good material detention conditions may tell you very little about what prisons are used for. Without a doubt, prison conditions in Azerbaijan often meet all the standards. But prison conditions can also be used as an instrument in international politics to achieve respectability (to the West and their monitoring bodies like the CPT). In several places of the new remand prison in Baku, a little sign is hanging which proclaims in interesting English: TORTURE NOT TO. Now who would be the intended audience of that?

Azerbijan taught me a lot about what independent monitors do and (do not) see. I believe Azerbaijan sees external monitoring like the CPT as an opportunity rather than as a threat. After reading Dostoyevsky, I once believed that you can truly learn something about the civilisation of a given country purely by taking a look at its prisons. My journey to Azerbaijan has convinced me that that belief is quite wrong-headed. Prisons, and particularly facilities officially designated as remand and/or convict prisons, can at most display a small slice of a country or even of its administration of justice. More to the point, they are like the Eurovision Song Contest: excellent opportunities to put on a bit of a show. What do prisoners' rights matter to those in power if the latter, in informal reality, have all the power and hold all the strings when it comes to the maintenance of law and order, crime detection, prosecution and sentencing?

# 5 Reflections

## 5.1 Locking Them Up and Locking Them Away

A prison can perform many different functions, even simultaneously. Prisons can be used to detain people awaiting a further decision (such as a sentence, a deportation order or something else). They can incapacitate people who are perceived to be dangerous in order to protect society (and themselves) from the damage they can wreak. Equally, they can be a means for punishing offenders. In that case, incarceration is aimed at retribution and revenge for suffering inflicted on the victim. However, deprivation of liberty can also be imagined as a therapy intended to change wrongdoers and rehabilitate them so that they are fit to resume their place in society, preferably without indulging in criminality again. Deprivation of liberty can also be used to restore a mutual reconciliation of perpetrator, victim and society. Alternatively, it can turn into a mechanism to pacify and unify a restive society through the judicious use of scapegoating.

During my prison visits I observed several of those functions at work, in many permutations and combinations, and in varying degrees. I also saw prisons performing functions which are hardly discussed in traditional penal theory. I dubbed the prisons of Azerbaijan 'Eurovision Europrisons' in order to highlight the public relations role they serve and the way in which the state invokes them in international relations. Prisons, and the resources that have been invested in them, can therefore have the function of creating a desired image. I could also have called the Azeri prisons that I visited 'Potemkin prisons', with a nod to that nobleman, the founder of Kherson and a great aficionado of Howard. Just as Potemkin became a byword in Russia for window dressing after he created entire fake villages and dolled up real villages to impress Catherine the Great on her visit to the Crimea in 1787, it seems as if today's Azeri policymakers have made the prison system part of their charm offensive and caviar diplomacy towards the West. I see a real challenge here for monitoring bodies (and to some extent also for researchers trying to measure prison performance (Liebling 2004)) which are predominantly preoccupied with collecting information about how well prisons perform with respect to certain standards. This information in itself does not always tell us very much about what prisons are used for in a specific context; it is merely an indicator for how well prisons function in accordance with certain formal standards. What its function is in a given context and how and why it is used for punishment remain largely hidden from view. Dostoyevsky was wrong. The degree of civilisation in a society cannot be judged by just looking at what happens in prisons, unless, one takes a (carceral tour) design that allows to include questions about the role of prisons in society.

In the other five countries I visited, I observed that two functions were in tension: incarcerating people for the good of society and attempting to change inmates so that they can return to society and live a law-abiding life. In Britain and France, the balance seems to have tilted strongly towards the protection of the public. Here people are being locked up predominantly to make society safer, and since incarceration is intended to be a punishment, one does not feel uncomfortable with the idea that it is a rather miserable experience. It is probably not a coincidence that I have observed the worst prison conditions in these two countries. I shall not forget the sight or the smell of the *parloir* at Fresnes. Obviously, even in France or Britain punishment is not the sole function of the prison; these countries also seem to embrace the ambition of rehabilitating inmates. Yet on the basis of what I have seen and read, I conclude that there is still much to be done before that aim can be achieved—and in these times of austerity, it is an even more distant prospect.

In Norway, the Netherlands and Italy, I found more of an equilibrium, although my impressions of Dutch prisons did not differ substantially from what I saw in Britain or France in this regard. For sure, security is also a dominant theme in the Netherlands when it comes to prisons and incarceration, and prison life there is largely organised around that function. The Dutch prison system invests a great deal in rehabilitation but it seems to be pretty picky about which prisoners can benefit. Like the British, the Dutch are firm believers in the idea that it is the individual responsibility of the convict to reform himself or herself. In such a model prisoners are being rewarded for their efforts and initiative with better conditions of detention and a more fully elaborated support framework for their process of rehabilitation. And, in a sense, such a system seems to work: those who do manage to get access to the evidence-based prison programmes really can leave prison 'better'. The flip side is that those who cannot or will not dance to that tune—the *niet-kunners*, in Dutch parlance—risk missing out in such a system, with very real consequences: they remain behind bars because they are perceived to be a continuing risk for public safety. Because of growing numbers of *refuseniks*, rehabilitation programmes tend to become more selective and exclusive.

During my visits I learnt that Norway and Italy have not merely listed rehabilitation as an official aim but that they have also implemented this objective within their prisons. It surprised me in particular that Italy scored so well in this respect. Before the start of my visit to Italy, I had only read about problems of severe overcrowding and abominable conditions. Besides, I had been under the impression that there was little scope for investment in prisons or prisoners. However, the spirit of Beccaria was still present in Italian prisons. Even the high-security facility that I visited had a clear focus on preparing inmates for their return to society. The well-equipped workshops, the cooperative production model and the humane, open atmosphere which I could observe in the Milan prison made me conclude that in these institutions rehabilitation is a day-to-day reality. It is evident that Italy, owing to its historical and political legacy in which prisons never were considered as trustworthy institutions, has never been so taken by the discourse of security as many other European countries have been. If the waters of rehabilitation ran dry elsewhere towards the end of the 1960s, they seem to still run clear and fresh in Italian prisons. The reality of rehabilitation efforts, however, is not without troubles. There is often a lack of resources and many initiatives fail. Rehabilitation is almost impossible for some inmates in the Italian prison system. What are the future prospects of low-ranking mafioso prisoners who sit singing Neapolitan ballads far from home at the foothills of the Alps?

When it comes to rehabilitation, the Norwegian penal system has a long tradition of working towards the rehabilitation of wrongdoers. But even in Norway, it seems as if the golden age of equality is over, and this tends to affect the role of rehabilitation in Norwegian prisons. What to do with the growing group of foreigners who have no place in Norwegian society but who nevertheless end up in its prisons? What does preparing for re-entry mean for people who will most probably be removed from the country as soon as their prison term has ended? As long as Norwegian prisons can devote themselves to assisting inmates for a return to Norwegian society, everything seems fine. But what does return to society mean in a multicultural and globalised age? And to what extent does this create and deepen inequalities between the group of prisoners regarded as worth the investment and those who are written off because the country will gain no benefit from them after the sentence has expired?

Even Norway is nowadays facing these challenges and there are no easy answers or quick-fix solutions. These challenges are also causing a shift in the functions of prisons. The Norwegian prison system is not exclusively geared towards rehabilitation. There is plenty of punishment being doled out too: sentences measured in days, which by nature are devoid of rehabilitative programmes, are still frequently imposed and served. Besides, foreign convicts in the country tend to serve a large part of their sentence (even of longer sentences) before being deported.

It seems to me that the level of equality in a society is a key indicator of what one can expect of its prison system. In social contexts where some form of equality is inherently present, or where there are paradigms of mutual respect and consensus-based politics, it seems to be more natural for prisons to be geared towards rehabilitation. In such countries, law breakers are not automatically locked away (or at least not further excluded from the mainstream than they already were) but are temporarily locked up, that is, until they are ready to re-enter society. In societies where there is a substantial degree of inequality, on the other hand, prisons become more easily dumping grounds for undesirables who are perceived to be a threat by the dominant social groups. In those social contexts, it is much harder to construct genuine rehabilitation programmes because prisoners are no longer regarded as members of society, if they ever were. This inequality often seeps into the very prisons so that a distinction is maintained between those inmates who deserve to be rehabilitated (and who justify that expense) and the rest of the convict crowd.

My travels with Howard have convinced me that understanding patterns of equality and inequality is crucial to understanding the functions prisons can have in a given context (Lappi-Seppälä 2011; Wilkinson and Pickett 2009). The equality/inequality debate and the question of inclusion also hark back to the historical roots of the prison. Prisons have always been places of confinement for people who must be excluded temporarily or permanently from society (McConville 1995). Those who did not fit or who were perceived to be dangerous were locked up. This exclusion was often the mere precursor to a subsequent punishment:

transportation to an overseas colony, a public corporal punishment that left its mark on the body for life or—the ultimate exclusion—the death penalty.

It was precisely to mitigate the element of exclusion suffered under the existing judicial penalties that custodial sentences were developed. Already in the context of the early-medieval Italian cities, and much before Howard's times, there are examples of prisons that used incarceration as a punishment, with a perspective on the return to society afterwards. In the French context, too, imprisonment became a kind of foreign body in the arsenal of existing punishments. The *lettres de cachet* were of course tools for locking people up without the trouble of going through the usual legal channels, and as such were inherently susceptible to capricious abuse. However, they were also—and perhaps even primarily—a consequence of the need to have an instrument to punish in other ways than killing, injuring or excluding people. Via *lettres de cachet*, capital punishments were stayed and commuted into temporary removals from society with a view to correcting the offender and then reinserting him into the mainstream.

When prisons lack a genuine determination to correct and to 'lock in' ex-offenders after they have done their time, they will inevitably be largely instruments of exclusion. It will be a self-perpetuating state of affairs in which always the same categories of people are being locked up and locked away. Some countries, such as Norway and England and Wales, are getting tough on foreign convicts by declaring them persona non grata and by expelling them. The practice of solving problems of incarceration and criminality by deporting undesirables overseas is mainly a thing from the past but many contemporary societies still seem to be wrestling with finding a functional substitute. What can be done with transients whose only connection to the country in which they are imprisoned is the crime they have committed while passing through? What does inclusion mean for them, and how and where should this inclusion be brought about? For me, these are the key challenges that the prisons of tomorrow will face if their ambition goes beyond the mere incarceration of people. My travels have convinced me that this particular issue is causing prison authorities throughout Europe the most headaches.

## 5.2 Capacity

Although it was not the specific aim of my carceral tours, I kept finding myself embroiled in discussions about prison capacity. I visited countries that had too many prisoners (England and Wales stand out here) and countries that seemed to have not enough prisons (France, the UK and Italy). I also visited countries which had too many prisons (the Netherlands and—if we are to believe the official statistics—Azerbaijan). Or should one perhaps say that they have too few prisoners? In countries which are eager to lock up people, it seems obvious that there are a lot of prisoners. It is therefore more probable that there will be an insufficient number of prison beds. This begs the question: is the shortage being caused by an insufficient number of prison places or by an excessive number of custodial sentences?

What do prison statistics reveal about the countries that we visited for our study? Azerbaijan had 210 prisoners per 100,000; England and Wales had 149; France had 102; Italy had 88; and Norway and the Netherlands both had 75 inmates per 100,000. The position of countries changes somewhat when we take prison capacity into account: France has an occupancy rate of 118.3 %; England and Wales, 112 %; Italy, 110.4 %; Norway, 94.1 %; Azerbaijan, 85.5 %; and the Netherlands has an occupancy rate of 77 % (International Centre for Prison Studies 2013a, b, 2014a, b, c, d). Why these differences between these countries? This is a difficult question. The intuitive explanation that countries which incarcerate relatively more people are countries with higher crime rates does not seem to hold true. Prison populations often do not correlate with a country's crime statistics (Lappi-Seppälä 2011). So what is the cause? It seems probable that the response to crime and a country's policy towards criminal behaviour are much more important than levels of crime as such. A nation's inclination to use the prison as a preferred response to crime and the increasing length of custodial sentences (by tightening early release procedures) seem to be much better predictors for the size of prison population and overcrowding levels.

That said, the jigsaw has certainly not been pieced together yet. It still strikes me how few countries have managed to get a grip on prison capacity management as a component of their penal policy. Surely, if capacity is largely a function of political choices, it must be possible to anticipate or react to changing numbers? However, measures to combat prison overcrowding seldom achieve the desired effect, and predictions of future capacity needs are often inaccurate and highly unreliable. Prison developments in the Netherlands offer a good illustration of the difficulties in getting to the bottom of how prison capacity works and to tackle the issues involved. In the 1970s, the Dutch had Western Europe's lowest incarceration rate (at just 18 inmates per 100,000 inhabitants); the prison population quadrupled between 1985 and 2005 and then plummeted again. While many (retrospective) explanations have been proffered for this huge yo-yo effect (see e.g. van Swaaningen 2013), it appears that policymakers were taken by surprise at every turn. They were surprised by the sudden flip in capacity, and above all they were unprepared for the intensity and wide ramifications of those fluctuations. Anyone who had stood up in the Netherlands 10 years ago and said that by now prisons would be closing on a large scale and their governors would be all but begging for more inmates would have been written off as a madman. Yet, that is the situation the country now finds itself in.

There has been no shortage in recent years of researchers seeking to understand these kinds of processes better and to come up with evidence-based explanations (Lappi-Seppälä 2011; Dünkel 2016). We can learn much from their efforts, and there are certainly parallels to be drawn between prison capacity and my research question of what prisons are for. When societies polarise and prisons are transformed into instruments to lock offenders away, there is a high probability that prison populations will rise accordingly (Lappi-Seppälä 2012). In these conditions, prisons become warehouses to be stuffed continuously with the same sort of people (often the very same people). However, this is only part of the story. Prisons are often hybrid systems playing a double role: locking people up as well as locking them away. Indeed, prisons can breed inequalities as a result of such a twin-track policy: it can give rise to some groups leaving prison promptly and quite well-prepared for life back on the outside, while other groups languish inside for many years (Boone 2012). These are all pieces of the larger puzzle, which is how to gain a sound understanding of prison capacity.

# 6 Conclusion

There is a strong argument to make for the added value of prison visits for those who want to learn something about prisons. There are things to learn during prison visits that other sources, which of course should always be used as well, cannot reveal.

When we compare the results of prison visits carried out by John Howard in the eighteenth century with those of a contemporary study inspired by Howard or the findings of monitoring bodies, then it becomes apparent that a carceral tour approach can lead to very different outcomes. And this is not a consequence of essential methodological differences or limitations inherent to the prison visit design. What one can learn from carceral tours depends to a large extent on the lens through which prisons are observed. If it is the intention to gather information about the performance of prisons with respect to specific standards—which is how most inspection and monitoring bodies operate—results of such an exercise can only be used to make statements in that respect. It is somewhat comparable to the measurements of temperature John Howard made before the prison fascination entered his life: they were exact but just measurements without any additional comments about their relevance or meaning. The same is possible for information on what happens in prisons. In many instances, it does tell us very little about the role and function of the prison or about the level of development or democracy (for an example in which information about prison performance is linked to what happens outside prisons and vice versa, see Liebling 2015). After all, prisons are just instruments of a criminal justice system. They can be adjusted to international standards without changing anything about the system and the purposes for which it is used. Prisons are always some kind of façade. To me, that is where the real challenge lies for those who study and assess prisons by entering the belly of the beast.

## Notes

1. This chapter is based on the foreword and epilogue of the English revised translation of an earlier original book published in Dutch (Vander Beken 2015a, 2016) and on (Vander Beken 2015b).

## Literature

Boone, M. 2012. *Eigen boeven eerst. Insluiting en uitsluiting in de sanctietoepassing*. Den Haag: Eleven International Publishing.

Casale, S. 2009. A System of Preventive Oversight. *Essex Human Rights Review* 1: 6–14.

Dey, E. 2009. Prison Tours as a Research Tool in the Golden Gulag. *Journal of Prisoners on Prisons* 18: 119–125.

Downes, D. 1988. *Contrasts in Tolerance: Post-war Penal Policy in the Netherlands and England and Wales*. Oxford: Clarendon.

Dünkel, F. 2016. The Rise and Fall of Prison Population Rates in Europe. *Newsletter of the European Society of Criminology* 15 (2): 2–5.

Howard, J. 1764. An Account of the Degree of Cold Observed in Bedfordshire. *Philosophical Transactions* 54: 118.

———. 1767. Extract of a Letter from John Howard, Esq; F.R.S. to William Watson, M. D. F. R. Giving Some Observations on the Heat of the Waters at Bath. *Philosophical Transactions* 57: 201–202.

———. 1771. Observations on the Heat of the Ground on Mount Vesuvius. *Philosophical Transactions* 61: 53–54.

———. 1791. *An Account of the Principal Lazarettos in Europe. With Various Papers Relative to the Plague: Together with Further Observations on Some Foreign Prisons and Hospitals; and Additional Remarks on the Present State of Those in Great Britain and Ireland*. London: Johnson, Dilly and Cadell.

———. 1792. *The State of the Prisons in England and Wales with Preliminary Observations, and an Account of Some Foreign Prisons and Hospitals*. 4th ed. London: Johnson, Dilly and Cadell.

Huckelbury, C. 2009. Tour de farce. *Journal of Prisoners on Prisons* 18: 126–128.

International Centre for Prison Studies. 2013a. Azerbaijan. *World Prison Brief*. http://www.prisonstudies.org/country/azerbaijan. Accessed 27 Sep 2016.

———. 2013b. Netherlands. *World Prison Brief*. http://www.prisonstudies.org/country/netherlands. Accessed 27 Sep 2016.

———. 2014a. France. *World Prison Brief*. http://www.prisonstudies.org/country/france. Accessed 27 Sep 2016.

———. 2014b. Italy. *World Prison Brief*. http://www.prisonstudies.org/country/italy. Accessed 27 Sep 2016.

———. 2014c. Norway. *World Prison Brief*. http://www.prisonstudies.org/country/norway. Accessed 27 Sep 2016.

———. 2014d. United Kingdom: England & Wales. *World Prison Brief*. http://www.prisonstudies.org/country/united-kingdom-england-wales. Accessed 27 Sep 2016.

Lappi-Seppälä, T. 2011. Explaining Imprisonment in Europe. *European Journal of Criminology* 8 (4): 303–328.

———. 2012. Penal Policies in the Nordic Countries 1960–2010. *Journal of Scandinavian Studies in Criminology and Crime Prevention* 13 (1): 85–111.

Liebling, A. 2004. *Prisons and Their Moral Performance*. Oxford: Oxford University Press.

———. 2015. Appreciative Inquiry, Generative Theory, and the 'Failed State' Prison. In *Advances in Criminological Theory*, ed. J. Miller and W. Palacios, 251–270. Piscataway: Transaction Publishers.

McConville, S. 1995. Local Justice. In *The Oxford History of the Prison. The Practice of Punishment in Western Society*, ed. N. Morris and D. Rothman, 297–327. New York: Oxford University Press.

Minogue, C. 2009. The Engaged Specific Intellectual: Resisting Unethical Prison Tourism and the Hubries of Objectifying Modality of the Universal Intellectual. *Journal of Prisoners on Prisons* 18: 129–142.

Nagelsen, S., and C. Huckelbury. 2009. The Prisoner's Role in Ethnographic Examinations of the Carceral State. *Journal of Prisoners on Prisons* 18: 111–118.

Pakes, F. 2015. Howard, Pratt and Beyond: Assessing the Value of Carceral Tours as a Comparative Method. *The Howard Journal of Criminal Justice* 54 (3): 265–276.

Piché, J., and K. Walby. 2009. Dialogue on the Status of Prison Ethnography and Carceral Tours: An Introduction. *Journal of Prisoners on Prisons* 18: 88–90.

———. 2010. Problematizing Carceral Tours. *British Journal of Criminology* 50 (3): 570–581.

———. 2012. Carceral Tours and the Need for Reflexivity: A Response to Wilson, Spina and Canaan. *The Howard Journal of Criminal Justice* 51 (4): 411–418.

Pratt, J. 2008a. Scandinavian Exceptionalism in an Era of Penal Excess. Part I: The Nature and Roots of Scandinavian Exceptionalism. *British Journal of Criminology* 48 (2): 119–137.

———. 2008b. Scandinavian Exceptionalism in an Era of Penal Excess. Part II: Does Scandinavian Exceptionalism have a Future? *British Journal of Criminology* 48 (3): 275–292.

Shalev, S. 2013. *Supermax. Controlling Risk Through Solitary Confinement.* Abingdon: Routledge.
Van Swaaningen, R. 2013. Reversing the Puntive Turn: The Case of the Netherlands. In *European Penology?* ed. T. Daems, D. van Zyl Smit, and S. Snacken, 339–360. Oxford: Hart Publishing.
Vander Beken, T. 2015a. *Howardreizen. De rol van de gevangenis in Europa.* Antwerp-Apeldoorn: Maklu.
———. 2015b. Travels with John: the Function of Prisons in Europe. *Independent Monitor* 115: 10–12.
———. 2016. *The Role of Prison in Europe. Travelling in the Footsteps of John Howard.* Basingstoke: Palgrave Macmillan.
Wacquant, L. 2002. The Curious Eclipse of Prison Ethnography in the Age of Mass Incarceration. *Ethnography* 3 (4): 371–397.
West, T. 2011. *The Curious Mr. Howard. Legendary Prison Reformer.* Hook: Waterside Press.
Wilkinson, R., and K. Pickett. 2009. *The Spirit Level: Why Greater Equality Makes Societies Stronger.* London: Allen Lane.
Wilson, D., R. Spina, and J.E. Canaan. 2011. In Praise of the Carceral Tour: Learning from the Grendon Experience. *The Howard Journal of Criminal Justice* 50 (4): 345–355.

**Tom Vander Beken** is a professor at the Institute for International Research on Criminal Policy, Ghent University, Belgium.

# Tracing the Impact of the Council of Europe Anti-torture Committee on Albania's Prison System

Brunilda Pali and Xhilda Vocaj

## 1 Introduction

Following the historic political changes in Central and Eastern Europe in the end of the 1980s, for all the countries of the region, the reform of the criminal justice system became a priority requirement in their path towards democracy (Walmsley 2005). Albania especially inherited an image of the criminal justice system in general, and of the prison system in particular, as a symbol of repression and violence, thus the challenges for reforming the criminal justice based on the rule of law and human rights were vital during the transition towards political pluralism, and as will be argued throughout the chapter, remain vital even today.

B. Pali (✉)
Leuven Institute of Criminology (LINC), KU Leuven, Leuven, Belgium

X. Vocaj
International Litigation and Arbitration, Paris, France



T. Daems, L. Robert (eds.), *Europe in Prisons*, Palgrave Studies in Prisons and Penology, DOI 10.1007/978-3-319-62250-7_5

In Albania, reform was needed at multiple levels: legislation, implementation, and infrastructure. This chapter analyses the country's criminal justice reforms, with the main emphasis on the role and impact of local and international prison monitoring and oversight as a key indicator in preventing, denouncing, and redressing violations of the rights of detained persons, in the framework of the application of national legislation and ratified international human rights treaties.

The presence and the role of monitoring bodies in Albania, especially in safeguarding the rights and treatment of imprisoned persons, cannot be taken lightly, given the legacy of torture, death, and disappearances in some of the country's infamous prisons and internment camps during the dictatorial regime. At the same time, the 'pressure' by the EU towards Albanian candidacy status has also been decisive. The focus on human rights and proper treatment of detained persons was one of the 12 key priorities of the 2010 EC's Opinion on Albania's application for membership of the EU (COM(2010)680: 12), and it still remains part of Albania's necessary reforms towards EU Integration.[1]

In this chapter, we first present some general information on the country's background, mainly as it relates to prison data and legislation. In the following section, we give a brief overview of the main monitoring bodies in Albania, but our chapter mainly focuses on the work and role of the Committee for the Prevention of Torture (CPT). After this overview, we organise the mapping of the role of the CPT in three core themes which seem to be central for Albania throughout the years: first, ill-treatment and human rights violations; second, overcrowding, pre-trial detention, and other poor material conditions; and third, health-related concerns.

## 2 Country Background, Prison Data, and Legislation

The communist regime in Albania lasted almost half a century (1944–1991) and is considered to have been one of the fiercest one-party dictatorships and totalitarian regimes in Europe, with its isolation, endless political murders, exiles, prisons, and forced-labour camps. It maintained an extensive system of prisons and forced-labour camps, more than 50 institutions, among which most institutions were for political prisoners (see Gashi 2012: 30–33; Musta 2000: 8–64). The rates in the first years were reported to have been 3 in 1 (political prisoners versus normal prisoners); thus, in January 1947, out of a total of 4,749 prisoners, 3,659 were political prisoners, a number that kept increasing fast in the years immediately after (Sufaj 2000: 106–110). The number of convicted persons serving imprisonment during the communist regime was very large and has changed in different periods. To date, we do not have accurate data on the exact number of convicted persons, but only different estimations. According to Musta (1993) and Zegalli (1999)—former political prisoners—during the dictatorship in Albania, there were about 20,000 people who served time in these prisons and labour camps, excluding about 2,500 people who were executed. Other authors, like Suli and Kaso (1995), mention a much higher number of political prisoners during the communist rule, like 600,000 prisoners. In 'Prison Nation', a short documentary about the crimes of communism in Albania, it is estimated that more than 5,000 people were killed, while another 70,000 were sentenced to years in jail. Despite the lack of clear data, we can conclude that at the end of the regime, there was a large number of prisoners in the small country of about three million inhabitants, a large number of whom—mainly the political prisoners—were released through amnesties that took place after 1991.[2]

Currently, there are 23 penal institutions in Albania, including prisons, pre-trial detention centres, and special centres (the prison hospital, the institution for minors in Kavaja, and a special institution in Kruja for the treatment of elderly inmates and inmates with chronic diseases). Prisoner numbers have increased regularly every year, with a total in April 2016 of 5,769 prisoners.[3] A similar amount of Albanian prisoners also are held in European prisons, mainly Greece and Italy.[4]

One of the priorities after 1991, besides the granting of amnesties and setting up commissions for the investigation of the crimes of the state mainly against political prisoners, was to design and improve the legal and quasi-legal framework[5] as well as to ratify a significant number of international legal instruments[6] which became part of the Albanian national legislation. The ratification of the European Convention on

Human Rights (ECHR) has ensured that victims of human rights violations are entitled to have their cases reviewed by the European Court of Human Rights (ECtHR).[7] Various legal and institutional reforms have been adopted to ensure that steps are taken within the prison system aiming at the approximation of this system with international norms and standards. However, as we argue in this chapter, while the legislative reform in Albania can be read as a success story, it is the implementation of these reforms that has either been delayed or not fully realised.

## 3 International and Domestic Monitoring Bodies in Albania

The first independent monitoring human rights organisation in Albania was the Forum for the Defense of Human Rights and Fundamental Freedoms, registered by the Albanian Ministry of Justice in January 1991. In August 1991, a second independent human rights group, the Association of Former Political Prisoners and Detainees was formed, and beginning with a visit in early March 1992 by a delegation of the Vienna-based International Helsinki Federation for Human Rights (IHF), in which Helsinki Watch participated, international monitoring organisations have been welcomed in Albania ever since.

The main monitoring and reporting body in Albania has been the CPT. The European Convention for the Prevention of Torture and Inhuman or Degrading Treatment or Punishment was signed and ratified by Albania in 1996, and the first visit of the CPT to Albania took place in 1997. In terms of Albania's history, the year 1997 was a very important one. The Albanian rebellion or unrest of 1997 (also referred to as Albania's civil war) was an uprising sparked by the pyramid (Ponzi) scheme failures which had started in 1991 and had been endorsed by a number of government officials in Albania. By January 1997, the pyramid schemes could no longer make payments to investors, an estimated two-thirds of the Albanian population. As a result, Albania descended into civil disorder and violence in which the government collapsed and more than 2,000 people were killed. Due to the significant breakdown of law and order, most Albanian prisons were emptied of their occupants, ransacked, or destroyed.[8] Following these acute political disorders, Albania ratified a constitution in 1998, establishing a democratic system of government based upon the rule of law and guaranteeing the protection of fundamental human rights.

The work of the CPT is designed to be an integrated part of the Council of Europe[9] system for the protection of human rights, creating a proactive preventive non-judicial mechanism alongside the existing reactive judicial mechanism of the ECtHR. The CPT implements its preventive function through two kinds of visits—periodic or regular visits and *ad hoc* visits undertaken in special cases. In Albania, from 1997 until 2016, there have been 11 visits in total, of which 5 periodic and 6 *ad hoc* visits.

Additionally, in 2003, the Albanian Parliament ratified the implementation of the UN Optional Protocol of the Convention against Torture (OPCAT). In compliance with the OPCAT, in 2008, the Parliament assigned to the Albanian People's Advocate[10] (PA, hereafter referred to as the Ombudsman) the function of the National Preventive Mechanism (NPM) against torture. The OPCAT ratification and establishment of the Albanian NPM was initiated as a cooperation between civil society and the Ombudsman under the motto 'Albania without torture'.

The preventive approach foreseen in the OPCAT is based on the regular and periodic monitoring of places of detention through visits to these facilities conducted by expert bodies in order to prevent abuses. In contrast, the Ombudsman only monitors the situation once he receives allegations of abuse, and therefore remains an institution characterised by a reactive approach in addressing human rights issues, instead of a preventive approach, as required by OPCAT. Until today, no consistent and comprehensive system of visits to places of detention has been developed, such as full inspection visits, follow-up visits, and ad hoc visits.[11] Other concerns have been expressed in relation to the weak power of Ombudsman's recommendations resulting often in the administration's non-compliance with them. An additional concern also remains its effective independence from the parliament, executive, and state institutions.

Other bodies and watchdog organisations that have played an important role in the process of prison monitoring, awareness raising on specific cases of ill-treatment, offering trainings, and recommendations are

Amnesty International (AI), the Albanian Helsinki Committee (AHC), the Organisation for Security and Cooperation in Europe (OSCE presence in Albania), the Council of Europe Commissioner for Human Rights ('the Commissioner'), the Albanian Rehabilitation Centre for Trauma and Torture (ARCT), the Children's Human Rights Centre of Albania (CRCA), and other national NGOs.[12]

## 4 Mapping the Role of the CPT in Albania

Throughout this section, we discuss some of the findings and recommendations of the CPT, based on its visits to the Albanian prison system throughout the years (1997–2016), trying to assess its impact based on concrete changes, either in legislation or in implementation. We start to assess the changes using as a baseline the first visit of the CPT, focussing on the main identified problems. During the first visit of the CPT in Albania in December 1997, the country was in a very difficult political, economic, and social context. Most of the prisons were ransacked and destroyed, so the CPT noted the overall limited possibility for building a better prison infrastructure. During this visit, the CPT identified as particular areas of concern, ill-treatment, mainly by the police, prison overcrowding, poor health and living conditions, poor infrastructure, lack of rehabilitation programmes, precarious living conditions of psychiatric patients, and failure in implementation of the law (CPT/Inf(2003)6, para 189). The lack of staff capacity, staff awareness, and motivation has remained an intersecting issue in prisons, pre-trial detention centres, police commissariats, and hospitals. In what follows we thematise the problems under three headings: first, ill-treatment and human rights violations; second, overcrowding, pre-trial detention, and other poor material conditions; and third, health-related concerns.

### 4.1 Ill-treatment and Human Rights Violations

Perhaps given the country's political heritage, it does not come as a surprise that one of the most long-standing problems in Albania has been the ill-treatment and serious human rights violations of detainees by law enforcement agencies, mainly the police. As mentioned above, already during its first visit in 1997, the CPT noticed serious ill-treatment cases and high risks of ill-treatment in pre-trial detention, police commissariats, and prisons, and therefore recommended, on the one hand, training for staff, and, on the other, serious investigation and prosecution of cases. In the following visit in 1998, the CPT noticed a few improvements of relations between staff and prisoners after the change of prison directors, and the Ministry of Justice had cancelled the security measures for death penalty offenders,[13] but nevertheless, in many cases, the degrading measures continued (CPT/Inf(2003)7, para 24). During the next visit in 2000, the CPT, revisiting the pre-trial detention centres and police commissariats, observed again with some concern that the cases of ill-treatment had seriously deteriorated, and quite a few cases could even be categorised as torture. They asked for investigations, for mandatory medical control, and for serious consideration of complaints (CPT/Inf(2003)9, para 20). In 2001, the CPT again confirmed multiple cases of ill-treatment in pre-detention centres and police commissariats. With the exception of launching a phone line to record complaints, no other important measures were taken by the government. The CPT recommended additionally that the Ombudsman's competences expand, and that the Ombudsman meets with the detainees without the presence of witnesses. They further recommended that a strong public message that condemns the violence against prisoners and detainees must be prepared by the Ministry of Public Order (CPT/Inf(2003)11, para 14). In the course of their 2003 visit, the CPT concluded that the lack of an effective and appropriate response from the prosecuting/judicial and disciplinary authorities could only foster a climate of impunity in the country (CPT/Inf(2006)22, para 7).

The 2005 CPT visit revealed that little progress had been made in the implementation of the recommendations previously made by the CPT, especially concerning the conditions of pre-trial detention. In the report based on that visit, the Committee called upon the Albanian authorities to take urgent action to improve the situation. The CPT visit report called upon Albanian state authorities that: '[s]teps should be taken without delay to ensure that the management of the detention center is placed under the exclusive responsibility of the Ministry of Justice. Further, the CPT wished to stress that it is not sufficient simply to change the legal status of the establishment concerned for the situation to be rendered satisfactory. Instead, steps should be taken to improve material conditions in these facilities, the regime offered to inmates must be radically improved, and staff should receive appropriate training' (CPT/Inf(2006)24, para 58).

Here, a reflection is needed to clarify (partly) the persistence of the problem. The prison system in Albania (as in many other countries of the same political heritage) had been under the Ministry of Public Order[14] and subsequently was caught for many years *in limbo* between this Ministry and the Ministry of Justice. For many years, the ambiguity of responsibilities and allocating of funding has been the reason for the delays in implementing the CPT recommendations (CPT/Inf(2003)10, p. 16 in response to paras 34, 35, 37, 38 of the CPT/Inf(2003)9). The transfer, which was instituted formally in 2001,[15] defined the authority of the Ministry of Justice over the pre-trial detention system,[16] but it took many years to be implemented. A complete transfer became possible only in 2007. This transfer was—among other things—a matter related to respect for human rights and fundamental freedoms of persons deprived of their liberty.[17] In fact, only in the course of the visit in 2008, the CPT observed some improvements both with regard to the conditions of detention in pre-trial detention centres and with regard to treatment of detainees whilst in police custody, although a number of allegations of physical ill-treatment were again received (CPT/Inf(2009)6, para 9). Furthermore, in December 2009 a 'Manual on the Treatment of Persons in Police Custody' was approved by the Director General of the State Police. The manual covers a wide range of issues concerning custody by the police, such as the procedures for admission to police custody cells (including mandatory medical checks), the rights and obligations of detainees during their stay in these facilities, conditions of detention therein, access to healthcare during police custody, technical parameters and layout of custody cells, the keeping of custody records, and so on.

Unfortunately, during the 2010 visit to Albania, the CPT reported that it had again received a significant number of allegations of physical ill-treatment of criminal suspects by the police (CPT/Inf(2012)11, paras

13). The allegations related mostly to ill-treatment inflicted at the time of questioning with a view to obtaining a confession or extracting information. The CPT expressed concerns about the many, consistent allegations of ill-treatment received from young persons, including allegations of psychological ill-treatment. The CPT also reported a lack of effective investigations into ill-treatment claims even when reported to a judge. The CPT made a number of recommendations in this regard, notably in relation to detainees' access to a lawyer and a medical doctor, notification to detainees of their rights, keeping of records during detention, and specific issues related to juveniles. The CPT stressed that whenever criminal suspects brought before judicial authorities allege ill-treatment, the allegations should be recorded in writing, a forensic medical examination (including, if appropriate, by a forensic psychiatrist) immediately ordered, and the necessary steps taken to ensure that the allegations are properly investigated. The CPT further noted that most of the staff (including senior officers) met by the delegation at local police stations had no knowledge of the above-mentioned manual's existence. As a result, some training sessions for law enforcement officials have been organised by the authorities in order to familiarise them with the contents of the manual.[18] The findings of this visit in prison establishments indicated that ill-treatment by staff is not a widespread phenomenon, but there is a 'need for constant vigilance' in the prison system (CPT/Inf(2012)11, para 46).

The following year is politically an important one for Albania, with the violent events of 21 January 2011 in Tirana, during which four persons were killed, several dozens of demonstrators and law enforcement officers were injured, and 113 individuals were arrested and placed in detention. There have been serious cases of ill-treatment by the police, as well as the lack of access to a lawyer, a medical doctor, and contact with family members. Furthermore, the police refused to execute the General Prosecutor's detention orders with regard to six senior officers of the Guard of the Republic with a view to taking their statements in relation to the events of 21 January. Only two law enforcement officials have been found guilty of involuntary manslaughter, while an investigation into human rights violations involving other security officials was dropped due to lack of evidence. In this context, the CPT conducted an *ad hoc* visit to examine the treatment of persons who had been taken into custody in the context of disturbances that had occurred in Tirana. The delegation interviewed all the persons (still) in detention (about 35) and examined relevant records at Tirana Prisons Nr. 302 and Nr. 313 and at several police establishments in Tirana. The CPT urged the Albanian authorities to pursue a policy of 'zero tolerance' of ill-treatment and formulated several recommendations to reinforce the safeguards afforded to persons detained by the police (in particular, as regards the right of access to a lawyer) (CPT/Inf(2016)11, para 16). It further recommended that the Albanian authorities have to reinforce their policy in respect of crowd-control operations, that in most cases involve persons being deprived of their liberty, and the training provided to police officers to act in such operations. Some measures taken by the government included amendments to the curricula of police staff training, concerning action and reaction in cases of massive arrests. The authorities earmarked €1.8 million for the State Police in order to improve its capacity and efficiency, and equipment has been modernised in the context of this investment.

In 2012, the United Nations Committee against Torture (UN CAT) also expressed its concern in relation to information that alleged victims of ill-treatment were not aware of complaint procedures beyond reporting their complaints to the police, which in some cases had refused to accept complaints concerning misconduct by the police (see also Leskoviku and Papavangjeli 2011). It also expressed concerns regarding the reported cases of ill-treatment of persons in a vulnerable situation who have declined to file complaints against the police out of fear of counter-complaints by the police or other forms of reprisals. It also expressed its deep concern at reports indicating that basic safeguards against ill-treatment during pre-trial detention in Albania were still not applied systematically and effectively (UN CAT 2012, para 13). It noted that detainees were not always fully informed of their rights from the outset of their deprivation of liberty, were deprived of timely access to a lawyer and a medical doctor and of the right to notify a family member or person of one's choice of an arrest and current place of detention, and were often not brought before a judge within the constitutionally prescribed periods.

The Ombudsman also noted in his 2012 annual report (2012: 56–57) that there was an almost twofold increase in the number of complaints it received against the police, compared to 2011 (234 and 119 respectively).

More specifically, in 2012, out of the 234 police-related complaints received by the Ombudsman, 71 related to ill-treatment, including torture. It submitted 26 recommendations to the relevant authorities, concerning 77 police officers, requesting that criminal and/or disciplinary proceedings be initiated. In this report, the Ombudsman noted that there was a need for continuous training of law enforcement officers on how to treat persons deprived of liberty, including the obligation to inform persons under arrest of their rights immediately upon arrest. The Ombudsman stressed that the registers on deprivation of liberty need to be standardised and should contain all information concerning the deprivation of liberty, notably the time and reason thereof, the physical state of the person (particularly whether there are any visible signs of physical injury), and information as to whether access to a lawyer and a medical doctor has been provided. Both the CPT and the Ombudsman often have stressed that surveillance systems should be installed as one of the measures to prevent ill-treatment in detention. The Ombudsman has recommended to the General State Police Directorate to adopt the necessary measures in order to ensure that psychologists and a lawyer are always present at proceedings involving juveniles, in compliance with the relevant provisions of the Criminal Procedure Code (i.e. art.35, 37, 48 and 296/1).

Ill-treatment by law enforcement agents has also been reported by local NGOs. For example, the ARCT reported about this problem extensively in its 2012 alternative report to UN CAT. In its 2012 monitoring report, according to Nil Muižnieks, Commissioner for Human Rights of the Council of Europe (2014), the European Institute of Tirana noted allegations of physical and psychological ill-treatment, including against juveniles, in 7 out of 17 pre-trial detention institutions visited (2012: 41). One of the cases concerned a juvenile who was allegedly beaten up for 10 minutes while his hands were handcuffed. The juveniles who witnessed the beating admitted that they had not complained out of fear of ill-treatment (ibid: 105). All the juveniles reported that the use of batons by law enforcement officers was a common practice, a problem also noted often by the CPT. In its 2013 judgement in the case of Kaçiu and Kotorri,[19] concerning, inter alia, the torture by the police of one applicant during interrogation, the ECtHR found Albania to be in violation of art. 3 of the ECHR. The Court noted that the applicant's beating was of such severity that he had to be carried to the courtroom by police officers. The Court added that even though the domestic authorities were made aware of the applicant being beaten, the prosecutor did not take any steps to investigate the applicant's repeated and serious allegations. Moreover, the judge at the initial hearing did not request that the applicant's clear physical discomfort be investigated, even though the applicant could not stand or walk.

There is a persistent lack of effective investigations into and prosecution of cases of serious human rights violations committed by law enforcement officials. For example, only one criminal proceeding relating to the criminal offence of torture[20] was initiated in 2012, and it was eventually dismissed in court. Furthermore, a pattern exists of classifying reported acts of ill-treatment, including torture, committed by law enforcement officials as criminal offences of 'abuse of power' or 'commission of arbitrary acts', under art. 248 and 250 of the Criminal Code, respectively,[21] and, in 2012, UN CAT (2012: para 8) called on the Albanian authorities to refrain from this practice.

In 2014, during its last periodic visit, the CPT concluded in its report that the situation had not improved, but that it had instead deteriorated. Therefore, it was required once again on the part of Albanian authorities to combat the phenomenon of police ill-treatment (CPT/Inf(2016)6, para 73). Given this persistent scenario, it is not surprising at all that one of the key priorities set for Albania in the context of the EU accession process (European Commission 2010: 12) concerns measures that need to be taken to improve the treatment of detainees and to ensure judicial follow-up of cases of ill-treatment. In May 2012, the government updated its action plan for the period 2012–2015 which outlines a list of measures to be taken in this regard, including the improvement of the legal framework for the treatment of inmates or remand prisoners, as well as of the legislation relating to the penitentiary and the police. During 2012–2013, the prison system also developed a protocol for handling complaints. Further harmonisation of legislation of the prison system with EU legislation (EU *acquis*, best practices, and standards) has been set as one of the strategic priorities of the General Directorate of Prisons. In order to improve the rights of treatment of the persons deprived of their liberty, amendments to the Law No. 8328 on the rights and treatment of prisoners and detainees (16 April 1998), and some amendments to Law

No. 10032 about 'Prison Police' (11 December 2008), have been proposed by the Ministry of Justice. In particular, these initiatives stipulate the general principles of treatment of persons with mental disorders, detainees and prisoners of foreign nationality, women and children, persons with disabilities, LGBT, members of ethnic and linguistic minorities, the elderly and people with long-term sentences in the prison system and other issues related to insurance health scheme request and complaints mechanism, disciplinary measures, rewarding and special leaves, transfer rules, protection of personal data, as well as a specific chapter on the rights and obligations of pre-trial detainees. Worth mentioning is that the General Directorate of Prisons has signed 14 cooperation agreements during 2013–2014, with various non-governmental organisations that deal with human rights. This cooperation is focussed on several aspects, such as prison monitoring, staff training in different aspects, compiling modules, and organising study visits in penal institutions of the EU.[22]

## 4.2 Overcrowding, Pre-trial Detention and Other Material Concerns

Prison overcrowding, overuse of pre-trial detention, and difficult material conditions of prisons and other detention centres have also been long-standing issues of concern for the Albanian prison system.[23] Prison overcrowding in Albania has reflected the significant increase in organised crime and in violent crimes against the person that followed the breakdown of law and order in 1997, which has led to a corresponding increase in the number of long-term prisoners. Prison overcrowding is also partly due to legal provisions designed to sharply deter not only violent crime against persons but also crimes against property. For example, under art. 134(2) of the Criminal Code, non-violent theft even of a relatively petty order, if committed by more than one person, carries a minimum sentence of five years imprisonment. Recently, polemic laws regarding unauthorised possession of firearms have come into force[24] which provide a sentence of 7–15 years of imprisonment.[25]

In addition, courts rely heavily on the penalty of imprisonment—as opposed to non-custodial penalties—mainly because the necessary administrative structures for enforcing alternative penalties are lacking.

Moreover, courts fail to take into account existing alternative, non-custodial restrictions on personal freedom, such as bans on leaving the country, release on bail, or judicial controls. Court decisions impose pre-trial detention ignoring individual reasoning, disregarding the presumption of innocence, and the recommendation that pre-trial detention must always be exceptional and justified.[26] Although alternative measures to pre-trial detention have been persistently recommended, judges have failed to consider the use of such alternatives. Furthermore, as mentioned in the beginning of the chapter, imprisonment rates have increased regularly every year, and currently, more than half of all prisoners are pre-trial detainees.

Pre-trial detention has been identified as a core concern by the CPT early on during its visits. The number of pre-trial detainees continues, nevertheless, to remain high and the duration excessive, without mentioning the high risks for ill-treatment. The problem of pre-trial detention is also related to the problem of excessive length of judicial proceedings.[27] In his 2012 Annual Report, the Ombudsman noted that out of 250 complaints he received concerning problems relating to the justice system, 90 related to excessive length of proceedings in domestic courts. The measure of pre-trial detention has also been used excessively for juveniles.[28]

Recommendations of the CPT regarding overcrowding have mainly been reflected in the construction of new prisons in Albania. For example, throughout the last years, new institutions (Fushë-Krujë, Rrogozhinë, Peqin, Vlorë, Korçë, Durrës, Kavajë, Berat, Fier, Lezhë, and Elbasan)[29] have been constructed with financial support mainly from the EU and in some isolated cases with support from the state budget. Among the plans of the government, privatisation of prisons is also being discussed as part of the plans for infrastructure improvement, but not the construction of semi-open and open prisons. The Albanian government tackled the situation further by implementing the new OSCE-supported probation system and by granting amnesty to certain convicts.[30]

Experience has shown, however, that overcrowding is not necessarily solved, at least in the long term, by increased prison capacity. In fact, as we can easily notice in Albania, as prisons continue to be built, the prison population also continues to increase. In fact, in the CPT standards, it is explicitly written that:

> To address the problem of overcrowding, some countries have taken the route of increasing the number of prison places. For its part, the CPT is far from convinced that providing additional accommodation will alone offer a lasting solution. Indeed, a number of European States have embarked on extensive programmes of prison building, only to find their prison populations rising in tandem with the increased capacity acquired by their prison estates. By contrast, the existence of policies to limit or modulate the number of persons being sent to prison has in certain States made an important contribution to maintaining the prison population at a manageable level. (CPT/Inf/E(2002)1—Rev. 2011, para 14)

Similarly, the Ombudsman, reflecting on this problem, in 2003 argued that:

> In our view, the problem of overcrowding in prisons cannot be solved simply by building new prisons. Above all, more importance should firstly be given to the preventive measures, which society and the Albanian state should undertake; secondly prosecutors and courts should apply a better policy in imposing other security measures. They should apply more frequently measures such as bail, or house arrest, and other forms of penalty, not only the penalty of imprisonment. The deprivation of liberty is an extreme measure, and should be used only when alternative measures would be inappropriate due to the extreme danger posed by the crime and its perpetrator. (Ombudsman, 2003: 120)

Besides overcrowding and pre-trial detention, since the first visit, other material conditions of prisons and other detention facilities in Albania have also been a major concern of CPT, but some improvement has been noticed in that regard throughout the years, although unevenly. The difficulty of properly assessing these changes relates to the fact that the conditions of the prisons in Albania started almost at level zero, so it will take many years, given the country's economic difficulties, to reach an acceptable level according to European standards. Starting with the first visit, where prisons were even destroyed and ransacked, already in 1998 CPT noticed improvement of some prison facilities which had been in miserable conditions the year before. Compared to 1997, the majority of the prisoners had their own bed, but a large number still had not even the basic sleeping conditions (CPT/Inf(2003)7, para 27).

In 2001, during CPT's visit in the Vlorë police station, the conditions were so poor that the CPT delegates concluded that the premises were probably beyond repair and should be torn down (CPT/Inf(2003)11, para 26), and accordingly some improvements were introduced in December 2003. In the report on that visit, CPT writes that:

> The conditions of the police custody cells which the delegation visited in Tirana and Vlorë continued to be worrying. These cells generally lacked any furniture, had poor lighting and were cold and dirty. The fact that police custody theoretically lasts for a relatively short period in Albania (48 hours) cannot reasonably justify not carrying out the recommendations already formulated by the CPT on this matter. (CPT/Inf(2003)11, para 26)

In February 2002, the Ministry of Public Order, in a response to the CPT, stated:

> The Ministry of Public Order and the General Police Department have ensured the funds for the reconstruction of all police commissariats which have detention areas, mostly in the direction of the sanitation, the places where the detainees meet with their family members, the refrigerator rooms for food supplies, bedding and cover and other human conditions. (CPT/Inf(2003)10, para 16)

AI, in their 2004 report based on their monitoring visits in 2002–2003, states that there were no visible signs of any such renovation, with the exception of the preventive detention facilities at Vlorë, where some improvements have been made. In its response to the CPT, the Ministry added that other problems, such as the need to extend cell space and exercise yards, could not be addressed, for technical and other reasons, and that even if provision were made for such expenses, they would go in vain, since in the near future the system of preventive detention, which so far has been a subordinate of the Ministry of Public Order, would pass into the charge of the Ministry of Justice (CPT/Inf(2003)10, paras 34, 35, 37, 38).

During their 2003 visit, the CPT visited the pre-trial detention facilities at Elbasan and Shkodra, finding extremely poor material conditions combined with a very restrictive regime (CPT/Inf(2006)22, para 60). As a result, four facilities were included in a general renovation and equipment of Shkodra district funded by the Government and United States Agency for International Development (USAID), completed by January 2004. In 2011, conditions of detention in police establishments had improved in several institutions, but it remained extremely poor in all the other establishments visited (CPT/Inf(2016)11, para 25). During the last visit in 2014, the lack of electricity and running water over a 24-hour period and the dilapidated and damp buildings as well as their overcapacity led the CPT to conclusions that the living conditions in these institutions are not in accordance with international standards (CPT/Inf(2016)6, para 52; see also European Commission 2011: 16).

## 4.3 Healthcare-Related Concerns

The provision of healthcare responding to the health needs of prisoners in all prisons continues to remain a challenge for the Albanian prison system. Even the cases reviewed by the ECtHR involve health-related issues in prison. One of the cases concerned the failure to provide due medical care to an applicant suffering from a serious disease,[31] and in another case, negligence in failing to prescribe adequate medical treatment and subsequent deterioration of the applicant's health due to the lack of medical treatment was reported.[32]

Already during its first visit in 1997, CPT visited prison hospitals, where they noted lack of care on behalf of the staff, the unclear status of the prison hospital, and the lack of implementation of the Law on Mental Health (1996) regarding the status of the patients that are in the psychiatric hospitals based on involuntary hospitalisation (CPT/Inf(2003)6, para 31). During the next visit in 1998, CPT noticed improvements in the prison hospitals, where mortality had been reduced from 11.3 % to 4.38 %, due to some improvements in food, hygiene, and heating. Nevertheless, the CPT noticed no improvements in staff behaviour, and no systemic monitoring of patients either at their entry moment or follow-up during their stay. Implementation of the Law on Mental Health of 1996 continued to be lacking. In its recommendations, the CPT asked for regular follow-ups of patients, a renovation plan for the infrastructure of the hospital, personalised treatment of each patient, training for hospital staff, a clear division of tasks within the hospital, and implementation of the Law on Mental Health (CPT/Inf(2003)7, paras 20, 38).

Almost all national and international actors who monitor the Albanian prison system have strongly highlighted the violation of the physical and mental security of persons subjected to mandatory medication as well as prisoners who are accommodated in the same premises as such patients. The CPT reports have repeatedly warned about the situation of forensic psychiatric patients and legal safeguards for involuntary hospitalisation. In 2000, with the exception of the minor improvement of the documentation and medical treatment, the CPT confirmed the same concerns as the previous years. The way in which the rehabilitation centre for minors in Berat was run: with no ill-treatment, with good conditions, and multiple programmes (CPT/Inf(2003)9, para 167), deserved praise. In 2001, the CPT repeated the same recommendations regarding the prison hospital (CPT/Inf(2003)11, para 34). The government has accordingly increased the budget by 40%, and has decided to create a special inter-ministerial commission to deal with the non-implementation of the Law of Mental Health.

In 2006, the CPT noted with regret that none of their specific previous recommendations, related to the medical examinations on admission to pre-trial detention facilities, had been implemented in practice. Moreover, there were no improvements regarding the general provision of healthcare in the establishments visited (CPT/Inf(2007)35, paras 23, 24). Even in 2008, there were no improvements related to the situation concerning the medical examination of the newly arrived. Moreover, the CPT expressed its concern related to specialised care, such as the limited access to a dentist on a regular basis in the detention and pre-trial detention facilities (CPT/Inf(2009)6, paras 33, 35). During their visit in 2010, they noted that in all the establishments visited, the healthcare facilities were of a poor quality, and the medical equipment was extremely limited. As regards the provision of psychiatric care, several detention facilities were not visited by a psychiatrist. This caused the need to transfer the prisoners to other establishments, with the risk of considerable delays (CPT/Inf(2012)11, paras 70, 74).

Nonetheless, the mental health system in Albania has experienced major changes during this period. A national programme of deinstitutionalisation of long-term psychiatric patients was launched, and 10 supported homes and six community mental health centres have been opened thus far in different parts of the country. In 2010, after numerous previous visits with no improvements, the CPT's delegation observed that the services for psychiatry and neurology in Shkodra Psychiatric Hospital have been totally separated, and an admission/observation unit has been opened within the psychiatric ward (CPT/Inf(2012)11, para 110). In 2011, during the *ad hoc* visit of the CPT, it was noted that a doctor was permanently available at the Directorate General and no complaints were lodged with regard to the access to a doctor. Furthermore, the persons with serious injuries were apparently transferred to a hospital without delay (CPT/Inf(2016)11, para 21). In 2012, a new Law on Mental Health entered into force, which provides for legal guarantees for the rights and treatment of persons subjected to mandatory medication measures.

Nevertheless, at the occasion of its last visit in 2014, the CPT has again expressed concern that the 2012 Law on Mental Health, which contains a number of important safeguards for psychiatric patients, has never been implemented in the context of involuntary hospitalisation. All the patients for whom an involuntary placement procedure had been initiated had subsequently been convinced by staff to sign a voluntary hospitalisation consent form. However, in practice, most of these patients were not allowed to leave the hospital unaccompanied and were thus *de facto* deprived of their liberty, without respecting the legal requirement of involving a court. Another major concern lies in the fact that the great majority of forensic patients who had been declared not criminally responsible continued to be held in prison establishments in breach of national legislation and severe violation of their rights. Moreover, many of them were being held at Kruja Special Facility[33] in conditions that, in the CPT's view, were likely to amount to therapeutic abandonment. This establishment did not have a single psychiatrist for over a year, the supply of psychotropic medication was seriously affected by prolonged shortages, and hardly any rehabilitative activities were offered to patients. The CPT called upon the Albanian authorities to take urgent measures to remedy these shortcomings and to speed up the creation of a specialised forensic psychiatric facility (CPT/Inf(2016)6). Overall, the CPT noticed a slight amelioration of the general healthcare in the prison system but also noted that the overall quality of healthcare in prison was undermined by the fact that all the prisons visited suffered from a severe shortage of medication. Moreover, in their report, they noted that, despite the repeated recommendations since their first visit to Albania, medical screening of newly arrived inmates was not systematic (CPT/Inf(2016)6, para 71).

## 5 Conclusion

The aim of this chapter was to understand the role and impact of the CPT (including other local and international civil society actors) on the prison system in Albania. Emerging from a dictatorial political heritage, the challenges for reforming criminal justice based on the rule of law and human rights were vital during the transition towards political pluralism, and as we argued throughout the chapter, remain vital even today. The presence and the role of monitoring bodies in Albania, especially in safeguarding the rights and treatment of imprisoned persons, cannot be taken lightly, given the legacy of torture, death, and disappearances in some of the country's infamous prisons and internment camps during the dictatorial regime. At the same time, the 'pressure' by the EU towards Albanian candidacy status—granted in 2014—has also been decisive. The focus on human rights and proper treatment of detained persons was one of the 12 key priorities of the 2010 EC's Opinion on Albania's application for membership of the EU (COM(2010)680, 2010, p. 12), and it still remains part of Albania's necessary reforms towards EU Integration.

In terms of legislation and ratification of European Conventions, it can be easily concluded that Albania is doing quite well; the problem remains rather at the implementation level. We mapped the role of the CPT through three core themes, which seem to have remained central for Albania throughout the years, namely, ill-treatment and violation of human rights; overcrowding, pre-trial detention, and other poor material conditions; and health-related concerns. Given the acute nature and persistence of basic problems of poor material conditions, ill-treatment, and health-related issues, the concerns regarding rehabilitation and reintegration in Albania seem almost luxurious. Nevertheless, Albanian legislation provides for the prospect of a successful return to society after release as the main purpose of punishment. However, the daily practice in penal institutions offers very little in the form of individualised treatment programmes, educational, rehabilitation, or release programmes. In most penal institutions, these programmes are totally lacking, and even when they do exist, they have tended to be formal and superficial (Pavavangjeli 2014). Already in 1997, the CPT noticed the total absence of such programmes, and in 1998, there was no improvement in prison programmes and activities. During the 2000 visit, lack of rehabilitation programmes remained a problem. Despite the 2009 amendments to the General Directorate of Prisons, which legally enable the realisation of labour in prisons as well as appropriate remuneration for prisoners' work, in practice, the remuneration of prisoners' work does not seem possible. In their last report, in 2014, the CPT noted that there have been some efforts to provide inmates with a scope of out-of-cell activities, such as work, education, and daily association sessions. However, it remains a matter of serious concern that the majority of inmates in the prison system were not involved in any employment or educational training (CPT/Inf(2016)6, para 57).

Despite what seems to be a long persistence of the problem of ill-treatment and other problems, the role of the CPT in Albania has been enormous. Especially because the CPT clearly increases its standards and recommendations as the country progresses with little steps in the directions indicated. Given the country's political heritage, it does not come as a surprise that one of the most long-standing problems in Albania has remained the ill-treatment and serious human rights violations of detainees by the law enforcement agencies, mainly the police. Even though it will be almost 20 years since the CPT started visiting Albania, given the long time it took to establish and transfer the responsibilities for the prison system to the Ministry of Justice, the implementation of the recommendations must be assessed therefore with this *in limbo* period in mind. Even then, difficult political events in the country have contributed towards regress in acute ways, as, for example, in 2011. These events, in fact, shed light on the fact that the problem of the prison system cannot be assessed separately from other problems that relate to the justice system, like corruption and impunity. As in all the countries that are struggling to find their path towards democracy, not all lives seem to matter the same way, and certainly on a scale of importance, detainees rank the lowest, when compared to law enforcement officials. An issue that was not addressed in the chapter but which is often 'the elephant in the room' when discussing the justice system in Albania is the issue of corruption. According to the 2012 Transparency International Corruption Perception Index, Albania ranks among the 10 most corrupt countries in Europe. In its 2013 progress report on Albania, the EC noted that corruption in the judiciary remains a particularly serious problem. The high level of corruption within the judiciary was also noted by the UN Human Rights Committee (UNHRC) in its 2013 Concluding Observations on Albania.

The *National Strategy for Development and Integration 2007–2013*, a core document concerning the prospects of Albania for European integration, stressed the government's intention to reform the judiciary and its administration according to European standards. A new national strategy launched for 2014–2020, also encompasses reforms pertaining to the judicial field. Various strategic documents and pieces of legislation concerning the justice system have been adopted in recent years, notably in the context of the implementation of obligations relating to Albania's candidacy to the EU. The most important developments were the adoption in 2011, by the Council of Ministers of Albania, of a comprehensive Justice Reform Strategy 2011–2013 and the accompanying action plan. By Order No. 261 of 29 October 2013 of the General Director of Prisons, a working group was also set up in order to draft the Anti-Corruption Strategy in the Prison System. A fundamental part of this strategy is the definition of the concrete measures and activities to prevent and denounce corruptive acts of the uniformed staff and civil staff, persons deprived of their liberty, and free citizens. In July 2016, Albania's parliament approved the judicial reform which aimed at battling organised crime and corruption. The reform is seen as a major step in Albania's journey towards EU membership.[34]

In relation to overcrowding, especially in pre-trial detention, although alternative measures to pre-trial detention have been persistently recommended by the CPT, judges have failed to consider the use of such alternatives. Furthermore, as mentioned earlier in the chapter, imprisonment rates have increased every year, and despite the emphasis of the CPT to solve problems of overcrowding in more systematic ways, the fact that Albania has only chosen to tackle this issue through a few amnesties and the building of new prisons, remains worrying. We believe, therefore, that the time has come for the CPT to formulate more clearly recommendations that go in other directions and drop overcrowding from its main concerns, otherwise Albania will end up once again becoming a 'prison country', in accordance with its past heritage. Problems that concern the material conditions of the buildings largely have to do with poor conditions of public institutions, in general, and can largely be tackled through foreign donors' support, as it already seems to be the case.

Next to the judiciary, corruption again comes as a crosscutting issue that relates also to the public healthcare sector. Once again, the lives that matter are the lives that can financially afford it. Another intersecting issue that remains a problem—as we mentioned throughout the chapter—is the professionalisation of staff in prisons, pre-trial detention centres, police commissariats, and hospitals. On the one hand, the political appointment of staff, on the other hand, their lack of adequate training, and once more their lack of motivation due to poor payment remain deep concerns in the country threatening the stability, professionalism, and credibility of staff. Based on the guidelines of the Albanian Government for the penitentiary system, for the period 2014–2017, a new Mid Term Strategy of the Penitentiary System and its Action Plan have been drafted. Among other priorities, the further consolidation of the prison system remains important, as is improving the physical infrastructure and material conditions of the penitentiary institutions; increasing partnerships for the respect of human rights in the prison system; and prevention, investigation, and prosecution of acts of corruption by the prison administration.

To conclude this chapter on an optimistic note, in light of the reforms and strategies announced and already under way, and especially given the expected start of Albania's EU membership negotiations in 2016, we have to remain hopeful that a new page will be written on Albania's prison system.

## Notes

1. See Albania 2013 Progress Report, SWD(2013)414 final, 8. Officially recognised by the European Union (EU) as a potential candidate country in 2000, Albania started negotiations on a Stabilisation and Association Agreement (SAA) in 2003, which was successfully agreed and signed on 12 June 2006. Albania applied for EU membership on 28 April 2009, and was awarded candidate status in 2014. Until now, no further progress has been made in this process, since the membership negotiations have not yet started.
2. In the late 1990s, the government began to release political prisoners in substantial numbers. According to the government, by March 1991, about 530 political prisoners had been released. On 2 July 1991, President Alia signed a decree granting amnesty to all prisoners convicted of espionage, sabotage, diversion, and terrorist acts, as well as those convicted of slandering high state organs. On September 30, the Parliament enacted an Amnesty Law recognising the innocence of all who had been convicted of 'crimes of conscience' under the previous regime. The Amnesty Law also established a method of compensation for former prisoners and included within its scope all persons deported or sent to internal exile for political reasons. According to Human Rights Watch, in 1992, there were approximately 950 common prisoners left in Albanian prisons (Human Rights Watch 1992).
3. For a total capacity of 5,455 prisoners. Of the total number of prisoners, about 110 are women and about 75 minors, and 2979 are pre-trial detainees (Statistics from the Albanian Prison Directorate, n.d., May 2016).
4. In 2013, a compulsory new deal was signed between the UK and Albania for the transfer of about 77 Albanian prisoners, but when brought into force in 2014, it resulted in three prisoners being transferred out of 334 present in the UK. To our knowledge, there has been no accepted EU

plan for the deportation of prisoners from the EU countries towards non-EU countries. On the other hand, a system has been established for transferring convicted prisoners back to their EU country of nationality, habitual residence, or another EU country with which they have close ties. This system was introduced through the Council Framework Decision 2008/909/JHA of 27 November 2008 on the application of the principle of mutual recognition for judgements imposing custodial sentences or measures involving deprivation of liberty.

5. The most important include Law no. 8328 on the rights and treatment of prisoners and detainees (16 April 1998) as amended; Law No. 8454 on the Ombudsman (4 February 1999) as amended; Regulation 1075 for the security and treatment of persons in preventive detention (15 September 1999); Decision of the Council of Ministers 327 on code of behaviour for police in prisons (15 May 2003); and Ministry of Justice order 3052/1 for rules on the behaviour of officials in the prison system (25 May 2005).
6. The most important include Universal Declaration of Human Rights (1948); European Convention on Human Rights (1950); Helsinki Final Act (1975); UN Minimum Standard Rules for the treatment of prisoners (1955); UN Convention against Torture and other Cruel, Inhuman or Degrading Treatment or Punishment (1987); European Convention for the Prevention of Torture and /or Cruel or Degrading Treatment (1987); UN set of principles on the protection of all persons against any form of detention or imprisonment (1988); UN basic principles for the treatment of prisoners (1990); and European Prison Rules (2006).
7. Some of the Albanian cases are *Grori v. Albania* (App. No. 25336/04), *Dybeku v. Albania* (App. No. 41153/06), *Caka v. Albania (*App. No. 44023/02), where Albania has been condemned for having violated art. 3 of the European Convention on Human Rights (ECHR).
8. On 13 March 1997 about 1,000 prisoners were released or broke out of prisons. On 16 March, more than 50 prisoners were pardoned by President Berisha and an amnesty law which passed at the end of March benefited more than 600 convicted persons (see Amnesty International 1997).
9. The Council of Europe Commissioner for Human Rights (the Commissioner) has also visited Albania several times, preparing detailed reports and recommendations (e.g. Report by Nils Muižnieks, Commissioner for Human Rights of the Council of Europe (2014) following his visit to Albania from 23 to 27 September 2013; the Compilation and Summary by the Human Rights High Commissioner 2016).

10. Most European countries have adopted what has been termed the 'ombudsman plus' model, in which the National Preventative Mechanism (NPM) function has been given to an existing ombudsman's office, whose powers have simply been enlarged. In these countries, the ombudsman carries out the NPM functions in collaboration with civil society organisations. Some countries have designated an existing National Human Rights Institution as the NPM and some have established completely new bodies to undertake the NPM functions, whilst others have assigned it to existing mechanisms and bodies, either with or without an overarching coordinating body.
11. For example, in its 2012 concluding observations United Nations Convention against Torture (UN CAT) expressed concerns about the lack of professional staff, financial resources, and methodological resources to carry out its functions effectively and independently (UN CAT 2012, para 11).
12. For example, Amnesty International (AI) has visited several preventive detention centres in 2002–2003 (Amnesty International 2004). The Albanian Helsinki Committee (AHC) carried out a systematic programme monitoring detention conditions between 1998 and 2001 (Albanian Helsinki Committee 2012). The Organisation for Security and Cooperation in Europe (OSCE) conducted a survey of 11 prisons in 2012 (OSCE 2013). In 2002, the Children's Human Rights Centre of Albania (CRCA) visited a number of police stations and usually monitors violations of children and juveniles rights. In 2003, the Community Assistance for Reconstruction, Development, and Stabilization (CARDS) Twinning Project, funded by the European Commission and supported by logistical aid and expertise from the Austrian Prison Service, also visited preventive detention centres. Albanian Rehabilitation Centre for Trauma and Torture (ARCT), starting in 2008, has performed more than 250 monitoring visits in all the penitentiary institutions, and since 2012, it has started monitoring the police commissariats (see ARCT 2012, 2015).
13. Albania committed itself on 29 June 1995 to 'sign, ratify and apply Protocol No. 6 of the European Convention on Human Rights on the abolition of the death penalty in time of peace within three years of accession, and to put into place a moratorium on executions until the total abolition of capital punishment' (Opinion No. 189 of the Parliamentary Assembly on the accession of Albania to the Council of Europe (1995), para 17.ii).

14. Currently Ministry of Interior.
15. Art. 6 of Law no. 8678 on the organisation and functioning of the Ministry of Justice (2001).
16. In accordance with the Decision of 15 March 2003 of the Council of Ministers (no. 327, on the transfer of the pre-detention system under the Ministry of Justice).
17. Art. 71 of the European Prison Rules stipulates that 'Prisons should be under the responsibility of public authorities, separate from military, police crime investigation authorities'.
18. During the almost three decades of developments that have taken place in the Albanian prison system since 1991, staff professionalism has been and remains among the top priorities. The lack of staff capacity, staff awareness, and motivation has remained an intersecting issue in prisons, pre-trial detention centres, police commissariats, and hospitals.
19. *Kaçiu and Kotorri v. Albania*, 25 June 2013, paras 97–100.
20. In 2007, the definition of torture contained in art. 86 of the Criminal Code was fully aligned with art. 1 of the UN CAT.
21. More specifically, 31 criminal proceedings relating to police misconduct in 2012 came under art. 250 of the Criminal Code. In 18 out of 31 cases, criminal charges were dismissed at the investigation phase. Out of 16 cases of law enforcement officials accused of this criminal offence in 2012, only three received prison sentences, while seven of them were fined.
22. EuropeAid/136–327/DH/ACT/AL. Support to the Penitentiary System and the Probation System in Albania. Annex C1. Standard Twinning Project Fiche.
23. The problem of overcrowding in recent years has been raised in a series of progress reports on Albania by the European Commission (2008: 12, 2009: 14, 2013: 42, 2014: 46).
24. Law nr. 144 in 2013 and Law nr. 98 in 2014 amending art. 278 of the Albanian Criminal Code.
25. The Constitutional Court ruled that these laws were unconstitutional by decision rendered the 10th December 2015.
26. Rec(2006)13 of the Committee of Ministers to member states on the use of remand in custody, the conditions in which it takes place, and the provision of safeguards against abuse.
27. For example, the average stay of pre-trial detained women is 22.3 months (Papavangjeli 2013).

28. Art. 37(b) of the Convention on the Rights of the Child, ratified by and binding on Albania, provides that states parties should ensure that no child is deprived of his or her liberty unlawfully or arbitrarily, and that any arrest, detention, or imprisonment of a child shall be in accordance with the law and shall be used only as a measure of last resort.
29. Worth mentioning are the assistance to the construction of four pre-trial detention centres and prisons, in Fier, Elbasan, Berat, and Shkodra (under IPA 2007, 2008, 2010, 2011); assistance to the construction of three pre-trial detention centres and prisons in Fushë Kruja, Korca and Vlora (under CARDS 2001–2005); and the construction of the re-integration centre in Kavaja (under CARDS 2004).
30. Based on the Law on amnesty provision, whose implementation started in April 2014, 813 people benefited from it.
31. See *Grori v. Albania*, App. No. 25336/04, 7 October 2009.
32. See *Dybeku v. Albania*, App. No. 41153/06, 2 June 2008.
33. In contrast, a number of improvements were observed at Vlora Psychiatric Hospital since the last visit to the establishment in 2005. In particular, the delegation received no allegations of ill-treatment of patients by staff or of violence amongst patients. Further, patients from all wards benefited from a relaxed open-door regime with free access around the hospital premises during the day, and the level of hygiene was generally adequate in all the wards. In addition, staffing levels had significantly improved. On the other hand, the Committee for the Prevention of Torture (CPT) recommends that urgent steps be taken to improve the poor material conditions in the wards for chronic patients.
34. On 22 July 2016, a Statement was made by High Representative/Vice-President Federica Mogherini and Commissioner Johannes Hahn on the adoption of judicial reform in Albania: 'Today the Parliament of the Republic of Albania adopted unanimously constitutional amendments which constitute provisions for a deep and comprehensive judicial reform. We congratulate the people of Albania, their leadership and all political forces who showed the maturity and responsibility to make this historical decision. This unprecedented step addresses a longstanding request by the overwhelming majority of the citizens for justice that is accountable, independent and transparent. It is also a major contribution to the fight against corruption and organised crime. These are all key priorities for Albania on its path towards integration into the EU. Now it is important that the implementation of the reform starts

immediately, with the view that the people of Albania are served by a justice system that is firmly based on European standards' (see the website of the European Neighbourhood Policy And Enlargement Negotiations: http://ec.europa.eu/neighbourhood-enlargement/news_corner/news/2016/07/20160722_2_en).

## Literature

Albanian Helsinki Committee. 2012. *Report: Pre-detention and Prison Conditions in Albania*. Tirana: Komiteti Shqiptar i Helsinkit.

Albanian Prison Directorate. n.d. *Statistics*. s.d., Tirana. http://www.dpbsh.gov.al. Accessed May 2016.

Albanian Rehabilitation Centre for Trauma and Torture. 2012. *Alternative Report*. Unpublished Report, Tirana.

———. 2015. *Monitoring of Places of Detention in Albania*. Unpublished report, Tirana.

Amnesty International. 1997. *Concerns in Europe: January–June 1997* (EUR 01/006/1997). London: Amnesty International. http://www.refworld.org/docid/45bf13272.html. Accessed 7 Sep 2016.

———. 2004. *Albania: Inhuman and Degrading Detention Conditions in Police Stations—Steps Towards Reform*. (EUR 11/001/2004). London: Amnesty International. https://www.amnesty.org/en/documents/eur11/001/2004/en/. Accessed Sep 2016.

Commissioner for Human Rights of the Council of Europe. 2016. *Compilation and Summary. Universal Periodic Review*. http://www.ohchr.org/EN/HRBodies/UPR/Pages/ALSession19.aspx. Accessed Sep 2016.

European Commission. 2008. *Progress Report on Albania 2008* (Com(2008)674). Brussels: European Commission.

———. 2009. *Progress Report on Albania 2009* (Com(2009)533). Brussels: European Commission.

———. 2010. *Commission Opinion on Albania's Application for Membership of the European Union* (COM(2010) 680). Brussels: European Commission.

———. 2011. *Progress Report on Albania 2011* (SEC(2011) 1205 final). Brussels: European Commission.

———. 2013. *Progress Report on Albania 2013* (SWD(2014) 304 final). Brussels: European Commission.

———. 2014. *Progress Report on Albania 2014* (COM (2014)700 Final of 8.10.2014). Brussels: European Commission.

European Institute of Tirana. 2012. Monitoring Report: Enhancing Access to the Justice System in Albania: Human Rights Protection in the Pre-trial Detention System, Tirana.

Gashi, R. 2012. Types of Prisons and Labour Camps and the Position of Convicted Persons in Albania During the Communist Dictatorship. *Thesis* 1: 27–50.

Human Rights Watch. 1992. Report on Albania. https://www.hrw.org/reports/1992/WR92/HSW-01.htm. Accessed 15 Sep 2016.

Leskoviku, M., and E. Papavangjeli. 2011. *On the Assessment of the Request and Complaint Mechanism in the Prisons*. Tirana: OSCE.

Muižnieks, Nils. Commissioner for Human Rights of the Council of Europe. 2014. Report following his visit to Albania from 23 to 27 September 2013 (CommDH(2014)1). Strasbourg: Council of Europe.

Musta, A. 1993. *Mandela's of Albania, 'Naim Frashëri'*. Tirana: Toena.

———. 2000. *Prisons of the Prison State*. Tirana: Toena.

Ombudsman. 2003. *2003 Annual Report*. Tirana. http://www.avokatipopullit.gov.al/. Accessed Mar 2016.

———. 2012. *2012 Annual Report*. Tirana. http://www.avokatipopullit.gov.al/. Accessed Mar 2016.

OSCE. 2013. *Report on Conditions in Albanian Prisons and Recommendations for Reform*. Tirana: OSCE. http://www.osce.org/albania/104571?download=true. Accessed Sep 2016.

Papavangjeli, E. 2013. *Convicted Women and Their Reintegration in Society—Gender Perspective in the Criminal Justice System*. Unpublished Ph.D., Tirana.

———. 2014. The Development of the Albanian Prison System in the Light of International Standards. *Security and Human Rights* 25 (1): 69–85.

Sufaj, F. 2000. *The History of Albanian Prisons During XX-th Century*. Tirana: Albin.

Sula, H., and P. Kaso. 1995. *The Dictatorship…*. Tirana: Alta.

Transparency International. 2012. *Corruption Perception Index*. https://www.transparency.org/.

UN CAT. 2012. *Concluding Observations on Albania*. CAT/C/ALB/CO/2. http://www.ohchr.org/EN/Countries/ENACARegion/Pages/ALIndex.aspx

UN Human Rights Committee. 2013. *Concluding Observations on Albania*. CCPR/C/ALB/CO/2. http://www.ohchr.org/EN/Countries/ALIndex.aspx

Walmsley, R. (2005). *Prisons in Central and Eastern Europe*. HEUNI Paper No. 22. The European Institute for Crime Prevention and Control, affiliated with the United Nations, Helsinki.
Zegalli, Z. 1999. *Confessions from the Prison of Communist Dictatorship*. Tirana: Koha.

**Brunilda Pali** is Senior Research Fellow at the Leuven Institute of Criminology (LINC), KU Leuven, Belgium.

**Xhilda Vocaj** is a lawyer specialised in international litigation and arbitration, Paris, France.

# Council of Europe Anti-Torture Committee and Prisons in Austria

Ursula Kriebaum

## 1 Introduction

The European Convention for the Prevention of Torture entered into force for Austria in 1989.[1] Austria was among the first round of countries selected by lot to receive a periodic mission.[2] Therefore, it received its first periodic mission already in 1990. At that time, the bulk of recommendations of the European Committee for the Prevention of Torture and Inhuman or Degrading Treatment or Punishment (hereafter CPT) was addressed to the Ministry of the Interior concerning interrogation methods used by the police, and only few recommendations concerned the prison system. This ratio has changed over time, and so have the responses of the Austrian government to CPT reports.

To explore the interaction between the CPT and Austria with regard to prisons,[3] this chapter focuses on the CPT's visits to Austria, the visited prisons, the findings concerning the individual institutions and the patterns of CPT recommendations to Austria as well as Austria's answers.

U. Kriebaum (✉)
University of Vienna, Vienna, Austria



T. Daems, L. Robert (eds.), *Europe in Prisons*, Palgrave Studies in Prisons and Penology, DOI 10.1007/978-3-319-62250-7_6

inally the development of the national prison inspection institutions is outlined.

## 2 CPT Missions to Austria

Austria received six periodic missions from the CPT so far: 20 May 1990 to 27 May 1990 (CPT/Inf(91)10), 26 September 1994 to 7 October 1994 (CPT/Inf(96)8), 19 September to 30 September 1999 (CPT/Inf(2001)8), 14 April to 23 April 2004 (CPT/Inf(2005)13), 15 February 2009 to 25 February 2009 (CPT/Inf(2010)5) and 22 September 2014 to 1 October 2014 (CPT/Inf(2015)34). They lasted from 8 to 12 days. The delegations comprised four members for the first and second visit and either five or six members for the following visits. They were accompanied by one or two experts, members of the secretariat and interpreters.

## 3 The Prison Institutions Visited

While during the first visit only prisons in Vienna had been visited, this changed and CPT delegations in later visits inspected prisons in several parts of Austria.

### 3.1 First CPT Visit—1990

In 1990 the delegation visited the *Vienna Court of First Instance Prison* (CPT/Inf(91)10, paras 29–39). The delegation did not receive any allegations of torture or inhuman or degrading treatment or punishment (CPT/Inf(91)10, para 31). It noted a certain overcrowding but found the conditions not to be unacceptable (CPT/Inf(91)10, para 33). Concerning regime activities the delegation noted a certain underuse of facilities such as workshops and the gymnasium due to lack of staff and asked for the reasons for this situation (CPT/Inf(91)10, para 34). With regard to confinement to an isolation cell for 14 days as disciplinary measures, the CPT underlined the need to be mindful of the principle of proportionality

(CPT/Inf(91)10, para 35). While the medical care was satisfactory (CPT/Inf(91)10, para 36), the delegation remarked that there was insufficient access to washing facilities (incl. clothes). This was especially the case for women (CPT/Inf(91)10, para 37). The delegation also noted difficulties in the communication between prisoners and staff due to language problems. This assessment was part of the general picture of a lack of educational facilities, especially German language courses (CPT/Inf(91)10, paras 38–39).

## 3.2 Second CPT Visit—1994

In 1994 the delegation visited two other prisons: *Stein* (CPT/Inf(96)28, paras 102–106) and *Schwarzau* (CPT/Inf(96)28, paras 110–112). As in 1990, the delegation received no allegation of torture or other forms of ill-treatment (CPT/Inf(96)28, para 98). In *Stein* the CPT noted a small overpopulation of 30 persons in relation to an official capacity of 650 detainees (CPT/Inf(96)28, para 96). It considered the material conditions of detention to be satisfactory (CPT/Inf(96)28, para 102) and remarked that the prison in general had a very developed programme of activities (CPT/Inf(96)28, para 105). However, the Committee mentioned that the more qualified work placements were only accessible to Austrian prisoners and wanted to receive explanations for this situation from the Austrian authorities (CPT/Inf(96)28, para 106).

The CPT considered that although it did not receive complaints, the availability of a general medical practitioner as well as the availability of nurses with a diploma should be increased. The same was true for the presence of a dentist in which case the CPT received complaints (CPT/Inf(96)28, para 117). Furthermore, only marginal medical files of inmates existed (CPT/Inf(96)28, para 123). It recommended that medical admission tests should follow as soon as possible after admission. The CPT considered the availability of one or two testing possibilities a week as too few (CPT/Inf(96)28, paras 125–126). It remained unclear whether HIV tests were made on a compulsory or on a voluntary basis, and the CPT pointed out that the result had to be covered by medical confidentiality (CPT/Inf(96)28, para 29). Furthermore, the delegation took note of a memorandum that described certain forms of solitary confinement (disciplinary, for security reasons, etc.). For one of these forms, the memorandum stipulated that the detainee must be naked when detained in a special cell and is not allowed to exercise daily in fresh air. The CPT considered the former to be degrading treatment and the latter to be inacceptable as well (CPT/Inf(96)28, para 147).

In *Schwarzau* a renovation programme was ongoing during the visit. This led to detention conditions which were far from ideal, and the CPT recommended an acceleration of the renovation process (CPT/Inf(96)28, paras 110–111). Furthermore, the CPT noted that its delegation heard numerous complaints about tensions among prisoners (CPT/Inf(96)28, para 99). The programme of activities was good (CPT/Inf(96)28, para 112).

The CPT considered that the availability of a general medical practitioner as well as the availability of nurses with a diploma should be increased (CPT/Inf(96)28, paras 118–119). As in *Stein*, only marginal medical files of inmates existed (CPT/Inf(96)28, para 123). Medical admission tests were not available frequently enough and, moreover, the conditions during medical admission tests were below an acceptable level of medical ethics (CPT/Inf(96)28, para 127). Furthermore, some inmates with psychiatric needs did not benefit from the therapeutic environment required (CPT/Inf(96)28, para 128).

A number of issues concerned both facilities: in general, the possibilities to remain in contact with the outside world were satisfactory in both prisons. However, only limited access to telephones was available for inmates (CPT/Inf(96)28, para 135). Although a number of initiatives had been undertaken to ameliorate the situation of foreign prisoners inside the institution, the situation had still remained problematic (CPT/Inf(96)28, para 137). There were still serious communication problems (CPT/Inf(96)28, para 138). The CPT took note in this context of art. §65a Strafvollzugsgesetz (StVG) (law of penal execution) that provided that needs of foreign prisoners should be taken into consideration, for example, with regard to acquisition of books and the offer of language courses (CPT/Inf(96)28, paras 137–140).

Concerning disciplinary sanctions, the CPT noted that there were no time limits foreseen concerning solitary confinement for reasons of maintaining order and security (CPT/Inf(96)28, paras 141–143). In *Stein* the CPT received a complaint that an inmate had not been informed of the reasons for and the length of his solitary confinement pursuant to art. 125 (2) StVG (CPT/Inf(96)28, para 146).

The CPT stressed the importance of prison monitoring Commissions (*Vollzugskommissionen*) and suggested that they should use their possibilities of visits and should publish an annual report of their activities (CPT/Inf(96)28, paras 149–151).

## 3.3 Third CPT Visit—1999

In 1999, the CPT delegation made two follow-up visits. It revisited the former Vienna Court of First Instance Prison that had been renamed into *Wien-Josefstadt* prison and the *Schwarzau* prison (CPT/Inf(2001)8, paras 78–124).

With regard to the *Wien-Josefstadt* prison, the overall situation had worsened. This was true concerning the finding of ill-treatment as well as with regard to the material conditions, the possibilities of regime activities and the medical services (CPT/Inf(2001)8, paras 78, 80). The delegation received allegations of ill-treatment especially in the context of the application of disciplinary measures which had been applied to disobedient prisoners in the so-called basement. But it was also informed of rude and dismissive behaviour in general and especially towards foreign detainees (CPT/Inf(2001)8, para 80). In general the situation in the prison was characterised by grave tensions between prisoners and staff as well as between the staff and the prison directorate.

The delegation stated that the material conditions in parts D and E of the prison were satisfactory; those in parts A, B and C were acceptable despite high occupancy rates (CPT/Inf(2001)8, para 83). Although access to showers had theoretically improved, it was still problematic due to staff shortages. The same was true for the possibility to wash clothes and access to hygienic products. Here the CPT mentioned that it had pointed out these difficulties already in 1990 and the situation had not improved in 1999. Furthermore, numerous complaints had been raised concerning nutrition that concerned the quantity as well as the variety of food offered (CPT/Inf(2001)8, para 85). This was true for 'ordinary prisoners' as well as for occupants of the mother/child unit (CPT/Inf(2001)8, para 86). No improvement had been made with regard to the underuse of facilities such as workshops and the gymnasium. The situation had even worsened (CPT/Inf(2001)8, paras 89–91).

While the delegation considered the availability of a general medical practitioner as satisfactory, the same was not true for dental and psychiatric care that should be improved (CPT/Inf(2001)8, para 93). The same was true for the level of nursing staff (CPT/Inf(2001)8, para 94). The CPT considered the medical examination on admission had improved concerning timeliness (within 24 hours), but it had still been too cursory (CPT/Inf(2001)8, para 106). Moreover, it pointed out that the indication of medical diagnostics on cell doors contradicted the obligation of doctor confidentiality (CPT/Inf(2001)8, para 110). The CPT stated that the medical records—like in 1994—were too cursory. They did not include medical observations. This had a negative influence on the quality of the medical service that can be provided (CPT/Inf(2001)8, para 107). Furthermore, the CPT noted a need for serious improvement of the therapeutic possibilities of the psychiatric unit in the prison. It found that unit Z6 for psychiatric patients did not have the necessary number of professionals. Especially, there was a lack of nurses with psychiatric training (CPT/Inf(2001)8, para 100). Moreover, the CPT raised concerns over the existence of 'cage beds' (metal bars) as a security measure and recommended their abolition (CPT/Inf(2001)8, para 105). A further concern was the fact that the health-care personnel for prisons were employed and supervised by the Ministry of Justice and not by the Ministry of Health (CPT/Inf(2001)8, para 112).

Other issues of concern were the possibility of investigating judges (*Untersuchungsrichter*) to be present according to section 45 para 3 *Strafprozessordnung* (StPO) (code of criminal procedure) at meetings between the inmates and their lawyer and to control their phone calls. This was against the principle of lawyer-client privacy (CPT/Inf(2001)8, para 113).

In general, the possibility for inmates to receive visitors was satisfactory. However, visitors were separated from the inmates by a glass wall. Visits without such a wall were possible, in principle, but long waiting periods had to be accepted (CPT/Inf(2001)8, para 114). Furthermore, the CPT observed several shortcomings with regard to the possibility of phone conversation and postal delivery (CPT/Inf(2001)8, paras 116–117). Other shortcomings concerned the fact that not all of the disciplinary cells (*Absonderungszellen*) had beds and inmates had to sleep on mattresses on the floor (CPT/Inf(2001)8, para 119). A lack of proper information about the internal regulations of the prison in a language prisoners understand led to complaints of inmates (CPT/Inf(2001)8, para 121). An issue of concern for the CPT was the fact that the security personnel wore fire arms during the night shift (3 pm to 7 am) (CPT/Inf(2001)8, paras 122–123). The CPT welcomed the existence of prison committees for the inspection of prisons that had been established to ensure adequate treatment of prisoners. However, it observed that their frequency of visits varied and strongly depended on the dedication of the Commission members (CPT/Inf(2001)8, para 124).

In contrast to the situation in *Wien-Josefstadt*, the CPT found the prison in *Schwarzau* to be in good shape. The renovation had led to a very high standard of material conditions of detention (CPT/Inf(2001)8, para 79, 88). The delegation did not receive any allegations of ill-treatment (CPT/Inf(2001)8, para 80). The facility provided for good access to various activities for prisoners (CPT/Inf(2001)8, para 92).

The CPT observed that its recommendation of 1994, to increase the presence of medical doctors, had not been implemented. A medical doctor had only been present twice a week (CPT/Inf(2001)8, para 97). There were still no organised consultations by paediatric experts in the mother-child unit (CPT/Inf(2001)8, 98). The poor quality of medical examinations had already been criticised in 1994. It had not been improved and the CPT still received complaints in 1999 (CPT/Inf(2001)8, para 108). In this context, the CPT took note of a judgment by the Austrian Constitutional Court of October 1999 concerning a complaint by an inmate of *Schwarzau*. There, it was decided that if a detainee had been denied an additional medical examination by the prison administration, although a medical specialist had deemed it necessary, the principle of the equality before the law had been violated (CPT/Inf(2001)8, para 109).

Concerning the possibility of maintaining contacts with the outside world, the CPT found that the good standards confirmed in 1994 were maintained (CPT/Inf(2001)8, para 114). As had been recommended in paragraph 135 of the CPT's report concerning its last visit, a card telephone had been installed in *Schwarzau* (CPT/Inf(2001)8, para 116). The disciplinary cells provided satisfactory conditions (CPT/Inf(2001)8, para 119). The CPT remarked with regret that the importance of the prison monitoring Commissions (*Vollzugskommissionen*) had been reduced and pointed out their fundamental role for the prevention of ill-treatment (CPT/Inf(2001)8, para 124).

The CPT visited *Göllersdorf* for the first time in 1999. *Göllersdorf* is a high-security prison for the criminally insane. Therefore, inmates are also designated as patients in the following. According to Austrian criminal law, placements in such institutions are of unlimited duration. The CPT did not receive any 'credible' allegations of physical ill-treatment (CPT/Inf(2001)8, para 127) but a number of allegations of verbal aggressiveness towards patients. Both staff and the director were familiar with this situation (CPT/Inf(2001)8, para 128). This situation was also due to a lack of special formation (CPT/Inf(2001)8, para 129). In the same spirit, the CPT noted that there was a lack of professionally educated staff (CPT/Inf(2001)8, para 130).

The material detention conditions of inmates were satisfactory (CPT/Inf(2001)8, para 132). However, the construction was unfavourable from a security perspective (CPT/Inf(2001)8, para 133). While the activities provided for inmates were on the whole satisfactory, the possibility to take a walk outside depended on the presence of a sufficient number of staff members during the day (CPT/Inf(2001)8, para 134). Ergo therapies and so on were underused, and therefore appropriate medical treatment was limited for a number of inmates to pharmacotherapy, making the patients apathetic (CPT/Inf(2001)8, para 135).

The CPT also found that restraint of agitated patients might have been more violent than necessary. Agitation led to immediate placement in separate units and if talking to the patient did not help, medication would have been used. If this also turned out to be insufficient, physical restraint had been used (CPT/Inf(2001)8, para 137). One of the cells for crisis intervention contained a cage with an Asian-style toilet and a mattress only. The other two were satisfactory (CPT/Inf(2001)8, para 138).

Furthermore, the CPT wanted information about the access to a judicial remedy for persons committed for an unlimited time to such institutions to review the necessity of their internment (CPT/Inf(2001)8, para 141). Other than that, the CPT observed that the consent of patients to medical/psychiatric treatment or objections against such treatment should always be set down in writing and not just orally. Exceptions to the principle of free and informed consent should only be possible under exceptional circumstances (CPT/Inf(2001)8, para 142).

## 3.4 Fourth CPT Visit—2004

In 2004 the CPT noted an increase of prisoners in Austria which led to overcrowding and less satisfactory detention conditions (CPT/Inf(2005)13, para 69). It received practically no allegations of ill-treatment by staff (CPT/Inf(2005)15, para 71). Prison staffing in terms of numbers and training was a general issue (CPT/Inf(2005)13, para 73).

The CPT's delegation carried out a follow-up visit to *Wien-Josefstadt*, but with a focus on juvenile prisoners. In general, the material detention conditions in the juvenile units were satisfactory (CPT/Inf(2005)13, para 86–87). As already observed during the 1999 visit, food was insufficient in terms of quantity and diversity. The hours of distribution were inconvenient (dinner at 3 pm) (CPT/Inf(2005)13, para 88).

The staff shortage had a negative impact on the daily schedule of juveniles and the possibility of out-of-cell activities. This was especially true for outdoor exercise and sports activities as well as recreational activities, religious worship and working possibilities (CPT/Inf(2005)13, paras 89–92).

With regard to health care, the CPT found the general level to be adequate but recommended to employ a fully qualified specialist in child/adolescent psychiatry (CPT/Inf(2005)13, para 95). Furthermore, the CPT recommended assuring that for juvenile prisoners taking part in medical research projects, informed consent of the legal representatives or parents is obtained (CPT/Inf(2005)13, para 95). Plans had been implemented to employ medical personnel by the Ministry of Health instead of the Ministry of Justice (CPT/Inf(2005)13, para 98). For juvenile prisoners access to phone cards was difficult, and they were only allowed to make phone calls in German or English. The CPT recommended only a selective supervision of phone calls ordered by investigating judges (CPT/Inf(2005)13, para 100).

Concerning disciplinary measures, the right to have a lawyer present during disciplinary hearings did not work in practice. Further, prisoners were not allowed to call witnesses on their behalf and to cross-examine evidence given against them (CPT/Inf(2005)13, para 102). The CPT raised concerns with regard to the practice to use other prisoners or staff members as interpreters during disciplinary hearings (CPT/Inf(2005)13, para 103). With regard to the segregation units, the recommendation to equip them with beds had been implemented (CPT/Inf(2005)13, para 104). The CPT was pleased that juveniles were not sanctioned for incidences of self-harm or suicide attempts although this had been provided for by the law. It recommended adapting the law (CPT/Inf(2005)13, para 105). The CPT noted that inspections by the prison monitoring committees (*Vollzugskommissionen*) only took place once a year and recommended a system of regular inspections by an independent body (CPT/Inf(2005)13, para 107).

With regard to internal regulations, the CPT noted that not all of the foreign prisoners received adequate information in their language. Furthermore, language problems led to communication difficulties between the staff and the inmates. A lack of money for phone calls led to difficulties for foreign prisoners to keep contact with the outside world (CPT/Inf(2005)13, para 108). As already addressed in 1999, the CPT raised concerns over the fact that the security personnel wore firearms during the night shift (CPT/Inf(2005)13, para 109).

The CPT visited the *Vienna-Mittersteig* prison for the first time. It received no allegations of ill-treatment. The material standard was good (CPT/Inf(2005)13, para 112). The number of medical doctors and specialists was adequate. However, the CPT recommended increasing the number of nurses qualified in psychiatric care (CPT/Inf(2005)13, para 113). The CPT gained a very favourable impression of the therapeutic activities offered to inmates (CPT/Inf(2005)13, para 115). The fact that most inmates could not afford a lawyer to assist in involuntary hospitalisation procedures was an issue of concern (CPT/Inf(2005)13, para 118).

The CPT also made a first-time visit to *Linz* prison. It received no allegations of ill-treatment, but complaints of occasional rude behaviour towards foreigners by certain staff members (CPT/Inf(2005)13, para 71). The material detention conditions were good (CPT/Inf(2005)13, para 75). However, the CPT was particularly concerned that some juvenile prisoners had to share cells with adults. This constituted a threat of domination and exploitation (CPT/Inf(2005)13, para 76). Furthermore, adequate access to natural light should be ensured for all cells (CPT/Inf(2005)13, para 79). All prisoners were entitled to daily outdoor exercise; but the yard had no shelters against rain and no benches (CPT/Inf(2005)13, para 80).

Work activities were only available for a third of the inmates. The CPT raised concerns since there were no educational classes, not even German language courses, no possibilities for vocational training, only some sports activities, and it was common for prisoners without work to spend 23 hours a day in their cell (CPT/Inf(2005)13, para 83). Concerning the health-care team, the CPT recommended an increase of the attendance hours of the general practitioner and to substantially increase the nursing cover. Furthermore, it should be guaranteed that someone qualified to provide first aid would always be present on the premises (CPT/Inf(2005)13, para 93). The CPT raised concerns that the initial medical examination of prisoners took place in the presence of non-medical prison staff. This would not facilitate detection of prior ill-treatment by the police (CPT/Inf(2005)13, para 96). The CPT recommended the introduction of more open visiting arrangements due to the fact that 95 % of the visits had to take place under closed conditions, for example, behind a screen, for juveniles with low plexi-glass (CPT/Inf(2005)13, para 99). Furthermore, it recommended a reform of the complaints procedures. Inmates should receive written reasoned answers within a reasonable time to internal complaints. Complaints should be possible on a confidential basis (CPT/Inf(2005)13, para 106).

## 3.5 Fifth CPT Visit—2009

In 2009 the CPT's delegation carried out full visits to *Gerasdorf* and *Innsbruck*, a follow-up visit to *Wien-Josefstadt* and interviewed some remand prisoners in *Klagenfurt* and *Linz*.

Generally, the CPT welcomed that the overall prison population had been reduced through legislative measures (reduction of waiting period for conditional release, non-custodial sanctions and stricter rules for imposition of remand detention) (CPT/Inf(2010)5, para 67). The CPT asked for information concerning a pilot project on electronic monitoring of released prisoners introduced in 2008 (CPT/Inf(2010)5, para 68).

The delegation did not receive allegations of ill-treatment by staff in any of the prisons (CPT/Inf(2010)5, para 69). However, allegations of inter-prisoner violence were raised in *Innsbruck* and *Wien-Josefstadt* (CPT/Inf(2010)5, para 70). With regard to staff policy, the CPT noted the very low rate of female prison officers in all of the prisons visited and recommended an increase in particular in sections for juveniles where mixed-gender staff should be the rule (CPT/Inf(2010)5, para 74).

The maximum period of solitary confinement was too long for juveniles (CPT/Inf(2010)5, para 102). Furthermore, the CPT recommended that disciplinary punishment should not include prohibition of family contact (CPT/Inf(2010)5, para 103). The involvement of prison doctors in disciplinary matters should be reviewed, especially with regard to the fact that according to section 117 StVG the medical doctor attests whether a patient is fit for punishment which could disturb the good relation to patients (CPT/Inf(2010)5, para 107). A further area of concern for the CPT was the carrying of firearms by staff inside detention areas. It recommended that it should cease (CPT/Inf(2010)5, para 114). Truncheons should be hidden from the view of inmates (CPT/Inf(2010)5, para 115), and pepper spray should not form part of the equipment (CPT/Inf(2010)5, para 116).

With regard to *Gerasdorf* the CPT reported that the prison management was able to organise a variety of out-of-cell activities and had a dedicated staff. However, it raised concerns about the decreasing staffing levels (CPT/Inf(2010)5, para 72). Furthermore, it noted that newly recruited staff that was working with juveniles should receive specialised training (CPT/Inf(2010)5, para 73). The material detention conditions were adequate (CPT/Inf(2010)5, para 80), and all inmates were involved in a good programme of activities (CPT/Inf(2010)5, para 84). However, the juveniles complained about the quality and quantity of food (CPT/Inf(2010)5, para 83). Furthermore, the CPT recommended a more frequent access to showers (CPT/Inf(2010)5, para 82). The CPT raised serious concerns about the insufficient level of health-care staffing in *Gerasdorf* (CPT/Inf(2010)5, para 94). In several of the visited prisons, prison officers with basic medical training were responsible for the distribution of medicines, had access to medical files and were present during medical consultations. The CPT recommended this practice to be discontinued (CPT/Inf(2010)5, para 95). The CPT noted delays of several days before the initial medical screening by a doctor, and those medical files were not properly completed and maintained (CPT/Inf(2010)5, para 98–99). The CPT considered the psychological care adequate (CPT/Inf(2010)5, para 101). With regard to disciplinary procedures, the CPT criticised that prisoners were not heard by the body deciding on the sanction and had no right to call witnesses. Furthermore, the inmates were not provided with a copy of the disciplinary decision in a systematic manner (CPT/Inf(2010)5, para 106).

In *Innsbruck* the CPT received allegations of inter-prisoner violence (CPT/Inf(2010)5, para 70). The CPT was concerned because of the poor staffing situation, night shifts starting at 2.30 pm with a small team of officers based in a central control office and with prisoners remaining locked up (CPT/Inf(2010)5, para 71). The material conditions of detention were good (CPT/Inf(2010)5, para 75), but the CPT recommended a more frequent access to showers (CPT/Inf(2010)5, para 82). As in *Gerasdorf*, the CPT noted delays of several days before the initial medical screening by a doctor, and those medical files were not properly completed and maintained (CPT/Inf(2010)5, para 98–99).

Although the prison offered in principle a good variety of activities and work facilities, these were hampered by staff shortage. There were hardly any out-of-cell activities for remand prisoners (CPT/Inf(2010)5, para 76–77). Juveniles profited from a good involvement in educational and sports activities (CPT/Inf(2010)5, para 85). The CPT raised concerns about insufficient health-care staff and psychological support for prisoners (CPT/Inf(2010)5, para 93, 101). It noted a widespread prescription of psychotropic medication for prisoners (including women and juveniles) at *Innsbruck* prison with concern (CPT/Inf(2010)5, para 100). With regard to visiting arrangements, the CPT noted that remand prisoners in *Innsbruck* and *Vienna* could receive visits only under closed conditions, where they were separated by glass from their visitors (CPT/Inf(2010)5, para 109). Concerning disciplinary procedures, the same concerns as in *Gerasdorf* were raised in relation to Innsbruck (CPT/Inf(2010)5, para 106).

Like in *Innsbruck* the CPT received allegations of inter-prisoner violence in *Wien-Josefstadt* (CPT/Inf(2010)5, para 70). Juvenile prisoners complained about the quality and quantity of food (CPT/Inf(2010)5, para 83). Furthermore, there was a poor staffing situation (CPT/Inf(2010)5, para 71) and insufficient access to activities (CPT/Inf(2010)5, para 86). Moreover, the CPT recommended a more frequent access to showers (CPT/Inf(2010)5, para 82). With regard to visiting arrangements, the CPT raised the same concerns as in *Innsbruck* (CPT/Inf(2010)5, para 109). The health-care staffing levels were overall considered adequate in *Wien-Josefstadt*. However, the CPT recommended not discontinuing a contract for a part-time adolescent psychiatrist who had been recruited in response to a 2004 visit but whose contract had not been prolonged (CPT/Inf(2010)5, para 92).

## 3.6 Sixth CPT Visit—2014

In 2014 the CPT's delegation carried out first-time full visits to *Feldkirch*, *Graz-Karlau* and *Graz-Jakomini* and targeted visits to *Stein* and *Wien-Josefstadt* prisons (CPT/Inf(2015)34, para 53). Although the CPT did not find a major problem of overcrowding in the Austrian prison system, most of the prisons visited operated above their official capacity (CPT/Inf(2015)34, para 55). Furthermore, no progress had been made concerning the staffing situation since the criticism formulated during the 2009 visit (CPT/Inf(2015)34, para 59). The CPT pointed out that staff shortages inevitably had a negative impact on out-of-cell activities (CPT/Inf(2015)34, para 59, 68).

While the delegation hardly received any allegations of physical ill-treatment, a number of allegations of verbal abuse (including racism) had been raised in *Feldkirch* and *Graz-Karlau* (CPT/Inf(2015)34, para 60). The delegation learned that a criminal investigation had been launched against one prison officer at *Graz-Karlau* prison, who was suspected of having beaten an agitated inmate (CPT/Inf(2015)34, para 61). Inter-prisoner violence was no major problem (CPT/Inf(2015)34, para 62). Efforts had been made by staff to prevent instances of inter-prisoner violence, and prison officers generally intervened in a timely and appropriate manner when they were confronted with such instances (CPT/Inf(2015)34, para 62).

The CPT found material detention conditions to be on the whole satisfactory (CPT/Inf(2015)34, para 64). Problems were noted with regard to access to natural light in *Graz-Karlau* (CPT/Inf(2015)34, para 64) and the limited size of cells in *Feldkirch* (CPT/Inf(2015)34, para 65). Furthermore, the CPT reported a general problem of underused facilities due to understaffing (working day ends early in the afternoon and therefore, only limited access to activities was possible) (CPT/Inf(2015)34, para 68). The CPT noted that the majority of adult sentenced prisoners in the establishments visited was provided with work and was offered a range of other organised out-of-cell activities (CPT/Inf(2015)34: 7, see also para 67). However, the CPT considered the regime for adult remand prisoners as not acceptable; for the vast majority of them, the only daily out-of-cell activity was an hour of outdoor exercise (CPT/Inf(2015)34, para 69).

For juveniles the material detention conditions were satisfactory in *Wien-Josefstadt* and good in *Graz-Jakomini* (CPT/Inf(2015)34, para 73). Significant improvements had been made regarding the regime in *Wien-Josefstadt* compared to the situation in 2009 (CPT/Inf(2015)34, para 75). They were offered a structured programme of purposeful activities and were able to spend most of the day outside their cell (CPT/Inf(2015)34: 7, see also para 75). Furthermore, the Austrian authorities had decided to no longer hold juveniles at *Wien-Josefstadt* (CPT/Inf(2015)34, para 75). In *Graz-Jakomini* the prison offered educational and vocational activities, but cells were closed already at 3:30 pm. The CPT recommended to improve this situation (CPT/Inf(2015)34, para 76).

As regards health care, the CPT expressed serious concern about the almost total lack of medical confidentiality in all the establishments visited. In particular, it remained the case that, in every prison, various health-related tasks that are normally reserved for qualified nurses were performed by prison officers with only basic health-care training (*Sanitätsbeamte*). These officers were usually present during medical consultations, had access to medical documentation and were responsible for the distribution of prescribed medicines. At the same time, they continued to perform custodial functions. The CPT emphasised that this practice should be abolished as it is in breach of the principle of medical confidentiality and compromises the perception of the professional independence of prison health-care staff (CPT/Inf(2015)34, paras 78–82). While overall the procedures for medical screening on admission were satisfactory, the CPT recommended with regard to *Feldkirch* that a comprehensive medical examination should be made within 24 hours of a prisoner's admission (CPT/Inf(2015)34, para 82). Concerning the presence of general practitioners and psychiatrists, the CPT recommended an increase in *Feldkirch*, *Graz-Karlau* and *Graz-Jakomini* (CPT/Inf(2015)34, para 79).

Further, the CPT formulated a number of specific recommendations regarding various other prison-related issues, such as prisoners' contact with the outside world, discipline and security. In particular, the Committee recommended that pepper spray no longer form part of the standard equipment of custodial staff and that the Austrian authorities reconsider their policy regarding the carrying of firearms by prison staff inside detention areas (CPT/Inf(2015)34, para 114–116).

Concerning contacts with the outside world, the CPT observed that remand prisoners should have a right to visits as a rule and only in case of risks like collusion should visits or calls be supervised (CPT/Inf(2015)34, para 85). It also recommended that closed visits should be the exception and open visits the rule (CPT/Inf(2015)34, para 86). Concerning sentenced prisoners, the CPT recommended to increase the visit entitlement to one hour per week (CPT/Inf(2015)34, para 87). With regard to the situation of foreign prisoners, the CPT recommended not to use fellow inmates as interpreters (CPT/Inf(2015)34, para 90) and was interested in receiving further information concerning a video interpretation pilot project in *Wien-Josefstadt* (CPT/Inf(2015)34, para 90).

The CPT raised concerns about disciplinary sanctions that, despite its recommendation of 2009, the sanction of solitary confinement still entailed a total prohibition of family contacts. Any restrictions on contacts should only be applied when the offence related to such contacts (CPT/Inf(2015)34, para 94). It considered the maximum period of four weeks of solitary confinement to be excessive. There should be a maximum of two weeks (CPT/Inf(2015)34, para 93). With regard to disciplinary procedures, the CPT repeated its concerns that prisoners were not heard by the body deciding on the sanction and that the inmates were not provided with a copy of the disciplinary decision in a systematic manner and in a language they understood (CPT/Inf(2015)34, para 95). As to the carrying of firearms by staff, the CPT reiterated its findings that it is undesirable and dangerous and repeated its recommendation to review the policy of carrying firearms inside detention areas. Pepper spray should not form part of the standard equipment of custodial staff (CPT/Inf(2015)34, paras 97–98).

In the context of its targeted visit to *Stein*, the delegation focused on offenders that were subjected to a court-ordered measure of forensic placement (*Massnahmenvollzug*). Material conditions were adequate in terms of repair, but not suitable for persons in need of therapy and assistance. *Stein* lacked facilities for therapeutic activities. The CPT raised concerns because of the limited psychiatric cover (CPT/Inf(2015)34, para 108). In general it raised concerns whether Stein was suited to a meaningful implementation of forensic placement (CPT/Inf(2015)34, para 109). The CPT had serious doubts whether free and informed consent of sexual offenders had been obtained concerning *anti-androgen treatment* (chemical castration) in *Stein* (CPT/Inf(2015)34, para 111).

## 4 Patterns of Recommendations and Austria's Answers

The comments of the Austrian government on the CPT report concerning its first visit to Austria comprised only 11 pages. The answers were rather general and did not deal with the individual recommendations one by one.

The answers to the reports on the following CPT visits were much more extensive and detailed. Those to the CPT report on the second visit (1994) set out the recommendation or inquiry and then answered each of them individually. In a case where statistics were not available and difficult to provide, the Austrian government said so and stated that it would take the CPT's request as incentive to establish a system of records in the recommended area (CPT/Inf(96)29: 35).

The same approach to restate the recommendation and to provide answers was adopted concerning the visits of 1999 and 2004. Unfortunately, it was not followed with regard to the visits of 2009 and 2014 where only the answers are provided and the recommendations have to be looked up in the CPT's report. Since the paragraphs are always indicated, it is possible to match the two.

In the following, both the information about recommendations and the answers thereto are taken exclusively from the reports of the CPT and the responses of the Austrian government.

## 4.1 Overcrowding

### 4.1.1 CPT

Overcrowding was a phenomenon that has existed in Austrian prisons since the first visit of the CPT in Austria (CPT/Inf(91)10: 11). In 1994 the CPT did not consider the slight overcrowding it found in *Stein* to raise concerns (CPT/Inf(96)28, paras 96, 102). It was only in 2004 when the CPT noted a further increase of prisoners in Austria which led to overcrowding and less satisfactory detention conditions and activities for prisoners (CPT/Inf(2005)13, paras 69, 138). The CPT recommended to the Austrian authorities to '...pursue vigorously the application of a range of measures designed to combat prison overcrowding, including policies to limit or modulate the number of persons sent to prison.' (CPT/Inf(2005)13, para 69). In 2014 the CPT mentioned that:

> ...the official capacity of the Austrian prison estate has been increased from 8,501 to 8,635 places. At the same time, the overall prison population has

increased by some 10% and stood at approximately 8,800 at the time of the 2014 visit. These figures would suggest that there is currently no major problem of overcrowding in the Austrian prison system. Nevertheless, as can be seen from the figures in paragraph 54, most of the prison establishments visited by the CPT in 2014 operated above their official capacity, which led to cramped detention conditions in certain parts of some of the establishments visited. (CPT/Inf(2015)34, para 55)

### 4.1.2 Reply

In its answer to the CPT report on its second visit, the Austrian government outlined a comprehensive reform of pre-trial criminal proceedings that led to a drop in the number of remand prisoners by 23.5 % in 1994 from 1993 and mentioned that this trend continued during 1995 (CPT/Inf(96)29, para 1.4). In its answer to the 2004 CPT report, where the CPT raised concerns about an increase in the number of prisoners, the Austrian government stated that it was continuing its efforts to reduce prison overcrowding. On the one hand, new space for inmates was created, and on the other hand, alternatives to imprisonment explored (CPT/Inf(2005)14, para 69). No statement of the Austrian government can be found concerning the CPT's remark in its report on the 2014 visit where it had stated that operating above the official capacity had led to cramped conditions in certain parts of the establishments visited (CPT/Inf(2015)34, para 55).

## 4.2 Staff Shortage—Regime Activities

### 4.2.1 CPT

Another recurring topic is a lack of access to activities and an underuse of facilities due to staff shortage. The CPT mentioned this problem already in its first report to the Austrian government (CPT/Inf(91)10: 11). The situation worsened from 2004 onwards. In 2004, the CPT even made an immediate observation on the low numbers of staff at the *Wien-Josefstadt* prison that had led to a drastic reduction of the activities offered to juvenile prisoners (CPT/Inf(2005)13, para 10). In 2009 the CPT raised concerns that the activities for prisoners in *Innsbruck* were heavily circumscribed by staff shortages (CPT/Inf(2010)5, para 76). In 2014 the CPT included this problem in the executive summary of its report and stated:

> …it is a matter of serious concern that, despite a specific recommendation made after the 2009 visit, major staff shortages were once again observed in the prisons visited, which inevitably had a negative impact on prisoners' access to out-of-cell activities. It also remained the case that the "night shift" of prison officers started at around 3 p.m. (and even at noon on Fridays and weekends), with the result that most prisoners remained locked up in their cells until the following morning. Whilst acknowledging the efforts being made by the Austrian authorities to recruit additional staff, the CPT calls upon the authorities to carry out a complete overhaul of the staffing situation in Austrian prisons. (CPT/Inf(2015)34: 7, see also paras 59, 68)

With regard to the regime of juveniles in *Wien-Josefstadt*, the CPT noted in its report on the 2014 visit that significant improvements had been made compared to the situation in 2009. The detention conditions of juveniles had improved significantly (less overcrowding, housing programmes, better activities, plans for separate detention facilities) (CPT/Inf(2015)34: 7).

### 4.2.2 Reply

In 2004 the Austrian government indicated that work is obligatory for sentenced prisoners. With regard to prisoners on remand, it indicated that it was very difficult to provide them with appropriate work because of their unpredictable release. The authorities indicated that they intended to provide for more activities for prisoners by changing working hours of prison staff and by transferring staff from the administration to the work with prisoners (CPT/Inf(2005)14, para 70). The recommendation to make 'strenuous' efforts to improve activities to prisoners at *Linz* was answered by a description of the existing system (CPT/Inf(2005)14, para 83). With regard to the situation of juveniles in *Wien-Josefstadt*, the government indicated that the range of activities has been increased and the number of inmates has considerably decreased since the CPT's visit (CPT/Inf(2005)14, para 92).

By letter of 28 January 2015, the Austrian authorities informed the CPT that an additional 100 prison staff positions and 55 civilian staff positions had been allocated to the prison administration, which would be filled in the following one and a half years. The CPT considered this to be a step in the right direction. However, it recommended rigorous measures in order to render the situation satisfactory (CPT/Inf(2015)34, para 59).

In its answer to the report on the 2014 visit, the Austrian authorities gave an overview of the development of staffing levels and indicated that they were committed to meet the requirements of a competent deployment of personnel in the prison service to be able to provide for meaningful activities concerning work as well as leisure (CPT/Inf(2015)35: 15).

## 4.3 Outdoor Activities

With regard to a lack of shelters and benches, the Austrian authorities indicated in a letter to the CPT of 2 August 2004 that instructions had been issued to place seats in the men's exercise yard and that it was intended to partially cover that yard (CPT/Inf(2005)13, para 80).

## 4.4 Medical Personnel and Health-Care Issues

### 4.4.1 CPT

An increase of qualified medical and psychiatric staff has been a recurring recommendation.[4] Further issues mentioned in the recommendations concerned the conduct of medical examinations, medical confidentiality, cage beds and employment of prison doctors by the Ministry of Health instead of the Ministry of Justice.

### 4.4.2 Reply

In its response to the report on the 1994 visit of the CPT, the authorities addressed the recommendations concerning the situation in the prisons *Stein* and *Schwarzau*.

With regard to *Stein*, the report announced that the government intended to employ qualified nurses as soon as staffing schedules and budgets would permit this. With regard to an increase in the number of medical doctors, the government indicated that the Ministry of Justice would try to improve the availability of medical doctors. However, it also indicated that the prison management as well as the medical doctors considered the existing coverage by medical doctors as sufficient. Concerning the psychiatric service, the government indicated that it had been able to improve the psychiatric services considerably. The dentist's attendance had been increased (CPT/Inf(96)29: 38).

Concerning *Schwarzau* the government indicated that the Ministry of Justice would review the medical service. With regard to an increase in nursing staff and an emergency service at night and weekends, it considered the recommendation not to be feasible because of a lack of resources and not absolutely necessary (CPT/Inf(96)29: 38).

The CPT's recommendation in 1999 to stop the use of 'cage beds' (metal bars) in *Wien-Josefstadt* led to an immediate response of the Ministry of Justice. It prohibited by phone the use of these beds in the prison. One month later, the use of 'cage beds' was prohibited everywhere in Austria. The use of 'net beds'[5] was regarded as permissible. No 'cage beds' have been used thereafter in Austrian prisons (CPT/Inf(2001)9: 45, para 105).

Other than that, the CPT recommended an increase in the dental and psychiatric care at *Wien-Josefstadt* prison (CPT/Inf(2001)8, para 93). The government in its answer to the CPT report considered both as sufficient and did not intend to increase them (CPT/Inf(2001)9: 43).

With regard to *Schwarzau*, the CPT found that its 1994 recommendations to increase the presence of a general practitioner had not been implemented (CPT/Inf(2001)8, para 97). In reaction to the reiteration of the 1994 recommendation by the CPT, the authorities reported the status quo. The former prison doctor had cancelled his contract, and negotiations for filling the vacancy were ongoing. In the meantime an agreement with the hospital Neunkirchen would provide for medical care (CPT/Inf(2001)9: 43). The government considered the situation as being 'repaired' (CPT/Inf(2001)9: 43, 45–46. The nursing care situation was considered as not appropriate by the authorities themselves (CPT/Inf(2001)9: 44). The authorities described any increase of ergo therapeutic care as impossible due to a lack of ergo therapists on the labour market (CPT/Inf(2001)9: 44).

With regard to the CPT's recommendation to give every new detainee a full preliminary medical examination, the authorities responded that this is not provided for by the Austrian prison system and also not a requirement met by doctors outside the prison system (CPT/Inf(2001)9: 45).

The Austrian government answered the recommendations to the 2004 visit by stating the status quo and by indicating that the situation in *Linz* was satisfactory. Nevertheless, it planned to contract more nursing staff (CPT/Inf(2005)14: 34). With regard to the employment of a specialist in child/adolescent psychiatry, the authorities implemented the CPT's recommendation (CPT/Inf(2005)14: 34). Concerning the recommendation to conduct medical examinations out of hearing and sight of non-medical staff, the authorities replied that this is done unless special security reasons would require the presence of non-medical staff (CPT/Inf(2005)14: 35). The recommendation to employ prison doctors by the Ministry of Health and not the Ministry of Justice was largely implemented. According to the reply, only three doctors throughout Austria were still employed by the Ministry of Justice (CPT/Inf(2005)14: 35).

With regard to the situation of a specialist in child/adolescent psychiatry in *Wien-Josefstadt*, the CPT recommended in its report on the 2009 visit to maintain his presence since it was unclear whether the contract would be prolonged. The government did not specify whether the contract was prolonged but only indicated that it was aware of the importance of proper care in this field (CPT/Inf(2010)6: 26).

Concerning the CPT's recommendation to review health-care staffing levels in *Gerasdorf* and *Innsbruck*, the government indicated that they were evaluated at the time of the drafting of the answer. With regard to psychiatric care in *Gerasdorf* and *Innsbruck*, the authorities stated that psychiatric care was ensured (CPT/Inf(2010)6: 26–27). They also indicated that it was not possible to abolish the practice of involving prison officers in the performance of health-care duties as recommended by the CPT. This was due to occupancy levels and staff shortage (CPT/Inf(2010)6: 27). The poor level of hygiene in *Wien-Josefstadt* had been remedied (CPT/Inf(2010)6: 27).

With regard to medical examinations after admission, the answer is not clear concerning *Innsbruck* where it only states that a new physician who was also in charge of the examinations had been employed (CPT/Inf(2010)6: 27). With regard to *Gerasdorf*, the authorities indicated that inmates are always transferred from other institutions to *Gerasdorf* and that therefore they already have undergone such an examination at the previous institution (CPT/Inf(2010)6: 27). The implementation of the recommendation on pharmacotherapy at *Innsbruck* cannot be assessed since the Ministry of Justice apparently directly answered the CPT's recommendation, and the outcome is not reported in the public answer of the government (CPT/Inf(2010)6: 28). The psychological service at *Innsbruck* was increased as recommended by the CPT (CPT/Inf(2010)6: 28).

In relation to the recommendations of the 2014 visit, the authorities indicated that an increase of general practitioners and psychiatrists was not possible due to the tight budgetary and personnel situation in these fields (CPT/Inf(2015)35: 16). Concerning the issue of confidentiality, the government mentioned that a decree covering the presence of prison officers in hospital wards had been issued. The content was not mentioned in the answer of the government (CPT/Inf(2015)35: 16). Prison officers would not have to perform health-related activities. Concerning the dispensing of medication, a system of blister packaging of medication had been introduced, so that prison officers without medical training could perform this task (CPT/Inf(2015)35: 16). The government also indicated that the system of electronic medical files had been developed according to the CPT's recommendations (CPT/Inf(2015)35: 17). The CPT's recommendation on the administration of pharmacological treatment at *Feldkirch* gave rise to a discussion with the officer involved and resulted in a change of the situation (CPT/Inf(2015)35: 17). Concerning the medical admission screening the government indicated that it had been expanded (CPT/Inf(2015)35: 17). A needle exchange programme was not allowed in Austrian prisons but was planned for the future (CPT/Inf(2015)35: 17).

## 4.5 Access to Showers

### 4.5.1 CPT

A further recurring topic in CPT reports is lack of access to shower facilities in some of the prisons. This matter already came up in 1990 concerning *Wien-Josefstadt* (CPT/Inf(91)10, para 37). The CPT raised it again with regard to juvenile (especially female) prisoners in 2009 (CPT/Inf(2010)5, para 82) as well as concerning the prison in *Feldkirch* in 2014 (CPT/Inf(2015)34, para 66). The criticism of 1990 with regard to the situation in *Wien-Josefstadt* was still valid in 1999. Although two showers per week had been authorised, they could not be guaranteed in practice for organisation reasons (CPT/Inf(2001)8, para 84).

### 4.5.2 Reply

Whether the criticism concerning the lack of access to showers of 1990 that had been repeated in 1999 has been taken up is unclear since the government's answer is silent on this point (CPT/Inf(2001)9: 41, where the rest of the recommendation is addressed). In its answer to the 2009 visit, the authorities pointed out that in *Innsbruck, Gerasdorf, Klagenfurt* and *Linz*, female prisoners could take as many showers as they wanted. With regard to *Wien-Josefstadt*, they indicated that juveniles were given more possibilities to shower than provided for by the law (CPT/Inf(2010)6: 25). Concerning the situation in *Feldkirch* in 2014, the answer stated that upon individual request, it was possible to take more frequent showers if this was possible from an organisational viewpoint. A general increase of showering possibilities would not be possible because of lack of facilities and personnel (CPT/Inf(2015)35: 15).

## 4.6 Communication with Foreign Prisoners

### 4.6.1 CPT

The CPT mentioned significant difficulties of communication between foreign prisoners and staff in all of its reports although it also noted that efforts had been made to overcome these problems.[6] In 2014 the CPT wanted to receive information about a video interpretation service for health-care purposes that had been introduced in *Wien-Josefstadt* (CPT/Inf(2015)34, para 91). The CPT also raised concerns about a lack of educational classes including German language classes for foreign prisoners (CPT/Inf(96)28, paras 138–140; CPT/Inf(2005)13, para 81) and language training for staff working with foreigners.[7] In its report of 2010, it mentions that the authorities made efforts to address the situation by offering German courses (CPT/Inf(2010)5, para 110).

### 4.6.2 Reply

While the reply in 1991 did not focus on this issue, the authorities gave an account of the status quo in their reply on the 1994 visit. There, they indicated that soon after 1989 the foreign prison population in Austria's prisons changed 'dramatically' and listed a number of measures that had been taken to cope with the phenomenon. They did not specifically address the recommendations (CPT/Inf(96)29: 43). In the answer to the 2004 visit, the authorities indicated that the prison regulations were available in 13 languages and handed out to prisoners on admission. Furthermore, they indicated that language courses were available in many of the penal institutions. Following a CPT recommendation, they were promoting these programmes in all of the institutions (CPT/Inf(2005)14: 38). In their reply to the 2009 visit, the authorities indicated that they followed the CPT's recommendation and offered more foreign language training. With regard to the phenomenon of using fellow prisoners as interpreters, they indicated that for 'economic and factual reasons' it would be impossible to get along without them (CPT/Inf(2010)6: 30). In their answer to the 2014 visit, the authorities indicated that they have introduced medical history questionnaires in 48 languages and were employing external interpreters and that communication in *Wien-Josefstadt* has been possible in 24 languages. Furthermore, they reported that the video-interpreting project for medical purposes in *Wien-Josefstadt* was very successful and has been prolonged (CPT/Inf(2015)34: 18–19).

## 4.7 Firearms

### 4.7.1 CPT

From 1999 onwards the CPT raised concerns over the fact that the security personnel in prisons wore firearms during the night shift (CPT/Inf(2005)13, para 109). Whenever it became necessary to open a cell, the officer who directly opened the cell door was unarmed, but there was always an armed security officer standing some distance away. The CPT considered this a dangerous and undesirable practice, which could lead to high-risk situations for both prisoners and prison officers. The CPT invited the Austrian authorities to reconsider the policy on the carrying of firearms by staff working within prison premises in 1999, 2004, 2009 as well as in 2014.[8]

### 4.7.2 Reply

This is the only recommendation where the Austrian government and the CPT disagreed from early on. In its reply to the 2004 visit, the government indicated that:

> Pistols are only used as a preventive measure in case of emergency and only by specially trained staff, who are responsible for the security. Custodial staff is never wearing a pistol, when working with inmates. In general the weapons are kept in a special office and must not be worn by the staff during day. They are only worn during night shift by specially trained security staff and only in particular areas of the prison (never in direct contact with inmates in the cell). (CPT/Inf(2005)4: 38)

In its response to the visit of 2009, the government reiterated its previous response and pointed out that Austria would observe its obligation under the European Convention on Human Rights to always use the most moderate weapon that achieves its objective. They noted that there had not been any complaints about any assaults on the part of prison officers and that the proportionate use of weapons had a preventive effect (CPT/Inf(2010)6: 30). The authorities saw no reason to change the practice (CPT/Inf(2010)6: 31). They repeated that without weapons there would be security risks and an emergency due to the low levels of staffing during the night. The officer carrying the firearm would never be in direct contact with inmates but would be covering the escape route (CPT/Inf(2010)6: 31). Also in the response to the visit in 2014, the Austrian authorities saw no reason to change this legislation (CPT/Inf(2015)35: 19).

## 4.8 Segregation

With regard to the segregation units in *Wien-Josefstadt*, the CPT's delegation in 2004 noted that the CPT's recommendation of 2001 to equip them with beds had been implemented (CPT/Inf(2005)13, para 104). As to the issue of segregation of juveniles and adults, the Austrian authorities indicated in a letter of 2 August 2004 to the CPT that the situation had been created by overcrowding and the lack of a separate juvenile unit. They expected to remedy the situation by an expansion of the open section in *Asten* (CPT/Inf(2005)13, para 76).

## 4.9 Discipline

With regard to confinement to an isolation cell for 14 days as disciplinary measures, the CPT underlined the need to be mindful of the principle of proportionality (CPT/Inf(91)10, para 95). In 2014 the CPT raised concerns with regard to recommendations on solitary confinement as a punishment in 2009 (CPT/Inf(2010)5, paras 102–103) that had not been implemented. The recommendations concerned the maximum periods of solitary confinement as well as the possibility of contacts with the outside world during this period and the disciplinary procedures (CPT/Inf(2015)34, paras 92–95). The government stated in its answer to the 2014 report that the implementation of the recommendation was assessed at the time of the answer. With regard to juveniles, the answer states that the provision concerning the maximum period of detention in house arrest as disciplinary sanction for juveniles would be limited to one week. This change had been made in December 2015.[9]

With regard to the recommendation in the report on the 2004 visit to review the relevant provision on self-harm and suicide attempts, the government recapitulated the legal situation and stated that the wording of section 107 para 1 no. 3 of the Law on the Execution of Sentences (StVG) would be re-examined. Apparently the wording has not been changed since.[10]

## 5 National Supervisory Institutions

Since its visit in 1994, the CPT has always inquired about a system of regular inspections of prison establishments by an independent body. In 1994 it stressed the importance of prison monitoring Commissions (*Vollzugskommissionen*) and suggested that they use their possibilities of visits and that they should publish an annual report of their activities (CPT/Inf(96)28, paras 149–151). With regard to its visit in 1999, the CPT stressed again the important function of the prison monitoring Commissions, raised concerns as to their practical impact and asked to sensitise them concerning their important task (CPT/Inf(2001)8, para 124). In 2004 the CPT considered that the fact that only one visit a year was undertaken by the prison monitoring Commissions (*Vollzugskommissionen*), significantly limited the effectiveness of this instrument. The CPT stressed that effective inspection procedures constitute a fundamental safeguard against ill-treatment in prisons. It recommended that the Austrian authorities develop a system of regular inspections of prison establishments by an independent body (CPT/Inf(2005)13, para 107).

In parallel, the CPT recommended already in 1990 with regard to the institution under the authority of the Ministry of the Interior 'the Austrian authorities to explore the possibility of empowering an independent body to inspect on a regular basis the conditions of detention in police jails' (CPT/Inf(91), para 87). In its report transmitted to the Austrian authorities after its second periodic visit in 1994, it recommended establishing without delay a body composed of independent persons to investigate thoroughly the interrogation methods used at the Vienna Security Bureau (CPT/Inf(96)28: para 19). It reiterated its former recommendation to create an independent inspection organ for police jails (CPT/Inf(96)28: para 94).

Only in 1999, the Austrian authorities set up the Human Rights Advisory Board (*Menschenrechtsbeirat*) (Kriebaum 2004; see also Holzinger 1999: 17, 2000: 16, 2003: 256; Pöschl 2001; Szymanski 2001: 76; Funk 2001: 570; Mahler 2002: 28; Nowak 2002), with a view to introducing a mechanism for inspecting conditions of detention in police establishments and monitoring the observance of human rights by law enforcement agencies (Sections 15a, 15b and 15c of the Security Police Act (*Sicherheitspolizeigesetz*, SPG) and Ordinance of the Federal Minister of the Interior No. 395/1999 (as amended by Ordinance No.260/2004)). The Council was composed of 11 members and 11 substitute members.[11]

To ensure an area-wide control of places of detention of the security authorities and of places where the security forces use coercive measures in the exercise of authority, six Commissions had been established. For each Higher Regional Court (Graz, Innsbruck, Salzburg and Vienna), one Commission had been set up on 29 June 2000 with the exception of Vienna, where three Commissions had been installed. The Commissions consisted of five to eight members and had each a secretariat at their disposal (in Vienna two of the Commissions shared one secretariat) (§15 (2) *Geschäftsordnung des Menschenrechtsbeirates*). The CPT served as a role model for the Commissions (Kriebaum 2004: 91).

Establishments administered by the Ministry of Justice were not covered by the mandate of the Austrian Human Rights Advisory Council. In 2004 the CPT invited the Austrian authorities to review the status of the Human Rights Advisory Council in various regards but also with a view to enlarge it to institutions administered by the Ministry of Justice (CPT/Inf(2005)13, paras 20, 107). It recommended developing a system of regular inspections of prison establishments by an independent body (CPT/Inf(2005)13, para 107).

It was only in view of the accession to the Optional Protocol to the Convention against Torture (OPCAT) that the Austrian parliament had decided to set up a monitoring body with a comprehensive mandate also including prisons. This was done by designating the Ombudsman Board as the National Preventive Mechanism (NPM) under the OPCAT (Kucsko-Stadlmayer 2013: 913; Ritter 2015). In this new role, it took over the functions of the former Human Rights Advisory Board and its six Commissions.

Based on an amendment of the Austrian Federal Constitution (*Bundes-Verfassunggesetz* (B-VG)) and the Ombudsman Board Act 1982 (*Volksanwaltschaftsgesetz* 1982), the Austrian Ombudsman Board and its Commissions assumed their new functions on 1 July 2012.[12]

The Austrian Ombudsman Board has a mandate that includes the monitoring of all the facilities where persons are deprived of their liberty, including prisons. To fulfil its task, the NPM maintained the six multi-disciplinary Commissions established by the Human Rights Advisory Board though with a slightly different composition. This was necessary to cope with its larger mandate. It includes not only traditional detention institutions like prisons or police detention units but also, for example, psychiatric facilities, homes for the elderly, long-term care facilities and facilities for persons with disabilities. Each of the Commissions consists of seven members and one head of Commission.[13]

In addition the Ombudsman Board as NPM has a Human Rights Advisory Council as an advisory body that is different from the former Human Rights Advisory Council. It is constituted of representatives of non-governmental organisations and federal ministries and supports the NPM.[14] In 2014 at the occasion of the sixth visit of the CPT to Austria, it met with the NPM and two heads of Commissions to share information. With regard to visits to prison institutions, the NPM made visits to 17 correctional institutions in 2012 (Volksanwaltschaft 2012: 21), 52 to correctional institutions in 2013 (Volksanwaltschaft 2013: 23) and 35 to correctional institutions in 2014 (Volksanwaltschaft 2014: 9). The annual reports do not indicate how often the individual institutions have been visited during one year. It is therefore not possible to assess the control density concerning individual prisons.

## 6 Concluding Remarks

Several types of reactions by Austria to the CPT and its recommendations can be identified over the years. The first type concerns specific recommendations with no immediate financial consequences. A number of those have been implemented on short notice, like the abolition of 'cage beds' or the equipment of segregation units with beds.

A second type concerns recommendations that the Austrian authorities rejected. An example for this approach is the reaction to the recommendation to reconsider the policy to carry firearms by staff working within prison premises.

A third type of reaction relates to recommendations concerning the increase of staffing levels for medical or other staff. Here, a readiness in principle to implement the recommendations meets with resistance to factually implement the recommendations. The non-implementation is often explained by budgetary constraints, or the recommendations are not really answered but only the status quo is described in the answer of the government. This is also the case with regard to recommendations concerning food. In financial neutral areas, recommendations concerning staff have been implemented such as the recommendation to employ prison doctors by the Ministry of Health and not the Ministry of Justice.

A fourth type of reaction relates to recommendations concerning disciplinary measures and the procedure concerning their promulgation. Here some movement can be discerned although the process is rather slow.

The last type of reaction concerns national supervisory institutions. Here a strong indirect influence of the CPT on the situation in Austria can be noticed. The CPT's recommendations on their own did not bring about the creation of the NPM with its Commission. But the CPT has heavily influenced the format of the Human Rights Advisory Council and its Commissions. The Commissions were replicas of the CPT both in their composition and their working methods. These Commissions have been 'transferred' to the NPM and still resemble the CPT in both their composition and their working methods. Since the annual reports of the NPM do not indicate the institutions visited, it is difficult to ascertain how many institutions are visited and how many of the visits are follow-up visits.

The reactions to the recommendations of the CPT show the mixed results of the CPT's work in Austria. On the one hand, it achieved important changes, some within a short time and mainly in areas without major financial implications. On the other hand, it was not always effective in bringing about reforms. This is shown by the repeated complaints of the CPT that recommendations already made on the occasion of one or sometimes even several earlier visits had not been implemented.

The mere fact that the mechanism exists and produces publicly available reports should not be underestimated. In this way the CPT creates transparency and a public record. This is itself of vital value.

Since the mechanism is based on cooperation rather than on findings of violations leading to State responsibility, it is for the national authorities and institutions to translate the CPT's findings into practice. Here, the NPM created in 2012 can play an important role in monitoring and ensuring the implementation of CPT recommendations in Austria and on the other hand in reporting back to the CPT what the obstacles for implementing some of its recommendations are.

## Notes

1. European Committee for the Prevention of Torture and Inhuman or Degrading Treatment or Punishment, ETS No. 126. Text amended according to the provisions of Protocols No. 1 (ETS No. 151) and No. 2 (ETS No. 152) which entered into force on 1 March 2002; for publications on the Convention, see, for example, Murdoch (2006), Morgan and Evans (2002), Kriebaum (2000, 2002), Evans and Morgan (1992, 1997, 1998), Evans (2002), Harris (2002), Association for the Prevention of Torture, Council of Europe and Geneva Police Service (1999), Kicker (2008), Council of Europe (2010), Myjer (2010). The Committee is also referred to as the Council of Europe anti-torture Committee.

2. The CPT decided the programme for the first round of periodic missions by lot to underline its impartiality (see 1st General Report CPT/Inf(91)3, paras. 19 and 52; Cassese (1994: 117)).
3. The chapter follows the distinction of the CPT in institutions administered by the Ministry of Justice and institutions administered by the Ministry of Interior. Only prisons administered by the Ministry of Justice are taken into consideration.
4. CPT/Inf (96)10, paras 117-119; CPT/Inf (2001)8, paras. 95, 97, 101; CPT/Inf (2005) 13, paras. 93, 95; CPT/Inf (2010) 5, paras. 92, 94; CPT/Inf (2015) 34, para. 79.
5. A net bed is similar to a cage bed, but instead of metal bars around the side and top of the bed, a net bed has netting, similar to the material used for fishing nets or rope.
6. CPT/Inf (91) 10, para 38; CPT/Inf (96) 10, para 138; CPT/Inf (2005) 13, para 108; CPT/Inf (2010) 5, paras 110, 111; CPT/Inf (2015) 34, para 90.
7. CPT/Inf (2005) 13, para 108; CPT/Inf (2010) 5, para 110; CPT/Inf (2010) 5, para 110.
8. CPT/Inf (2001) 8, paras 122, 123; CPT/Inf (2005) 13, paras 109, 142; CPT/Inf (2010) 5, para 114; CPT/Inf (2015) 34, p. 8, see also para 97.
9. §58 Jugendgerichtsgesetz (Juvenile Court Law) (9) Federal Law Gazette 599/1988 as amended by Federal Law Gazette I No. 154/2015.
10. Federal Law Gazette No. 144/1969 as amended by Federal Law Gazette I No. 26/2016: §107 (1).
11. §15a(2) SPG. The Federal Minister of the Interior appointed all the members and substitute members of the Council. Three of the members and their substitutes were selected directly by the Minister of the Interior. Five NGOs which may nominate members were selected by the Minister of the Interior as well. The rest of the members and their substitutes were nominated by ministries which are closely related with the subject under consideration. The members were appointed for a period of three years and acted on a voluntary basis. (§15b(1) SPG).
12. Art. 148a B-VG (2). The ombudsman board is ex officio entitled to investigate its suspicion of maladministration by the Federation including its activity as a holder of private rights, mainly of violations of human rights it assumes.

    (3) For the protection and the advancement of human rights, it is incumbent on the Ombudsman Board and the Commissions appointed

by it (Art. 148 h para 3) in the area of the administration of the Federation including its activity as holder of private rights
    1. to visit and inspect the location of deprivation of liberty,
    2. to watch and check in advisory manner the conduct of the organs authorised to exert direct administrative power and compulsions as well as
    3. to check respectively visit certain institutions and programmes for handicapped persons.
13. §12(1) *Volksanwaltschaftsgesetz* determines that there have to be six Commissions and together they have to consist of at least 42 members (BGBl. Nr. 433/1982 idF BGBl I Nr. 1/2012).
14. On the new Human Rights Advisory Council, see Vogl (2013).

## Literature

Association for the Prevention of Torture in Co-operation with the Council of Europe and the Geneva Police Service. 1999. *A Visit by the CPT – What's It All About? 15 Questions and Answers for the Police*. Geneva: Council of Europe.

Cassese, A. 1994. The European Committee for the Prevention of Torture and Inhuman and Degrading Treatment or Punishment Comes of Age. In *Towards More Effective Supervision by International Organizations. Essays in Honour of Henry G. Schermers*, ed. N. Blokker and S. Muller, vol. I, 115–126. Dordrecht: Martinus Nijhoff Publishers.

Council of Europe. 2010. *New Partnerships for Torture Prevention in Europe. Proceedings of the Conference. Strasbourg, 6 November 2009*. Strasbourg: Council of Europe.

Evans, M. 2002. Getting to Grips with Torture. *International and Comparative Law Quarterly* 51 (2): 365–383.

Evans, M., and R. Morgan. 1992. The European Convention for the Prevention of Torture: Operational Practice. *International and Comparative Law Quarterly*. 41 (3): 590–614.

———. 1997. The European Convention for the Prevention of Torture: 1992–1997. *International and Comparative Law Quarterly*. 46 (3): 663–675.

———. 1998. *Preventing Torture. A Study of the European Convention for the Prevention of Torture and Inhuman or Degrading Treatment or Punishment*. Oxford: Oxford University Press.

Funk, B.-C. 2001. Der Menschenrechtsbeirat, Präsentation und erste Ergebnisse. *Zeitschrift für Verwaltung* 26: 570–574.

Harris, D., ed. 2002. *Yearbook of the European Convention for the Prevention of Torture*. Nottingham: University of Nottingham, Human Rights Law Centre.

Holzinger, G. 1999. Der Menschenrechtsbeirat – Organisation, Aufgaben, Möglichkeiten. *Die Bundespolizei* 6: 17.

———. 2000. Der Menschenrechtsbeirat beim Bundesministerium für Inneres. *Juridikum* 16–18.

———. 2003. Der Menschenrechtsbeirat als Instrument des präventiven Menschenrechtsschutzes. In *Norm und Normvorstellung. Festschrift für Bernd-Christian Funk zum 60. Geburtstag*, ed. I. Eisenberger, I. Golden, K. Lachmayer, G. Marx, and D. Tomasovsky, 255–264. Vienna: Springer Verlag.

Kicker, R. 2008. Das Europäische Komitee zur Verhütung von Folter (CPT): Rückblick und Ausblick. In *Rechtsschutz gestern – heute – morgen. Festgabe zum 80. Geburtstag von Rudolf Machacek und Franz Matscher*, ed. A. Bammer, G. Holzinger, M. Vogl, and G. Wenda, 589–600. Vienna: NWV Verlag.

Kriebaum, U. 2000. *Folterprävention in Europa. Die Europäische Konvention zur Verhütung von Folter und unmenschlicher oder erniedrigender Behandlung oder Bestrafung*. Vienna: Verlag Österreich.

———. 2002. *Prevention of Torture in Europe. CPT Modus Operandi*. Geneva: APT.

———. 2004. The Austrian Human Rights Advisory Council. In *Univerzita Karlova V Praze, Evropské Informační, International Conference on the Implementation of the Optional Protocol to the UN Anti Torture Convention Under the Auspice of the Czech Minister of Foreign Affairs*, ed. H.C. Scheu and S. Hýbnerová, 88–106. Prague: Facultas Juridica Universitatis Carolinae Pragensis.

Kucsko-Stadlmayer, G. 2013. Die Volksanwaltschaft als 'Nationaler Präventionsmechanismus'. *Österreichische Juristenzeitung* 20: 913–925.

Mahler, C. 2002. Die Kommissionen des Menschenrechtsbeirates. *MRM – MenschenRechtsMagazin* 3: 132–135.

Morgan, R., and M. Evans. 2002. *Combating Torture in Europe – The Work and Standards of the European Committee for the Prevention of Torture*. Strasbourg: Council of Europe.

Murdoch, J. 2006. *The Treatment of Prisoners. European Standards*. Strasbourg: Council of Europe.

Myjer, E. 2010. About the Human Rights Success Stories of the Council of Europe: Some Reflections on the Impacts of the CPT Upon the Case-Law of the European Court of Human Rights. In *Fervet Opus. Liber Amicorum Anton*

*van Kalmthout*, ed. M. Groenhuysen, T. Kooijmans, and T. de Roos, 161–174. Antwerpen/Apeldoorn: Maklu.
Nowak, M. 2002. Verhütung von Menschenrechtsverletzungen durch präventives Besuchssystem: Controlling der Sicherheitsexekutive durch Menschenrechtsbeirat in Österreich. In *Strafrecht, Strafprozeßrecht und Menschenrechte – Festschrift für Stefan Trechsel zum 65. Geburtstag*, ed. A. Donatsch, M. Forster, and C. Schwarzenegger, 55–78. Zürich: Schulthess Verlag.
Pöschl, M. 2001. Der Menschenrechtsbeirat. *Journal für Rechtspolitik* 47–63.
Ritter, M. 2015. Präventiver Menschenrechtsschutz. Menschenrechtsmonitoring der Sicherheitsbehörden in Österreich – Veränderungen durch die Umsetzung von OPCAT. *SIAK-Journal – Zeitschrift für Polizeiwissenschaft und polizeiliche Praxis* 1: 12–27.
Szymanski, W. 2001. Der Menschenrechtsbeirat – Berater des Bundesministers für Inneres in Menschenrechtsfragen. In *Neue Wege des Grundrechtsschutzes. Band 16*, ed. Österreichische Juristenkommission, 75–80. Vienna: Verlag Österreich.
Vogl, M. 2013. Der neue Menschenrechtsbeirat bei der Volksanwaltschaft. In *Verwaltung im demokratischen Rechtsstaat. Festschrift für Harald Stolzlechner zum 65. Geburtstag*, ed. K. Giese, G. Holzinger, and C. Jabloner, 679–704. Vienna: Verlag Österreich.
Volksanwaltschaft. 2012. *Report of the Austrian Ombudsman Board on the Activities of the National Preventive Mechanism 2012.* Vienna: Volksanwaltschaft. http://volksanwaltschaft.gv.at/en/reports#anchor-index-2950
———. 2013. *Report of the Austrian Ombudsman Board on the Activities of the National Preventive Mechanism 2013.* Vienna: Volksanwaltschaft. http://volksanwaltschaft.gv.at/downloads/48h64/Austria_Report%20on%20Activities%20of%20NPM_2013.pdf
———. 2014. *Report of the Austrian Ombudsman Board on the Activities of the National Preventive Mechanism 2014.* Vienna: Volksanwaltschaft. http://volksanwaltschaft.gv.at/downloads/66ouj/Report%20on%20the%20activities%20of%20the%20NPM%20-%202014.pdf

**Ursula Kriebaum** is Professor of Public International Law at the University of Vienna, Austria.

# Europe in Belgian Prisons: Assessing the Impact of the Council of Europe Anti-Torture Committee and the European Court of Human Rights

Tom Daems and Luc Robert

## 1 Introduction

Belgium is a small country that neighbours France, Germany, the Netherlands, its small cousin the Grand Duchy of Luxembourg and, across the North Sea Channel, the United Kingdom. This geographical position made it one of the fighting grounds during both World Wars. The inter- and supranational levels have been important ever since, and its strong presence on the international political scene needs to be understood against this historical background of promoting peace and diplomacy. Belgium is one of the founding fathers of the Council of Europe

T. Daems (✉)
Leuven Institute of Criminology (LINC), KU Leuven, Leuven, Belgium

L. Robert
National Institute of Forensic Sciences and Criminology (NICC), Brussels, Belgium



T. Daems, L. Robert (eds.), *Europe in Prisons*, Palgrave Studies in Prisons and Penology, DOI 10.1007/978-3-319-62250-7_7

and the European Union. Many politicians with a major role in domestic politics have also been important on the European level, elaborating and supporting a European agenda. The country's capital, Brussels, is also referred to as the home of the European Union, or at least as its first place of residency (the second is Strasbourg) and the prime locus of European decision-making. The long-standing and intimate relationship with key European institutions makes Belgium an interesting case to study. Does the proximity of and strong historical adherence to 'Europe' imply that Belgian prisons are strongly affected by European institutions?

The question of the impact of 'Europe' in Belgian prisons is broached by focusing on two major institutions, respectively of a preventive and reactive nature. On the preventive level, we assess the visits of the European Committee for the Prevention of Torture and Inhuman or Degrading Treatment or Punishment (CPT) to Belgian prisons. As for the reactive dimension we present a case study about the European Court of Human Rights (ECtHR) in its dealings with internees incarcerated in Belgian prisons. The impact of the CPT and the ECtHR are assessed separately first. In the conclusion, we offer some further observations and reflections about both institutions and their impact.

## 2 Belgium and the CPT

Belgium was quite late to ratify the European Convention on Torture and Inhuman or Degrading Treatment or Punishment: it signed the Convention already on 26 November 1987 but ratification only took place on 7 June 1991 (Parmentier 1992, 1999). At the time of writing (September 2016) Belgium had been visited nine times by the CPT. Six visits took place as part of the CPT's scheme of periodic visits. The reports of these visits (1993, 1997, 2001, 2005, 2009 and 2013) as well as the replies of the Belgian authorities to these reports have been published. Interestingly, in the early years the Belgian authorities also issued press statements when they granted permission to publish in order to clarify or justify their position immediately upon the report's release. These (often lengthy) press statements offered already first replies before the formal (intermediary) government responses became available and they quickly became object of intense debate in Belgium in those first years (see Geboers et al. 1995; Parmentier 1999). From 23 to 27 April 2012 the CPT conducted its first ad hoc visit to Belgium. This visit focused in particular on two issues which it had already addressed repeatedly in previous periodic visits: living conditions in prisons (in particular, as a result of overcrowding in institutions holding remand prisoners) and the adverse and at times fatal consequences of industrial action by prison officers for prisoners' well-being (CPT/Inf(2012)36). The ad hoc visit took place amidst—and added fuel to—a great deal of public and political debate of the state of Belgium's prison infrastructure and safety regulations. Next to these six periodic visits and the 2012 ad hoc visit we also need to mention the CPT's 2011 periodic visit to the Netherlands. As part of this visit the CPT's delegation paid a visit to the Dutch prison of Tilburg which housed Belgian inmates. Following a 2009 agreement between Belgium and the Netherlands, and in order to curb problems of persistent overcrowding, the Belgian government decided to hire 650 places of detention in Tilburg. Unsurprisingly, this unusual way of solving internal problems of prison capacity by exporting prisoners across Belgian borders had captured the attention of the CPT. A second ad hoc visit was organized from 7 to 9 May 2016 following large-scale industrial actions in Belgian (mostly francophone) prisons; it also led to high-level talks on 21 June 2016 of representatives of the CPT with the Belgian Minister of Justice, aimed at discussing the introduction of a guaranteed minimum service in prisons during strikes and other industrial actions by prison staff.

Throughout this section we will discuss some of the findings and recommendations of the CPT, based on its visits to Belgian prisons. We will focus on three major areas, that is, physical conditions, social conditions and safeguards against ill-treatment. These have been three core areas the CPT focuses upon when it visits places of detention (see, e.g. CPT/Inf(1991)3: para 48). An exhaustive treatment of all observations and recommendations would lead us too far. We will discuss a number of recurrent themes (i.e. prison overcrowding, strikes by prison officers, legal safeguards and independent monitoring) which raise questions about the impact of the CPT. Somewhat reminiscent to what sociologists of law refer to as 'Is law important?' (see, e.g. Griffiths 1979), we will explore the question: 'Is the CPT important for Belgian prison(er)s?'

## 2.1 Physical Conditions: Prison Overcrowding

Topics that can be grouped under the heading of 'physical conditions' have always occupied a large part of the CPT's reports related to Belgium. Prison overcrowding in Belgian institutions has been, from the very beginning, one of the central problems that has attracted the attention of the CPT.[1] In 1993, during its first periodic visit, the CPT visited the prisons of Bruges (St. Andries), Lantin and St. Gilles. All three institutions suffered from overcrowding: Lantin (133 %), male inmates in Bruges (130 %) and St. Gilles (143 %) (CPT/Inf(1994)15: para 81–83). In its report the CPT highlighted that these findings were corroborated by a note of 27 May 1992, where the then Minister of Justice depicted detention conditions as 'medieval' (CPT/Inf(1994)15: para 84). The situation was particularly worrying in the prison of St. Gilles: the 'perverse combination', so the CPT argued, of surpopulation, lack of adequate sanitary facilities, an insufficient offer of activities as well as the dilapidated condition of the building amounted to what the CPT referred to as 'an inhuman and degrading treatment' (CPT/Inf(1994)15: para 85)—and this notwithstanding the efforts of the local prison governors to improve the conditions in the institution which were welcomed by the then President of the CPT Claude Nicolay in an interview in the Belgian press (Meskens 1994).

During its 1997 visit the CPT noted that in three of the four visited institutions more than half of the inmates could not participate in any activity. In terms of prison overcrowding, there was even a further deterioration of the situation in the prison of Lantin (the occupancy rate stood now at 147 %) (CPT/Inf(1998)11: para 96). The situation had slightly improved in St. Gilles. Nonetheless, the hygienic circumstances and shared cells remained substandard. In the prison of Mons the situation was far from optimal: overcrowding, problems with hygiene, old mattresses placed on the prison floor, slopping out, ... Such circumstances were, in the CPT's view, 'inhuman and degrading' (CPT/Inf(1998)11: para 119).

Against this background of persistent problems of overcrowding (see also CPT/Inf(2003)32; CPT/Inf(2006)15; CPT/Inf(2010)24; CPT/Inf(2016)13) it is not surprising that this was one of the main reasons for the CPT's ad hoc visit of April 2012. On the first day of its visit to the prison of Forest there were 706 inmates whereas the capacity was at 405. The CPT discussed briefly a report of November 2011 that it had received from a member of the Supervision Commission of the prison of Forest which painted an 'alarming panorama' of the situation in the prison. Certain wings had an occupancy rate of 235 %. Living conditions were bad and tensions between inmates were rampant (CPT/Inf(2012)36: para 10). The situation would not improve in the months thereafter. The CPT again used strong words to denounce what it had observed in some of the wings in the prison: conditions could be considered 'inhuman or degrading treatment'. It noted that the Belgian authorities did not contest these findings during conversations at the occasion of the visit (CPT/Inf(2012)36: para 19). In its report the CPT drew attention to a 2011 report from the Belgian Court of Audit in order to temper the Belgian authorities' optimism of their capacity to tackle overcrowding by means of measures it had brought to the attention of the CPT since many years. The CPT supported the conclusion of the Court of Audit that a wide-ranging political strategy is missing (CPT/Inf(2012)36: para 74). It also repeated that it remains convinced that building extra prison cells cannot be the only—and for sure not the most adequate—solution.

How have Belgian authorities responded? Interestingly, in a press statement of 14 October 1994—which was released on the day the report of the first visit was made public—Belgian authorities were clearly not amused with the CPT's assessment that the living conditions in St. Gilles were 'inhuman and degrading': such a 'serious appreciation' of the situation was the full responsibility of the CPT (see CPT/Inf(95)6: annexe III). Nonetheless, the authorities stressed that the administration had never been in denial about the poor quality of the prison conditions. Indeed, it would have been difficult to deny this since, as we discussed above, the CPT quoted from a 1992 paper from the Minister himself where living conditions were labelled as 'medieval'. In its official response the government pointed at a long-term plan to modernize existing prisons and build new institutions as well as various other initiatives that would bring down the prison population (such as removing illegal entrants from the prisons, relaxing of early release procedures, individual and collective pardon, etc.) (CPT/Inf(1995)6; CPT/

Inf(1996)7). Subsequent Belgian responses to the CPT's repeated insistence that the problem of overcrowding needed to be tackled urgently had a roughly similar structure: on the one hand, pointing at various initiatives to invest in alternative sanctions (penal mediation, non-execution of short prison sentences, and—later on—the autonomous sanction of the work penalty and electronic monitoring, etc.) and, on the other hand, creating new prison space as well as renovating old institutions. Progress proved to be slow, however. In its 2016 reply to the report for the 2013 periodic visit Belgian authorities again acknowledged that the situation was far from perfect. But, nonetheless, the situation was slowly improving: one year after the CPT's visit, overcrowding had been reduced by 12 % (CPT/Inf(2016)14: 14).

## 2.2 Social Conditions: Industrial Action by Prison Officers

For the social conditions we focus on a theme that has been at the centre of the CPT's dialogue with Belgian authorities since its 2005 visit: strikes by prison officers. In its 2006 report (fourth periodic visit, April 2005) the CPT pointed at the special circumstances of the visit: just before the start of the delegation's visit the prison system had been deeply affected by a long and intense industrial action which had serious consequences for life behind bars in the prison of Andenne. The industrial action in this Walloon prison had lasted nine days and nine nights. The CPT was particularly concerned about the incidents that took place during a previous industrial action (17–22 September 2003): two inmates committed suicide in these circumstances (CPT/Inf(2006)15: para 107). The CPT regretted that these tragic events had not initiated a fundamental debate at the highest level to end such spontaneous strikes which endanger the lives of inmates. Against this background the CPT suggested that implementing a guaranteed minimum service offers the 'only solution' ('la seule solution') to avoid such incidents in the future (CPT/Inf(2006)15: para 117). At the occasion of its 2009 periodic visit the CPT, again, paid a great deal of attention to strikes in the prison system. During its visit to the prison of Lantin it received a copy of the report of the local Supervision Commission with details about a prison strike that had lasted from 29 June until 3 July 2009. This report—which was quoted in extenso by the CPT in its report (CPT/Inf(2010)24: para 83)—paints a grim picture of living conditions during that action. The prison officers had left the prison in the hands of a small number of police officers. In this context one inmate who was detained in a disciplinary cell committed suicide. The report also pays attention to events in the prison of Forest where in September and October 2009 police officers took over control of the prison during a prison officers' strikes. The details were particularly worrisome: violence and degradation towards inmates; threats towards prison governors and non-striking prison officers; and a suicide attempt (CPT/Inf(2010)24: para 84–85). Against this background the CPT repeated its recommendations to introduce without further delay a guaranteed minimum service (CPT/Inf(2010)24: para 87).

The recommendation fell, again, on deaf ears. Indeed, one of the triggers for the ad hoc visit of 23–27 April 2012 were the enduring problems that followed in the wake of prison officers' strikes. This explains why the CPT visited the prison of Andenne, where a strike had taken place the week before the start of its visit (8–16 April 2012). On the basis of the information it received and discussions with prison governors and police forces at the occasion of the visit the CPT came to the conclusion that the protocol of April 2010 is 'far from satisfactory' and that it does not guarantee a 'reasonable functioning' of prison institutions in times of strike (CPT/Inf(2012)36: para 86). It repeated therefore, once more, its recommendation to provide a minimum guaranteed service. After observing, again (in September–October 2013), that no sufficient action had been taken to implement the previous recommendations, the CPT decided at its March 2014 plenary meeting to initiate the procedure stipulated in art. 10, §2 of the Convention. This would make it possible for the CPT to make a public statement if Belgium continued failing to improve the situation in the light of the CPT's recommendations (CPT/Inf(2016)13: para 51). At the time of writing (September 2016) no such public declaration had been made yet but the CPT has, once again, addressed the issue at the occasion of its second ad hoc visit to Belgium (7–9 May 2016) as well as during high-level talks on 21 June 2016 with the Minister of Justice and a member of the Private Office of the Belgian Prime Minister.[2]

How did the Belgian authorities respond to these findings and recommendations? In its reply to the 2005 visit report, the government mentioned that a protocol had been negotiated with the prison officers' unions in order to minimize the impact of the strikes (CPT/Inf(2006)40: 51–52). A guaranteed minimum service was, therefore, not necessary, so it argued. At the occasion of its fifth periodic visit, however, the CPT came to the conclusion that the consultation procedure which was elaborated in the protocol mentioned by the government had failed in a number of cases (CPT/Inf(2010)24: para 82). In its reply Belgium suggested that the problems had been solved in the meantime: a new protocol of 19 April 2010 between the Minister of Justice and the representative trade unions had been agreed upon in order to strengthen the social dialogue and to solve conflicts in the prison system. A guaranteed minimum service was therefore, in its view, again not required (CPT/Inf(2011)7: 27). After the 2012 ad hoc visit, Belgian authorities limited their reply to a mere repetition of what the Agreement of the Federal Government (December 2011) stipulated on this issue (i.e. 'more constraining measures' will be taken when the protocol is evaluated negatively or when the procedure is not being followed during strikes) and mentioned briefly two parliamentary initiatives to introduce a guaranteed service during industrial action (CPT/Inf(2012)37: 17). The government response also disclosed that an evaluation of the protocol had taken place in the meantime but that it was subject to an 'internal analysis'. The objective of the evaluation, so one can read in the Belgian reply, was to guarantee the basic rights of inmates by adapting the protocol and to introduce an instrument to manage strikes (CPT/Inf(2012)37: 17). In the (incomplete) reply to the 2013 periodic visit the Belgian government did not address the issues raised by the CPT concerning the strikes (CPT/Inf(2016)14). These have been taken up, however, in the Agreement of the Federal Government (10 October 2014): here the (new) federal government briefly mentioned the critique of the CPT and announced that a guaranteed service will be introduced during its term of government (2014–2019) (Gouvernement 2014: 122–123).

## 2.3 Basic Safeguards: Prisoners' Rights and Independent Monitoring

Since its first visit to Belgium (in 1993), the CPT has repeatedly highlighted the lack of adequate complaint procedures and independent monitoring mechanisms. In its 1994 report, it insisted that Belgium should introduce a complaint procedure as well as a monitoring mechanism. It also drew attention to the lack of formal rights for inmates in Belgian prisons (CPT/Inf(1994)15: para 245–248). In addition, the CPT pointed at problems with the disciplinary procedure and detention in high security wings (in the prisons of Bruges and Lantin). At the occasion of its second visit, the CPT paid less explicit attention to the problematic legal position of inmates. Nonetheless, it mentioned again problems with the disciplinary process (CPT/Inf(1998)11: para 188–197). In this context the CPT referred to the Commission Dupont (which had been created in order to prepare a draft Prison Law) and hoped that its recommendations would be taken into account (CPT/Inf(1998)11: para 190). After the third visit (in 2001) the CPT again raised a number of issues about the disciplinary procedure: it was exclusively oral and offered no possibility to appeal for the inmates who were subjected to disciplinary sanctions. The CPT observed that the Commission Dupont had finalized its report and that it had addressed the critiques of the CPT. The CPT insisted that the Belgian authorities should study the report swiftly so that the law could be voted and implemented (CPT/Inf(2002)25: para 96). At the occasion of its fourth visit (April 2005) the Prison Law had finally been voted (12 January 2005) but the CPT regretted that the required Royal Decrees had not been adopted yet. It urged the government to take the necessary steps (CPT/Inf(2006)15: para 88). However, also during its next visits the CPT could not observe much progress in this respect. In its 2010 report, the CPT devoted special attention to the topic of maintaining order and the uncertainty that characterized the disciplinary process. It called upon the Belgian authorities to speedily implement Title VII of the Prison Law (which deals with prison discipline) (CPT/Inf(2010)24: para 148). It deplored that one of Belgium's largest prisons (Bruges) did not have a functioning Supervision Commission and asked for action to make it operational. It also insisted to implement the complaint procedure, as stipulated in Title VIII of the Prison Law (CPT/Inf(2010)24: para 158). At the occasion of the 2012 ad hoc visit the CPT again insisted on the further implementation of the Prison Law and expected 'resolute measures' from the government (CPT/Inf(2012)36: para 87). It also highlighted the importance of independent monitoring and deplored the resignation of the Central Supervision Council in March 2012. The CPT suggested to create a 'Committee D' which would be connected to Parliament and no longer depend on the Minister of Justice for logistical support. Belgium should also ratify the Optional Protocol to the UN Convention Against Torture (CPT/Inf(2012)36: para 88). After its 2013 periodic visit, and in view of the lack of sufficient progress, the CPT repeated again that the Belgian authorities should 'without further delay' take all necessary measures in order to assure the full implementation of the Prison Law (CPT/Inf(2016)13: para 57).

How did the Belgian authorities respond? It is interesting to first discuss briefly the immediate response in the press briefing of 14 October 1994: here the government questioned the sense of urgency to rectify the lack of legal guarantees and informed the CPT that it preferred to wait for an additional protocol to the European Convention of Human Rights (see CPT/Inf(95)6: annexe III). In its intermediary reply to the 1993 visit report the government contested the assessment of the CPT on the inadequate legal position: existing instruments (Royal Decree of 1965 and Ministerial Circulars) offered sufficient guarantees, so it argued (CPT/Inf(1995)6: 59–60). In the final reply to the CPT's report the tone changed somewhat: here it announced that an expert had been appointed to prepare a draft prison law on the fundamental principles of deprivation of liberty, including a complaint procedure, the legal position of inmates and early release (CPT/Inf(1996)7: 38). From the second periodic visit onwards the Belgian government continued this line of responding to the CPT's findings and recommendations, that is, by reporting on the progress made towards drafting and implementing the Prison Law (see CPT/Inf(1999)6: 72ff; CPT/Inf(1999)11: 12ff; CPT/Inf(2003)32: 39).

In its response to the fourth periodic visit, the government referred several times to the Prison Law of 12 January 2005 which had been approved by Parliament in the meantime, in particular to address comments on the disciplinary cells in Andenne (i.e. that the norms for such cells were being investigated for a draft Royal Decree of the Prison Law) and to clarify that the solitary cellular regime would be regulated by the Prison Law. More in general, the government informed the CPT that it worked towards a phased implementation of the Prison Law by means of eight working groups (CPT/Inf(2006)40: 45–47). In its reply to the fifth report, Belgian authorities used the political crisis (the federal government had resigned on 22 April 2010, and there was, at the time of the reply, no new government with full executive powers yet) as an excuse for their inaction with respect to the failure to implement Titles VII and VIII of the Prison Law (CPT/Inf(2011)7: 45–46). In addition, Belgian authorities responded that it was not their responsibility that there was no local Supervision Commission at the prison of Bruges: all efforts to find a solution had proven ineffective, so it explained. However, the more general recommendation of the CPT, that is, that all Supervision Commissions should receive sufficient support in order to fulfil their monitoring obligations, received no reply from Belgium (CPT/Inf(2011)7: 46). The CPT's comments after the 2013 periodic visit report received a brief but somewhat more promising response: the Belgian authorities pointed at the Agreement of the federal government (October 2014) which stipulated that the Prison Law would first be amended and, then, implemented in full (CPT/Inf(2016)14: 16).

## 2.4 Is the CPT Important for Belgian Prison(er)s?

Is the CPT important for Belgian prison(er)s? In this section we will explore the question of the CPT's impact which has some affinity with what sociologists of law usually ask about the importance—or the lack thereof—of law (Griffiths 1979). What has the CPT (not) achieved? Did it have any impact and, if so, where, how and under what conditions? It has been argued at several occasions that it is difficult to evaluate or measure the impact of the CPT. Indeed, as Morgan and Evans (2001: 158) pointed out: '… the links between the recommendations of the CPT and final outcomes are generally shrouded in some mystery'.

At times the impact of the CPT seems to be tangible and obvious. This is particularly the case when the CPT called upon the Belgian authorities to remedy a situation within 3 months following 'immediate observations' (in accordance with art. 8, §5 of the Convention). On 15 March 2002, for example, Belgium informed the CPT that the psychiatric annex of the prison of Lantin which was, again (for the third time in a row), heavily criticized at the occasion of the third periodic visit (CPT/Inf(2002)25: para 60), would close its doors the latest on 15 April 2002 (CPT/Inf(2002)25: para 61). But also in other situations it is sometimes possible to identify a direct link between the CPT's findings or recommendations and action by the Belgian authorities. This is most often the case in what one might refer to as 'quick fix/quick win' situations which do not require much effort, for example, when the government responded immediately favourably to the CPT's recommendation to abolish the obligation to work for female inmates in the prison of Bruges (CPT/Inf(1995)6: 48) or when it informed the CPT that a failing heating system in cell no. 6212 in the prison of Jamioulx had been repaired (CPT/Inf(2011)7: 35).

On the other hand, and at the other extreme, it is often also clear when there has been no impact at all. This is particularly the case when the CPT itself reports on a state's failure to implement its recommendations. In its 2010 and 2012 reports, for example, the CPT explicitly referred to the persistent lack of follow-up of recommendations that had been made repeatedly such as its recommendations concerning a guaranteed service during prison strikes or its recommendations related to prison overcrowding (CPT/Inf(2010)24: para 7; CPT/Inf(2012)36: para 7). In such instances the CPT insisted that Belgian authorities should take 'decisive action'. It is interesting to note that in these cases the CPT had threatened to invoke art. 10, §2 of the Convention, that is, to apply the only 'sanction' it has at its disposal, namely to issue a public declaration in case Belgium does not cooperate or fails to improve the situation in view of the CPT's recommendations.

Between both extremes—impact or no impact—there is a large grey zone where the CPT becomes one (key) player amongst many others which try to influence prison policy. Sometimes these other players are also European institutions and forces are joined—such as can be observed from the recent linkages between the CPT and the ECtHR. Notwithstanding the fact that the ECtHR and the CPT are very different institutions which abide to a very different logic—reactive versus preventive (see further)—there have been some interesting interactions in the recent past. Indeed, also in the case of Belgium the ECtHR has been keen to use the CPT as a fact-finding body. The case of *Aerts v. Belgium* (1998, see *infra*) offers an early illustration: here the Court used observations of the CPT about the failure to provide psychiatric treatment in the prison Lantin. More recently, the CPT's reports featured prominently in the case of *Vasilescu v. Belgium*.[3] In such cases, then, there is no direct impact of the CPT but its findings become important factual descriptions of the 'truth' of detention across Europe. Moreover, given the recurrent cycle of its visits it will often be possible to document *histories* of substandard treatment or punishment. In view of its unlimited access to places where persons are deprived of their liberty and its reputation throughout Europe the reports of the CPT have therefore become a rich archive of detention practices in Europe spanning over a quarter of a century.

Linkages are also established with other monitoring bodies. Indeed, the CPT is not the only institution which visits places of detention and which engages in a dialogue with state authorities. In recent times institutions with a similar *modus operandi* have become operational at the global (the Subcommittee for Prevention Torture), national (National Preventive Mechanisms)[4] and regional/local levels. The CPT, then, becomes a knot—an important and experienced knot—in a (global) network of monitoring bodies. At times one can observe a two-way interaction between the CPT and other monitoring mechanisms. For example, the CPT decided to organize an ad hoc visit to Belgian prisons in 2012 because it had received important information—in particular via a report from a member of the Supervision Commission of the prison of Forest (CPT/Inf(2012)37; see *supra*). The vice-president of the Supervision Commission explained later in the media that the Commission had decided—as a measure of last resort—to get in touch with the CPT in order to force a breakthrough to improve the unacceptable living conditions in the prison of Forest (Heyvaert 2012). At the same time the CPT also uses the local expertise of such Supervision Commissions. For example, at the occasion of its 2009 visit it could usefully draw upon a report of the Supervision Commission of the prison of Lantin to document the impact of prison staff industrial action (CPT/Inf(2010)24; see *supra*). In such cases, then, the CPT relates to other (local) monitoring bodies as if *they* were fact-finding instruments.

Linkages are not restricted to monitoring bodies. It is in the interest of the CPT that its findings and recommendations are spread throughout civil society. Indeed, given the fact that the CPT usually visits each member state every 4 to 5 years (and, in addition, that it has to be selective during such periodic visits), the role of *Einzelganger* is not the most attractive option: '…the baton must pass on to others' (Evans and Morgan 2001: 150). This has also happened in the case of Belgium: NGO's such as the Flemish and Francophone Leagues of Human Rights and the Belgian section of the *Observatoire International des Prisons* (OIP) have, for example, at the occasion of the publication of the CPT's report on its fourth periodic visit used that opportunity to bolster their demand for an immediate and full implementation of the Prison Law (X 2006a, b); or when the CPT's report on the visit to the (Dutch) prison of Tilburg was released, to question once more this unusual way of tackling prison overcrowding in Belgian prisons (X 2012). In his 2009 report, the Council of Europe Commissioner for Human Rights endorsed many of the CPT's recommendations related to prison overcrowding, the treatment of internees, the need to implement the Prison Law and to take action to minimize the adverse consequences of prison strikes by providing a guaranteed service (Hammarberg 2009). Even prison governors have at times welcomed the CPT's findings and recommendations, for example at the occasion of the 2012 ad hoc visit—in the hope that an intervention by the CPT would move the government to take action (X 2012).

The linkages between the media and the CPT are more unpredictable. The Belgian press usually gives a more or less fair account of some of the issues that have been raised by the CPT in its reports. However, this has not always been the case. The press coverage on the 2009 periodic visit in the French-language media (Wallonia), for example, was completely different from the press coverage in the Dutch-language media (Flanders) (Daems 2010). In the Flemish media headlines appeared on websites of newspapers with titles such as 'Belgium gets good points from Europe for prison policy' (X 2010). In the French-speaking media, however, the tone and focus was very different: 'Report condemns seriously our prisons' (Gutierrez 2010). Some French-speaking commentators even argued that the CPT should have been harsher for the Belgian authorities (such as the president of the OIP, Delphine Paci, with respect to Belgium's reluctance to implement the Prison Law in full). Indeed, the length of the CPT's reports and the wide range of institutions it usually visits invite journalists to be selective in their coverage. When the report of the third visit was released, a newspaper based in Antwerp highlighted that the governors and officers in the local prison received an 'excellent report' and that the CPT was 'very positive' about them (De Wit 2002)—but, obviously, this was only part of the story.

Joining forces and establishing linkages is undoubtedly important and can, indeed, increase the impact of the CPT's work but this is not necessarily so. In the large grey zone (between immediate impact and no impact) that we discussed above, we can also identify a number of issues which have worried the CPT for many years and which were not satisfactorily addressed by Belgian authorities. Indeed, with the coming of age of the CPT it becomes possible to document and analyse how certain themes have been dealt with over a longer period of time. If, for example, after 10, 15 or 20 years of debate on issues such as complaint procedures for prisoners or tackling prison overcrowding, there is no or insufficient evidence of improvement (see *supra*), does this then imply that the CPT has failed? But also: how do state authorities formulate their replies to recommendations that have been repeatedly made (Daems 2017)? At times it seems obvious that the CPT and the Belgian authorities are not entirely on the same footing. The recent history of prison strikes is quite interesting and revealing in this respect. Belgium is one of the few countries in Europe which does not have a guaranteed service in such circumstances. During strikes a limited number of local police officers usually take over the tasks of the prison officers. Given the CPT's repeated recommendation to provide a guaranteed service in such circumstances (see *supra*), it remains to be seen how the CPT will deal with Belgium's persistent failure to implement this recommendation. Belgian authorities carry a very large responsibility in this case: in 2003 and 2009 inmates have died during industrial actions, so the CPT disclosed in its reports. Moreover, presenting the protocol of 19 April 2010 as a solution to the problem (CPT/Inf(2011)7; see *supra*) was a contentious move of the government as voices outside as well as inside the government had criticized and questioned the protocol's potential to end wild prison strikes. Indeed, one month after the conclusion of the protocol, two major prison trade unions were already on strike. The Minister of Justice was angry and called it a 'political strike'. Towards the end of 2010 police forces criticized the fact that they had to replace striking prison officers, in particular during the festive season. The Minister of Internal Affairs shared their critique and pled openly for such a guaranteed service (Daems 2011a, b).[5] Against this background it seemed inappropriate that the Belgian authorities presented this failing protocol early 2011 as the solution for the serious problems which were repeatedly highlighted by the CPT.

## 3 Interned Offenders in Belgian Prisons: Is the European Court of Human Rights Coming to the Rescue?

In this section we will assess the impact of the ECtHR in one particular case, that is, interned offenders locked up in Belgian prisons. For decades the plight of internees in Belgian prisons has been a cause of national and international criticism. In 1998 the ECtHR convicted Belgium for the first time for violating fundamental rights of an interned prisoner. Since then and especially in the last years, many convictions have followed, up to the point that (shortly before finishing our research for this chapter) the ECtHR has decided in a pilot judgment that there exists a structural problem that exceeds individual complaints launched against the Belgian state (see *infra*). In what follows, first, the situation of internees in Belgian prisons is briefly sketched. Next, the pilot judgment and important preceding decisions are presented. This section concludes with an assessment of the impact of the ECtHR on the situation of internees in Belgian prisons.

## 3.1 Internees in Belgian Prisons

In Belgium offenders deemed not criminally responsible for their offences can be interned by the courts. Internment was created as *a measure of social defence* by the Act of 9 April 1930. It was changed under the influence of new social defence ideas, with the Act of 1 July 1964 that remained in vigour for more than half a century, until 30 September 2016 (see *infra*). Art. 1 of the Act of 1 July 1964 refers to 'a state of lunacy, a grave state of mental disturbance or feeblemindedness that make him [the offender] unfit to control his actions' and who is determined to be socially dangerous because of his mental state (see also Naudts et al. 2005: 149; Cosyns et al. 2007: 46–47) as the grounds for interning a person who, according to art. 7, committed a felony or a crime (only excluding the misdemeanours, dealt with by the police courts). Internment is an *indeterminate* social defence measure: the termination of the internment of a person, either institutionalized or supervised in the community, can only be decided by the Commission for Social Defence; if no release is granted, the internment can last for the remainder of a person's life. An interned offender can be released (under conditions) 'when his mental state has sufficiently improved and the conditions for his reintegration are fulfilled' (art. 18 Act of 1 July 1964). In Belgium, internment is a one-off measure, in that a person is either deemed fully responsible or not responsible at all, without any in-between (as was the case in the past, prior to 1931, and as is the case in countries such as the Netherlands, where a sliding scale of criminal responsibility is used) (e.g. Goethals 1991, 1997; Hanoulle 2009).

Internment takes place in an institution assigned by the Commission for Social Defence. In theory, this means interned offenders are sent to institutions for social defence, to forensic psychiatric centres, or, based on therapeutic grounds and with specific motivations for the decision, a placement can be ordered in an institution deemed appropriate both for security and care. Prior to being sent to an institution assigned by the Commission for Social Defence, the internment temporarily can take place in the psychiatric unit of a prison. The law requires the existence and availability of sufficient places for interned offenders so that they can be treated in an institution adapted to their specific needs and it assumes that treatment and therapy, aimed at improving their mental health, is being provided. On both counts, a problem exists for internees in ordinary prisons, even when placed in the psychiatric annexe. From internment's inception onwards, an important group of internees has resided in prisons, without sufficient places available in specialized institutions or units and without the real availability of treatment and care (for these and other criticisms, e.g. De Waele 1983; Goethals 1991, 1997: 30–31; Casselman 1997: 54–55; Cartuyvels et al. 2010). '[T]he Belgian authorities appear to have been satisfied that it met its aim of "protecting" society. The inadequate conditions and the lack of treatment for the internee, however, were of less concern to them' (Naudts et al. 2005: 149–150), so psychiatrists observed a decade ago. The problem persists until today, with some internees spending decades in the regular prison system without recourse to treatment or an adapted environment that is more suited to their needs.

Statistics about this population are rather scarce. At the end of 2013 there were 3820 internees, of which 1087 people were residing in a prison (Dheedene et al. 2015: 4). The number of internees in prisons increased markedly over the last decades. On 1 March 2000, 640 internees were in prisons and institutions for social defence, in all 7 % of the total prison population, while on 1 March 2011, this had gone up to 1103, representing 10 % of the Belgian prison population (Court of Audit 2012: 117). The latest annual report by the prison administration mentions an average daily population of 903.6 internees, which represents 8.2 % of the total prison population in 2015 (Directorate-General Penitentiary Institutions 2016: 40). The problematic situation of internees has recently again moved to the centre of political and public debate, this time in the context of euthanasia. An internee in the prison of Merksplas had spent more than three decades in prisons, without any real treatment; he was deemed untreatable according to psychiatrists. He saw no way out of his psychological suffering other than through filing for euthanasia. Since December 2011, 11 internees have filed for euthanasia (on grounds of intolerable psychological suffering), with serious doubts about whether and how their hopeless situation *as an internee* contributed to their application to have their life ended, with fears that some of them are asking to inflict a death sentence on themselves (see Snacken et al. 2015).

## 3.2 Internees Challenging Belgium Before the ECtHR

Although the situation of internees in prisons gives them prima facie many reasons to turn to the ECtHR, the reality shows otherwise. This may be explained, first and foremost, by the vulnerabilities of this group. Descriptive studies of the profile of internees show a population struck by a high percentage of co-morbidity, with figures ranging between 69 and 73.4 % (Cosyns et al. 2007; Dheedene et al. 2015: 7–8; Goethals et al. 2010: 17). An important segment (circa 45 %) of interned offenders in Belgian prisons is assessed as 'high care', and circa a third of imprisoned internees are assessed as 'high care' and 'high risk' (Court of Audit 2012: 122). These vulnerabilities may lead to difficulties in securing access to domestic courts and, further down the judicial path, to the ECtHR. A study of the Court's case law covering a period of over 50 years (September 1953–31 December 2004) shows that out of 118,000 cases only 108 concern psychiatric commitment, referring to 'persons of unsound mind, alcoholics or drug addicts or vagrants' (art. 5 §1 e of the ECHR) (Niveau and Materi 2006). Niveau and Materi (2006: 434) explicitly relate this small number of cases to the vulnerabilities of the concerned population.

Another reason has to do with their legal defence. For lawyers, there might be little interest in taking up the defence of an interned offender (who as a client may pose particular difficulties to work with, and perhaps also lacks the financial means). This regularly boils down to legal defence by *pro deo* lawyers whose experience is often too limited to use the 'European tools', including finding their way to the ECtHR when the case has exhausted the domestic means (Van Steenbrugge 2005: 321; see also, on 'the degree of support offered', Niveau and Materi 2006: 434). The vulnerabilities of this group and their possible difficulties of acceding to the courts have led some to plead for a 'class action suit' for internees in Belgian prisons (Hanoulle and Merckx 2012: 211).

Against this background it should not come as a surprise that it took so long before the predicament of internees in Belgian prisons ended up at the table of the Strasbourg judges. After the important 1998 case of *Aerts v. Belgium*,[6] it took over a decade until the next judgment with a violation followed.[7] However, especially since 2012 internees are more easily finding their way to the ECtHR. Statistics by the ECtHR (1959–2014) mention 205 judgments wherein Belgium was a party, including 148 judgments where at least one violation was found (European Court of Human Rights 2015). By the end of 2014, there were 15 cases concerning internees where at least one violation had been found; this represents 10 % of all Belgian cases with a violation. These numbers (and a further nine cases, of which eight in 2015 and one in 2016) suggest that internees (or at the very least their lawyers) have become more aware of the ECtHR as an additional (subsidiary) avenue for their griefs, which may be related to developments in the case law of the ECtHR itself. The Court's evolutive and dynamic interpretation of the ECHR makes the Convention 'a living instrument' (Van Zyl Smit and Snacken 2009: 369; Gerards and Fleuren 2014: 2), and the treatment of 'persons of unsound mind' is no exception to this (for a general evolution of the Court's treatment of and case law concerning persons of unsound mind, see Tulkens and Dubois-Hamdi 2015). Changing interpretations and extended, more far-reaching protections of fundamental rights of 'persons of unsound mind' might make lawyers more confident about bringing the case before the ECtHR.

## 3.3 Violating Human Rights of Internees: From the Individual Case to a Structural Deficit

Over the last few years, a rising number of ECtHR judgments have found violations in cases involving internees in Belgian prisons. Concurrently, the ECtHR has changed the way it approaches some aspects of the practice of internment. On 6 September 2016, the ECtHR decided in a pilot arrest that when it comes to dealing with internees, the structural deficiencies in Belgium need to be addressed in a systematic manner.[8] In this section we first discuss the key judgments in the run-up to that pilot judgment. The pilot judgment is particularly interesting as it illustrates how the Court can surpass the level of the individual case.

Internees in psychiatric annexes have repeatedly challenged Belgium for a violation of art. 5 §1 e). Intended to protect persons against arbitrary or unlawful detention, the ECtHR states that a certain link has to exist between the purpose of detention and the conditions, viz. the regime in which this takes place. In the case of an interned offender, the Court explicitly states that detention would only be 'regular' if it takes place in a hospital, a clinic or another appropriate institution.[9] The ECtHR first found a violation of this article against an internee in Belgium in the case of *Aerts v. Belgium* in 1998. This judgment became an important case law reference of the Court (see, inter alia, Van Zyl Smit and Snacken 2009: 95; Tulkens and Dubois-Hamdi 2015).

In *L.B. v. Belgium*, 2013, the ECtHR started to refer to structural issues in the context of a violation of art. 5 §1 (e) (Hanoulle 2013a). It explicitly pointed at the fact that in Belgium, '...numerous internees are awaiting a transfer to an institution for social defence or a private institution and find themselves in a situation comparable to that of the claimant, deprived of therapeutic care that could contribute to a successful reintegration into social life'.[10] The Court mentioned numerous national and international sources that establish this structural deficiency.[11] Since that case, the Court considered the violation of art. 5 §1 (e) as a structural problem in Belgium. This is the most recurring violation found in cases that internees have launched against the Belgian state. In no less than 23 out of 24 cases with a violation against the fundamental rights of internees, Belgium has been found guilty of violating this article. Furthermore, this structural flaw also affects how the Court takes into consideration other cases.

In *Claes v. Belgium*, 2013, the ECtHR convicted Belgium for a violation of art. 3, which was strongly linked to a violation of art. 5 §1 (e). A mentally handicapped man had been kept in psychiatric annexes of prisons for almost 15 years. The ECtHR again referred to national and international sources (including CPT reports)[12] according to which psychiatric annexes in prisons are inadequate as a place to detain persons of unsound mind, such because of lack of staff, poor quality and absence of continuous care, the degraded state of these annexes, prison crowding and a structural lack of places in the external psychiatric circuit.[13] The Court advanced this argument and stated that the claimant's situation 'results, in reality from a structural problem', consisting of two important elements. Next to the insufficient staffing in psychiatric annexes of prisons, the Court also mentioned that a placement outside a prison often is impossible either for a lack of available places in psychiatric hospitals or because the legislation does not allow the instances of social defence to impose a placement in an institution other than prison.[14] The ECtHR also brought to mind the weak position of internees against government[15] and argued that the difficult situation of the claimant being held in a psychiatric annexe without any real hope for change and without appropriate medical treatment and such for almost 15 years had subjected him to a suffering that far exceeds the inevitable suffering inherent to detention.[16] Since this decision, two more violations of art. 3 have been found in cases of internees in Belgian prisons.[17]

Since the *Claes v. Belgium* case, the ECtHR took the structural difficulties in treating internees in prisons as a starting point when new cases were brought before the court (Hanoulle 2013b). The burden of proof seemed to have shifted from the internee towards the government: 'it is up to government to show that the appropriate treatment was provided that was adapted to the pathology of the claimant' (Tulkens and Dubois-Hamdi 2015: 82, our translation). Together with the *Aerts v. Belgium* and *L.B. v. Belgium* cases, this judgment has become a reference for judging cases filed by internees against the Belgian state.

These cases have set the scene for a further ruling by the Court, one that goes beyond the individual level, while being based on a concrete case. In 2006, W.D. had been interned for sex offences and ended up in the prison of Merksplas, awaiting transfer to a specialized institution. The examination revealed that he suffered from several problems, including poor cognitive functioning (low I.Q.), an autism spectrum disorder and traits of paedophilia. W.D. failed to get a transfer to a more appropriate setting. The ECtHR stated that '…maintaining him in a psychiatric wing without a realist hope of change, without suited medical assistance and during a significant period constitute a particularly troublesome proof that he has been submitted to a level of distress that exceeds the suffering inherent to detention' (our translation) and found a violation of art. 3 (degrading treatment) in his case.[18] Furthermore, W.D. was held in 'a location not adapted to his health situation', which for the Court constituted a violation of art. 5 §1. Additionally, the ECtHR concluded that W.D. could not enforce his fundamental rights because of 'the lack of adapted places in the external circuit' (i.e. in specialized institutions) and 'the lack of qualified personnel in psychiatric wings of prison'.[19] These conditions, together with the violation of art. 3, made the ECtHR decide that Belgium had also violated art. 5 §4 (judicial control of lawfulness of detention) and art. 13 (right to an effective remedy).[20]

The Court not only found four violations; it also pulled out its judicial bazooka. It treated this case according to the pilot procedure and, therefore, rendered a pilot judgment, in which it pointed at structural deficiencies that needed to be tackled in a more systematic manner. For the ECtHR it was clear that the case of W.D. was not unique: 'The situation of the claimant cannot be dissociated from the general problem that has its origins in a structural dysfunction proper to the Belgian system of internment that has touched upon and is susceptible to touch upon the future of numerous persons. According to the Court, the observed situation is constitutive of a practice that is incompatible with the Convention' (our translation).[21] The ECtHR set out a deadline for change: it gave Belgium two years to tackle the structural problems. In the meantime, the Court suspended the treatment of 50 separate cases by internees launched against the Belgian state (see also Robert 2016).[22]

### 3.4 Has the ECtHR Impacted Upon What Happens with Internees in Belgian Prisons? An Assessment

In assessing the impact and influence of the ECtHR, two dimensions can be identified. The first concerns a dimension that stretches from the highly specific individual case up to a structural, systemic issue; the second dimension extends from a direct impact to an indirect impact.

The case of internees in Belgian prisons is particularly interesting in light of the first dimension. Strictly speaking, the ECtHR is there to judge specific cases. States that have violated the human rights of a claimant can face three types of obligations: the payment of compensation, the adoption of general measures such as legislative reform, and the adoption of individual measures (such as a reopening of domestic proceedings) (see the scheme of 'the life of an application', Sharpe 2010: 67), all three situated at two extremes of the individual-structural dimension.

As far as imprisoned internees are concerned, it is interesting to observe how the Court, after a number of similar violations and also based on its changing case law, gradually started to shift from stressing individual considerations to highlighting structural difficulties and problems, to then adopt the pilot procedure and cast a judgment that aims at bringing about the adoption of general measures. In terms of impact and influence, the Court first envisaged stopping the rights violations in individual cases. The impact then is mainly on an *individual* level (but see the next dimension). By casting its pilot judgment, the ECtHR is of the opinion that too many individuals have been or risk being struck by the structural deficiencies in the system of internment. With its pilot judgment, the Court intends to bring about structural changes in the way Belgium deals with internees, that is, it envisages a *structural* impact. Although this dimension suggests that a judgment of the ECtHR has an impact, be it individual or structural, this is not necessarily the case. The exact impact relates to how Belgium (or any country found to have violated fundamental rights) implements the Court's judgments.[23]

Another way of looking at the influence of the ECtHR relates to the directness of the impact of judgments by the Court, ranging from a direct impact to an indirect impact. The ECtHR and the ECHR have a direct impact both on the domestic courts as well as on legislation. First, domestic courts have dealt with internees' complaints about a lack of treatment in the past, sometimes leading the courts to decide in favour of the internee and his right for treatment (Idomon 2006–2007; Hanoulle and Merckx 2012). The ECtHR's position is subsidiary to the domestic courts, but the decisions reached by the Court have a *res interpretata* effect in Belgium, they have 'interpretative authority' (Schaiko et al. 2014: 104). The relationship between the ECtHR and domestic courts has been the subject of extensive analyses (see Gerards and Fleuren 2014; Gerards 2014; for Belgium, Schaiko et al. 2014). In general, much importance is given to the case law of the ECtHR, and its case law is also incorporated into domestic case law, beginning with the highest courts of the country (Schaiko et al. 2014: 123–127). As far as internees are concerned, the ECtHR judgments led the Court of Cassation to a shift in 2010 towards considering the protection of society and the treatment or care of internees as being on a par, rather than the latter as secondary to the first (Hanoulle and Merckx 2012). In addition to changes in domestic case law, domestic courts can also make use of the case law by the ECtHR and the ECHR as sources to decide over a local case.

Second, albeit harder to assess in its exact scope and depth, the ECtHR and the Convention also have an impact on legislation. In Belgium, an a priori review of legislation is undertaken by the Council of State, providing the legislator with advisory opinions on its conformity with higher norms in the legal order, including the ECHR (Schaiko et al. 2014: 106). The Constitutional Court also conducts a constitutional review of new legislation and has come to interpret the rights and freedoms entailed in the Belgian Constitution in light of the ECHR, thus providing a very direct link between the ECHR and its 'evolutive' interpretation by the ECtHR and domestic legislation (Schaiko et al. 2014: 120). Furthermore, Belgian courts may also review legislation in light of international legal norms for those matters not related to the Belgian constitution in itself (Schaiko et al. 2014: 110, 121). As far as legislation related to internment and internees is concerned, things are on the move in Belgium. The plight of internees has led the legislator to vote a law in 2007 (Act of 21 April 2007), which for a number of reasons has never been applied. The legislator, in part spurred by the convictions of Belgium by the ECtHR, set out to work on new legislation, which became the Act of 5 May 2014 (Hanoulle 2015: 290). The current minister of Justice decided to update the legal position of internees and to amend the new Act on a number of issues. This new legislation responds to a number of concerns dealt with by the ECtHR (such as the legal assistance of internees by a lawyer) (see also Hanoulle 2015).

Further down the continuum of the directness of impact, the ECtHR and the ECHR can affect and influence policy, practice and wider penal culture also indirectly. The ECtHR judgments enjoy 'considerable prestige' and are looked at and commented upon across Europe and in Belgium, which means a violation of a State also boils down to a *blamage*, even a moral shaming of the State (Van Zyl Smit and Snacken 2009: 365). Some judgments about controversial issues are picked up by the national media and may trigger a wider public debate, as has happened when Belgium had violated the fundamental rights of internees (e.g. Schaiko et al. 2014: 139). This can affect and influence the minds and mores of political, intellectual and cultural elites, although the impact thereof upon policies and practice concerning internees in prisons will often be indirect and implicit and thus hard to disentangle from other elements. It is also important not to overstate the influence of the ECtHR, as the moral indignation about the situation of internees in psychiatric annexes is not only driven by ECtHR judgments[24] and, indeed, the critical debate was already there before Strasbourg entered the discussion.

However, something seems to have changed in recent years and it may well be that the ECtHR has played an important role in this. Even though the plight of internees in prisons has not yet been resolved, the mores seem to be changing for the better and important steps have been taken to tackle the manifold problems, including plans for the construction of three forensic psychiatric institutions (one opened in early 2015, a second is under way and a third is planned), the opening of a unit for female internees and the construction of a long stay unit for internees with negative prospects of release (Vander Laenen 2015). These extra places will help reducing the use of the prison for this vulnerable population.

## 4 Conclusion

As our discussion of the CPT and the ECtHR demonstrates, it is not possible to offer a conclusive, all-encompassing assessment of the impact of 'Europe' in prisons in Belgium, one of the most 'European' countries on the old continent. Each institution and each specific problem require a separate analysis which may lead to different conclusions. If anything, our assessment reveals similarities between the impact of the CPT and the ECtHR, in that the impact of both institutions ranges from no impact to a very direct (positive) impact. Furthermore, there is some correspondence between the scope of the impact of the CPT and the ECtHR. For the ECtHR, the impact can be expected to be much more straightforward (either the case refers to an individual issue or to a structural issue), although difficulties in implementation raise doubts about this, and as the above discussion shows, the Court itself adjusts its stance depending on previous similar cases, with a possible shift from the individual case to the observation of structural dysfunctions. For the

CPT, as an institution with a preventive aim, the nature of the impact is less straightforward. Our analysis (and more extensively, see Daems 2017) reveals the CPT recommendations are answered along a similar continuum, with many possibilities between no impact at all and a (positive) impact.

# Notes

1. The problem of prison overcrowding has also been addressed at length in the 2009 report by Thomas Hammarberg, the then Council of Europe Commissioner for Human Rights, following the first visit to Belgium. Hammarberg visited the prisons of Forest and Antwerp. See Report by the Council of Europe Commissioner for Human Rights, Thomas Hammarberg, on his visit to Belgium 15–19 December 2008 (CommDH(2009)14, Strasbourg, Council of Europe, 17 June 2009). In September 2015 the current Commissioner for Human Rights Nils Muižnieks paid a visit to the psychiatric ward of the Forest prison. In the press release the Commissioner '...stressed the urgency of measures to prevent violations of the rights of detainees with psycho-social and intellectual disabilities, in line with the relevant judgments of the European Court of Human Rights against Belgium' (Commissioner for Human Rights 2015).
2. http://www.cpt.coe.int/documents/bel/2016-06-22-eng.htm.
3. *Vasilescu v. Belgium*, App. No. 64681/12, 25 November 2014.
4. At the time of writing, Belgium had not yet ratified OPCAT. It signed OPCAT on 24 October 2005.
5. Interestingly, when this Minister of Internal Affairs (Annemie Turtelboom) became Minister of Justice in the next federal government (2011–2014) she did not take any steps to implement such a guaranteed service. On the contrary, from early 2012 onwards she succumbed fully to the powerful trade unions and initiated inter alia a (failed) attempt to amend the Prison Law in order to make routine strip-searches possible (on this, see Daems 2014).
6. *Aerts v. Belgium*, App. No. 61/1997/845/1051, 30 July 1998. The ECtHR found violations of art. 5 §1 and art. 6.
7. *Houtman and Meeus v. Belgium*, App. No. 22945/07, 17 March 2009.
8. *W.D. v. Belgium*, App. No. 73548/13, 6 September 2016.

9. For example, *Aerts v. Belgium*, App. No. 61/1997/845/1051, 30 July 1998, para 46.
10. *L.B. v. Belgium*, App. No. 22831/08, para 96.
11. Ibid., para 72–75.
12. *Claes v. Belgium*, App. No. 43418/09, para 70–72.
13. Ibid., para 98.
14. *Claes v. Belgium*, App. No. 43418/09, para 99.
15. Ibid., para 101.
16. Ibid., para 100.
17. *Lankester v. Belgium*, App. No. 22283/10, 9 January 2014; *W.D. v. Belgium*, App. No. 73548/13, 6 September 2016.
18. *W.D. v. Belgium*, App. No. 73548/13, 6 September 2016, para 114.
19. Ibid., para 151.
20. Ibid., para 154.
21. Ibid., para 164.
22. Ibid., para 164.
23. On this, see the chapter by Anagnostou and Skleparis in this book or the recent comment from Nils Muižnieks (2016), the Commissioner for Human Rights of the Council of Europe.
24. The President of the Flemish League for Human Rights, in a 2014 Conference on internment with the telling title 'No Exit', made the analogy of the ECtHR with economic rating bureaus (Vandervelpen 2014). Violations against fundamental rights would qualify as lowering the human rights ratings of a country.

## Literature

Cartuyvels, Y., B. Champetier, and A. Wyvekens. 2010. La défense sociale en Belgique, entre soin et sécurité. Une approche empirique. *Déviance et Société* 34 (4): 615–645.

Casselman, J. 1997. Internering: huidige situatie. In *Internering*, ed. J. Casselman, P. Cosyns, J. Goethals, M. Vandenbroucke, D. De Doncker, and C. Dillen, 39–61. Leuven: Garant.

Commissioner for Human Rights. 2015. Press Release: Visit to Belgium. September 18.

Cosyns, P., C. D'Hont, D. Janssens, E. Maes, and R. Verellen. 2007. Geïnterneerden in België. De cijfers. *Panopticon* 28 (1): 46–61.

Court of Audit. 2012. *Maatregelen tegen de overbevolking in de gevangenissen.* Brussels: Central Printing Press of the House of Representatives.

Daems, T. 2010. Mooi, het leven is mooi. *Panopticon* 31 (6): 1–16.

———. 2011a. De ene staking is de andere niet: over (de gevolgen van) syndicale acties in de Belgische gevangenissen. *FATIK: Tijdschrift voor Strafbeleid en Gevangeniswezen* 130: 3–4.

———. 2011b. Een gevangenis is geen koekjesfabriek. *De Juristenkrant* 228: 13.

———. 2014. 'Ceci n'est pas une fouille à corps': The Denial of Strip Searches in Belgian Prisons. In *Punishment and Incarceration: A Global Perspective*, ed. M. Deflem, 75–94. Bingley: Emerald Group Publishing.

———. 2017. Slaves and Statues: Torture Prevention in Contemporary Europe. *British Journal of Criminology* 57 (3): 627–643.

De Waele, J. 1983. Enkele dysfuncties van de wet tot bescherming van de maatschappij. *Panopticon* 3: 231–245.

De Wit, J. 2002. Europa geeft Antwerpse gevangenis goed rapport. *Gazet van Antwerpen*, October 19.

Dheedene, J., K. Seynnaeve, and A. Van der Auwera. 2015. De geïnterneerdenpopulatie in Vlaamse gevangenissen: enkele cijfergegevens. *FATIK: Tijdschrift voor Strafbeleid en Gevangeniswezen* 145: 4–9.

Directorate-General Penitentiary Institutions. 2016. *Jaarverslag 2015*. Brussels: Federal Government Service.

European Court of Human Rights. 2015. *Violations by Article and by State—1959–2014*. Strasbourg: European Court of Human Rights. http://www.echr.coe.int/Documents/Stats_violation_1959_2014_ENG.pdf. Accessed Oct 2015.

Evans, M., and R. Morgan. 2001. Torture: Prevention versus Punishment? In *Torture as Tort*, ed. C. Scott, 135–153. Oxford: Hart Publishing.

Geboers, J., G. Smaers, and W. Van Laethem, eds. 1995. *Detentie in België. Een kritische analyse van het rapport van het Europees Comité ter Preventie van Foltering over hun eerste bezoek aan België*. Ghent: Liga voor Mensenrechten.

Gerards, J. 2014. The European Court of Human Rights and the National Courts: Giving Shape to the Notion of 'Shared Responsibility'. In *Implementation of the European Convention on Human Rights and of the Judgments of the ECtHR in National Case-Law*, ed. J. Gerards and J. Fleuren, 13–93. Antwerp: Intersentia.

Gerards, J., and J. Fleuren. 2014. Introduction. In *Implementation of the European Convention on Human Rights and of the Judgments of the ECtHR in National Case-Law*, ed. J. Gerards and J. Fleuren, 1–12. Antwerp: Intersentia.

Goethals, J. 1991. *Abnormaal en delinkwent. De geschiedenis en het actueel functioneren van de wet tot bescherming van de maatschappij*. Antwerp: Kluwer.

———. 1997. De wet tot bescherming van de maatschappij in een historisch perspectief. In *Internering*, ed. J. Casselman, P. Cosyns, J. Goethals, M. Vandenbroucke, D. De Doncker, and C. Dillen, 11–38. Leuven: Garant.

Goethals, J., B. Maes, and S. Verlinden. 2010. De internering van verstandelijk gehandicapte geïnterneerden. *FATIK: Tijdschrift voor Strafbeleid en Gevangeniswezen* 126: 16–22.

Gouvernement. 2014. *Accord de Gouvernement*. Brussels. October 10.

Griffiths, J. 1979. Is Law Important? *New York University Law Review* 54: 339–374.

Guttierrez, R. 2010. Un rapport condamne lourdement nos prisons. *Le Soir*, August 8.

Hammarberg, T. 2009. *Report by the Council of Europe Commissioner for Human Rights, Thomas Hammarberg, on His Visit to Belgium 15–19 December 2008*. Strasbourg: Council of Europe.

Hanoulle, K. 2009. Te gek om los te lopen of net niet? De vergeten groep van de verminderd toerekeningsvatbare daders in het Belgische strafrecht. In *Van pionier naar onmisbaar. Over 30 jaar Panopticon*, ed. W. Bruggeman, E. De Wree, J. Goethals, P. Ponsaers, P. van Calster, T. Vander Beken, and G. Vermeulen, 370–384. Antwerp: Maklu.

———. 2013a. Straatsburg gunt België geen respijt meer: interneren moet gelijk staan aan behandelen. *Rechtspraak Antwerpen Brussel Gent* 1: 7–13.

———. 2013b. Trieste primeur: Straatsburg veroordeelt België wegens onmenselijke behandeling geïnterneerde. *Rechtspraak Antwerpen Brussel Gent* 8: 460–464.

———. 2015. Een nieuwe interneringswet, een nieuwe wind door het interneringslandschap? *Panopticon* 36 (3): 289–296.

Hanoulle, K., and T. Merckx. 2012. Recht op behandeling van de geïnterneerde: evenwaardig met of ondergeschikt aan bescherming van de maatschappij? *Tijdschrift voor Strafrecht* 4: 207–212.

Heyvaert, J. 2012. Comité tegen foltering in Vorst. *De Standaard*, April 24.

Idomon, C. 2006–2007. Bevoegdheid van de kortgedingrechter en van andere instanties inzake betwistingen omtrent de voorwaarden van detentie en internering. *Rechtskundig Weekblad* 2: 42–48.

Meskens, J. 1994. Le plus grave? La surpopulation pénitentiaire. *Le Soir*, October 15.

Morgan, R., and M. Evans. 2001. *Combatting Torture in Europe*. Strasbourg: Council of Europe Publishing.

Muižnieks, N. 2016. *Non-implementation of the Court's Judgments: Our Shared Responsibility*. Council of Europe, The Commissioner's Human Rights Comments, August 23. https://www.coe.int/en/web/commissioner/-/non-implementation-of-the-court-s-judgments-our-shared-responsibility. Accessed Sep 2016.

Naudts, K.H., P. Cosyns, T. McInery, K. Audenaert, F. Van Den Eynde, and C. Van Heeringen. 2005. Editorial. Belgium and Its Internees: A Problem for Human Rights and a Stimulus for Service Change. *Criminal Behaviour and Mental Health* 15 (3): 148–153.

Niveau, G., and J. Materi. 2006. Psychiatric Commitment: Over 50 Years of Case Law from the European Court of Human Rights. *European Psychiatry* 21: 427–435.

Parmentier, S. 1992. Kijken achter tralies. België en het Europees Verdrag voor de preventie van foltering en onmenselijke en vernederende behandeling. *Panopticon* 13: 468–499.

———. 1999. The Validity and Impact of CPT Standards with Regard to Belgium. In *Protecting Prisoners. The Standards of the European Committee for the Prevention of Torture in Context*, ed. R. Morgan and M.D. Evans, 181–196. Oxford: Oxford University Press.

Robert, L. 2016. System error. Een pilootarrest over internering in Belgische gevangenissen. *FATIK: Tijdschrift voor Strafbeleid en Gevangeniswezen* 151: 3–4.

Schaiko, G., P. Lemmens, and K. Lemmens. 2014. Belgium. In *Implementation of the European Convention on Human Rights and of the Judgments of the ECtHR in National Case-Law*, ed. J. Gerards and J. Fleuren, 95–143. Antwerp: Intersentia.

Sharpe, J.L. 2010. Current Organization and Procedures. In *The Conscience of Europe. 50 Years of the European Court of Human Rights*. Council of Europe, ed. E. Myjer, L. Berg, P. Kempees, G. Malinverni, M. O'Boyle, D. Spielmann, M.E. Viliger, and J.L. Sharpe, 66–85. London: Third Millennium Publishing Ltd.

Snacken, S., C. Devynck, W. Distelmans, S. Gutwirth, and C. Lemmens. 2015. Demandes d'euthanasie dans les prisons belges. Entre souffrance psychique, dignité humaine et peine de mort. *Criminologie* 48 (1): 101–121.

Tulkens, F., and C. Dubois-Hamdi. 2015. Prison et santé mentale. La jurisprudence de la Cour européenne des droits de l'homme. *Criminologie* 48 (1): 77–99.

Van Steenbrugge, W. 2005. Geïnterneerden en mensenrechten. In *Vrijheden en vrijheidsbeneming: mensenrechten van gedetineerden*, ed. E. Brems, S. Sottiaux, P. Vanden Heede, and W. Vandenhole, 307–322. Antwerp: Intersentia.

Van Zyl Smit, D., and S. Snacken. 2009. *Principles of European Prison Law and Policy. Penology and Human Rights*. Oxford: Oxford University Press.

Vander Laenen, F. 2015. Van het interneringsfront veel nieuws. *FATIK: Tijdschrift voor Strafbeleid en Gevangeniswezen* 148: 3–4.

Vandervelpen, J. 2014. De veroordelingen door het Europees Hof voor de Rechten van de Mens. In *No Exit. De interneringsproblematiek naar Belgisch recht*, ed. High Council for Justice, Brussels. http://www.csj.be/nl/inhoud/no-exit-er-hoop-voor-geinterneerden-video. Accessed June 2016.

X. 2006a. Liga voor Mensenrechten dringt aan op toepassing wet Dupont. *Belga*, April 20.

———. 2006b. La Ligue des Droits de l'Homme veut voir la loi Dupont appliquée. *Belga*. April 20.

———. 2010. België krijgt goede punten voor gevangenisbeleid. *De Morgen*, July 23.

———. 2012. Gevangenis Tilburg: 'afwezigheid Vlaamse Gemeenschap grootste zorg'. *Belga*, June 26.

**Tom Daems** is an Associate Professor of Criminology at the Leuven Institute of Criminology (LINC), KU Leuven, Belgium.

**Luc Robert** is a Research Fellow at the National Institute of Forensic Sciences and Criminology (NICC), Brussels, Belgium.

# Europe in Irish Prisons: Not Quite the 'Good European'

Claire Hamilton

## 1 Introduction

Ireland presents as a particularly appropriate prism through which to consider the influence of Europe in prisons and penal policy, poised as it is between the cold winds of punitivism occasionally blowing from the west and the perhaps more measured approach to punishment espoused by fellow Europeans (Daems et al. 2013). Picking up this theme in a consideration of the Irish law on parole and life sentences, Griffin and O'Donnell (2012: 613) describe it as 'an apparent outlier to both the human rights or punitive approaches, or perhaps a hybrid of sorts'. The discussion which follows in this chapter does little to contradict arguments concerning Ireland's idiosyncratic approach to criminal justice, with the same singularity of approach evident as regards European influences on prisons (on 'Hibernian exceptionalism' see further: Hamilton 2015; Griffin and O'Donnell 2012; Healy and O'Donnell 2005; Healy 2012; Vaughan and Kilcommins 2008). Despite a general lack of judicial

C. Hamilton (✉)
Maynooth University, Maynooth, Ireland





T. Daems, L. Robert (eds.), *Europe in Prisons*, Palgrave Studies in Prisons and Penology, DOI 10.1007/978-3-319-62250-7_8

zeal towards the case law of the European Convention of Human Rights (ECHR) (Doyle and Ryan 2011; Farrell 2013; Rogan 2014a) and a profound state apathy towards serious human rights breaches in many areas of prison policy, the influence of European human rights norms and standards has been palpable in some areas, namely, prisoner voting, and (to a lesser degree) the provision of in-cell sanitation facilities and the investigation of prisoner deaths (Hamilton 2014). This influence has, however, largely manifested at a political rather than a legal level. As yet, there have been no cases resulting in a judgment by the European Court of Human Rights (ECtHR) on prison conditions in Ireland (the only decision concerns release procedures) and no successful litigation invoking the Convention domestically.[1]

In order to elaborate more clearly this 'complex of competing characteristics' (Griffin and O'Donnell 2012: 613) it is proposed to provide readers first of all with a brief overview of Irish penal policy and prison law. Having described both the less developed nature of the jurisprudence on prisons in Ireland and the more pragmatic approach often taken to policy in this area, the chapter then moves to consider a number of areas in which Irish prison law can arguably still be said to fall short of European standards, such as the law on parole and the continued use of the practice of 'slopping out' in certain prisons. Particular consideration is given here to what has been described by McCullagh (2002: 595) as the 'democratic deficit' with regard to accountability in the Irish penal system, which compares unfavourably with that of our closest neighbours. On a more sanguine note, the next part examines a key area of Irish prison law and policy where reforms have ostensibly been effected in order to secure compliance with the Convention. In this regard, the 2007 change in the law on prisoner voting may be regarded as perhaps the clearest instance of a process of 'controlled liberalisation' or tactical concession to forestall potential criticisms (Risse and Ropp 1999 cited in Vaughan and Kilcommins 2010). The chapter concludes with some observations on the factors within Irish penal policy militating for and against a more European approach together with some views on the use of the ECHR in this area in the future.

Overall, it is the aim of this brief survey of some of the most contentious areas of Irish prison law and policy to provide some flavour of the approach of the authorities to the Convention and other European human rights norms, and more particularly their role as agents for change. Given the unique perspective of the book, it barely needs stating that the below does not purport to be a comprehensive assessment of Ireland's compliance with the ECHR in the area of prison law and readers interested in such an assessment may find much to consider elsewhere (Hamilton and Kilkelly 2009; Herrick 2009; Rogan 2014a, c).

## 2 Irish Penal Policy and Prison Law: An Overview

In comparative terms, Ireland's imprisonment rate of 81 per 100,000 in March 2016 is quite low (ICPS 2016). We are ranked near the bottom of the Council of Europe's table of prisoners with a detention rate closer to that of Switzerland (84) or Norway (71) than our closest neighbours, England and Wales (147) and Scotland (141) (ibid). Sentences also tend to be short, with 83 per cent of those received into prison in 2014 serving less than six months, a factor which may be relevant to the less developed body of prison law in this jurisdiction (Irish Prison Service 2015; Rogan 2014b). These imprisonment rates have been arrived at from a very low base, however, rising to current rates from 2185 (61 per 100,000) in 1992 (Hamilton 2014). Whether this state of affairs is due to a hardening of attitudes or increased punitiveness akin to that witnessed in certain western jurisdictions over the last few decades is difficult to gauge. Rogan (2013: 106) has characterised decision-making in this area as 'pragmatic' arguing that '…it is difficult to state what precisely is the particular ideology—or political or penal philosophy—driving change within Irish penal policy'.

As with many other western jurisdictions over this period, therefore, change is certainly a feature of the Irish penal landscape, but in the Irish case mingled with the stagnation which appears endemic to Irish criminal justice (O'Donnell 2008). This is perhaps best illustrated by the poor physical conditions affecting many Irish prisoners, particularly those accommodated in the dilapidated nineteenth-century prisons. As will be discussed presently, the practice of 'slopping out' night waste continues to affect many hundreds of Irish prisoners despite sustained and trenchant criticism from the European Committee for the Prevention of Torture (CPT) and indeed the Irish government's own pledge to provide in-cell sanitation in all places of detention by 1999 (Prison Hygiene Policy Group 1997).

A similar degree of apathy may also be said to have stymied the development of a significant corpus of prison law in Ireland which has only recently begun to emerge as a discrete area of legal practice.[2] Herrick (2009) attributes the underdeveloped nature of Irish prison law to factors such as the small size of the jurisdiction, the absence of legal aid for prison cases, as well as practitioner 'passivity' and a traditionally non-interventionist approach adopted by the Irish judiciary to prisoner cases. The reticence shown by the Irish courts in this area may be attributed to the problems of non-justiciability and the related view that the courts should be reluctant to direct the executive on the allocation of resources (Hamilton and Kilkelly 2009). It may also be explained by reference to the principles developed in the older jurisprudence which recognise that prisoners' rights were *necessarily* diminished by virtue of their imprisonment.[3] As observed by Hamilton and Kilkelly (2009), this position is in contrast to the case law of the ECtHR which has continued to assert the fundamental rights of prisoners beyond the prison gates, save of course for the right to liberty. Nor, given the absence of a set of minimum enforceable standards, is the relatively underdeveloped nature of the case law compensated for by the legislative schema. A Prison Act was enacted in 2007 but deals largely with planning and administrative issues, prison discipline and the Office of the Inspector of Prisons. Similarly, the Prison Rules 2007, which take the form of secondary legislation or a statutory instrument, do not confer directly justiciable rights but contain important procedures which must be followed in the disciplinary context, and so on. A set of *Standards for the Inspection of Prisons* published by the Inspector of Prisons in 2009 lay out best practice for the treatment of prisoners and management of prisons based on international human rights standards (such as the ECHR) but have yet to be placed on a statutory footing.

There are signs, however, that things are beginning to change in this area, something which can be attributed, at least in part, to increased practitioner awareness of the potential use of the ECHR. Under the European Convention on Human Rights Act 2003 state bodies in Ireland must perform their functions in a manner compatible with the state's obligations under the Convention and courts must interpret domestic law in light of the Convention, insofar as is possible. Writing some years ago, Liam Herrick (2011a), former director of the Irish Penal Reform Trust, cites the two decisions of *Mulligan v. The Governor of Portlaoise Prison*,[4] and *Kinsella v the Governor of Mountjoy Prison*,[5] as the beginning of significant movement in the courts' approach to prisoner litigation. From the instant perspective, *Mulligan* holds greater significance given its analysis of the Convention case law on prison conditions and the parameters it established for future litigants. While, as will be discussed further below, the court did not find that the requirement to 'slop out' night waste constituted a breach of the plaintiff's rights on the facts of the particular case, suggestions in the judgment that a different set of factual circumstances could meet with more success in the courts, have seen the most dramatic improvements in the Irish prison estate in decades. It is important, however, not to overstate the impression made by the Convention in Irish prison law and policy. Rogan (2014a: 2) describes its impact in this area (as elsewhere) as fairly 'muted' and cites in support the decision of Judge Hogan in *DF v Garda Commissioner (No 3)*[6] in which he held that many of the protections in the Convention are already in place under the Irish Constitution (e.g. art. 3 of the Convention goes no further than the protection of the person under art. 40.3.2 of the Irish Constitution).

## 3 Conditions in Irish Prisons and the Impact of the ECHR

It is by now well established in the ECHR case law that seriously deficient prison conditions may constitute inhuman and degrading treatment contrary to art. 3. While the ECtHR was traditionally reluctant to declare prison conditions inhuman or degrading in the absence of proof of the deliberate infliction of suffering, a more robust line of case law no longer requires intention on behalf of state authorities to find a violation under art. 3 (Snacken and van Zyl Smit, 2013). This brings the ECHR jurisprudence more in line with rule 4 of the Basic Principles of the 2006 European Prison Rules[7] which holds that 'Prison conditions that infringe prisoners' rights are not justified by the lack of resources'. Indeed, evolving standards in relation to the threshold for inhuman and degrading treatment have led to the ECtHR holding in a number of recent decisions that severe overcrowding could *per se* constitute conditions which contravene art. 3 of the Convention.[8] This holds much relevance in an Irish context given that overcrowding is a feature of many of our prisons and doubling up ('double bunking') in prison cells has been the norm for many years (Herrick 2011b). Indeed, the recent expansion in the prison population has led to the inclusion of two-person occupancy cells as a formal part of Irish prison accommodation policy in contravention of European Prison Rules (JCFJ 2012).

Increasingly, in making determinations on conditions of detention in member states the Strasbourg Court has relied on reports by the CPT which has fulfilled the role of 'fact finding instrument' of the Court (Myjer 2010, cited in Snacken and van Zyl Smit 2013). In its reports on Ireland, the Committee has raised overcrowding as an issue on several occasions. In 1998, it described the problems of overcrowding in Irish prisons as 'endemic', a concern which it repeated in 2002, before moving in 2006 to identify overcrowding as an exacerbating factor for other systemic problems such as poor cell conditions, poor regimes and inter-prisoner violence (Martynowicz 2011). In its 2011 report, the Committee (CPT 2011) reiterated its assessment of conditions in some Irish prisons as 'unsafe', stating: 'As was the case in 2006, the de facto overcrowding, combined with the conditions in certain of the old and dilapidated prisons, raises real concerns as to the safe and humane treatment of prisoners' (CPT 2011: para 21). While the Committee acknowledged the significant measures taken by the Irish authorities to address the problem in its most recent report (CPT 2015), overcrowding was still a matter of concern in a few prisons, notably the Dóchas Centre (women's prison) and Cork Prison.

In addition to severe overcrowding, Ireland holds the dubious distinction of being one of the few western European jurisdictions to persist with the practice of 'slopping out' in its prisons (IPRT 2010). 'Slopping out' refers to the practice of prisoners using a bucket/chamber pot to collect human waste while locked in their cells overnight and emptying these buckets/chamber pots the following morning (IPRT 2011). This, combined with the conditions outlined above, has attracted much criticism from both national and international monitoring bodies (see, e.g. Prison Hygiene Policy Group 1997; UN Human Rights Committee 2008; Inspector of Prisons 2013). For its part, the CPT has repeatedly (since 1993) condemned as 'degrading' and 'humiliating' the use of slopping out in the Irish prison system, adding that it also debased the prison officers who supervised it. The government's response has been dilatory to say the least: while slopping out was finally ended in Mountjoy, Ireland's largest prison, in 2013, more recently followed by Cork prison, it continues in Limerick and Portlaoise prisons. This is despite a commitment as far back as 1997 to provide in-cell sanitation in all places of detention by 1999 (Prison Hygiene Policy Group 1997).

Fresh impetus has been brought to this area by the decision in *Napier v. Scottish Ministers*,[9] which held that the overcrowded conditions in Scottish prisons—which included slopping out—were contrary to human dignity under art. 3 ECHR. This resulted not only in Mr. Napier winning his case, but in urgent measures being taken to eliminate the practice throughout the Scottish prison estate. Following *Napier*, hundreds of prisoners in Ireland have instituted proceedings in relation to slopping out in Irish jails. While none of these cases have been successful in the courts, the prospect of paying out large amounts in compensation has prompted more strenuous efforts by state authorities in recent years to reduce the number of prisoners exposed to the practice. The landmark case in this regard is *Mulligan v. Governor of Mountjoy Prison*[10] where the High Court held that a lack of in-cell sanitation was not inhuman or degrading either under the Irish Constitution or under the Convention in circumstances where the prisoner was not sharing a cell and the conditions of detention were otherwise good. A notable feature of *Mulligan* is that, while the High Court made no declaration of unconstitutionality or incompatibility with the Convention *on the particular facts of the case*, it may have left the door open for future cases. Judge MacMenamin referred in his judgment to a number of ECtHR decisions in which the combination of 'slopping out' and other negative aspects of imprisonment (such as overcrowding, double bunking and particular health vulnerabilities on the part of an individual prisoner) led to a situation where prisoners' rights were adversely affected. Indeed, given that many Irish prisoners will have experienced slopping out in considerably worse conditions than the plaintiff in *Mulligan*, the Irish Penal Reform Trust (2010) views the judgment as a significant step towards the ending of the practice of slopping out in Ireland. This was the view also taken by the State Claims Agency which warned following the judgment 'of [the] significant financial risk faced by the State in relation to the lack of in-cell sanitation' (State Claims Agency, cited in Thornton Hall Project Review Group 2011). The state has subsequently financially settled three cases brought by prisoners and, as noted, has finally committed the necessary resources to eliminate the practice from a large part of the prison estate (Tighe 2015). Despite its impact, however, the judgment remains illustrative of the *de minimis* approach taken by the Irish courts to the Convention case law. As subsequently observed by counsel for the petitioner in the Scottish decision in *Greens v. Scottish Ministers*[11] Judge MacMenamin's analysis was informed by out-of-date case law on slopping out from the ECtHR (Rogan 2012). Herrick (2010) is similarly critical of the judgment's failure to consider the absolute nature of the art. 3 provision combined with the sustained inaction- spanning several decades - on behalf of the authorities on this issue.

## 4 European Human Rights Norms, Politics and Parole

Given the poor conditions described above it is perhaps surprising that Ireland has not been the subject of a judgment from the ECtHR. The only Irish prison law case to appear before the Strasbourg Court has in fact been an (unsuccessful) challenge to the procedure governing the release of prisoners, or more specifically, the role of the Minister for Justice and Equality in deciding whether to grant a prisoner early release. The area of parole/release is one in which the jurisprudence of the ECtHR has been influential, particularly through its insistence on clarity in the scope of the penalty (*Kafkaris v. Cyprus*)[12] and the independence of the body reviewing sentence. Under art. 5(4) of the Convention, a person enjoys the right to have the lawfulness of their detention determined speedily by a 'court' and this has been interpreted by the ECtHR to require certain features such as independence from the executive.[13] Its influence has been particularly keenly felt in the UK, where the ECtHR case law has played a crucial role in the transformation of the Parole Board from an entity controlled by the executive to an independent and formal decision-making body (Griffin and O'Donnell 2012). In stark contrast to the ECHR-driven reforms in the UK and other European jurisdictions,[14] the release process in Ireland has not changed substantially for over half a century. In yet another instance of Hibernian exceptionalism, Griffin and O'Donnell (2012: 613) describe parole in Ireland as '[developing] in a vacuum, largely immune to broader pressures of transformation, with the country showing a reluctance to look beyond its own cultural, political and historical realities'.

While the ECtHR case law is applicable to Ireland, the Irish position differs somewhat to that in Britain, as the life sentence is not divided into punitive and preventative elements. The role of the judge is therefore simply to impose a life sentence with the decision on release made by the Minister for Justice and Equality on the advice of the (non-statutory) Parole Board. As Rogan (2014c) observes, the Irish Parole Board is in a peculiar position in that, while it reviews the prisoner's progress and may recommend release, it has no power to direct release. Although in practice most recommendations are accepted by the Minister, the involvement of a politician in the process is problematic as it leaves the process open to charges of populism or manipulation for political gain. A further anomaly concerns the ambiguous legal status of parole in Ireland: released prisoners may consider themselves to be 'on parole', but the word actually has no legal meaning in Ireland and the nature of the release granted is actually temporary release (a form of release used for many other purposes from compassionate leave to easing pressure on the prison population).[15]

Irish prisoners sentenced to life imprisonment are eligible for release after 7 years, and this threshold also applies to prisoners sentenced to 14 years or more who wish to be considered for release. It should be noted that while the minimum term which must be served is stated in Parole

Board practice, it is not contained in statute, in contravention of the Council of Europe's Recommendation on Conditional Release.[16] The minimum threshold of seven years is low by European standards but the de facto length of a life sentence has crept upwards over the years with recent statements indicating that prisoners serve an average of 17 years prior to being released (IPRT 2012a).[17] Comparing the release system in Ireland with other European jurisdictions, Griffin and O'Donnell (2012: 617) note that it is not the gradual increase in time served prior to release that sets Ireland apart, rather 'it is the lack of certainty that surrounds this process'. High levels of uncertainty also abound in relation to the criteria for release: while there are certain statutory criteria in place, these are vague, with no real indication provided as 'to the priority to be accorded to the various individual and social interests involved' (O'Malley 2008). During a recent visit by the CPT a number of complaints were received from life sentence prisoners regarding the lack of a structured sentence plan making it difficult to know what the Board required of them when they became eligible for release (CPT 2011: para 53). Again, this would appear to contravene the Council of Europe Recommendation on release which requires that the criteria which prisoners have to fulfil to qualify for release 'should be clear and explicit' as well as realistic (para 18) (IPRT 2012a). The problem is further compounded by the Board's tendency to take into account factors extraneous to the offender's circumstances; a failure to provide prisoners with reasons for refusal of their release; and significant delays in parole hearings (IPRT 2012a; Griffin and O'Donnell 2012).

The question of the compatibility of the current arrangements with art. 5(4) of the Convention was considered by the Irish courts in *Whelan and Lynch v. Minister for Justice and Equality*.[18] The argument that neither the Minister nor the Parole Board could be considered to be sufficiently independent for the purposes of compliance with the Convention was rejected on the grounds that sentences in Ireland did not contain a preventative detention component as in England and the article was therefore not engaged. Distinguishing the ECtHR's decision in *Kafkaris*, the Supreme Court held that the power to grant temporary release was exclusively an executive function, and there was no separate decision to extend a person's detention (IPRT 2012a). Despite strong academic criticism of this decision (Hamilton 2009; Griffin and O'Donnell 2012), the ECtHR has upheld the Supreme Court's decision, holding that the Minister's discretion to grant temporary release did not affect the legality of his current imprisonment which remained in conformity with the original life sentence. The Court also noted the availability of judicial review by the Irish courts. They accordingly held the application to be manifestly ill-founded and inadmissible.[19]

Despite the lack of success in Strasbourg, there remains an unease at European level with political involvement in release decisions[20] which, combined with long-standing domestic criticism (see, e.g. McCutcheon and Coffey 2006; O'Malley 2008; Law Reform Commission 2008; Hamilton 2009; IPRT 2012a; Griffin and O'Donnell 2012; Griffin 2015), may have finally nudged the system of parole closer to reform. Following the recommendations of the Penal Policy Review Group (2014) in November 2014 the government indicated its intention to review the current system and in particular to bring forward legislation to place the Parole Board on a statutory footing.[21] The extent to which core principles articulated in the main Council of Europe instruments are embedded within this legislation will be particularly interesting to observe, providing as they do a blueprint for reform (IPRT 2012a).

## 5 Accountability

In the closed world of the prison, the importance of an effective system of inspection and monitoring to implement human rights standards and best practice solutions cannot be overemphasised (Gostin and Staunton 1985). In this relation, there has historically been evidence of what McCullagh (2002) has termed a 'democratic deficit' in the Irish prison system which serves to reinforce views that the system adopts an indifferent attitude towards its duty of accountability. For example, the publication of Annual Reports on Prisons was quite sporadic until 2000 and the information provided within them at times extremely limited. As it currently stands, the main domestic accountability mechanisms in Ireland are the Prison Inspectorate and the Visiting Committees which visit prisons, meet with prisoners and publish annual reports. Both the

Inspector's reports and the reports of the Visiting Committees are publicly available on the Department of Justice website but neither of these bodies have the power to compel the Prison Service to adopt their recommendations.

It is beyond doubt that the Prison Inspectorate, which has operated on an administrative basis since 2002 and a statutory basis since 2007, has played a very significant role in securing the rights of prisoners in this jurisdiction. The office is independent in the performance of its functions and has demonstrated this independence on several occasions through the publication of a number of reports critical of the Prison Service (see, e.g. the recent damning report on the separation unit in Mountjoy which led to its closure: Inspector of Prisons 2014). The effectiveness of the Visiting Committee system is more difficult to assess. While some Committees have taken their role extremely seriously (such as the reports of the Mountjoy Committee), others have been less rigorous, and displayed a tendency to view prison life through what O'Mahony (1994) has termed 'a pair of pleasantly rose-tinted spectacles'. Moves are afoot, however, to strengthen the independence and effectiveness of the Visiting Committees with the planned Inspection of Places of Detention Bill to include provisions establishing a link between the Visiting Committees and the Inspector of Prisons (Fitzgerald 2015). As part of these plans, it is intended that Visiting Committees will report regularly to the Inspector (Fitzgerald 2015).

While the above measures represent real progress in this area, the absence of a *fully* independent prisoner complaints mechanism can be viewed as the most significant weakness in the accountability system governing Irish prisons at present. It is not clear what the ECtHR would consider to be a satisfactory system of complaints; however, both the CPT and the European Prison Rules have laid emphasis on the need for independence from the prison administration in any such system (Rogan 2012). In its recent reports on Ireland, the CPT (CPT 2007; CPT 2011; CPT 2015) has been critical of oversight in this area, noting problems in resourcing the Inspectorate, a failure to properly investigate complaints and a lack of prisoner confidence in the complaints system. This is perhaps unsurprising in light of the fact that complaints by Irish prisoners about their treatment may only be addressed to the

Visiting Committee, the governor or the Department of Justice and Equality, all of which may be viewed as partial. Following such criticism, a new comprehensive prisoner complaints system was introduced in November 2012 based on a model recommended by the Inspector of Prisons who has independent oversight of the process.[22] This was followed in 2013 by amendments to the Prison Rules to support and give effect to the new procedures for the investigation of prisoner complaints. These provide that prisoner complaints under Category A (assault, serious intimidation by staff etc.) will be examined by investigators from outside the Prison Service to ensure an effective and impartial investigation. It cannot be gainsaid that these reforms bring a level of independence to the prisoner complaints system in Ireland for the first time, however, the establishment of an oversight mechanism *fully* independent of both the Irish Prison Service and the Minister for Justice, such as a Prisoner Ombudsman, remains a desirable objective (IPRT 2013, 2014). Indeed, this is the conclusion reached by the recent review of the new system by the Inspector of Prisons (2016: para 7.2) which identified 'a litany of failures, at all levels of the service…to adhere to statutory obligations or defined duties' concerning the investigation of many categories of complaint.

A final aspect of accountability which would appear lacking in an Irish context concerns the specific obligations on the authorities in the event of a death in prison. Under case law deriving from art. 2 of the ECHR, it is incumbent on the State to ensure that an effective, independent investigation is carried out following any death in state custody. This issue has been thrown into sharp relief in an Irish context following the tragic death of Gary Douch in Mountjoy Prison in 2006 at the hands of another inmate. The subsequent report of the Committee of Investigation into that death revealed very serious problems within the Irish prison system relating to severe overcrowding, failures in respect of mental health care and inadequate systems for transferring information (McMorrow 2014). In addition to these substantive concerns, however, the controversy surrounding Mr. Douch's death and the long delay in publishing the Committee's report raise questions about procedural fairness in relation to the investigation of deaths in custody. Although since January 2012 the death of any prisoner in custody or on temporary release is the subject of an independent investigation by the Inspector, there remain questions as to whether this secures compliance with the Convention under art. 2. While the Inspector's reports do appear to fulfil the requirement under art. 2 of providing an opportunity to learn lessons from a death, the Inspector cannot hold any individual to account for the death of the prisoner in the form of civil or criminal responsibility (Rogan 2014c). In particular, the Inspector of Prisons does not have the power to require witnesses (such as prison officers) to attend or give evidence, nor does he have the legal power to require people to give him documents relevant to the investigation. Without these powers of discovery and compellability availed of by the Committee of Investigation into Douch's death, investigations carried out by the Inspector may still not meet the art. 2 requirements (Mullally 2014). It is also important that the Inspector puts in place procedures to deal with families in order to safeguard their interests as thus far the reports suggest that families of deceased prisoners are not always consulted (Rogan 2014c). The failure to afford families an opportunity to comment on any draft report and to ask questions of the prison authorities raises additional concerns about art. 2 compliance (IPRT 2012b).

## 6 The ECtHR and Prisoner Voting

While the above account testifies more to the institutional torpor which has, at least until recently, dominated Irish penal affairs, the system is also capable of abrupt change. The Convention's role as a catalyst for such change in Ireland is perhaps best illustrated by the reforms which took place following the ECtHR decision of *Hirst v. UK*[23] on prisoner voting rights in 2004. The Court held in *Hirst* that the British ban on prisoner voting was in breach of art. 3, Protocol 1 of the Convention prompting the Irish government to enact legislation enabling prisoners to cast a postal vote in 2006.[24] Hitherto, as Hamilton and Lines (2009: 205) have observed, 'Ireland had occupied a strange no man's land in relation to the voting rights of its prisoners'. Prisoners were not divested of those rights by legislation and therefore in theory continued to enjoy the right to vote under art. 16 of the Constitution. They were, however, denied the practical means to exercise the franchise through the failure of the authorities to provide an administrative means through which they could access a ballot (Hamilton and Lines 2009; Behan and O'Donnell 2008). Challenges to this position before the courts had met with little success and indeed provide a good illustration of the differing approaches of the Irish and Strasbourg courts (Hamilton and Kilkelly 2009). The Irish Supreme Court in *Breathnach v. Ireland*[25] following the earlier decision in *Murray v. Ireland*,[26] held that the right to vote was *necessarily* suspended with the loss of liberty. This conclusion was arrived at without any explanation as to why it was necessary that voting rights be curtailed, when the provision of voting facilities was clearly within the Executive's power. Indeed, counsel for the State conceded in *Breathnach* that accommodating prisoners' votes would not present undue administrative difficulties, and the Chief Justice himself had remarked that it would not be 'wholly impractical'. In contrast, in *Hirst (2) v. UK*,[27] the ECtHR rejected the notion that the ECHR does not follow prisoners into prison. Indeed, in their concurring opinion in *Hirst*, Judges Tulkens and Zagrebelsky noted '[t]here are no practical reasons for denying prisoners the right to vote…and prisoners in general continue to enjoy the fundamental rights guaranteed under the Convention, except for the right to liberty'. The *Hirst* decision and several others issued by the European Court therefore illustrate the practical significance of an approach whereby prisoners are not deemed to have shed their rights at the prison gates (the so-called doctrine of inherent limitations). As Livingstone (2000: 311) writes: 'Prisoners can invoke the same rights which people assert on the outside. Their essential humanity, even after imprisonment, is thus judicially recognized'.

Given the conservative position adopted by the Irish courts on the issue, the *Hirst* decision offered a new opportunity for prisoner rights campaigners in Ireland to build momentum for change through political rather than legal channels (Hamilton and Lines 2009). Organisations such as the Irish Penal Reform Trust were active in raising awareness of the judgment and worked with opposition parties in advancing the issue in the Oireachtas (legislature). This work was to prove particularly significant given that it was a proposed private members bill on the issue from Fine Gael TD[28] Gay Mitchell that finally spurred the government into action and secured a commitment to legislation (Hamilton and Lines 2009). Introducing the Electoral (Amendment) Bill to the Dáil, the Minister for Environment, Heritage and Local Government, Dick Roche, explicitly stated that the legislation would meet the government's obligations under the provisions of the ECHR (Behan 2014). Referring to the *Hirst* judgment, he argued that while the legal position in the UK differed significantly from Ireland, 'in light of the judgment it is appropriate, timely and prudent to implement new arrangements to give practical effect to prisoner voting in Ireland'.[29]

It is to the credit of both the government and the opposition parties in Ireland in 2006 that they avoided the temptation to manipulate the issue for cynical political gain unlike their counterparts in the UK (Hamilton and Lines 2009). It is striking that no parliamentarian spoke against the enfranchisement of prisoners and that parliamentary questions on the issue of prisoner enfranchisement were submitted to the government by parties on both the left and right of the political spectrum. Considering the reasons for Ireland and the UK's divergent approaches, Behan (2014) identifies three factors, namely, the attitude to European influences, media interest and the political dynamic behind the issue. With regard to the first point, discussion on Europe in Ireland is much more positive than in the UK. Unlike the hostility to European 'interference' and 'foreign courts' present in some of the English parliamentary debates, there was a desire amongst Irish political representatives to bring Ireland into line with European norms. In an interview with Cormac Behan (2014) in November 2007, the Minister responsible for introducing the legislation observed that there was 'an obligation under the European Convention of Human Rights and Fundamental Freedoms which guarantees the right to vote', and there 'is a moral responsibility on member states that if you sign the Charter, you abide by the Charter'. While recognising the differences between Irish and English law on the issue, he thought it was 'better to deal with it at our pace, of our own volition than have a challenge to us in the Court of Human Rights' (Behan 2014). Behan also draws attention to the lack of media interest in the issue in Ireland and the specificities of the Irish situation concerning voting arrangements. As already noted, unlike other jurisdictions, Ireland already had legislation in place setting out the practicalities of registration, making enfranchisement easier to legislate for rather than having to repeal other legislation. This important factor 'eased the passage of legislation' without the 'need to use up any political capital' (Behan 2014).

## 7 Conclusion

As a small jurisdiction on the fringes of Western Europe, one could be forgiven for assuming that Irish penal policy may take its influence from its larger neighbours. Smaller jurisdictions may be more likely to adopt criminal justice changes from elsewhere than countries with a longer history or hegemonic power such as England (Karstedt 2015: 377). As indicated at the beginning of this chapter, however, Ireland has sought to forge its own path in matters of criminal justice, and this is true also of its prisons. The influence of European human rights norms on the penal field is therefore highly inconsistent. On the one hand, there are the legal reforms relating to prisoner voting as a clear instance of a process of 'controlled liberalisation' or tactical concession to forestall potential criticisms from Europe (Risse and Ropp 1999 cited in Vaughan and Kilcommins 2010). A desire to avoid litigation based on Convention law has also driven improvements in prison conditions and, more speculatively, accountability measures relating to deaths in custody. On the other hand, the inertia evident in addressing many of these problems (some of which are ongoing) as well as the failure of successive administrations to reform the parole process, speaks more to the Hibernian exceptionalism presaged at the beginning of this chapter. Perhaps the best conclusion when it comes to prison law and policy in Ireland is that influences have traditionally been local rather than international (see further Hamilton 2014). Even in the area of prisoner voting, the clearest instance of Ireland acting as a 'good European', Behan (2014) draws attention to the crucial role played by local factors such as the existence of legislation already setting out the practicalities of registration, a quiescent media and the absence of political opposition.

Looking ahead, there are factors both militating for and against further European influence in this area. A major stumbling block remains the deeply conservative approach taken by the judiciary to the use of the

Convention in the prison context (and indeed criminal justice more broadly), as well the more limited interpretative obligation required by the ECHR Act 2003 (Farrell 2013; Doyle and Ryan 2011). The Irish legislation, while similar to the English Act, contains a much more qualified interpretive obligation than that of the UK and constitutional issues are to be determined by the courts prior to ECHR compatibility issues.[30] Development of Convention jurisprudence in the area of penal law and policy is also hampered by the absence of legal aid for cases not relating to the legality of a prisoner's detention, something which may itself engage art. 6 of the Convention (Rogan 2014b). Even within these parameters, however, 'there are many islands of hope' (Rogan 2014b: 3). The late blossoming of Irish prison law, if somewhat overdue, will no doubt see future claims grounded in both the provisions of the Irish Constitution and the Convention. The Irish litigation spawned by the *Napier* case has certainly raised awareness of the Convention's potential in this area and may disturb the complacency which has historically surrounded the use of the Convention in matters of criminal justice (Ni Raifertaigh 2007). It should not be forgotten, moreover, that policy and practice in prison matters can always move ahead of the law and legal norms (Rogan 2014b). European human rights frameworks such as the ECHR and European Prison Rules featured prominently in two recent review reports commissioned by the State into the future needs of the prison system (Thornton Hall Project Review Group 2011; Strategic Review of Penal Policy 2014). Further, it is not an overstatement to say of the recent developments in the fields of accountability, prison conditions, and so on detailed above that they are suggestive of new receptiveness to change and to international influences amongst officials in the Department of Justice and Equality.[31] A recent damning report on the 'closed' and 'secretive' culture within the Department (following a whistle blower saga, a ministerial resignation and a change of police commissioner) provides an important context in this regard, with a new Minister for Justice and Director General of the Irish Prison Service keen to mark a change from the past (Toland 2014; Lally 2014). In light of these factors, it may well be, as Rogan (2015) contends, that a 'rare policy window' has opened up in the Irish prison system. How best to utilise this window, and leverage international standards to alter prison law and policy, now presents the challenge for NGOs such as the Irish Penal Reform Trust and other agitators for change in the Irish criminal justice system. While one may be cynical about lasting change in Irish penal policy (O'Donnell 2008), it is at least certain that European human rights norms can provide the resources to capitalise on this opportunity, as the sweeping reforms of Irish policing in the 2000s can attest (Vaughan and Kilcommins 2007).

## Notes

1. *Lynch and Whelan v. Ireland*, App. No. 70495/10 and 74565/10, 8 July 2014.
2. See, for example, Rogan (2014b: 3): 'I think we are where the ECtHR was in the 90s in terms of the matters with which we have grappled…'.
3. See *Breathnach v. Ireland* [2001] 3 Irish Reports [IR] 230; *Murray v. Ireland* [1991] Irish Law Reports Monthly [ILRM] 465.
4. [2010] IEHC (Irish High Court) 269 (Date of Delivery: 14/07/2010) available at: http://www.bailii.org/.
5. [2011] IEHC (Irish High Court) 235 (Date of Delivery: 12/06/2011) available at: http://www.bailii.org/.
6. [2014] IEHC (Irish High Court) 213 (Date of Delivery: 11/04/2014) available at: http://www.bailii.org/.
7. Rec(2006)2 of the Committee of Ministers to member states on the European Prison Rules.
8. *Lind v. Russia*, App. No. 25664/05, 6 December 2007; *Kantyrev v. Russia*, App. No. 37213/02, 21 June 2007; *Andrey Frolov v. Russia*, App. No. 205/02, 29 March 2007; *Labzov v. Russia*, App. No. 62208/00, 16 June 2005.
9. *Napier v. Scottish Ministers*, [2005] SC (Session Cases) 229 (Date of Delivery: 10/02/2005) available at: http://www.bailii.org/.
10. *Mulligan v. Governor of Mountjoy Prison* [2010] IEHC (Irish High Court) 269 (Date of Delivery: 14/07/2010) available at: http://www.bailii.org/.
11. *Greens v. Scottish Ministers* (2011) CSOH (Scottish Court of Session) 79 (Date of Delivery: 12/05/2011) available at: http://www.bailii.org/.
12. *Kafkaris v Cyprus*, App. No. 21906/04, 12 February 2008.
13. See, for example, *Weeks v. UK*, App. No. 9787/82, 2 March 1987.

14. Griffin and O'Donnell (2012) cite the Sentence Implementation Court (Belgium), the Supervision Tribunal (Italy) and the Court for the Execution of Sentences (Germany).
15. Criminal Justice Act 1960 as amended by the Criminal Justice (Temporary Release of Prisoners) Act 2003.
16. Rec(2003)22 of the Committee of Ministers to member states on conditional release.
17. In her text on prison law, Rogan (2014c: 128) observes that one prisoner was released in 2012 after serving 13 years, the implication being that this was now an unusual event.
18. *Whelan and Lynch v. Minister for Justice and Equality* [2010] IESC (Irish Supreme Court) 34 (Date of delivery: 14/05/2010) available at: http://www.bailii.org/.
19. *Lynch and Whelan v. Ireland*, App. No. 70495/10 and 74565/10, 8 July 2014.
20. See further van Zyl Smit and Snacken (2009), commenting on the opinion of Judge Bratza in *Kafkaris v. Cyprus*.
21. As indicated in the ECtHR decision in *Lynch and Whelan v. Ireland*. See further Dail Debates, written answers, 19 February 2015 https://www.kildarestreet.com/wrans/?id=2015-02-19a.76.
22. As noted in the Prisons Act, 2007, 'it is not a function of the Inspector to investigate or adjudicate on a complaint from an individual prisoner'.
23. *Hirst v. United Kingdom*, App. 7405/01, 30 March 2004.
24. Electoral Amendment Act 2006.
25. [2001] 3 Irish Reports [IR] 230.
26. *Murray v. Ireland* [1991] Irish Law Reports Monthly [ILRM] 465.
27. *Hirst v. United Kingdom (no. 2),* Application No. 74025/01, 6 October 2005.
28. Fine Gael (Lit: Family or Tribe of the Irish) is one of the largest political parties in Ireland. It is liberal-conservative and Christian democratic in orientation. TD stands for Teachta Dala which means member of Dáil Éireann (the Irish Parliament).
29. Dáil Debates, 2006, vol. 624, col.1978.
30. *Carmody v Minister for Justice, Equality and Law Reform* [2010] 1 IR [Irish Reports] 635; [2009] Irish Supreme Court [IESC] 71 (date of delivery: 23/10/2009) available at: http://www.bailii.org/ie/cases/IESC/toc-C.html.

31. In Ireland, the Department of Justice and Equality retains control of prison policy while operational matters are dealt with by the Irish Prison Service.

## Literature


Behan, C. 2014. Embracing and Resisting Prisoner Enfranchisement: A Comparative Analysis of the Republic of Ireland and the United Kingdom. *Irish Probation Journal* 11 (October): 156–176.

Behan, C., and I. O'Donnell. 2008. Prisoners, Politics and the Polls: Enfranchisement and the Burden of Responsibility. *British Journal of Criminology* 48 (3): 319–336.

Daems, T., D. van Zyl Smit, and S. Snacken, eds. 2013. *European Penology?* Oxford: Hart Publishing.

Doyle, O., and D. Ryan. 2011. Judicial Interpretation of the European Convention on Human Rights Act 2003: Reflections and Analysis. *Dublin University Law Journal* 33: 369–392.

Farrell, M. 2013. 10 Years on Ireland's Human Rights Act Has Failed to Deliver. *The Journal*, December 29. http://www.thejournal.ie/readme/10-years-on-irelands-human-rights-act-has-failed-to-deliver-1236617-Dec2013/#comments

Fitzgerald, F. 2015. Opening Comments: Securing Responsibility in the Prison Service. Irish Penal Reform Trust Conference 2015: Securing Accountability, Dublin, September 27. http://www.justice.ie/en/JELR/Pages/SP15000615

Gostin, L., and M. Staunton. 1985. The Case for Prison Standards: Conditions of Confinement, Segregation and Medical Treatment. In *Accountability and Prisons: Opening Up a Closed World*, ed. M. Maguire, J. Vagg, and R. Morgan, 81–96. London: Tavistock.

Griffin, D. 2015. The Release and Recall of Life Sentence Prisoners: Policy, Practice and Politics. *Irish Jurist* 53: 1–35.

Griffin, D., and I. O'Donnell. 2012. The Life Sentence and Parole. *British Journal of Criminology* 52 (3): 611–629.

Hamilton, C. 2009. Detention. In *ECHR and Irish Law*, ed. U. Kilkelly, 2nd ed. Bristol: Jordan Publishing.

———. C. 2014. *Reconceptualising Penality: A Comparative Perspective on Punitiveness in Ireland, Scotland and New Zealand*. Farnham: Ashgate.

———. 2015. Penal Policy in Ireland: Notes from a Small Country. In *Routledge Handbook of Irish Criminology*, ed. C. Hamilton, D. Healy, Y. Daly, and M. Butler, 450–466. London: Routledge.

Hamilton, C., and U. Kilkelly. 2009. Detention. In *The ECHR and Irish Law*, ed. U. Kilkelly, 2nd ed., 277–304. Bristol: Jordans.
Hamilton, C., and R. Lines. 2009. Prisoner Voting Rights in Ireland. In *Democracy and Punishment: International Perspectives in Criminal Disenfranchisement*, ed. A. Ewald and B. Rottingham, 205–220. Cambridge: Cambridge University Press.
Healy, D. 2012. Advise, Assist and Befriend: Can Probation Supervision Support Desistance? *Social Policy and Administration* 46 (4): 377–394.
Healy, D., and I. O'Donnell. 2005. Probation in the Republic of Ireland: Context and Challenges. *Probation Journal* 52 (1): 56–68.
Herrick, L. 2009. Prisoners' Rights. In *The ECHR and Irish Law*, ed. U. Kilkelly, 2nd ed., 325–352. Bristol: Jordans.
———. 2010. Fresh Challenge to Slopping Out May Follow Court Ruling. *Irish Times*, July 26.
———. 2011a. Guest Blog, Liam Herrick, Director Irish Penal Reform Trust: The Prospects for Prison Law in Ireland. December 1. http://www.kodlyons.ie/index.php/news/single/guest_blog_liam_herrick_director_irish_penal_reform_trust
———. 2011b. Human Rights in Prison. IHRC/Law Society Conference, Ireland's Human Rights Record Under the Spotlight, Law Society of Ireland, Blackhall Place, Dublin. October 22. http://www.ihrec.ie/download/pdf/liam_herrick_irish_penal_reform_trust.pdf
Inspector of Prisons. 2013. *Annual Report 2012*. Nenagh: Office of the Inspector of Prisons.
———. 2014. *An Overview of the Mountjoy Prison Campus with a Particular Emphasis on the Separation Unit*. Nenagh: Office of the Inspector of Prisons.
———. 2016. *Review, Evaluation and Analysis of the Operation of the Operation of the Present Irish Prison Service Prisoner Complaints Procedure*. Nenagh: Office of the Inspector of Prisons.
International Centre of Prison Studies (ICPS). 2016. World Prison Brief. http://www.prisonstudies.org/world-prison-brief
Irish Penal Reform Trust (IPRT). 2010. IPRT Disappointed at Slopping Out Decision. July 14. http://www.iprt.ie/contents/1750
———. 2011. *Policy Briefing Paper on Sanitation and Slopping Out in the Irish Prison System*. Dublin: IPRT.
———. 2012a. *Position Paper 9: Reform of Remission, Temporary Release and Parole*. Dublin: IPRT.
———. 2012b. *IPRT Information Booklet: Deaths in Prison Custody: Information for Families and Others Affected*. Dublin: IPRT.

———. 2013. IPRT Welcomes Laws Strengthening Internal Prisoner Complaints System But Need for Independent Complaints Mechanism Remains. *Media Advisory*, January 22. http://www.iprt.ie/contents/2468
———. 2014. Failures in Accountability Structures in Irish Prisons 'Extremely Disturbing'—IPRT. *Media Advisory*, October 9. http://www.iprt.ie/contents/2671
Irish Prison Service. 2015. *Annual Report 2014*. Longford: Irish Prison Service.
Jesuit Centre for Faith and Justice (JCFJ). 2012. *The Irish Prison System: Vision, Values, Reality*. Dublin: Jesuit Centre for Faith and Justice.
Karstedt, S. 2015. Cultural Peers and Penal Policies: A Configurational Approach Toward Mapping Penal Landscapes. *Punishment and Society* 17 (3): 374–396.
Lally, C. 2014. Brave New Leadership is the Key to Reform of the Department of Justice. *Irish Times*, July 30.
Law Reform Commission. 2008. *Report on Homicide: Murder and Involuntary Manslaughter*. LRC 87–2008.
Livingstone, S. 2000. Prisoners' Rights in the Context of the European Convention on Human Rights. *Punishment and Society* 2 (3): 309–324.
Martynowicz, A. 2011. Oversight of Prison Conditions and Investigations of Deaths in Custody: International Human Rights Standards and the Practice in Ireland. *Prison Journal* 91 (1): 81–102.
McCullagh, C. 2002. The Social Analysis of the Irish Prison System. In *Criminal Justice in Ireland*, ed. P. O'Mahony, 595–614. Dublin: Institute of Public Administration.
McCutcheon, P., and G. Coffey. 2006. *Report into the Determination of Life Sentences Submitted to the Irish Human Rights Commission*. http://www.ihrc.ie/download/pdf/report_determination_life_sentences.pdf
McMorrow, G. 2014. *Report of the Committee of Investigation into Gary Douch*. Dublin: Department of Justice and Equality.
Mullally, S. 2014. Speech at the Launch of the Irish Human Rights and Equality Commission (IHREC) Designate Report on Ireland's Fourth Periodic Review of Its Compliance with the International Covenant on Civil and Political Rights. Jervis House, Dublin 1, June 16. http://www.ihrec.ie/download/pdf/prof_siobhan_mullally_ihrec_designate_speech_launch_of_report_on_iccpr_16_june_2014.pdf
Myjer, E. 2010. About the Human Rights Success Stories of the Council of Europe. Some Reflections on the Impact of the CPT upon the Case-law of the European Court of Human Rights. In *Fervet opus: liber amicorum Anton*

*van Kalmthout*, ed. M. Groenhuijsen, T. Kooijmans, and T. de Roos, 161–174. Antwerp: Maklu.

Ni Faifertaigh, U. 2007. The European Convention on Human Rights and the Criminal Justice System. *Judicial Studies Institute Journal* 2: 18–49. http://www.jsijournal.ie/html/volumes_7_2.htm

O'Donnell, I. 2008. Stagnation and Change in Irish Penal Policy. *Howard Journal of Criminal Justice* 47 (2): 121–133.

O'Mahony, P. 1994. The Annual Report on Prisons and the Issue of Accountability. *Irish Law Times* 12 (1): 6–9.

O'Malley, T. 2008. The Ends of Sentence: Imprisonment and Early Release Decisions in Ireland. Paper Delivered at Fitzwilliam College, Cambridge, June 2008, p. 12. Available at http://www.irishsentencing.ie/en/ISIS/Pages/WP09000222 (accessed various dates).

Prisons Hygiene Policy Group. 1997. *Report of the Prisons Hygiene Policy Group*. Dublin: Stationery Office.

Rogan, M. 2012. *Prison Conditions under Irish Law and the European Convention on Human Rights*. Dublin: Dublin Institute of Technology/Irish Penal Reform Trust.

———. 2013. Pragmatism, Neglect and the Effects of Austerity. In *Punishment in Europe: A Critical Anatomy of Penal Systems*, ed. V. Ruggiero and M. Ryan, 86–110. Basingstoke: Palgrave Macmillan.

———. 2014a. Judicial Conception of Prisoners' Rights in Ireland: An Emerging Field. *Academy of European Law, 'Improving Conditions Related to Detention'*, Council of Europe, Strasbourg, November 6–7.

———. 2014b. The Rule of Law and Access to Justice in Prisons. *Burren Law School*. http://arrow.dit.ie/aaschlawcon/5/

———. 2014c. *Prison Law*. Dublin: Bloomsbury.

———. 2015. The Policymaking Process and Penal Change. In *Routledge Handbook of Irish Criminology*, ed. D. Healy, C. Hamilton, Y. Daly, and M. Butler, 434–449. London: Routledge.

Snacken, S., and D. van Zyl Smit. 2013. Distinctive Features of European Penology and Penal Policy-Making. In *European Penology?* ed. T. Daems, D. van Zyl Smit, and S. Snacken, 3–26. Oxford: Hart Publishing.

Strategic Review of Penal Policy. 2014. *Final Report*. Dublin: Department of Justice and Equality. http://www.justice.ie/en/JELR/Strategic%20Review%20of%20Penal%20Policy.pdf/Files/Strategic%20Review%20of%20Penal%20Policy.pdf

Thornton Hall Project Review Group. 2011. *Report of the Thornton Hall Project Review Group*. Dublin: Department of Justice and Equality.
Tighe, M. 2015. State Pays Out to Prisoners with Slop-Out Cases. *Sunday Times*, May 17. http://www.thesundaytimes.co.uk/sto/news/ireland/News/article1557353.ece
Toland, K. 2014. *Report of the Independent Review Group on the Department and Equality*. Dublin: Department of Justice and Equality. http://www.justice.ie/en/JELR/Independent%20Review%20Accessible.pdf/Files/Independent%20Review%20Accessible.pdf
UN Human Rights Committee. 2008. *Concluding Observations in Respect of the Third Periodic Report Submitted by Ireland under Article 40 of the International Covenant on Civil and Political Rights*. CCPR/C/IRL/CO/, July 3.
Van Zyl Smit, D., and S. Snacken. 2009. *Principles of European Prison Law and Policy. Penology and Human Rights*. Oxford: Oxford University Press.
Vaughan, B., and S. Kilcommins. 2007. The Europeanisation of Human Rights and the Limits of Authoritarian Policing in Ireland. *European Journal of Criminology* 4 (4): 437–459.
———. 2008. *Terrorism, Rights and the Rule of Law: Negotiating Justice in Ireland*. Cullompton, Devon: Willan.
———. 2010. The Governance of Crime and Negotiation of Justice. *Criminology and Criminal Justice* 10 (1): 59–75.

**Claire Hamilton** is Senior Lecturer in Law at Maynooth University, Ireland.

# Best in Class? Norwegian Incarceration and the Pragmatic Production of Legitimacy

Thomas Horn and Thomas Ugelvik

## 1 Introduction: Doing Good on a Global Scale

If you are among the smallest children in your class, trying to bully the big boys is probably not a good idea. As a small country, Norway has historically seen it as in its interest to be in favour of peace and understanding between nations. Norway has backed the United Nations since its formation (the Norwegian lawyer Trygve Lie was the UN's first Secretary General from 1945 to 1953) and the country has been a firm believer in law and order in international relations. Thus, as a pure matter of realpolitik, Norway would be (and indeed is) a strong supporter of international law and international Human Rights (HR). One might

T. Horn (✉)
Schjødt Law Firm, Oslo, Norway

T. Ugelvik
Department of Criminology and Sociology of Law, University of Oslo, Oslo, Norway



T. Daems, L. Robert (eds.), *Europe in Prisons*, Palgrave Studies in Prisons and Penology, DOI 10.1007/978-3-319-62250-7_9

even say that the respect for HR is so deeply embedded in Norwegian social values that it transcends trivialities like realpolitik. Norwegians want all citizens of the world to benefit from universal HR, because HR are *good,* and Norwegians want to do and be good. And the aim of 'doing good' is in most cases self-explanatory; it needs no further justification. Critics have argued that the Norwegian political system has been dominated by such a 'regime of goodness' to the extent that all other arguments have been marginalized (Tvedt 2006).

In general, and only as a slight exaggeration, one might say that the Norwegian self-image is one based on pride in the fact that Norwegians are good at doing good. The country has been described as a humanitarian superpower. HR violations, when they happen, happen elsewhere, and as Norwegians, it is our job—our duty even—to try to intervene in a non-violent and constructive way. This chapter examines what happens when a self-styled humanitarian superpower receives external HR-based criticism. To what extent have the European Court of Human Rights (ECtHR) and the European Committee for the Prevention of Torture (CPT) influenced Norwegian prisons and Norwegian penal policy and jurisprudence? How has this criticism been understood, what has been the response and what have been the effects at the practical level—if any?

To answer these questions, we will first discuss Norwegian self-perception and attitudes toward HR and penal policy. Then, we will briefly describe the influence of the ECHR, before we will elaborate further on the influence of CPT visits. Concerning the CPT, we will discuss three specific cases that we believe will contribute to a deeper understanding of the issues raised in this chapter. All cases are not, strictly speaking, drawn from the prison estate. Two of them concern the closely related fields of immigration detention and police arrest. Finally, we will make our concluding remarks.

## 2 The Norwegian Context, Part 1: A Human Rights Superpower

The horrors of two world wars showed that citizens' rights could not be effectively protected by constitutions at the national level. This paved the way for the tremendous collective effort that was the birth of the international

Human Rights conventions. For Norwegians, HR have predominantly been seen as a matter of foreign policy and the conventions as instruments designed to protect the rights of less fortunate victims of maltreatment and atrocities elsewhere. As recently as in 1974, the Norwegian Supreme Court dismissed an HR plea by declaring that it was 'inconceivable' that Norwegian criminal procedure could be in breach with the European Convention on Human Rights (ECHR).[1] The a priori conclusion was that that sort of thing simply does not happen in Norway.

Still, over the last 20 years, the Norwegian Parliament has chosen to give HR a stronger and stronger position in Norwegian national law. In 2012, section 2 of the Norwegian Constitution was amended to state: 'The fundamental values lie within our Christian and humanitarian heritage. This Constitution should protect the democracy, rule of law and the Human Rights.' Even earlier, in 1999, the Norwegian Human Rights Act stated that core HR conventions like the ECHR should trump all other Norwegian sources of law.

Clearly, there is no doubt that the protection of HR enjoys a strong position in Norwegian law.[2] It is interesting, however, that this is the result of a development initiated by the Ministry of Foreign Affairs, not the Ministry of Justice. Norway has strong ambitions in promoting HR in other countries, and our credibility as a successful 'HR missionary' depends on a strong protection of HR at home.

The latest HR-related development was the 2014 incorporation of the main part of the ECHR into the Norwegian Constitution. The explicit goal of this manoeuvre was to 'cement' HR in the Norwegian society for the benefit of future generations. The pretext of this major constitutional amendment was the 200-years anniversary of the Constitution and the large-scale celebrations of our Norwegian self that accompanied it. The Norwegian Constitution has a strong symbolic position in itself. The national day—a grand annual celebration every 17th of May, when flag-waving Norwegians flock to the streets dressed in folk costumes—is actually a celebration of the 1814 drafting of the nation's constitution. The inclusion of HR formally into this almost sacred document was celebrated as irrefutable evidence of how strongly Norwegians believe in the HR project.

The protection of Norwegian citizens has not been the key issue in this development. The attitude has largely been that Norwegian law by default is in compliance with HR. Any discrepancies must surely have been due to a regrettable oversight, a silly glitch that should be quickly remedied.

## 3 The Norwegian Context, Part 2: Humanitarian, Welfare-Oriented Punishment

In Norwegian law, as in many other legal systems, a prison sentence is defined as a form of punishment and thus as a penalty that is supposed to be experienced as an evil by prisoners (Christie 2007). But in the Norwegian Correctional Service's policy documents, a prison sentence is also described as much more than that (MoJ 2008; Ugelvik 2011b). In the current Correctional Services white paper, a prison sentence is first and foremost described as an opportunity, a potential arena for rehabilitation and successful reintegration. A spell in prison is supposed to change prisoners in a way as to make it less likely that they will return to the institution in the future and more likely that they will choose to lead a law-abiding life upon finishing their sentence. All aspects of the everyday life in a prison are supposed to be tailored to this future goal: to create a well-oiled and harmonious society where people can live in peace and prosperity through transformation of individual offenders.

If Norwegian prisons are ambitious social engineering machines, the welfare state is supposed to be the engine. The point is, through cooperation between a complex assemblage of different welfare state agencies, policies and practices, to provide aid and give opportunities to prisoners to make them able and willing to turn their lives around and recreate themselves as productive members of society. Welfare logics and welfare state agencies are integrated parts of the operations of the Norwegian prison service. The prison system is shot through with welfare state optics, logics and policies to the degree that it might make sense to say prisons are welfare state institutions (Smith and Ugelvik 2017).

In addition to the infliction of a penalty, a prison sentence is supposed to fulfil needs and create new future options for prisoners. The Norwegian government actually believes so strongly that a prison sentence should have ambitious future goals that they have made it a guarantee. The so-called reintegration guarantee was launched by the Norwegian government in 2005. It states that any prisoner shall, when relevant, upon release be offered employment, education, a suitable housing accommodation, medical services, addiction treatment services and debt counselling. The slogan for what is called the 'seamless sentence' is that the prisoner belongs to the municipality before, during and after imprisonment (Fridhov 2013), meaning that prisoners' home municipalities—the local government running the area where they are likely to live post-release—need to consider them a part of the population for which they are responsible also during their sentence. The main goal of the guarantee is to decrease recidivism by strengthening prisoners' ability to live a law-abiding life. The guarantee provides no new legal rights, however, nor is it a guarantee in any legal sense. Rather, it is a political and inter-ministerial acknowledgement that prisoners' rights vis-à-vis the welfare state system are the responsibility of the welfare state as a whole, not just the criminal justice sector.

A vital part of the rationale of the Norwegian welfare-oriented prison system is the so-called principle of normality (Bronebakk 2012; MoJ 2008). It states that all aspects of life inside a prison should resemble life in society outside the prison walls as much as possible, with the obvious exceptions of the security and control measures that are necessary in institutions like prisons. Any deviation from this principle has to be justified explicitly. It also states that no prisoner shall serve her or his sentence under a higher-security regime than what is necessary. Differently put, one could argue that the punishment element of a prison sentence is supposed to consist solely of the deprivation of liberty for a period specified by the courts.

In practice, this is solved through the so-called importation model, the brainchild of the late and great Nils Christie (1970). This model is explicitly understood as a direct result of the principle of normality (MoJ 2008: 22). The correctional system imports services such as health care, education and cultural and social services from the external public welfare system on the other side of the wall. The prison healthcare system is thus part of the public healthcare system of Norway; the education department is part of the public school system. The prison librarian is hired by the municipality where the prison is located, and the prison library is part of a national system of public libraries. The Correctional Services are, in short, seen as a fully integrated part of the wider national welfare state system. Together with the various relevant state and municipal welfare state agencies, prisons are supposed to provide prisoners with the same level of welfare services that are available outside.

An important by-product of this model is that it can be argued that Norwegian prisoners in important ways are still included in the community outside; they are still acknowledged as citizens with important citizen's rights, even when they are serving a custodial sentence. The prison is part of the society surrounding it. The model also gives these public service institutions regular access to the prison, making the prison accountable to a wide range of potential critics on an everyday basis.

## 4 The Influence of the ECHR in Norway

To this day, there are only 40 judgments from the Court in Strasbourg that concern Norway. Only 12 of these cases are within the penal sphere; none concern prisons but rather different aspects of penal procedure according to art. 6 of the ECHR.[3] Hence, the main influence of the ECHR at the national level will be the application of ECHR decisions by Norwegian courts and other national decision makers.

The ECHR applies as part of Norwegian law. However, there can be several possible interpretations of law. As the wording of the ECHR is very vague, the influence of the Convention does to a large extent depend on the style of interpretation of law applied by the courts, as the courts are supposed to take account of both Norwegian legislation as well as the Convention. In different legal cultures, the courts could show 'judicial restraint' or be more progressive in favour of HR. Prior to the adoption of the Human Rights Act, the courts in Norway exercised a certain 'judicial restraint'. The Supreme Court held that the interpretation of the

ECHR had to be 'quite clear' in order to establish sufficient basis for trumping Norwegian national legislation. However, when the Norwegian Parliament adopted the Human Rights Act in 1999, the National Assembly made it clear that the ECHR should trump all other Norwegian legislation. Thus, since 2000, the Norwegian Supreme Court has developed a style of interpretation that is very loyal to the Strasbourg Court, seeking to apply the same method of interpretation as the ECtHR does itself.[4] This has sparked some debate about the democratic legitimacy of the Strasbourg Court. Critics have been met by the Supreme Court argument that the Human Rights Act has been adopted by Parliament itself, which is, of course, a democratically elected body.

Since the adoption of the Human Rights Act in 1999, the Norwegian Supreme Court has frequently ruled on the basis of the ECHR, and it has several times held Norwegian legislation to be in contravention with the Convention. Landmark cases that belong to the penal sphere concern, inter alia, the prohibition of double jeopardy, the right to adversarial proceedings, the presumption of innocence, the prohibition of retroactive punishment, the jury system, the reasoning of dismissals of applications for leave to appeal, the right to a lawyer, the right to trial within reasonable time and so on. However, very few Supreme Court cases concern prisons specifically,[5] and there are not many available cases from the lower courts.[6]

Does this mean that the Norwegian penal system conforms perfectly with the ECHR? Certainly, Norwegian prisoners are in many ways better off than prisoners in many other countries. However, the absence of court cases about prisoners' rights is not a sure sign of ECHR influence. A major practical problem is that it is very difficult for prisoners to get to know and understand their HR situation. Concomitantly, it may also be difficult to enforce those rights. The legal complexity involved in interpreting the Convention goes far beyond what most people can cope with. Not even public defenders know a great deal about the ECHR. Assistance from public defenders would be confined to the penal case itself, and prisoners do not normally benefit from legal aid after their court cases are over and they have started serving their sentence. To a large extent, pinpointing HR issues is left to a select group of NGOs, a few defence lawyers with a special interest in the ECHR and a handful of legal scholars.

One interesting example is the Norwegian 2014 so-called strip cell case (*glattcellesaken*). In Norway, all persons taken into police custody are placed in bare security cells. Detainees are held in solitary confinement, without even considering the need for the use of solitary confinement. The security cell placement can go on even after the prisoner is formally remanded by the court and can in extreme cases last for as long as 8 or even 10 days. In 2014, the courts held that this was in breach of art. 8 of the ECHR. This case was not initiated by a prisoner but by the Norwegian Bar Association and a few dedicated defence lawyers, on the basis of recent legal research.

Another recent high-profile case was the case where Anders Behring Breivik, the terrorist responsible for the 2011 bomb attack on an Oslo government building and mass killings at a political youth summer camp at Utøya, sued the Norwegian state because he claimed that the conditions of his imprisonment were in breach of the prohibition against inhuman and degrading treatment in art. 3. When the case came to trial, Breivik had been kept in solitary confinement in a special high-security wing for almost five years, under a very strict security regime. The district court held that the Correctional Services had not managed to make balanced and reasoned assessments of the situation and that they had failed to take into account the impact of the long-lasting solitary confinement Breivik had had to suffer. According to the court, the Correctional Services had failed to consider Breivik's mental illness, and they had also failed to consider whether a somewhat lower-security regime would be sufficient. The district court also pointed out that Breivik earlier had been subjected to total searches as a daily routine even when he had not been seeing anybody, although this practice had ended at the time of trial. Furthermore, for the first year of imprisonment, Breivik was awoken every 30 minutes every night because officers had to check that he was still alive. The few visits Breivik did receive (mainly from his lawyer and a visiting priest) happened through a security glass window, allowing no possibility for direct human contact. This arrangement was kept in place two years after the psychiatrist responsible for risk assessment had found that there was no need to continue. In contrast to what national and international newspaper headlines might lead one to believe, the essence of Breivik's case against Norway is not about the use of PlayStation 4 or the quality of prepared meals.

The district court ruling partially in favour of Breivik was a shock for Norwegian society. No doubt, this case has put the Norwegian society on severe tests. But with regard to the rule of law and the respect for HR, both the public and the courts have certainly passed the test; the consensus seems to be that human rights apply to *all* humans and that even someone like Breivik should have access to the courts. Also, on the part of the Norwegian society, if not on the part of Breivik himself, the proceedings took place with dignity and were based on an open and transparent procedure. As for the Correctional Services, however, it remains to be seen whether they can be said to have been sufficiently aware of the HR challenges in this difficult case. The Norwegian government has filed an appeal, and even if the Correctional Services might be rightfully criticized for some aspects of the security approach in the Breivik case, it is not obvious that the result will be that the court of appeal will agree that the regime Breivik is being held under constitutes a breach of art. 3.

Do Norwegian authorities remedy breaches of the ECHR? Disregarding a judgment from the ECtHR itself would indeed be 'unconceivable' (even though one serving minister once complained that the Strasbourg Court panel of judges included a judge from Azerbaijan, implying that someone from that part of the world could hardly teach a Norwegian anything about HR). If a Norwegian court has found that Norwegian authorities act in breach of the ECHR, one would also certainly expect the government to immediately remedy the situation. In real life, however, one could perhaps fruitfully distinguish between HR breaches that can be rightly seen as nothing more than mishaps due to the circumstances of the individual case that can be easily remedied and more serious systematic breaches. When ECHR breaches occur on a systematic basis—for example, due to flaws of the legislation itself, or due to Norwegian tradition or culture—remedying the situation will be much more difficult. One example is the above-mentioned 'strip cell case', which did in fact *not* lead to the abolishment of systematic use of police custody in breach of art. 8 of the ECHR. We elaborate on this below.

Also, different branches of government are used to operate on the basis of their own rules and their own way of thinking. Again, the Breivik case is a good example: Following the district court's ruling, the Correctional Services were asked if they would consider abolishing the glass partition wall if the wall was unnecessary and constituted a breach of art. 3. The prison authorities plainly rejected this, on the ground that the wall could only be abolished if the Prison Act was amended. Thus, the Correctional Services revealed that they had not at all grasped the essential point about the Norwegian Human Rights Act adopted by Parliament, incorporating the ECHR as Norwegian law trumping all other Norwegian legislation. Business as usual is a powerful way of thinking.

Moving from the ECHR to the UN Convention on the Rights of the Child (UNCRC), we have recently seen some impact on Norwegian prisons. According to art. 3 of the UNCRC, the best interests of the child shall always be a primary consideration. This has led the Supreme Court to significantly lower the threshold for use of community service as an alternative to prison for minor offenders.[7] Parliament has also abolished the use of some sorts of solitary confinement for underage prisoners.[8] The number of children being placed in police strip cells has also significantly reduced in recent years, due to pressure from NGOs and the Norwegian National Ombudsman for Children. On the other hand, children being put in immigration detention seems increasingly to be an issue. For unaccompanied minors, the Police Immigration Service has decided to use the minimum age of criminal responsibility found in the penal law as a guideline; unaccompanied minors under the age of 15 will not be detained in the high-security Police Aliens Holding Centre at Trandum. Younger children accompanying their parents, however, can be held at Trandum along with their parents.

## 5 The Influence of the CPT in Norway

There is no doubt that Norwegian authorities are eager to cooperate with the CPT. Even if the CPT is a preventive body, and not a court of law, HR monitoring bodies are seen as vital for the improvement of the HR situation abroad. The various relevant government agencies certainly muster their senior officials when the committee comes calling. It seems to be very important to avoid CPT criticism. It is thus fair to say that it was quite an unexpected blow to the Norwegian self-esteem, when the CPT in 1993 concluded its first inspection by criticizing Norway on several points. Since then, the use of police custody, the use of solitary confinement, the treatment of mentally ill prisoners and the Police Aliens Holding Centre have repeatedly been put under critical CPT scrutiny. How does the Norwegian government react to critical reports from the CPT? In the following, we briefly consider three cases: the prison-like Police Aliens Holding Centre (Norway's single high-security immigration detention centre), the use of solitary confinement for remand prisoners as well as the above-mentioned case of the pre-trial use of strip cells.

The Police Aliens Holding Centre at Trandum is Norway's only high-security immigration detention centre. It is conveniently located about 40 minutes' drive north of Oslo and right next door to Norway's main international airport. Trandum built two new cellblocks in 2012 and 2013, which meant that it could finally discontinue the use of the old and run-down army barrack that it had, up to that point, used to house detainees. The facilities were explicitly taken up to 'the Norwegian prison standards', meaning bright and well-furnished single occupancy cells with en-suite bathrooms in the style that has made Norwegian prisons famous worldwide for being exceptionally decent and humane institutions (Pratt 2008a, b; Pratt and Eriksson 2012).[9] In addition to six wings for adult men, Trandum has smaller wings for adult women, families travelling together and unaccompanied minors. It also has two separate activity wings with a library, game rooms, two gymnasiums and various smaller exercise rooms. The current capacity is 137 detainees, but this will increase in the near future, as new wings will open in 2016.

Although Trandum is not legally a prison, it does look like one in many ways. Detainees are strip-searched and required to squat naked on a mirror on the floor upon entering the institution and following every visit. Officers at Trandum can arm themselves with truncheons when needed, and they wear uniforms resembling prison officers' garb. The high fences surrounding the institutions are adorned with a number of CCTV cameras and topped with razor wire. The main difference between Trandum and a regular Norwegian prison is the legal status of the people incarcerated there. Detainees at Trandum, unlike prisoners, have committed no crime in the classical sense; they have violated the Immigration

Act, not the Penal Code, and are thus held at Trandum not as a punishment but as a precautionary and practical administrative measure. Unlike the goal of a Norwegian prison, then, the point of Trandum is not to rehabilitate people and bring them back into society but to make deportation as efficient as possible.

Trandum has been a controversial institution in the eyes of the Norwegian public since its opening. It lacks the strong legitimacy foundation the Norwegian prison system rests on. Wasvik (2015) summarizes the public sphere criticism of Trandum since its opening. She described a number of cases where the detention centre has received critical media attention, like the 2007 suicide in the security wing toilet, the coverage of the 2014 'child detainee scandal' where the detention of children was called unconstitutional by critics and the 2011 so-called Amelie case, where a young woman was detained and deported to Russia in the middle of what can only be described as a media storm (Ugelvik 2013). Throughout its brief history, Trandum has been visited twice by the CPT, in 2005 and in 2011. Both visits happened when detainees still occupied the old army buildings. Nevertheless, Trandum officials still scrambled to engage with the criticism that was voiced within the limits of the old and run-down buildings.

The first CPT visit to Trandum happened in 2005 (CPT/Inf(2006)14). The delegates noted that although most detainees spent only a relatively short time at Trandum—most detainees were released in a matter of days—a minority ended up spending longer; in one extreme case, a detainee had spent more than a year at the centre. The report points to problems of overcrowding, especially in the men's wing, where up to eight people were detained in bedrooms that were only very sparsely furnished. It also questioned the amount of training that Trandum officers—at that time hired through a private security company—received. Finally, the CPT also concluded that the two special bare security cells at Trandum were unsuitable for detention of any kind because they lacked natural lighting and a calling/communications system.

As criticism goes, the issues raised by the CPT were all of a very concrete and practical nature, and Trandum officials did not waste time engaging with the recommendations. According to the Norwegian government's response document (CPT/Inf(2006)34), they immediately took the capacity of the bedrooms in the men's wing down to six detainees and soon further down to four. It discontinued the use of the bare security cells, until windows and a calling system could be introduced. The contract with the security company was also terminated; officers were rehired as state employees and given more appropriate training. Nowadays, they are formally civilians employed in the police service. Requirements include a minimum of three years secondary education and a four-week course at the Norwegian Correctional Services College. Critics have argued that this still is not an adequate background for personnel-performing police authority and that this practice is watering down the important principle of the police being the only legitimate enforcer of violence. The Police Immigration Service has countered this criticism by arguing that the transport attendants have only limited authority and that they have received adequate training. The arrangement was seen as satisfactory in the 2011 CPT report.

The CPT representatives revisiting Trandum in 2011 were impressed by the wide range of activities available for detainees (CPT/Inf(2011)33). By and large, the institution was seen as adequate for its purpose, at least for the majority of detainees whose stay at Trandum is relatively brief. An issue not really addressed by the CPT was the lack of meaningful daytime activities for the minority of detainees who for some reason end up staying in detention for longer periods. The CPT did voice a concern about the lack of on-site nursing staff. At the time, a doctor visited the centre three afternoons per week, but there was no permanent medical staff presence to perform a screening of new arrivals.

The history of Trandum can be described as the history of an institution that rapidly and proudly has corrected the flaws CPT has pointed to. Following the 2011 visit, Trandum soon hired a permanent full-time nurse. Again, the CPT visit became an opportunity to show that HR issues are seen as very important. Every flaw corrected may be used to further the self-image of an institution (and a government) that takes HR very seriously indeed. Trandum was recently visited by the National Preventive Mechanism against Torture and Ill-treatment.[10] The visit resulted in a new wave of criticism (Sivilombudsmannen 2015). Trandum was said to, among other things, be unsuited for children, despite efforts made by the institution to make the family wing more child friendly. It remains to be seen whether Trandum will continue its tradition of making quick changes following such criticism.

The second case concerns the use of solitary confinement for remand prisoners, an ongoing issue since the first CPT inspection in Norway in 1993.[11] HR standards make it clear that solitary confinement can only be used when 'strictly necessary' and as 'a last resort'. Nevertheless, solitary confinement for remand prisoners has been in extensive use in all Scandinavian countries and has even been termed by international scholars as 'a peculiar Scandinavian phenomenon' (Evans and Morgan 1998; Morgan and Evans 2002). Prior to 2002, approximately 40 % of all remand prisoners in Norway were subjected to solitary confinement. Still, even under heavy criticism from CPT, the Norwegian authorities seemed reluctant to acknowledge the problem (see inter alia CPT/Inf(98)3). But in 2002, the Act on Criminal Procedure was amended. The rate dropped to approximately 15 % only by stating that solitary confinement should be decided by a court order. This was of course a big leap forward, but the rate is still high in an international perspective, and international bodies have called for further reductions.[12] As Denmark has managed to all but end the use of solitary confinement for remand prisoners, such reductions should be quite possible.[13]

However, again the authorities have chosen to respond by pragmatism rather than by taking a principled approach. Receiving further CPT criticism, the authorities have reminded the prosecutors and the courts that solitary confinement should only be used when strictly necessary but without contemplating to incorporate this important principle in the Act on Criminal Procedure. Rather, in conformity with the general tendency to opt for pragmatic solutions and to avoid rules of principle, the legislator has left the courts with almost unlimited discretionary powers, and a mere risk of collusion is sufficient to order solitary confinement. Thus, the legislator trusts that judges will always find the best solution, even in situations involving important issues of principle and even if the judges in cases like this often have very limited possibilities to make accurate predictions on the risk of collusion. No wonder then, that business as usual prevails.

The third case we will discuss is the Norwegian use of solitary confinement and police 'strip cells' for remand prisoners. The use of police strip cells has been a constant issue for HR monitoring bodies like the CPT and the Committee Against Torture (CAT) over the last 20 years. Every time Norwegian authorities are criticized by such bodies, as they were in 2011 when CPT recommended putting an end to this practice, and again in 2012 when CAT recommended that Norway 'should abolish' it, the external criticism sparks fierce public debate in Norway. The Norwegian government does acknowledge that the systematic use of strip cells for all persons detained by the police is 'bad' and should be stopped—but only in principle. Even if HR is a matter of principle, according to Norwegian mentality, problems should not be solved on the basis of principles but rather by trustworthy officials on the basis of pragmatic considerations in each and every case. Hence, during the last 20 years, the Norwegian response has always been the same; the use of strip cells is regrettable but necessary on a temporary basis due to a lack of ordinary prison cells. Therefore, a practice which is rooted in more than a century of police history is only 'temporary'; this regrettable practice will stop once a new prison is built, once a temporary peak of criminal activity has receded and so on. Even though adhering to HR principles and taking criticism by monitoring bodies like the CPT seriously, it seems that HR should not force Norway to abandon its essential pragmatism for the sake of abstract principles.

The Statute on Police Detention Cells illustrates this very well. This Statute was adopted in 2006, as a direct response to critical reports from HR monitoring bodies. Surprisingly, section 3.1 clearly states that police detention cells (strip cells) should not be used for periods exceeding 48 hours. Such a rule would of course be a clear-cut principled approach in line with the international recommendations. However, the statute goes on to say that the rule does not apply if a timely transfer to an ordinary prison 'is not possible due to practical reasons', meaning that no ordinary prison cells are available. Hence, the principled approach does only serve as façade legitimation and is totally undermined and trumped by the pragmatic approach. Again, pragmatism seems to be the first principle.

One could argue that recommendations from the CPT are not legally binding and cannot be compared to obligations under the ECHR. Nevertheless, as mentioned above, the Norwegian courts have declared the systematic use of solitary confinement in police strip cells to be in breach of art. 8 of the ECHR. But even so, Parliament turned down a proposal for an absolute time limit of 48 hours, effectively meaning that the statutory reservation that longer periods are allowed due to 'practical reasons' does still apply.[14] Pragmatism won the day once again, as Parliament stated that the problem would hopefully disappear if more ordinary prison cells were built, that the police should try to reduce the number of breaches and also try to make the strip cell experience a little more pleasant. The reason was pragmatic: More remand prisoners in ordinary prisons would contravene the goal of reducing the time that convicted criminals have to wait to serve their sentences. But at this point, the Norwegian Parliament, being used to pragmatic considerations, failed to acknowledge that rights under the ECHR cannot be subject to pragmatism. The Constitution takes the principled approach, and Parliament is not free to introduce or uphold legislation that is in breach of the ECHR.[15] In real life, however, pragmatism is powerful, and the ECHR is still violated on a systematic basis.[16]

## 6 Concluding Remarks: Trust in a Trustworthy Government?

So why did the Norwegian Parliament not acknowledge that the use of solitary confinement in police strip cells had to be abolished, as a matter of principle? One way of understanding this decision could be that Norwegians are not used to think of Norwegian authorities as HR violators. Instead, we place great trust in our authorities; Norway is routinely at or close to the top of 'trust in government' surveys. The composition of the National Monitoring Board for Police Cells may be an illustration. This board was established in 2006 as a consequence of the critical reports from the various HR bodies. Interestingly, it was composed of one senior official in the Police Directorate and one representative of the public prosecutor. Who watches the watchmen?

Another, related, perspective would be to consider the fact that Norwegians place great trust in their own traditions and certain

Norwegian ways of doing things. Great HR ambitions on behalf of the rest of the globe, combined with a self-perception as 'best in class', do not create an atmosphere where self-critical questions thrive. Once again the police detention cells are illustrative: The Norwegian police and Norwegian authorities have had to deal with HR monitoring bodies criticizing Norwegian police detention cells for the last 20 years. In spite of this, in 2014, the Police Directorate made a brand new manual for the design and construction of police detention cells without even considering whether the building of these cells would raise HR issues that ought to be considered. A visual example is that the manual minutely described how every holding facility should be equipped with a metal bar meant for handcuffing the detainees to the wall, even though both the CPT and the National Police Detention Monitoring Board had repeatedly recommended that such metal bars should be removed.

As self-confessed HR missionaries, it is more than a little awkward to be forced to acknowledge that sometimes there is something rotten even in the Kingdom of Norway. Being criticized by HR bodies somehow seems to be at odds with Norwegian self-perception as 'best in class'. HR values are deeply embedded in the Norwegian society. HR could even be seen as part of what constitutes the self-perception of the Norwegian nation. However, the adherence to HR is kept at a rather abstract level. For Norwegians, HR-related questions are primarily a matter for the Department of Foreign Affairs. The natural state of mind would be that it goes without saying that how we do things in Norway is in line with HR and that we do not easily manage to view ourselves from the outside.

Due to high ambitions in the HR sphere, as well as the strong humanistic foundation of the penal system, the general HR situation in Norwegian prisons is quite good. However, the Norwegian system places great trust in the authorities, leaving considerable room for discretion. Procedural systems and formal complaint mechanisms are sparse, the ideal being that decisions are best made on a pragmatic basis by the officer on the spot. It can be argued that there is a tension between this pragmatic approach and the principled approach establishing limits that cannot be crossed that HR are built on.

This tension is probably most easily solved in cases like Trandum Aliens Holding Centre, where many problems were addressed on a practical ad hoc basis. In such cases, criticism from monitoring bodies like CPT has the greatest potential to provoke change in favour of HR. When the CPT points to a lack of natural lighting, a new window can be installed within days. The lack of light may easily be written off as a regrettable glitch in an otherwise decent and humane system, fortifying the HR superpower self-image in the process: We may not be absolutely perfect, but we take our problems seriously and correct them quickly.

The police detention strip cells point at a more profound systematic problem. Norwegian authorities are still likely to hang on to the pragmatic approach, weighing HR against pragmatic considerations according to the ordinary Norwegian way of thinking, even where the courts have stated that the practice is in contravention with the ECHR.

In cases like this, the HR approach would probably benefit from a more continuous HR dialogue, not only at the international level (with CPT and CAT as interlocutors) but also at the national level. Such a dialogue would reach much farther than the standard 'problem identified, problem solved' approach favoured by the Norwegian government. This is in line with the international trend focusing on National HR Institutions and National Preventive Mechanisms, like the NPMs under OPCAT. A major task for the new Norwegian National Institution for HR is to demand that national authorities, like the Department of Justice, enter into a responsible dialogue to reduce the possibility that the more principled HR issues are simply ignored as 'not practical'.

## Notes

1. Supreme Court verdict, Rt. 1974 p. 935.
2. However, it did spark some debate when one legal scholar, employing a religious imagery, wrote that Norwegian law is 'confessing' to the Human Rights, cf. Strand (2009) and E. Smith (2011a).
3. Two cases concerning the right to adversarial proceedings (*Botten v. Norway*, App. No. 16206/90, 19 February 1996; *Kaste and Mathiesen v. Norway*, App. No. 18885/04 and 21166/04, 9 November 2006—both

violations). One case concerning the right to trial within reasonable time (*Beck v. Norway*, App. No. 26390/95, 26 June 2001—no violation). Six cases concerning the presumption of innocence (*Hammern v. Norway*, App. No. 30287/96, 11 February 2003; *O. v. Norway*, App. No. 29327/95, 11 February 2003; *Ringvold v. Norway*, App. No. 34964/97, 11 February 2003; *Y. v. Norway*, App. No. 56568/00, 11 February 2003; *Orr v. Norway*, App. No. 31283/04, 15 May 2008; *N.A. v. Norway*, App. No. 27473/11, 18 December 2014—four violations, two non-violations). Three cases concerning art. 6 and the impartiality of judges (*Ekeberg and others v. Norway*, App. No. 11106/04, 11108/04, 11116/04, 11311/04 and 13276/04, 31 July 2007; *Kristiansen v. Norway*, App. No. 1176/10, 17 December 2015; *Procedo Capital Corporation v. Norway*, App. No. 3338/05, 24 September 2009—two violations, one non-violation).

4. Supreme Court decision Rt. 2000s. 996.
5. Supreme Court decisions: Rt. 2003s. 1100—disciplinary sanctions in prison not a violation of double jeopardy rule in ECHR P7-4. Rt 2005 s. 140—conditions in high-security wing not a violation of art. 3. Rt. 2011s. 347—retroactive amendments of law concerning conditional release no violation of art. 7. Rt. 2015s. 921—standard of evidence concerning decision transferring prisoner from an open prison to a security prison, no violation of art. 6.
6. Published decisions: TOSLO-2002-1580—placement in high-security wing not a violation of art. 3. TTRON-2006-148273, no violation of art. 8 and right to family. LG-2007-83941, disciplinary sanctions in prison not a violation of double jeopardy rule in ECHR P7-4.
7. Court decision Rt. 2010s. 1313.
8. Act on Penal Procedure § 186a.
9. The Scandinavian/Nordic exceptionalism thesis has been discussed extensively, see inter alia Andersson (2011), Barker (2012), Bruhn et al. (2011), Johnsen and Granheim (2011), Mathiesen (2011), Pratt and Eriksson (2011), Shammas (2014), P.S. Smith (2011b), Ugelvik and Ugelvik (2013) and Ugelvik (2011a). Even the critics would usually agree that newly built Norwegian prisons are comparatively good, materially speaking.
10. The Norwegian National Preventive Mechanism against Torture and Ill-treatment was established in 2013 as a consequence of Norway finally adopting the Optional Protocol (OPCAT) to the UN Convention

Against Torture (CAT). The Preventive Mechanism ('*Forebyggingsenheten*') is part of the Norwegian Ombudsman for civil affairs. As the ombudsman's activity has always been judicial and reactive (reacting on complaints). Taking on a new role as a preventive non-judicial mechanism therefore posed a challenge. But being aware of this new mission, and organizing the preventive mechanism as a separate unit within the ombudsman's office, the preventive mechanism has proved itself to be a great success, producing thorough inspection reports often creating a basis for public debate.

11. Cf CPT/Inf(94)11, CPT/Inf(97)11, CPT/Inf(2000)15, CPT/Inf(2006)14. For a discussion of the CPT's findings on this topic for its 2011visit to Norway (CPT/Inf(2011)33), see also in extenso Horn (2017: 124).
12. CPT/Inf(2006)14, Human Rights Committee (2006), Committee Against Torture (2008), Working Group on Arbitrary Detention (2007), Human Rights Committee (2011), Committee Against Torture (2012). The statistics that were discussed with respect to the 2011visit (CPT/Inf(2011)33) are commented upon in Horn (2017: 124).
13. In 2014, only 36 remand prisoners (0.7 %) were subjected to solitary confinement in Denmark, cf. letter from the Danish General Prosecutor to the Department of justice of 9 July 2015.
14. Parliament decision, 10 June 2014, cf. Innst. 165L (2013–2014).
15. Cf inter alia the Norwegian Constitution section 92.
16. Cf the annual report for 2015 of the National Institution for Human Rights (an entity established by the Parliament itself and reporting directly to Parliament) as well as inter alia the report from the National Preventative body under OPCAT (cf. note 10) concerning the police detention cells in Bergen (May 2016).

## Literature

Andersson, R. 2011. A Blessing in Disguise: Attention Deficit Hyperactivity Disorder Diagnosis and Swedish Correctional Treatment Policy in the Twenty-First Century. In *Penal Exceptionalism? Nordic Prison Policy and Practice*, ed. T. Ugelvik and J. Dullum. London: Routledge.

Barker, V. 2012. Nordic Exceptionalism Revisited: Explaining the Paradox of a Janus-Faced Penal Regime. *Theoretical Criminology* 17 (1): 5–25.

Bronebakk, K.B. 2012. Hvis Det Var Mitt Barn. In *Festskrift Til Inger Marie Fridhov*, ed. Y. Hammerlin and B. Johnsen. Oslo: KRUS.

Bruhn, A., O. Lindberg, and P.-Å. Nylander. 2011. A Harsher Prison Climate and a Cultural Heritage Working Against It: Subcultural Divisions Among Prison Officers. In *Penal Exceptionalism? Nordic Prison Policy and Practice*, ed. T. Ugelvik and J. Dullum. London: Routledge.

Christie, N. 1970. Modeller for Fengselsorganisasjonen. In *I Stedet for Fengsel*, ed. R. Østensen. Oslo: Pax.

———. 2007. *Limits to Pain*. Eugene: Wipf & Stock.

Committee Against Torture. 2008. *Consideration of Reports Submitted by States Parties Under Article 19 of the Convention. Conclusions and Recommendations of the Committee Against Torture, Norway*. CAT/C/NOR/CO/5, February 5.

———. 2012. *Concluding Observations on the Combined Sixth and Seventh Periodic Reports of Norway, Adopted by the Committee at Its Forty-Ninth Session (29 October to 23 November 2012)*. CAT/C/NOR/CO/6–7, December 13.

Evans, M.D., and R. Morgan. 1998. *Preventing Torture. A Study of the European Convention for the Prevention of Torture and Inhuman or Degrading Treatment or Punishment*. Oxford: Clarendon Press.

Fridhov, I.M. 2013. Norge: Tilbakeføringsgarantien Og Forvaltningssamarbeid. In *Løsladelse: Planlægning Og Samarbejde I Danmark, Norge Og Sverige*, ed. A. Storgaard. Aarhus: Nordisk Samarbejdsråd for Kriminologi.

Horn, T. 2017. *Fullstendig isolasjon ved risiko for bevisforspillelse: Rettspolitiske vurderinger*. Bergen: Fagbokforlaget.

Human Rights Committee. 2006. *Consideration of Reports Submitted by States Parties Under Article 40 of the Covenant. Concluding Observations of the Human Rights Committee, Norway*. CCPR/C/NOR/CO/5, April 25.

———. 2011. *Consideration of Reports Submitted by States Parties Under Article 40 of the Covenant. Concluding Observations of the Human Rights Committee, Norway*. CCPR/C/NOR/CO/6, November 18.

Johnsen, B., and P.K. Granheim. 2011. Prison Size and the Quality of Life in Norwegian Closed Prisons in Late Modernity. In *Penal Exceptionalism? Nordic Prison Policy and Practice*, ed. T. Ugelvik and J. Dullum. London: Routledge.

Mathiesen, T. 2011. Scandinavian Exceptionalism in Penal Matters: Reality or Wishful Thinking? In *Penal Exceptionalism? Nordic Prison Policy and Practice*, ed. T. Ugelvik and J. Dullum. London: Routledge.

MoJ. 2008. *Straff Som Virker – Mindre Kriminalitet – Tryggere Samfunn. St.meld. nr. 37 (2007–2008)*. Oslo: Ministry of Justice and the Police.

Morgan, R., and M. Evans. 2002. *Combating Torture in Europe. The Work and Standards of the European Committee for the Prevention of Torture*. Strasbourg: Council of Europe Publishing.

Pratt, J. 2008a. Scandinavian Exceptionalism in an Era of Penal Excess, Part I: The Nature and Roots of Scandinavian Exceptionalism. *British Journal of Criminology* 48 (2): 119–137.

———. 2008b. Scandinavian Exceptionalism in an Era of Penal Excess, Part II: Does Scandinavian Exceptionalism Have a Future? *British Journal of Criminology* 48 (3): 275–292.

Pratt, J., and A. Eriksson. 2011. In Defence of Scandinavian Exceptionalism. In *Penal Exceptionalism? Nordic Prison Policy and Practice*, ed. T. Ugelvik and J. Dullum. London: Routledge.

———. 2012. *Contrasts in Punishment: An Explanation of Anglophone Excess and Nordic Exceptionalism*. London: Routledge.

Shammas, V.L. 2014. The Pains of Freedom: Assessing the Ambiguity of Scandinavian Penal Exceptionalism on Norway's Prison Island. *Punishment and Society* 16 (1): 104–123.

Sivilombudsmannen. 2015. *Besøksrapport: Politiets utlendingsinternat på Trandum 19–21 mai 2015*. Oslo: Sivilombudsmannen.

Smith, E. 2011a. Vil de som er imot, rekke opp hånden? Om menneskerettigheter, (annen) rett og demokrati. *Nytt Norsk Tidsskrift*, 49–60.

Smith, P.S. 2011b. A Critical Look at Scandinavian Exceptionalism: Welfare State Theories, Penal Populism, and Prison Conditions in Denmark and Scandinavia. In *Penal Exceptionalism? Nordic Prison Policy and Practice*, ed. T. Ugelvik and J. Dullum. London: Routledge.

Smith, P.S., and T. Ugelvik. 2017. Introduction: Punishment, Welfare and Prison History in Scandinavia. In *Scandinavian Penal History, Culture and Prison Practice: Embraces by the Welfare State?* ed. P.S. Smith and T. Ugelvik. London: Palgrave Macmillan.

Strand, V.B. 2009. Forskjellsbehandling på grunn av religion og livssyn ved ansettelser i tros- og livssynssamfunn. In *Arbeid og rett. Festskrift til Henning Jakhellns 70-årsdag*, ed. V.B. Strand and H. Aune. Oslo: Cappelen Damm Akademisk.

Tvedt, T. 2006. Utviklingshjelp, Utenrikspolitikk Og Den Norske Modellen. *Historisk tidsskrift* 85 (1): 59–85.

Ugelvik, T. 2011a. The Dark Side of a Culture of Equality: Reimagining Communities in a Norwegian Remand Prison. In *Penal exceptionalism?*

*Nordic prison policy and practice*, ed. T. Ugelvik and J. Dullum. London: Routledge.
———. 2011b. Hva Er Et Fengsel?: En Analyse Av Manualen Til En Sosial Teknologi. *Retfærd* 34 (1): 85–100.
———. 2013. Hvem Er Maria Amelie? Fortellinger Om Ulovlighet. In *Krimmigrasjon? Den Nye Kontrollen Av De Fremmede*, ed. N.B. Johansen, T. Ugelvik, and K.F. Aas. Oslo: Universitetsforlaget.
Ugelvik, S., and T. Ugelvik. 2013. Immigration Control in Ultima Thule: Detention and Exclusion, Norwegian Style. *European Journal of Criminology* 10 (6): 709–724.
Wasvik, M. 2015. Trandum Utlendingsinternat: En Historie Om Overgrep Og Skandaler. *Radikal Portal.* http://radikalportal.no/2015/04/22/trandum-utlendingsinternat-og-historien-om-overgrep-og-skandaler/. Accessed 25 Aug 2016.
Working Group on Arbitrary Detention. 2007. *Report of the Working Group on Arbitrary Detention, Addendum, Mission to Norway*. A/HRC/7/4/Add.2, October 11.

**Thomas Horn** is a lawyer and partner at Schjødt Law Firm in Oslo, Norway.

**Thomas Ugelvik** is Professor at the Department of Criminology and Sociology of Law at the University of Oslo, Norway.

# European Prison Policy and Spanish Prison Practices: Understanding Confluences and Gaps

José Cid and Ariadna Andreu

## 1 Introduction

Following van Zyl Smit and Snacken (2009), we perceive European prison policy (EPP, hereafter) as a body of principles that may be derived from different sources, in particular: (a) the judgments of the European Court of Human Rights (ECtHR, hereafter); (b) the recommendations on penal matters of the Committee of Ministers of the Council of Europe; (c) the reports of the European Committee for the Prevention of Torture and Inhuman or Degrading Treatment or

The research for this chapter has been funded by the Spanish Ministry of Economy and Competitiveness (Project 'Imprisonment and Recidivism' ref. DER2014-55315-P) and by the Catalan Government (AGAUR) (Project: 'Research Group on Desistance and Reentry', ref. 2014SGR1481). We are grateful to Mr. Javier Nistal (from the General Spanish Administration of Prisons) and Ms. Eulalia Luque (from the Catalan Administration of Prisons) for making unpublished data available and to the editors of this book for their insightful comments to a draft version of this chapter.

J. Cid (✉) • A. Andreu
University of Barcelona, Barcelona, Spain





T. Daems, L. Robert (eds.), *Europe in Prisons*, Palgrave Studies in Prisons and Penology, DOI 10.1007/978-3-319-62250-7_10

Punishment (CPT, hereafter); and (d) the framework decisions of the European Union concerning penal matters, in particular those related to the mutual recognition of sentences.[1]

We believe there are three main principles that are fundamental to the development of EPP: first, the limitation of the use of imprisonment (i.e. alternatives to imprisonment should be the normal sanction to a criminal offence and therefore imprisonment should only be used as a last resort and, when used, reduced to a reasonable length); second, normalization of prison life (i.e. the rights and quality of life of imprisoned persons should approximate as close as possible to the rights and quality of life enjoyed by citizens in the free society); and third, reintegration as a principal aim of imprisonment (i.e. prisoners should be able to participate in rehabilitation programs during their prison time and be assisted on their way to a successful transition to the community).

This chapter aims to analyze the influence of EPP on Spanish prison practice[2] since the start of the democratic period (since 1978) or, in case there has been no or only a limited impact in practice, to flesh out the reasons for this lack of influence. The chapter will be divided in three sections, each section focusing on one of the three principles that we just mentioned. These sections will be structured as follows: first, we will define the principle; then we will introduce and discuss criteria which will enable us to assess its influence on Spanish practice. In the final section of the chapter, we will offer a general conclusion about the confluences and gaps between EPP and Spanish prison practices.

# 2 Limitations of the Use of Imprisonment

## 2.1 Definition of the Principle

The principle of imprisonment as a last resort has been established in EPP at least since 1965 when it was stated that imprisonment should only be imposed when it is needed to achieve the aims of punishment.[3] This principle has been justified both in terms of rehabilitation, that is, imprisonment is only justifiable when no other sentence may achieve the aim of rehabilitation,[4] and proportionality—imprisonment is only justifiable when the seriousness of the offence makes no other sanction as appropriate.[5] The principle has been most clearly formulated in the 2006 European Prison Rules (EPR, hereafter): 'No one shall be deprived of liberty save as a measure of last resort.'[6] Imprisonment should be an exceptional answer not only because it deprives the person of a fundamental right[7] but also because it involves other deprivations for prisoners and their families;[8] it produces adverse effects on rehabilitation[9] and it has a high economic cost.[10]

Alternatives to imprisonment should be the normal response to a criminal offence because they are able to accomplish the aims of punishment: they may offer a proportional response to a criminal offence[11]; when they attend to the risks and needs of the offender, they are appropriate to protect the community[12]; they may be conducive to the rehabilitation of the offender when they attend to the criminogenic needs and desistance factors[13]; and they may promote the responsibility of the offender to the community and to the victim.[14] Alternatives should also be possible at the pre-trial stage; indeed, pre-trial detention should also be considered as an exceptional response.[15]

When imprisonment is considered to be the right sentence for the offender and the offence, then the length of imprisonment should be as short as possible in order to avoid long terms of imprisonment. In a 1992 Recommendation, this is formulated as follows: 'Where a custodial sentence on this ground is held to be justified, that sentence should be no longer than is appropriate for the offence(s) of which the person is convicted.'[16] The 1999 Recommendation on prison overcrowding adds the following: 'Efforts should be made to reduce recourse to sentences involving long imprisonment, which place a heavy burden on the prison system.'[17] Furthermore, in the execution of the prison sentences, parole should be used as an early release mechanism: 'Parole should be regarded as one of the most effective and constructive measures, which not only reduces the length of imprisonment but also contributes substantially to a planned return to the community.'[18]

However, as van Zyl Smit and Snacken (2009) argue, this preference for a reductionist position, as it is supported by various European Recommendations mentioned above, needs to be matched by a similar orientation at the level of the case law of the ECtHR. Only then will it be possible to conclude that '…the principle that imprisonment should be used only as a last resort is an integral part of the human rights framework that underpins the European prison law and policy' (van Zyl Smit and Snacken 2009: 359).

## 2.2 Evolution of the Use of Imprisonment in Spain During the Democratic Period

EPP seems to give a clear message to European states that they should strive toward reducing the use of imprisonment as much as possible. In order to test to what extent Spain has followed this guidance, it is useful to present data on the evolution of imprisonment during the democratic period[19] and to offer some explanation (Fig. 1).

There are four periods in the evolution of imprisonment (for the first three periods, see Cid 2008; Cid and Larrauri 2009).

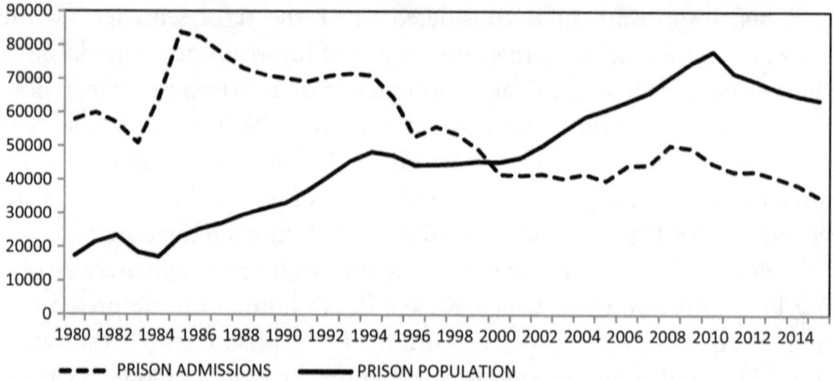


**Fig. 1** Prison admissions and average prison population (1980–2015). Own elaboration. Sources: Dirección General de Instituciones Penitenciarias (Spain: General State Administration) and Direcció General de Serveis Penitenciaris i Rehabilitació (Catalonia). For some years with no information in the official publications, the numbers were made available to the authors by the two administrations

### 2.2.1 Increase of Rates of Imprisonment in a Context of High Rates of Prison Admissions (1980–1994)

During the 1980s, Spain was confronted with an important increase in crime and this produced a big pressure on the prison system. A high level of admissions per year, mainly of pre-trial prisoners (69,000 entries per year on average), resulted in an increase of the average prison population. It is in this context that Spain introduced in 1987 for the first time a sentence of probation for drug-addicted offenders in its legislation. The new law offered judges the opportunity to suspend prison sentences if the offender agreed to follow treatment to overcome his or her drug addiction.

### 2.2.2 Stability of Rates of Imprisonment in a Context of a Decreasing Trend in Prison Admissions (1995–2001)

During this second period, the number of admissions to prison per year decreased considerably (51,000 per year on average) and the prison population stabilized. There are two explanations for this reduction in prison admissions.

First, the case law of the Constitutional Court required a rigorous standard to impose pre-trial detention which led to less use of pre-trial detention by judges. The code of Criminal Procedure that Spain adopted in the period of the transition to democracy did not establish clear safeguards to limit the use of remand prison by judges. Since its creation in 1980, the Constitutional Court made an interpretation of the constitutional guarantees to impose pre-trial detention that followed the case law of the ECtHR (De la Quadra-Salcedo 2013). The leading decision arrived in 1995 when the Court established that pre-trial detention is only constitutionally acceptable in order to assure the presence of the defendant at trial, to protect evidence or to prevent new crimes.[20] Although other factors were also relevant, Fig. 2 shows that pre-trial detention decreased in the following years.

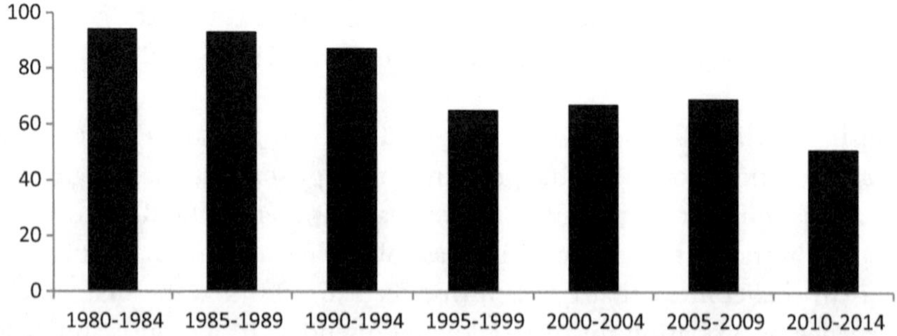


**Fig. 2** Prison admissions. Percentage of pre-trial prisoners (1980–2014). Sources: See footnote for Fig. 1

Second, in 1995, a new criminal code was adopted which entered into force one year later. In this new criminal code, we see the influence of EPP with respect to the introduction of new alternatives to prison and to the seriousness of offences which allowed judges to use alternatives to prison.

Until that moment, the main sanctions were the fine, the suspended sentence and prison. The new criminal code introduced day fines, community service and suspended sentence with probation. The convergence with Europe in this respect had been advocated by Spanish scholars (Cid and Larrauri 1997). Furthermore, the new criminal code extended the threshold of alternatives: previously only prison sentences up to one year of imprisonment could be suspended; with the new criminal code, prison sentences up to two years could be suspended or replaced by fines.

The impact of the new criminal code was small with respect to the use of the new community sanctions—community service and probation—(Cid and Larrauri 2002), but the increase in the use of suspended sentences by judges had a very significant decarcerative effect and contributed greatly to the stability of the prison population during these years (Cid 2005b).

### 2.2.3 Increase in the Rates of Imprisonment Despite a Decreasing Trend in Prison Admissions (2002–2010)

The third period is characterized by somewhat contradictory trends. We observe an important increase in the prison population (reaching, in 2010, a peak for the democratic era, with 78,000 prisoners and a ratio of 166 prisoners per 100,000 inhabitants) but, at the same time, the trend of decreasing admissions to prison is even more pronounced in this period (44,000 per year on average).

The further reduction of prison admissions can be explained by developments in the system of alternatives to imprisonment—community service and probation—which were introduced by a reform of the criminal code for offences of domestic abuse (in 2003 and 2004) and for driving offences (in 2003 and 2007) and which were extensively applied by judges (Anton and Larrauri 2009; Blay and Larrauri 2015).[21]

The expansion of the prison population in this context of decreasing prison admissions can be explained by the introduction of the new criminal code of 1995 which abolished good-time credits.[22] Good-time credits were an institution that reduced sentences automatically by one-third and by one-half when prisoners took part in rehabilitative activities in prison. The effect of this reform—which only applied to offences committed after the entry into force of the new code—was paramount. The increasing length of imprisonment had much more impact than the reduction in prison admissions and therefore the average prison population increased during these years (Cid 2008).[23]

### 2.2.4 Reduction in the Rates of Imprisonment in a Context of Decreasing Prison Admissions and Reforms That Affect the Length of Imprisonment (2011–2015)[24]

In 2011, we observed a new trend: a new fall in the prison population had started (from 79,000 prisoners in 2010 to 64,000 in 2015 and from a ratio of 166 prisoners per 100,000 inhabitants in 2010 to a ratio of 137

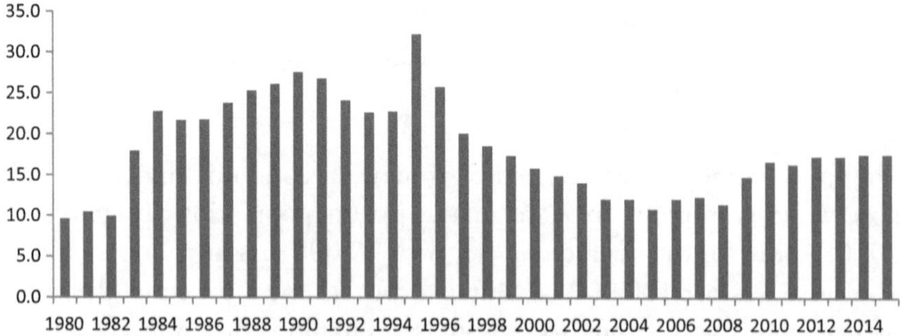


**Fig. 3** Number of paroles granted per year per 100 convicted prisoners (1980–2015). Sources: Direcció General de Serveis Penitenciaris i Rehabilitació (Catalonia) and Dirección General de Instituciones Penitenciarias (General State Administration). With respect to the data of the General State Administration, when no data were available in the official reports (annual reports of the Home Office Ministry or the Prison Directorate) the missing data were provided by the Spanish Prison Directorate

prisoners per 100,000 inhabitants in 2015). The decreasing number of prison admissions in this period (40,000 as average) does not seem large enough to explain this reduction of the prison population. There are two further reasons for this fall: firstly, a 2010 criminal law reform which reduced sentences for drug dealing and which was applied retroactively to sentenced prisoners; and secondly a change in parole policies, with a tendency to increase the use of parole in recent years. Figure 3 illustrates how the decreasing use of parole in the third period (of prison expansion) (with an average of 13 paroles granted per 100 convicted prisoners) is being reverted in the last period with the ratio of paroles rising to 16 per 100 convicted prisoners.[25]

## 2.3 Discussion

From the above exposition, we can draw three conclusions about the influence of the principle of the limitation of the use of imprisonment of EPP.

First, the ECtHR has been very influential—through the mediation of the Spanish Constitutional Court—in creating a more demanding standard for the use of pre-trial detention. This case law was converted into law in 2003 and has been important for the reduction of the number of admissions to prison since 1995. Furthermore, the European Recommendations promoting the use of alternatives to prison[26] and supporting the idea that imprisonment should be used as a last resort[27] have also been advocated by Spanish scholars and have contributed to the inclusion of new alternatives in the criminal code (in penal reforms of 1995, 2003 and 2007) and the creation of a probation system after the introduction of community alternatives by the criminal code of 1995.[28]

Second, there is a lack of influence of the principle with respect to reducing the length of imprisonment, both in the trial stage (making sentences no longer than is needed for the aim of punishment) and in the execution stage (granting parole as a way of reducing the effective length of sentences). Contrary to this principle, the Criminal Code of 1995, which is also referred to as the 'democratic criminal code', adopted a 'truth in sentencing' policy, which was mainly based on abolishing good-time credits.[29] This policy has had more impact than the one aimed at expanding the use of alternatives and therefore Spain was confronted with an important increase in the prison population during the first decade of the twentieth century.[30]

Third, in the context of the economic crisis of 2008, and with a reduced budget for the correctional system after 2010, policies aimed at reducing the length of imprisonment have started to emerge, both at the sentencing stage and in the execution of prison sentences. We do not have direct evidence that the changes in policy were driven by the shortened budget for the prison system, but we have some evidence that the previous policy of dealing with the increasing prison population by building new prisons (see further) came under critical scrutiny.[31] In any case, it seems that the context of the economic crisis has been favorable for adopting policies more aligned with the European Recommendations and the views of the CPT in favor of reducing the length of imprisonment.

Finally, the cumulative effect of the trend toward the reduction of prison admissions that started in 1995[32]—reaching in 2015 the lowest level since 1980—and the policies that have reduced the length of imprisonment have finally reversed the trend of an increasing prison population that had its origins in the 'truth in sentencing' policy that was introduced by the criminal code of 1995.

# 3 Normalization of Prison Life[33]

## 3.1 Definition of the Principle

The normalization of prison life—that is, the principle which states that prisoners' rights and life in prison should be as similar as possible to the conditions of free citizens—has been developed since the introduction in 1973 of the European Standard Minimum Rules for the Treatment of Prisoners (ESMR, hereafter). These Rules sought to adapt the United Nations Standard Minimum Rules for the Treatment of Prisoners (1955) to the European context. In 1987, the ESMR were redrafted and the new rules were referred to as the EPR. In 2006, they were again revised.

The principle of normalization was already clearly formulated in the ESMR of 1973:

> Imprisonment and other measures which result in cutting off an offender from the outside world are, by the deprivation of liberty, a punishment in themselves. Therefore the prison system shall not, except as incidental to justifiable segregation or the maintenance of discipline, aggravate the suffering inherent in such a situation. The regime of the institution should seek to minimize any differences between prison life and life at liberty which tend to lessen the responsibility of the prisoners or the respect due to their dignity as human beings[34]

The principle was further developed in rule 65 of the EPR of 1987:

> Every effort shall be made to ensure that the regimes of the institutions are designed and managed so as: a. to ensure that the conditions of life are compatible with human dignity and acceptable standards in the community; b. to minimize the detrimental effects of imprisonment and the differences between prison life and life at liberty which tend to diminish the self-respect or sense of personal responsibility of prisoners.

In the most recent edition of the EPR (2006) the principle is being included as part of the basic principles: '5. Life in prison shall approximate as closely as possible the positive aspects of life in the community.'

## 3.2 Evolution of Prison Conditions During the Democratic Era

The Spanish Constitution of 1978 elevates the principle of normalization to a constitutional status. Art. 25, 1 of the Spanish Constitution states that: 'Prisoners continue to benefit from the constitutional rights, subject to limitations derived from the judgment, the meaning of the punishment and the prison law.'[35] The prison law also established the principle of normalization in different dimensions of prison life such as the right to be accommodated in humane cells; the right to receive appropriate food; the right to health care; the right to work; the right to communicate with the outside world; the right to free time outside the cell; the right to be treated with respect; and the right to receive legal aid (García-Valdés 1982).

In this section, we explore to what extent these principles have been respected in practice. More specifically, we aim to assess the influence of the principle of normalization by analyzing the reports of the CPT (which has been visiting Spain since 1991) and the Spanish Ombudsman. Our analysis will be restricted to three important dimensions of prison life: accommodation, health care and respectful treatment.

### 3.2.1 Accommodation

Our first dimension refers to the idea that every prisoner is to be accommodated in one place. Prison overcrowding affects the quality of life in prison and is, therefore, to be avoided. The CPT has developed specific standards with respect to living space per prisoner in prison establishments. In a recent document, it stipulates that there should be a minimum of 6 $m^2$ of living space for a single-occupancy cell and 4 $m^2$ of living space per prisoner in a multiple-occupancy cell (see CPT/Inf(2015)44). CPT reports often document what adverse consequences overcrowding has for prison life: cramped and unhygienic accommodation; a constant lack of privacy (even when performing such basic tasks as using a sanitary facility); reduced opportunities in terms of employment, education and other out-of-cell activities; overburdened health-care services; increased tension and hence more violence between prisoners and between prisoners and staff (CPT/Inf(2013)8).

According to the CPT, prison overcrowding—which has been labeled as inhuman and degrading in early reports (see CPT/Inf(96)9)—has always been an important and persistent problem in Spain. Since its first visit to Spain (1991) the CPT has observed that almost all establishments it has visited were suffering from overcrowding. The CPT's recommendation has always been the same: 'every effort should be made to meet the goal of bringing the number of prison places (calculated on the basis of single occupancy) and the number of inmates into balance' (CPT/Inf(2000)5). The response of the Spanish government to this recommendation has always sounded similar: to build new prisons as the only and feasible solution to the problem of overpopulation.

In its response to the 1998 visit report, the government explained that '…from 1991 there is up and running a project for the building of new prisons, ten of which have already been inaugurated,…'; 'we are waiting for another four prisons to be inaugurated next year 2000'; 'and there are another two establishments which are being built; we have also to add other twenty-four establishments intended for social rehabilitation of prisoners in "tercer grado" regime who are benefiting from the "open plan" scheme' (CPT/Inf(2000)6). Ten years later, this answer was almost literally repeated: the government responded that it had adopted a plan to increase the prison estate through the construction of 18 new prison establishments, 32 open centers for social reintegration and 5 secure units for mother-child accommodation (CPT/Inf(2011)12). On the other hand, the Catalan government approved a renovation plan for the prison system, which involved constructing eight new prisons and closing down six establishments by 2010 (CPT/Inf(2011)12). Despite the building plan, the problem of overcrowding reappeared in the first decade of the twenty-first century as a consequence of a rising prison population. Figure 4 shows the trend of overcrowding in this period.

In its report for the 2007 visit, the CPT discussed for the first time possible causes for prison overcrowding in Spain: the use and length of time on remand, the underdeveloped use of alternatives to imprisonment, the increasing length of sentences and the reduced possibilities for conditional release. In its response to the 2011 visit, the Spanish

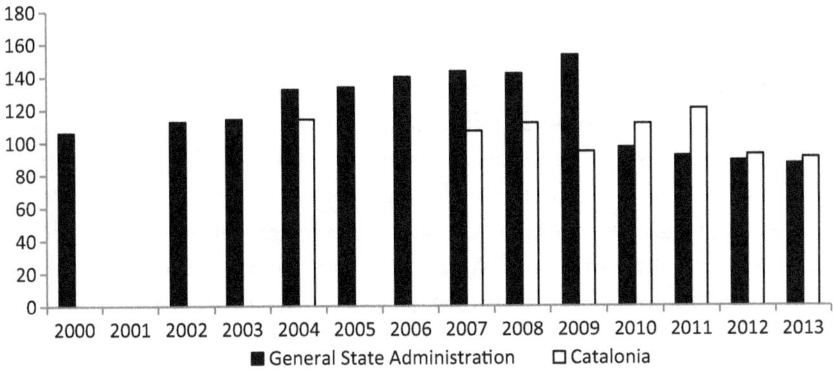


**Fig. 4** Prison density. General State Administration and Catalonia, 2000–2013. Source: Council of Europe Annual Penal Statistics (SPACE), http://wp.unil.ch/space

government addressed for the first time other remedies to tackle overcrowding, such as the promotion of the use of the open regime, alternative measures to imprisonment, programs designed to prepare for social reintegration and outside contact for detainees (CPT/Inf(2013)7).

In conclusion, it seems that the Spanish government was focused for years on the construction of new centers and the refurbishing of existing prisons. It is not until 2007 that the authorities began to consider other solutions, such as developing alternatives to imprisonment. However, on the basis of the information available in the CPT's reports, it remains unclear as to what extent the CPT's recommendations with respect to tackling overcrowding have sparked this change in the government's position.

### 3.2.2 Health Care

Health care is an important aspect of the normalization of prison life, not only to assure that inmates have access to services of a similar quality as people in the general population but also because it offers opportunities to detect ill-treatment and torture. It is therefore important to explore how the CPT has evaluated the health service in Spanish prisons.

Since its first visit to Spain (1991) the CPT's observations have been more or less the same. The CPT has usually observed that the visited establishments had, for the most part, adequate numbers of medical and nursing staff and the medical facilities were satisfactory. However, it has also identified major shortcomings with respect to psychiatric and dental care services and these were still a cause for concern in the most recent reports. With respect to psychiatric care, the CPT criticized the insufficient number of psychiatrists and psychologists in prison to provide for the needs of inmates as well as the lack of treatment programs in order to work toward rehabilitation.[36] With respect to the provision of dental services, the situation does not seem to have improved either. In its response to the CPT visit from 21 to 28 April 1997 (see CPT/Inf(98)10), the government affirmed that in every prison there is a dentist who offers specialized attention to the inmates in accordance with art. 208 of the Prison Regulations. This article stipulates that medical and health care in prison must be equivalent to that provided to the rest of citizens. Given the fact that the Spanish social security system only covers dental extractions, this also extends to inmates. However, in the same response, the government states that some other services may be provided taking into account the inmate's lack of financial means to pay for these. Nevertheless, in its most recent reports, the CPT notes that dental services are still limited and this situation should be revised.

With respect to the shortcomings in specialized psychiatrists and psychologists, the government answered on several occasions that it is aware of this need and it has promised to increase the number of specialists in these areas. However, in its recent reports, the CPT felt the need to repeat that these shortcomings were still present.

On the other hand, in its first report, the CPT suggested that the government should intensify efforts to establish a satisfactory level of cooperation between prison medical services and the civil hospital structure. The Spanish government seems to have addressed this recommendation because in its response to the report following the CPT's visit from 10 to 22 April 1994 (see CPT/Inf(96)10) a new model for prison health care was announced. According to this model, prisons should have health facilities that enable them to offer basic medical services that are equivalent to what is offered by the public health services outside prison. However, when inmates need specialized services then these are provided by the public health services. As a result of this new model, the General Penitentiary Hospital was closed in 1995.

A final issue that is often stressed in the CPT's reports is the key role the medical service needs to play in order to detect possible forms of ill-treatment. In its report related to the visit from 19 September to 1 October 2007, the CPT reiterated that '...steps [should] be taken to ensure that any signs of violence observed when a prisoner is medically screened on his admission should be fully recorded, together with any relevant statements by the prisoner and the doctor's conclusions (...). The same approach should be followed whenever a prisoner is medically examined following a violent episode in prison (CPT/Inf(2011)11: 73). The persistence of the CPT seems to have borne fruit. Indeed, at the occasion of its 2011 visit, the CPT could observe that the Director of the Prison Administration had issued instructions which introduced in every prison a register of injuries as recorded by the doctor upon admission and during detention within the establishment (CPT/Inf(2013)6: 71). However, this system did not seem to be working effectively because during its 2012 visit to a Catalan prison, the CPT observed on the basis of an examination of individual cases that '...only the objective findings were recorded and sent to the director, whereas relevant statements of the inmates were not written down and doctors did not draw up any conclusions on the injuries sustained by prisoners' (CPT/Inf(2013)8: 22).

### 3.2.3 Respectful Treatment

The normalization principle also implies that inmates are being treated respectfully. During its first visit to Spain, the CPT heard allegations about ill-treatment and recommended '...that the Spanish authorities examine whether prison officers in the young offender units are on occasion abusing their authority and, if necessary, take remedial action' (CPT/Inf(96)9, Part 1: 94).

Since its first visit to Spain, the CPT has been worried about the living conditions in institutions that are part of grade 1 of the prison system (closed regime) as well as about the conditions for prisoners included in the list of 'File for Inmates requiring Special Supervision' (FIES, Spanish acronym). Another point of concern was the means of coercion, such as sprays, which, if used in an inappropriate way, may amount to ill-treatment.

The Spanish government, in its response to the CPT visit of 1991, rejected the CPT's recommendation to forbid the use of sprays as a measure of restraint, but it accepted to introduce measures in order to minimize the risk of abuse. The government also agreed with the CPT's recommendation to create a book to register the use of means of coercion. Finally, the government accepted the CPT's recommendation to modify the rules that apply to the closed regime and to redefine the FIES. These reforms were implemented in the new prison regulations of 1986 and by the instructions 7 and 8/1995.

Although the Spanish government had agreed at several occasions to create a centralized register to record the relevant facts concerning the use of means of coercion, the CPT observed in its report of the 1998 visit that this had not been created yet (CPT/Inf(2000)5). However, in its reply to the 1998 visit, the government listed the activities carried out by the prison authorities to guarantee the good use of means of coercion (CPT/Inf(2000)6): (1) the newly created Instruction 21/1996 which sets out the procedure to follow when applying any means of coercion; (2) a new direction issued by the Prisons Management Subdirectorate General to report to Supervisory Judges, when applying any means of coercion so as to facilitate the supervision by the judicial authority of the correct use of means of coercion; and (3) the Inspection Service visits all prison establishments under the authority of the Directorate General for Prisons in order to verify onsite that means of coercion are applied in compliance with the instructions delivered.

In addition, the CPT has repeatedly pointed at problems with respect to the use of restraint/fixation measures in Spanish prisons. In its response to the 2007 periodic visit report, the Spanish government listed the initiatives taken to address such problems (see CPT/Inf(2011)12): (1) the circulation of several circulars which explain how methods of restraint must be applied and how to use means of physical containment[37] (moreover, the so-called Superman position (diagonal arms binding) which had been disputed and reported at the occasion of several visits was formally banned by the 2/2007 circular); (2) Prison Authority stressed that every received complaint had been investigated; and (3) the Spanish Penitentiary Administration and the Justice Department of Catalonia approved codes of ethics, which detail all the deontological rules that all prison officers have to respect.

Since its first visit in 1991, the CPT received complaints about torture and ill-treatment in the visited prisons. Although the situation improved in the following years (with no allegations of torture during the visit of 1998 and some allegations of ill-treatment that remained restricted to cases where inmates were held in solitary confinement), the reports of the CPT of the twenty-first century continued to underline mistreatment as a major problem in some Spanish prisons. For example, during the 2003 visit, some inmates told the CPT delegation that certain prison officers had physically mistreated inmates (e.g. striking them with batons) while they were held in the disciplinary unit (CPT/Inf(2007)28). During the 2007 visit, the delegation met a number of prisoners in several sections in prison who alleged that they had been ill-treated by prison officers both in Catalonia and in prisons governed by the General State Administration (CPT/Inf(2011)11). Some of these cases were considered to be very severe by the CPT. Similar allegations about ill-treatment were reported and denounced in the reports related to the 2011 and 2012 visits (CPT/Inf(2013)6; CPT/Inf(2013)8); most of these consisted of punches and kicks and concerned primarily those inmates who were either transferred to or accommodated in special sections.

The judgments by the ECtHR regarding the violation of art. 3 of the ECHR, for not conducting an appropriate investigation of allegations of torture in police stations, raise questions on whether these allegations of mistreatment have been appropriately investigated by Spanish authorities.[38] On the other hand, the Spanish Ombudsman highlighted that the decrease in reports of mistreatment during the 1990s might be due to the lack of confidence of inmates in the Administration's ability to carry out impartial investigations (Defensor del Pueblo 2001, 2002).

## 3.3 Discussion

The main conclusion is that the principle of normalization of EPP has had an important impact on Spanish prison practice. In this respect, the principal actor of EPP has been the CPT. In our view, the relevance of the CPT in making the principle of normalization applicable throughout the Spanish prison system has been paramount. Although its recommendations are not always followed by the government, it seems clear that its continuous monitoring of the Spanish prison system and its insistence that improvement is needed in key areas of Spanish prisons have put a great deal of pressure on the Spanish government.

The influence of the CPT in the three areas under consideration may be summarized as follows:

(1) The two Spanish prison administrations (the General State Administration and Catalonia) have adopted policies aimed at tackling overcrowding by prison expansion. Building new prisons has for long been the preferred solution but in recent years, and probably stimulated by the financial constraints of the recent economic crisis, new policies oriented at increasing the use of open prisons and parole have also been used.
(2) The improvement in health care in prison also seems to be influenced by the criticisms of national and international committees of the deplorable situation in the 1990s when health problems related to drug addiction were very prevalent in Spanish prisons.[39] Nowadays medical care offered in the health-care units in prisons is similar to medical care that exists for citizens in free society, although there is still room for improvement, in particular, with respect to mental health and dental care.
(3) Finally, the CPT's visits seem to have had an impact on the disappearance of torture in the 1990s. However, allegations of ill-treatment, in particular related to the transfer to segregation units, continue to exist today. Moreover, it seems probable that there have been shortcomings with respect to the investigation of allegations of ill-treatment.

## 4 Reintegration

### 4.1 Definition of the Principle

There are two dimensions to the principle of reintegration: the right to participate in treatment activities and the right to receive assistance for the return to the community. With respect to the first dimension, the following was stipulated in the 1987 EPR:

> As soon as possible after admission and after a study of the personality of each prisoner with a sentence of a suitable length, a programme of treatment in a suitable institution shall be prepared in the light of the knowledge obtained about individual needs, capacities and dispositions, especially proximity to relatives.[40]

The second dimension focuses on the preparation for the return to the community, intended as the assistance that every released prisoner should receive, including that they are provided with appropriate documents and identification papers and that they obtain immediate financial means of subsistence while receiving assistance in finding suitable accommodation and work.[41] The recommendation on conditional release of 1970 already suggested to the governments of the member states of the Council of Europe the following:

> To review and develop, especially in the light of current innovations, the means intended to facilitate the transition from institutional life to freedom on release. In particular specific and detailed plans for release should begin at an appropriate moment during the sentence.[42]

In order to make a successful transition to the community, sentenced prisoners must receive assistance:

> Sentenced prisoners shall be assisted in good time prior to release by procedures and special programmes enabling them to make the transition from life in prison to a law-abiding life in the community.[43]

One of the release programs specifically stressed by EPP is parole:

> In order to reduce the harmful effects of imprisonment and to promote the resettlement of prisoners under conditions that seek to guarantee safety of the outside community, the law should make conditional release available to all sentenced prisoners, including life-sentence prisoners.[44]

## 4.2 The Principle of Reintegration in Practice in the Democratic Era

Art. 25, 2 of the Spanish Constitution of 1978 stipulates that 'prison sentences are oriented towards reeducation and social reintegration.' This principle, developed by the prison law of 1979, should be seen against the background of the evolution of the EPP at that time and, in particular, of Resolution (73)5 on standard minimum rules for the treatment of prisoners.[45]

With respect to the first dimension of the principle (the right to participate in treatment), the law established the obligation for the penitentiary administration to offer convicted prisoners the treatment they may need to address their criminogenic needs. The prison law (and the Spanish prison rules of 1996) regulates different kinds of programs that should exist in prison in order to address the needs of sentenced prisoners: education, vocational training, work, leisure and specific treatment programs. With respect to the second dimension (the preparation for the return to the community) the prison law introduced a progressive model: the prison sentence starts with a period in ordinary prison during which the criminogenic needs are addressed and is followed, after having served one-fourth of the sentence, with the preparation of the inmate's return to the community through home leaves, transfer to open institutions (where prisoners can work or participate in treatment outdoors during the day and return to the open prison at night) and parole. This progressive system implies that prisoners can only benefit from home leaves, open regime and parole if they have successfully completed their specific treatment programs.[46] This feature of the model is important because it may explain some of the gaps of the Spanish prison policy with respect to EPP.

The implementation of the prison law of 1979 has produced important changes in the prison system. It is true that the implementation of the law has taken a long time, but this seems understandable taking into account that the penitentiary system during the dictatorship (1939–1975) was not oriented to provide for the criminogenic needs of the prisoners; rehabilitation in that period consisted of a combination of discipline, religion and work (Cid 1994; Roldán 1988). It seems reasonable therefore that the introduction of the new models of rehabilitation and the new systems of supervision in the community took time.

Firstly, new professionals specialized in rehabilitation and reintegration have joined the prison staff: Spanish prisons now have 'surveillance personnel' (whose task is to maintain order and security within the prison) and 'treatment personnel'. The mission of the treatment personnel—composed of psychologists, social educators, social workers and lawyers[47]—consists of evaluating the needs of every sentenced prisoner, to work out a treatment plan and to offer to prisoners the means to challenge their needs. Secondly, new treatment programs have been introduced into the prison system. In the first stage of the development of the new prison system (1979–1995) rehabilitation was mainly directed at offering prisoners the opportunity to spend their time productively, that is, through work, education, training, sport and cultural activities. Their participation in such activities was being stimulated by a good-time credits system. In the second stage (from 1996 onward), and as a consequence of the influence of the 'what works' movement,[48] the system of treatment was complemented by specific treatment programs that are directly oriented to specific criminogenic needs or to specific kinds of offenders (e.g. programs targeting drug users, sex offenders, domestic violence as well as other forms of violence) (Cid 2005a). Thirdly, a system of early release has been developed. Open prisons (i.e. low-security institutions which accommodate prisoners only at night and where staff is directed at the follow-up of the resettlement plan in the community) were created and a service was founded which aims to assist prisoners with employment during early release, in open regime and in parole.[49]

Based on our discussion so far, readers may feel tempted to conclude that the Spanish penitentiary system is fully adapted to EPP with respect to the principle of reintegration. However, before drawing any conclusions, we need to look at how the system has worked in practice.

Figure 5 presents data (percentages) on prisoners who are serving their sentence in an open institution. Our data cover the period 1996–2014, that is, a period when the penitentiary law had been fully implemented (see supra). Three observations seem to be relevant to us: first, the two prison administrations (General State Administration and Catalonia) seem to have different policies with respect to the use of open regimes (i.e. it is more frequently used in Catalonia than in the rest of Spain) (Cid 2005b); second, during this period, 1996–2014, there is no clear trend toward a more intensive use of open regimes; third, and more importantly,

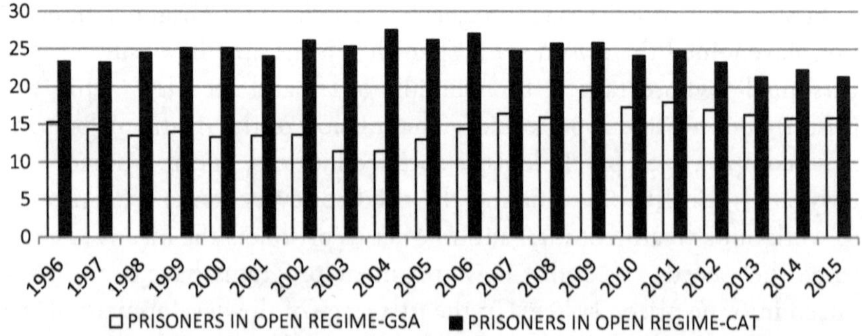


**Fig. 5** Percentage of sentenced prisoners in open regime. General State Administration (GSA) and Catalonia (CAT), 1996–2015. Sources: Dirección General de Instituciones Penitenciarias (General State Administration) and Direcció General de Serveis Penitenciaris (Catalonia)

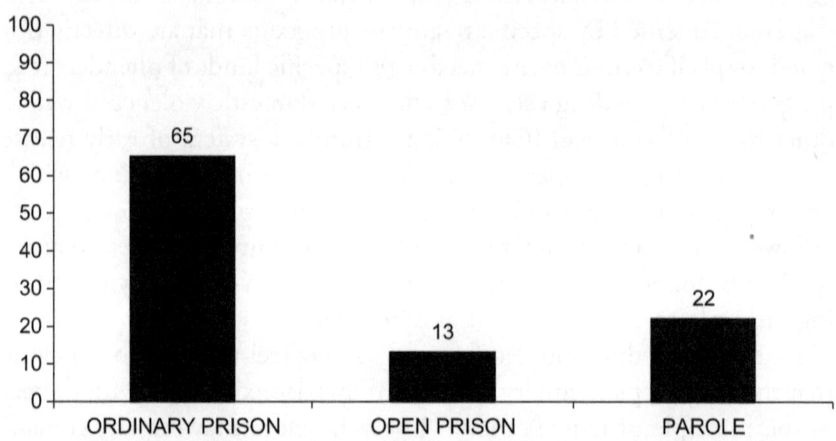


**Fig. 6** Classification at the expiration of the prison sentence. Catalonia (Average, 1996–2010). Unpublished data were made available to the authors by the Direcció General de Serveis Penitenciaris i Rehabilitació (Catalonia). Data on prisoners released from an ordinary prison (second degree) includes a small percentage (2 %) released from a closed institution (first degree). The data do not include prisoners who were not classified at the moment of release. (this concerns mainly prisoners who were serving short sentences.)

our data on the use of open regimes suggest that reality is far removed from the ideal of the progressive system: only a minority of inmates are able to spend their prison time in a more open regime.

One can also evaluate the performance of the penitentiary system with respect to reintegration by looking at how prisoners reach the end of their sentence. Data with respect to Catalonia (see Fig. 6) indicate that the expiration of the sentence after a transitional period—in open regime or parole—is not the rule; indeed, most prisoners are released without any transitional period.[50]

Research on recidivism in Catalonia indicates that the rates of reincarceration are lower for those who have benefited from early release than for those who are released at the expiration of the sentence (Capdevila 2015). It also reveals that early release is one of the factors that explains the better rates (Luque et al. 2005).

## 4.3 Discussion

From the previous exposition, we may conclude the following about the influence of the principle of reintegration of EPP in the Spanish penitentiary system.

First, this principle was fully recognized in the Spanish legislation because the idea that prison sentences should be oriented toward rehabilitation and social reintegration was included in the Constitution and further developed in the prison law.

Second, in the process of implementing the penitentiary law, the necessary means—treatment personnel, programs for rehabilitation and assistance programs for resettlement—were provided in order to comply with the EPR.

Third, available data on the performance of the prison system (as measured by the number of inmates who succeed in the rehabilitation programs and who progress to open regimes) suggest, however, that Spanish prison policy fails to comply with the principle that every prisoner should be assisted in the transition from prison to the community. Moreover, as we discussed above, this failure reduces the possibilities of reintegration and it increases the rates of reincarceration.

# 5 Conclusions

In this final section, we will draw some general conclusions about the influence of EPP on Spanish prison policy, and we will discuss to what extent there are still gaps and whether these may be overcome in the future.

The main conclusion of our chapter is that EPP—in its main dimensions, as discussed throughout this chapter—has been very influential on Spanish prison practice. The relevant actors have been the Committee of Ministers, the ECtHR and the CPT. The EU has had a more limited influence until now but this may increase in the future. While we think the influence of the Council of Europe has contributed to making Spanish prison practice more progressive—that is, more in line with the principles of the limitation of the use of imprisonment, normalization and reintegration—we are not sure that the influence of the EU would necessarily go in the same direction.[51]

The ECtHR case law with respect to the use of pre-trial detention has been most influential in limiting the use of imprisonment. Art. 10, 2 of the Spanish Constitution requires that the principles of the Constitution are being interpreted taking into account the international conventions on human rights.[52] On the basis of the case law of the ECtHR, the Spanish Constitutional Court has established that pre-trial detention is only acceptable when imprisonment is needed to tackle a danger of absconding, a risk of reoffending or for protecting the integrity of the evidence. As a result of this case law, and the legal reforms that followed from it, Spanish judges have become more restrictive in using pre-trial detention. This change in practice has influenced the rate of admissions to prison. This is probably the most important and visible illustration of the influence of the ECHR on Spanish prison policy. In addition, the recommendations of the Council of Europe favoring the use of alternatives to imprisonment have also impacted upon Spanish prison practice. In 1995, somewhat belatedly compared to most other countries in Europe, Spain reformed its system of alternatives to prison: community sentences were made available to judges and the possibilities of avoiding the use of prison were extended. The implementation of this new system had notable decarcerating effects and contributed to Spain becoming a country with one of the lowest numbers of admissions to prison in Europe.

With respect to the principle of normalization, the CPT has been very persistent in highlighting the main problems of the Spanish penitentiary system, in particular prison overcrowding, inadequate health care and ill-treatment. The CPT has put a great deal of pressure on the Spanish government in order to improve the situation and, as a result, some of the problems have been solved in the meantime. This does not imply that everything has been solved by now but at least the government has acknowledged that these problems exist and that they need to be tackled. In recent years, the ECtHR has also condemned Spain for violating art. 3 of the ECHR. Although the case law refers basically to torture and ill-treatment in police stations, the fact that the ECtHR has found a violation of art. 3 for not having taken appropriate measures to investigate cases of torture seems to have made judicial authorities more willing to conduct investigations into allegations of ill-treatment in prisons. Moreover, also the CPT has repeatedly insisted that such allegations should be subject to an independent inquiry.

Finally, the confluence with the recommendations of the Council of Europe's Committee of Ministers is very clear with respect to the principle of reintegration. The Spanish Constitution is one of the few in Europe that explicitly states that prison sentences should be oriented toward rehabilitation and reintegration. Moreover, as we discussed above, the Prison Law (1979) further developed the principle of rehabilitation and reintegration by granting prisoners the right to receive treatment and, once the person is ready for reintegration, to be assisted in this process. Moreover, the prison system has been equipped with personal and material resources to make rehabilitation and reintegration a real perspective for prisoners.

However, our discussion in this chapter has revealed two major gaps between EPP and Spanish prison practice. On the one hand, the principle of limiting the use of imprisonment by reducing the length of imprisonment has been ignored in Spanish practice. The decision taken by the legislator in 1995 to abolish good-time credit in the Criminal Code has resulted in a doubling of the length of time spent in prison. This has played an important role in the overall increase of the prison population, passing from 46,594 prisoners in 2001 to 78,140 in 2010, a 60 % increase in 9 years. It is only in the wake of the economic crisis that some reforms affecting the length of sentencing have been adopted. These have, in combination with the long trend to the reduction of prison admissions, produced a new era of decreasing imprisonment rates.

On the other hand, the principle of reintegration, which includes the idea that every sentenced prisoner is being assisted in the transition from prison to community, does not seem to apply to most prisoners who are released at the expiration of the sentence (see Fig. 6 above).

How can we understand these two gaps? The gap with respect to the excessive lenght of imprisonment is probably due to the lack of influence of reductionist ideals among penal elites (Cid and Larrauri 2009). During the long process of elaborating the new criminal code of 1995, it was argued that the idea of proportionality should be the main principle to decide about punishment; rehabilitation was only perceived as a secondary rationale for non-serious offences and for granting early release to prisoners if this was conducive to addressing their criminogenic needs (Cid 1994). The abolition of good-time credits was clearly a concession to the principle of proportionality. Moreover, this focus on proportionality probably was also inspired by the presence of terrorism in Spanish society at that time because the new criminal code would also apply to persons convicted of terrorism.

The gap with respect to the principle of reintegration can be explained by the discretionary system of early release that has been adopted in Spain. EPP pleads for a universal system of reintegration in which every prisoner is assisted on his or her way to a successful resettlement in the community. This aim is probably more coherent with a mandatory system of early release. However, like several other European countries (see Padfield et al. 2010), Spain has adopted a discretionary system in which the progression to a more open regime depends on rehabilitative efforts during the time served in an ordinary prison (Cid and Tébar 2010). Although the European Recommendation on parole[53] states that both models—mandatory and discretionary—are able to fulfill the ideal of universal reintegration, it may be the case that only the mandatory system of parole can guarantee that all prisoners have a period of assisted transition from prison to community and that therefore none are being excluded of this intermediate period for lack of progress in terms of rehabilitation or for other reasons (Cid and Tébar 2010).[54]

We do not know whether these gaps will be closed in the future. On the one hand, we are pessimistic. Retributive thinking continues to be very influential in Spanish parliament. This became clear in a recent reform of the criminal code (2015) which increased the period of parole and extended the time needed to seal a criminal record.[55] However, other aspects of the Spanish context make us more optimistic about the further confluence of Spanish prison practice with EPP. The rehabilitative model can count on widespread support among academics and practitioners (García-España and Díez Ripollés 2012), and, in the wake of the economic crisis, politicians may come to realize that imprisonment is an expensive answer to respond to crime and that therefore it may become attractive to them to adopt and support policies to reduce the length of imprisonment.

## Notes

1. Van Zyl Smit and Snacken (2009) distinguish between European prison law (basically the judgments of the ECtHR) and the other sources that are not legally binding. Given the interactions between these two sources with respect to the influence they may have at a national level, we prefer to use the label 'EPP' in a broader meaning.
2. In Spain, there are two administrations in charge of the prison system: the Catalan administration (which deals with prisons in Catalonia) and the General Administration of the State (which deals with prisons in the rest of Spain). Throughout this chapter, we use data referring to the whole prison system (Spain) and data referring only to one part of the territory: the Catalan prisons (Catalonia) and the prisons of the rest of Spain (General Administration of the State).
3. Resolution (65)1 of the Committee of Ministers on suspended sentence, probation and other alternatives to imprisonment, Foreword.
4. Resolution (65)1 of the Committee of Ministers on suspended sentence, probation and other alternatives to imprisonment, Foreword.
5. Rec(99)22 of the Committee of Ministers concerning prison overcrowding and prison population inflation, art. 1.
6. Rec(2006)2 of the Committee of Ministers on the European prison rules, Foreword.
7. Rec(2006)2 of the Committee of Ministers on the European prison rules, Foreword.
8. Rec(99)22 of the Committee of Ministers concerning prison overcrowding and prison population inflation, art. 8.
9. Rec(2003)22 of the Committee of Ministers on conditional release (parole), Foreword.

10. Rec(2003)22 of the Committee of Ministers on conditional release (parole), Foreword.
11. Rec(2006)2 of the Committee of Ministers on the European prison rules, Foreword; Rec(92)16 of the Committee of Ministers on the European rules on community sanctions and measures, art. 6.
12. Resolution (65)1 of the Committee of Ministers on suspended sentence, probation and other alternatives to imprisonment, art. 1; Rec(2010)1 of the Committee of Ministers on the Council of Europe probation rules, art. 54.
13. Rec(2000)22 of the Committee of Ministers on improving the implementation of the European rules on community sanctions and measures, art. 22; Rec(2010)1 of the Committee of Ministers on the Council of Europe probation rules, art. 1.
14. Rec(2000)22 of the Committee of Ministers on improving the implementation of the European rules on community sanctions and measures, art. 22; Rec(2010)1of the Committee of Ministers on the Council of Europe probation rules, art. 1.
15. Rec(99)22 of the Committee of Ministers concerning prison overcrowding and prison population inflation, art. 11; Rec(2006)13 of the Committee of Ministers on the Use of remand in custody, the conditions in which it takes place and the provision of safeguard against abuse, art. 7c.
16. Rec(92)17 of the Committee of Ministers concerning consistency in sentencing, art. 5a.
17. Rec(99)22, of the Committee of Ministers concerning prison overcrowding and prison population inflation, art. 14.
18. Rec(99)22 of the Committee of Ministers concerning prison overcrowding and prison population inflation, art. 24.
19. The Spanish transition to democracy started after the death of Franco (1975). In 1977, the first democratic elections were held and in 1978 the new democratic Constitution was approved. The new prison law [Ley Orgánica General Penitenciaria, 1/1979] was approved in 1979.
20. Spanish Constitutional Court Decision, 128/1995, 26 July 1995. In this decision, the Constitutional Court declared that pre-trial detention is only acceptable when it is needed for procedural objectives (risk that the offender makes the evidence disappear and risk of absconding) or for the protection of society (risk of recidivism) and when there are no other measures available to reach these objectives. Moreover, pre-trial detention is only constitutional when the judge offers concrete evidence to prove the need to impose pre-trial detention for the objectives mentioned.

21. The criminalization of offences of non-serious domestic abuse (which passed from being a misdemeanor [falta] to a crime [delito]) and of driving offences (with more infractions now being treated as criminal offences rather than administrative offences) produced the effect of diminishing the seriousness of offences dealt with by judges and consequently increased the use of alternatives to prison. Antón and Larrauri (2009) studied the application of the new laws for offences of domestic violence and demonstrated that 90 % of the offenders convicted for such offences received an alternative sanction.
22. See the criticism of González (2011) who argues that we should not look at the immediate reasons for the increase of imprisonment rates (the Criminal Code of 1995) but at the causes of this change in the criminal law.
23. Apart from abolishing good-time credits, the criminal code of 1995 increased the penalty of some offences in comparison to the previous criminal code of 1973 (Tamarit 2007).
24. At the moment of writing (September 2016), the trend toward a decreasing prison population continued. In July 2016, the prison population stood at 61,000 prisoners, a ratio of 131 prisoners per 100,000 inhabitants (Source: Secretaría General de Servicios Penitenciarios).
25. Montero and Nistal (2015) argue that another factor that has contributed to the reduction of the prison population in this period is the use of deportation as an alternative of imprisonment or as substitution of early release for foreigners. They demonstrate how in this period the ratio of foreign prisoners in the General Administration of the State has been reduced.
26. Resolution (65)1 of the Committee of Ministers on suspended sentence, probation and other alternatives to imprisonment, foreword.
27. Rec(92)17 of the Committee of Ministers concerning consistency in sentencing, art. 5.
28. The influence of Spanish criminal law scholars in the introduction of new alternatives to imprisonment in the Criminal Code of 1995 and in further reforms may be observed by two indicators: first, in many of their publications, they advocated the introduction of new alternatives to imprisonment and, second, since the late 1970s, criminal law scholars played an important role in the commissions which elaborated the drafts of the new criminal code.
29. The Spanish Supreme Court made an interpretation of the Criminal Code that, in practice, extended the abolition of good-time credits to

persons sentenced for crimes committed before the enforcement of the new Criminal Code of 1995. The decision was considered constitutional by the Spanish Constitutional Court but contrary to the prohibition of retroactive application of punishment by the ECtHR in *Del Rio Prada v. Spain*, App. No. 42750/09, 21 October 2013. On this judgment, see Molina (2016).

30. The Council Framework Decision 2008/675/JHA of 24 July 2008 on taking account of convictions in the member states of the European Union in the course of new criminal proceedings may reduce the length of sentences for those prisoners with convictions in different countries. But the Spanish law that transposes this framework decision in the Spanish legal system has made a rather restrictive interpretation. In Molina (2016), there is a discussion of the case law regarding this issue.
31. See the interview Cid and Contreras (2014: 84) conducted with Mr. Ramon Parés, the former director of the Catalan prison system in which he argued that 'Before the economic crisis probably we spent too much, especially with the construction of new prisons.'
32. As argued in this chapter, the reduction of prison admissions in the period 1995–2015 (with the exception of the period 2005–2010) is probably due to the combination of three factors: a decrease in the use of pre-trial detention; an increase in the use of alternatives to prison; and less serious cases arriving to the courts. The reduction of prison admissions is not due to the reduction of the number of offenders sentenced for crimes: these went up from 117,000 in 1995 to 218,000 in 2014 (Source: Spanish National Institute of Statistics).
33. A more general description of the conditions of imprisonment in Spain can be found in González (2012).
34. Resolution (73)5 of the Committee of Ministers on the standard minimum rules for the treatment of prisoners, art. 58.
35. The importance of art. 25, 2 of the Spanish Constitution for the principle of normalization is situated in the idea that prisoners have the constitutional rights of every citizen, and limitations to these rights should be justified by the need to protect other relevant constitutional principles. In its case law, the Spanish Constitutional Court has made the principle of normalization more effective in areas such as the right to communicate free from interference (judgment of the Spanish Constitutional Court 73/1983, 30 July 1983 and 175/1997, 27 October 1997) and the right to defense in disciplinary procedures (judgment of the Spanish Constitutional Court 74/1985, 18 June 1984). Other judg-

ments of the Constitutional Court with respect to issues such as the prohibition of inhuman or degrading treatment and its compatibility with solitary confinement (judgment of the Spanish Constitutional Court 2/1987, 21 January 1987) have been more controversial. For more information on this issue, see Cid (2005a).

36. The Spanish Ombudsman has also pointed at the shortcomings in the treatment of inmates with mental health problems such as the prevalence of pharmacological treatment over a more integrated approach to caring for mental illness and the fact that mentally ill prisoners were often abandoned after their release from prison (Defensor del Pueblo 1998).
37. Circular 6/2004 concerning ex-post procedure following the use of any coercive measure; Circular 2/2007 ruling mechanical binding procedures; Circular 3/2004 on procedures to be followed in case of violence toward patients in psychiatric wards; Instruction 2/1994 on inmates' transfer and Circular 5/2004 on emergency inmates' transfers.
38. *Martínez Sala and others v. Spain*, App. No. 58438/00, 2 November 2004; *Etxebarria Caballero v. Spain*, App. No. 74016/12, 7 October 2014; *Otamendi Egiguren v Spain*, App. No. 47303/08, 16 October 2012; *Ataun Rojo v Spain*, App. No. 3344/13, 7 October 2014; *Arratibel Garciandía v Spain*, App. No. 58488/13, 5 May 2015. See also Queralt (2013).
39. In 1999, 18 % of Spanish prisoners were suffering from AIDS (European Monitoring Centre for Drugs and Drugs Addiction (EMCDDA) 2001). For more information on the policies adopted by Spanish authorities to prevent contagious diseases in prisons, see Cid (2005a)
40. Rec(87)3 of the Committee of Ministers on the European prison rules, art. 68. In the revised European prison rules of 2006, this sounds as follows: 'As soon as possible after such admission, reports shall be drawn up for sentenced prisoners about their personal situations, the proposed sentence plans for each of them and the strategy for preparation for their release' (Rec(2006)2 of the Committee of Ministers on the European prison rules, art. 103.3).
41. Rec(87)3 of the Committee of Ministers on the European Prison Rules, art. 70.1; Rec(2006)2 of the Committee of Ministers on the European prison rules, art. 33 (3, 7 and 8).
42. Resolution (70)1 of the Committee of Ministers on the practical organization of measures for the supervision and aftercare of conditionally sentenced or conditionally released offenders, art. 2e.
43. Rec(2006)2 of the Committee of Ministers on the European prison rules, art. 107.1.

44. Rec(2003)22 of the Committee of Ministers on conditional release (parole), art. 4 a.
45. Art. 65 of Resolution 73(5) states: 'The duty of society does not end with a prisoner's release. There should, therefore, be governmental and private agencies capable of providing efficient after-care for the released prisoner and directed towards lessening prejudice against him and towards his social rehabilitation.' See Resolution (73)5 of the Committee of Ministers on the standard minimum rules for the treatment of prisoners.
46. In case the person does not need to stay in an ordinary prison to have his/her criminogenic needs addressed, he/she may be classified in third degree and serve the prison sentence in an open institution.
47. It may seem strange that lawyers are part of the 'treatment personnel'. Initially, the prison law referred to 'personnel with a legal and criminology background' but since there was no degree in criminology in Spain at that time, the requirement for this dual training was eliminated. This explains why people with only a background in law are part of the treatment personnel in Spanish prisons.
48. Two Spanish academic members of this movement (Santiago Redondo and Vicente Garrido) had an important influence on the new policies adopted by the two penitentiary administrations in Spain.
49. In Spain, there are two systems of early release: open regime (here inmates are on the outside during the day and spend the night in an open prison or under a home detention curfew) and parole (here inmates leave the prison and reenter the outside world but they are under the supervision of a parole officer). Only prisoners who benefit from an open regime are eligible for parole. For more details, see Cid and Tébar (2010).
50. We do not have data from the General Administration of the State with respect to early release or release at the expiration of the sentence. However, the data on the use of open regime (see Fig. 5) indicate that the rates of prisoners who end their sentences through early release (in open regime and parole) are not very dissimilar between the two penitentiary administrations.
51. See Melloni, Case C-399/11, 26 February 2013, of the Court of Justice of the European Union. Here it was concluded that the execution of a European Arrest Warrant (EAW) is not conditional upon the conviction rendered in absentia being open to review in the issuing member state. In the wake of this decision, the Spanish Constitutional Court has modified its case law, establishing than the Spanish Constitution is not being violated (as it was until then) when a person is convicted in absentia (see

Izquierdo 2016). The EAW has been transposed in Spanish law by the law 3/2003 of 14 March 2003 (Baras 2012).

52. On the influence of the ECtHR on the Spanish Constitutional Court, see also Andrés (2014), Candela (2008) and López-Guerra (2013).
53. Rec(2003)22 of the Committee of Ministers on conditional release (parole).
54. The debate between mandatory or discretionary models of parole has of course many other dimensions. Authors who favor a discretionary model argue that this model increases the stimulus for rehabilitation and reduces the rates of recidivism (Petersilia 2003). See further Cid and Tébar (2010).
55. Ley Orgánica 1/2015, 30 March 2015, reforming the Criminal Code of 1995. Apart from the reforms mentioned in the chapter, the new law has introduced life sentences in Spain for crimes of genocide, aggravated murder and terrorism.

## Literature

Andrés, P. 2014. Acerca del papel del Tribunal Europeo de Derechos Humanos y de la tentación de desacreditar al mensajero. *Teoría y Realidad Constitucional* 33: 198–218.

Antón, L., and E. Larrauri. 2009. Violencia de género ocasional. Un análisis de las penas ejecutadas. *Revista Española de Investigación Criminológica* 7: 1–26.

Baras, M. 2012. *El espacio penitenciario Europeo*. Madrid: Ministerio del Interior.

Blay, E., and E. Larrauri. 2015. Community Punishments in Spain: A Tale of Two Administrations. In *Community Punishment: European Perspectives*, ed. G. Robinson and F. McNeill. London: Routledge.

Candela, M. 2008. The Reception Process in Spain and Italy. In *The Impact of the ECHR on National Legal Systems*, ed. H. Keller and A. Sweet. Oxford: Oxford University Press.

Capdevila, M., ed. 2015. *Tasa de reincidencia penitenciària 2014*. Barcelona: Centro de Estudios Jurídicos y Formación Especializada.

Cid, J. 1994. *¿Pena justa o pena útil?* Madrid: Ministerio de Justicia.

———. 2005a. The Penitentiary System in Spain. The Use of Imprisonment, Living Conditions and Rehabilitation. *Punishment and Society* 7 (2): 147–166.

———. 2005b. Suspended Sentences in Spain: Decarceration and Recidivism. *Probation Journal* 52 (2): 169–179.

———. 2008. El incremento del encarcelamiento en España: diagnóstico y remedios. *Revista Española de Investigación Criminológica* 6: 1–31.

Cid, J., and M. Contreras. 2014. Interview with Ramon Parés, former director of the Catalan Prison System. In *Trends in Corrections: Interviews with Corrections Leaders Around the World*, ed. M. Henderson Hurley and D.K. Das, vol. 2. Boca Raton: CRC Press.

Cid, J., and E. Larrauri, eds. 1997. *Penas alternativas a la prisión*. Barcelona: Bosch.

———, eds. 2002. *Jueces penales y penas en España*. Valencia: Tirant lo blanch.

———. 2009. Development of Crime, Social Change, Mass Media, Crime Policy, Sanctioning Practice and Their Impact on Prison Population Rates. *Sistema Penal & Violência* 1 (1): 1–21.

Cid, J., and B. Tébar. 2010. Spain. In *Release from Prison. European Policy and Practice*, ed. N. Padfield, D. Van Zyl Smit, and F. Dünkel. Cullompton: Willan Publishing.

De la Quadra-Salcedo, T. 2013. Scott c. España (STEDH de 24 de octubre de 1996): El derecho del sujeto en prisión preventiva a ser juzgado en un plazo razonable o a ser puesto en libertad durante el procedimiento. In *Conflicto y diálogo con Europa. Las condenas a España del Tribunal Europeo de Derechos Humanos*, ed. R. Alcácer, M. Beladíez, and J.M. Sánchez. Madrid: Cívitas.

Defensor del Pueblo. 1998. *Informe anual*. Madrid: Cortes Generales.

———. 2001. *Informe anual*. Madrid: Cortes Generales.

———. 2002. *Informe anual*. Madrid: Cortes Generales.

European Monitoring Centre for Drugs and Drugs Addiction (EMCDDA). 2001. *An Overview Study: Assistance to Drug Users in European Union Prisons*. Wimbledon: Cranstoun Drug Services Publishing.

García-España, E., and J.L. Díez-Ripollés, eds. 2012. *Realidad y política penitenciarias*. Valencia: Tirant lo Blanch.

García-Valdés, C. 1982. *Comentarios a la legislación penitenciaria*. Madrid: Cívitas.

González, I. 2011. Aumento de presos y código penal. Una explicación insuficiente. *Revista Electrónica de Ciencia Penal y Criminología*. 13 (4): 1–22.

———. 2012. La cárcel en España: mediciones y condiciones del encarcelamiento. *Revista de derecho penal y criminología* 8: 351–402.

Izquierdo, A. 2016. La callada configuración de los derechos fundamentales por el tribunal de justicia de la Unión Europea. In *La tutela multinivel del principio de legalidad penal*, ed. M. Pérez-Manzano and J.A. Lascurain. Madrid: Marcial Pons.

López Guerra, L. 2013. El diálogo entre el Tribunal Europeo de Derechos Humanos y los tribunales españoles. Coincidencias y divergencias. *Teoría y realidad constitucional* 32: 139–158.
Luque, E., M. Ferrer, and M. Capdevila. 2005. *La reincidencia penitenciaria en Cataluña*. Barcelona: Centre d'Estudis Jurídics i Formació Especialitzada.
Molina, F. 2016. Las cicatrices jurídicas del terrorismo: la doctrina Parot y otras interpretaciones irrazonables de la ley. In *La tutela multinivel del principio de legalidad penal*, ed. M. Pérez-Manzano and J.A. Lascurain. Madrid: Marcial Pons.
Montero, E., and J. Nistal. 2015. La evolución de la población reclusa en España entre 1995 y 2014. Algunas causas explicativas. *Cuadernos de Política Criminal* 116: 159–200.
Padfield, N., D. van Zyl Smit, and F. Dünkel, eds. 2010. *Release from Prison. European Policy and Practice*. Cullompton: Willan Publishing.
Petersilia, J. 2003. *When Prisoners Come Home. Parole and Prisoner Reentry*. Oxford: Oxford University Press.
Queralt, A. 2013. Martinez Sala c. España (STEDH de 2 de Noviembre 2004): la vertiente procedimental del derecho a no sufrir torturas ni penas o tratos inhumanos o degradantes. In *La tutela multinivel del principio de legalidad penal*, ed. M. Pérez-Manzano and J.A. Lascurain. Madrid: Marcial Pons.
Roldán, H. 1988. *Historia de la prisión en España*. Barcelona: Publicaciones del Instituto de Criminología de Barcelona.
Tamarit, J.M. 2007. Sistema de sanciones y política criminal. *Revista Electrónica de Ciencia Penal y Criminología* 9 (6): 1–40.
Van Zyl Smit, D., and S. Snacken. 2009. *Principles of European Prison Law and Policy. Penology and Human Rights*. Oxford: Oxford University Press.

**José Cid** is Associate Professor of Criminology and Criminal Law at the Autonomous University of Barcelona, Spain.

**Ariadna Andreu** is a former Research Fellow at the Autonomous University of Barcelona, Spain. Currently she is Research Fellow at the University of Barcelona, Spain.

# Monitoring the Implementation Gap: A Comparative Perspective

Jonas Visschers and Tom Daems

## 1 Introduction

The European Committee for the Prevention of Torture and Inhuman or Degrading Treatment or Punishment (CPT) has become a key actor in the field of prison policy throughout Europe. The coming of age of the CPT, which celebrated its 25th anniversary in 2015, makes it possible to reflect upon its successes as well as its failures. More in particular, over a quarter of a century of monitoring Europe's prisons by the CPT offers academics as well as human rights activists the opportunity to explore more in-depth what happens in the post-visit phase. Indeed, as the CPT already indicated in the early 1990s: 'The transmission of the report… is…to be seen as the beginning, not the end, of a process' (CPT/Inf(91)3: para 33). But what exactly happens after a report has been transmitted?

There are some indications that the CPT, like the European Court of Human Rights (ECtHR) (see, e.g. Anagnostou 2013; Anagnostou and Skleparis, this volume), is often and increasingly being confronted with

J. Visschers (✉) • T. Daems
Leuven Institute of Criminology (LINC), KU Leuven, Leuven, Belgium



T. Daems, L. Robert (eds.), *Europe in Prisons*, Palgrave Studies in Prisons and Penology, DOI 10.1007/978-3-319-62250-7_11

an implementation gap. Indeed, in recent years, the CPT has at various occasions complained about a lack of follow-up of its recommendations. In its 24th general report, for example, the CPT observed the following:

> …it is a matter of concern to the Committee that, in respect of several states parties, it has been obliged to repeat recommendations made in the context of earlier visits, having found no significant improvement or, in some cases, even a worsening of the situation. In the same vein, the responses of some states parties limit themselves to merely invoking the domestic legislative framework, whereas the CPT's recommendations in question pointed to the need for practical improvements, policy changes or even the amendment of legislation. (CPT/Inf(2015)1: 6)

Moreover, unlike the ECtHR which has a formal supervision mechanism (i.e. the adoption of execution measures is being supervised by the Committee of Ministers of the Council of Europe), the 1987 Convention does not foresee a similar mechanism that would allow for a systematic supervision of the implementation process of the CPT's recommendations. The CPT's recommendations form part of the ongoing dialogue that is being maintained with the authorities of the Council of Europe member states, but apart from the formal reply by the States or the high-level talks the CPT can initiate in rather exceptional circumstances, there seems to be no real follow-up of its recommendations.

However, notwithstanding this lack of an institutionalised follow-up mechanism, it is possible to say something about how European states deal with the recommendations of the CPT. The coming of age of the CPT implies that it has, by now, paid multiple periodic visits (usually every four to five years) as well as ad hoc visits to all member states of the Council of Europe. Close study of the CPT's reports related to a country, as well as the formal replies from state authorities in that country, should therefore enable observers of the work of the CPT to assess whether problems that have been identified by the CPT in a member state's prison system have been addressed by responding favourably to the CPT's recommendations or, alternatively, how these problems have been left untouched over a longer period of time (Daems 2017). The CPT's reports and the member states' replies, which over the years in fact have come to constitute a grand European archive containing hundreds of documents dealing with prison practice throughout Europe, are freely accessible through the CPT's website and will, hopefully, be searched further in future research by penologists throughout Europe.

Our ambition in this chapter is more modest. We will offer a first step towards describing and analysing the interactions between the CPT and three European states by focusing on one key theme, that is, prison regime. Countries included in this chapter are Norway, Poland and Spain. All three have a long-standing relationship with the CPT[1] and, therefore, the CPT maintains with each of them a so-called ongoing dialogue on the challenges their prison systems face and the ways in which these, in the CPT's view, might be most productively addressed. What has the CPT observed about the prison regime in Norway, Poland and Spain and how did state authorities respond to questions and recommendations of the CPT? What can we learn about the implementation gap?

This chapter is structured as follows: the next section briefly discusses the CPT's standards with respect to prison regime. We then continue with an overview of the major issues that have been identified by the CPT with respect to prison regime in Norway, Poland and Spain as well as the responses that have been formulated by the state authorities of the three selected countries. The chapter will conclude with a brief discussion.

## 2 Prison Regime and CPT Standards

Ever since its first visits, the quality of prison regime has been a constant preoccupation for the CPT. In its second general report (published in 1992), the CPT already stressed that prisoners should be offered a range of varied purposeful activities, including work, vocation, education, sport and recreation. Remand prisoners should be able to spend eight hours or more a day outside their cells engaged in such activities, and for sentenced prisoners, the regime should be even more favourable (CPT/Inf(92)3: para 47; CPT/Inf(2015)44: appendix). As for outdoor exercise, the CPT emphasised that all prisoners should be given the opportunity to exercise outdoors at least one hour per day, in yards which are spacious and suitably equipped to allow them to exert themselves physically, and equipped with a means of rest and shelter against inclement weather (CPT/Inf(92)3: para 48; CPT/Inf(2015)44: appendix).

Over the years, the CPT has devoted special attention to the needs of specific groups of prisoners. In the CPT's view, prisoners who are considered to be dangerous should benefit from a more relaxed regime as compensation for their more severe custodial situation. Hence, they should be offered activities as diverse as possible and a good deal of choice about the activities they want to participate in. The CPT also stresses that, notwithstanding their exclusion from several types of work because of security concerns, dangerous prisoners should not only be offered work of a tedious nature. Moreover, a good internal atmosphere should be provided in units accommodating dangerous prisoners with contact between prisoners and positive relations between staff and prisoners (CPT/Inf(2001)16: para 32). For prisoners held in solitary confinement, the CPT insists that their cells should meet the same minimum standards as ordinary cells and adds that they should not be subjected to more restrictions than absolutely necessary, given their situation. Further, the CPT asks for a clear differentiation between the regimes applicable to prisoners placed in solitary confinement, depending on the type of solitary confinement. For example, remand prisoners placed in solitary confinement by court order should be treated as far as possible as ordinary prisoners, while those placed in solitary confinement as a disciplinary sanction should never be totally deprived of family contact, and they should be offered—and even encouraged to take—one hour of outdoor exercise and be provided with diversified reading material (CPT/Inf(2011)28: para 61). Prisoners placed in administrative solitary confinement for preventative purposes should be provided with individual regime plans, geared towards addressing the reason(s) for the measure. Such plans '…should attempt to maximise contact with others—staff initially, but as soon as practicable with appropriate other prisoners—and provide as full a range of activities as is possible to fill the days' (CPT/Inf(2011)28: para 61). Furthermore, staff should encourage prisoners placed in administrative solitary confinement to take part in activities. Lastly, with respect to prisoners held in solitary confinement for protection purposes for prolonged periods, '… special efforts should be made to identify other prisoners with whom the prisoner concerned could safely associate and situations where it would be possible to bring the person out of cell' (CPT/Inf(2011)28: para 61).

# 3 Prison Regimes in Three Countries

## 3.1 Solitary Confinement in Norway

At the occasion of its visits to Norway, the CPT has repeatedly expressed its concerns about the regime offered to remand prisoners held in solitary confinement by court order. In the establishments visited in 1993, such prisoners were held 23 hours a day isolated in their cells, without being able to engage in activities other than daily outdoor exercise (CPT/Inf(94)11: paras 61–63). In 1999, the CPT noted some improvements to the regime for this particular group of inmates (such as in-cell activities, recreational activities and contact with staff) but, nevertheless, these prisoners remained locked up in their cell for 22–23 hours a day, without being able to communicate with other inmates (CPT/Inf(2000)15: para 40). The CPT, therefore, welcomed the adaptations made by the Norwegian authorities, but in its view, the regime offered to such prisoners remained 'impoverished' (CPT/Inf(2000)15: para 40). During the 2005 visit, the delegation was informed about and welcomed the fact that legislative and regulatory amendments had come into force aimed at improving the regime offered to prisoners held in solitary confinement (e.g. priority for such prisoners for participation in activities and contact with staff). However, the delegation observed little improvement in practice, as it met once more prisoners held in solitary confinement being locked up in their cells for 22–23 hours a day and having little contact with staff and other inmates (CPT/Inf(2006)14: para 55–56). Finally, in 2011, the Committee acknowledged the efforts of the management of the prisons visited to provide inmates held in solitary confinement by court order with in-cell activities and human contact. However, out-of-cell activities for such prisoners remained rather limited at one of the establishments visited. The situation was more favourable in the other prison, where this group of inmates was allowed to go to the gym for one to two hours a day, in addition to the daily hour of outdoor exercise (CPT/Inf(2011)28: para 75).

How did Norway respond to the CPT's concerns? Initially, the Norwegian authorities stressed that prisoners subjected to solitary confinement or held under restrictions for an extended period would, '...as far as personnel and other resources permit, be offered various activities..., opportunities for physical exercise and contact with prison staff' (CPT/Inf(94)12: 15). After the 1999 visit, the response changed somewhat: the authorities now also mentioned that activities for prisoners held in solitary confinement or under restrictions were limited because of the available funds and budgetary limits. Nevertheless, the Ministry of Justice had asked the prison governors to consider whether activities and contact for such prisoners could be increased by redistributing the available funds and would continue its work to improve their situation (CPT/Inf(2000)16: 18). After the 2005 visit, the response strategy of the Norwegian authorities changed once more. In their reply, the authorities declared that they tried '...to provide activities and appropriate human contact for as many remand prisoners held in solitary confinement and/or under restrictions as possible' (CPT/Inf(2006)34: 17), but also that the limits on the number of remand prisoners that can be held in solitary confinement or under restrictions without additional activities needing to be offered, were not exceeded at the time of the visit. Nevertheless, it was also indicated that the correctional services aimed '...to increase the number of remand prisoners offered activities' (CPT/Inf(2006)34: 17). However, it was unclear whether the Norwegian authorities were referring to remand prisoners in general or to remand prisoners held in solitary confinement or under restrictions in particular. Finally, after the 2011 visit, the Norwegian authorities explained that the limited out-of-cell activities for prisoners held in solitary confinement by court order in one of the establishments visited by the CPT was caused by the limited number of exercising rooms at this establishment. This would improve with the completion of the replacement of the building (CPT/Inf(2012)20: 26).

### 3.2 Work in Prison and Dangerous Offenders in Poland

The CPT has consistently highlighted that the availability of activities, in particular work, is insufficient in the Polish prison system. During its first visit to Poland (in 1996), the delegation observed that the employment situation in the establishments visited was far from satisfactory, '…a problem which apparently exists throughout the Polish penitentiary system' (CPT/Inf(98)13: para 71). In this context, the CPT stressed that '...the employment situation within the prison system should not be dictated exclusively by market forces', and that, 'if necessary, special measures should be introduced with a view to promoting work for prisoners' (CPT/Inf(98)13: para 71). But also the provision of other types of activities (such as training, education or sport) was being criticised at several occasions in the report (e.g. CPT/Inf(98) 13: paras 81–83, 94–96, 109–110). In 2000, the delegation observed that the measures taken by the Polish authorities to address the problem of prisoner work availability (in particular, a special law aimed at facilitating the employment of prisoners outside the prison system) had failed to bear fruit, as only 20 % of the inmates had work. The CPT repeated that prisoner employment should not solely be determined by market forces and added that 'a wider range of voluntary unpaid work activities should also be offered to prisoners' (CPT/Inf(2002)9: para 62). In addition, the CPT was again critical of various aspects of the programme of activities, other than work, offered to prisoners at the visited establishments (e.g. CPT/Inf(2002)9: paras 77–78, 88, 101–102, 115). After the third periodic visit (in 2004), the Committee stated that '...the situation as regards the provision of work, training and education to inmates in the prison establishments visited was far from satisfactory, a problem which apparently exists throughout the Polish penitentiary system' (CPT/Inf(2006)11: para 65). Focusing, in particular, on employment, the delegation was informed during the visit that only 23 % of the prisoner population had paid or unpaid work. The Committee acknowledged the efforts of prison management to create more jobs, but in its view, these would most probably only result into small improvements. Real reform, so the CPT clarified its position, requires that the Polish approach towards prison work changes fundamentally, that is, work in prison should be '...geared towards rehabilitation and resocialisation rather than towards financial profit' (CPT/Inf(2006)11: para 65). In 2009, the CPT again referred to the situation with respect to organised activities (work, training, education, sports, etc.) as generally unsatisfactory (CPT/Inf(2011)20: para 84). It also stressed that this situation affected, in particular, remand prisoners, rendering their prison experience more punitive than the one of sentenced prisoners. The delegation was informed that efforts were made to improve the provision of purposeful activities and work, but it stressed that more remained to be done (CPT/Inf(2011)20: para 84). Four years later, the CPT came to a similar conclusion: during its 2013 visit, the Committee noted that '...the provision of organised activities...was still generally very unsatisfactory' and repeated that the lack of activities for remand prisoners '...rendered their situation considerably worse than that of sentenced prisoners' (CPT/Inf(2014)21: para 43).

How did the Polish authorities respond to the CPT's observations and recommendations? After the 1996 visit, the Polish authorities indicated that the new 'Penal Executory Code' would create opportunities for new kinds of employment for prisoners (e.g. the possibility to work as freelancer), that a new law would introduce several measures to reduce production costs and increase employment of detained persons, and that '... prison service officers for employment of detained persons take actions to keep employment of the same level and even increase it in workshops outside prison establishments' and '...also look for new places of work' (CPT/Inf(1998)14: 34–35). As for other activities, it was mentioned that improvements had been made at two of the three establishments that were visited by the CPT in 1996 (CPT/Inf(1998)14: 22–23). No further information was provided with regard to the situation in the third establishment. After the second visit (in 2000), the Polish authorities again declared that different steps were being taken to offer more inmates the opportunity to work (CPT/Inf (2002)10: 21–22) and that the CPT's concerns with respect to other types of activities had been addressed (CPT/Inf (2002)10: 29–35). After the 2004 visit, the Polish authorities responded that several legal amendments had already been introduced and further steps were envisaged to make employment of prisoners common practice. However, they also played down the extent of the problem somehow by adding that inmates had already access to education and higher courses of vocational training (CPT/Inf(2006)12: 19–21). In its reply to the fourth visit (in 2009), the Polish authorities stressed that efforts were being made to allow large groups of inmates to participate in various cultural (educational) and sports activities and that, despite difficulties in organising activities for remand prisoners, they would attempt to ensure that such prisoners could participate in the largest number of out-of-cell activities possible (CPT/Inf(2011)21: 41–42). After the 2013 visit, the Polish authorities highlighted that reintegration programmes as well as work were, as far as possible, on offer to both remand and sentenced prisoners and repeated (cf. the Polish response to the previous visit) that, in spite of the difficulties in organising activities for remand prisoners, the penitentiary authorities had taken—and were still taking—measures to offer remand prisoners the opportunity to participate in the largest number of out-of-cell activities possible (CPT/Inf(2014)22: 29).

The regime for inmates who are classified 'dangerous' has been a particular concern of the CPT throughout its periodic visits to Poland. During the 1996 visit, the Committee noticed that dangerous prisoners were subject to an impoverished regime (e.g. limited out-of-cell time and in-cell activities, and exclusion from work or activities involving other prisoners; CPT/Inf(98)13: para 144). The CPT stressed that such prisoners should 'enjoy a relatively relaxed regime... by way of compensation for their severe custodial situation' (e.g. they should be permitted to mix freely with fellow prisoners and to move without restrictions in a small physical space, and activities offered to them should be as diverse as possible; CPT/Inf(98)13: para 145). The CPT did not observe any improvement during the 2000 visit: the regime for dangerous prisoners was still '...characterised by a total absence of organised activities and a paucity of human contact' (e.g. limited out-of-cell time and in-cell activities and restricted contact with prison officers; CPT/Inf(2002)9: para 71). The Committee repeated that it had serious misgivings about such a regime and stressed that it is up to the Polish authorities to provide all prisoners, regardless of the gravity of the offences they are accused or convicted of or their dangerousness, with appropriate stimulation and adequate human contact (CPT/Inf(2002)9: para 71). In 2004, the CPT retained its misgivings about the very restrictive regime applied to dangerous prisoners (e.g. limited out-of-cell time and absence of contact with prison officers) and stressed once more that prisoners, regardless of gravity of offences or dangerousness, should be given appropriate stimulation and human contact (CPT/Inf(2006)11: para 77). However, it seems as if its words again fell on deaf ears: the regime observed in 2009 was similar to the one observed in 2004 (CPT/Inf(2011)20: para 91). The delegation was informed that the Polish authorities had attempted to provide dangerous prisoners with in-cell work in two prisons that were visited by the CPT, but that these efforts had been discontinued. At the other establishment visited, individual plans were being developed and regular staff meetings were organised to discuss the situation of each dangerous prisoner. However, '...there appeared to be little to no structurally planned intervention...of the staff to provide appropriate mental and physical stimulation to [dangerous] prisoners' (CPT/Inf(2011)20: para 91). The CPT concluded that the regime for dangerous prisoners should be fundamentally reviewed by establishing inter alia a structured programme of constructive (and preferably out-of-cell) activities and encouraging such inmates to take part in this programme. It also repeated that such prisoners should be provided with appropriate stimulation and human contact (CPT/Inf(2011)20: para 91). But radical reform again did not take place: the situation observed during the 2013 visit was similar to the one observed during the two previous visits (CPT/Inf(2014)21: para 50). However, the Committee noted and welcomed the efforts of staff working with dangerous prisoners at the establishments visited to maintain regular interaction with them and to facilitate contact with the outside world. Nevertheless, the CPT repeated that the regime for such prisoners should be fundamentally reviewed as suggested after the 2009 visit (CPT/Inf (2014)21: para 50).

How did the Polish authorities respond to these concerns? Initially, after the first visit, they replied that dangerous prisoners '…are subject to intensified penitentiary actions according to individual programme' (CPT/Inf(1998)14: 41). However, the authorities failed to clarify the content of these 'intensified penitentiary actions'. After the second visit (in 2000), the Polish reply stressed more clearly that various activities were offered to dangerous prisoners and that such inmates had many possibilities to get in contact with the outside world (CPT/Inf(2002)10: 26–27). The response strategy of the Polish authorities changed somewhat after the next visit (in 2004): now it was announced that despite the fact that dangerous prisoners do have the same rights with respect to activities (even though it was acknowledged that certain activities may be filled in differently) and human contact as other prisoners, recommendations on how to treat such prisoners, worked out by the Prison Service, were already implemented in some establishments (CPT/Inf(2006)12: 26). The response to the CPT's concerns as expressed in the reports of the 2009 and 2013 visit, however, sounded very similar. Dangerous offenders, so it was argued, can choose whether they serve their sentence in an ordinary prison regime (where individual stimulation plans are not developed, but participation in activities is possible) or in a so-called programmed impact system (where individual plans are developed, aimed at providing appropriate mental and physical stimulation) (CPT/Inf(2011)21: 49–50; CPT/Inf(2014)22: 35–36).

## 3.3 Activities and Dangerous and 'Unadapted' Prisoners in Spain

Interestingly, the CPT has at several occasions observed and applauded that prisoners in Spain are being offered extensive out-of-cell time (e.g. CPT/Inf(96)9[Part 1]: para 158). However, over the years, the Committee has also identified and pointed at a number of weaknesses in the regime activities offered to inmates. For example, in 1991, the CPT noticed that the activities (e.g. workshops, educational and vocational courses and sports activities) were underdeveloped (CPT/Inf(96)9[Part 1]: paras 160–162). This was somehow confirmed during the second periodic visit (in 1994) when the Committee noted in two establishments that '...there was much enforced idleness among the prisoners, as activity programmes could not match the demand; for many, out-of-cell activities consisted essentially of exercise and watching television' (CPT/Inf(96)9[Part 2]: para 129). However, in the third prison it visited, the CPT welcomed the fact that several '...efforts had been made to ensure that all prisoners were offered activities' (CPT/Inf(96)9[Part 2]: para 130). In 1998, the CPT noted that by no means all prisoners were provided with purposeful activities, particularly work, during their extensive out-of-cell time (CPT/Inf(2000)5: para 73). But the Committee did stress that the observed situation represented '...a considerable improvement as compared to that which was found in certain establishments visited on previous occasions by the CPT' (CPT/Inf(2000)5: para 77). However, the CPT also insisted that the programmes offered to prisoners could be further developed, in particular, because the facilities set aside for activities were under-utilised. During the fourth periodic visit (in 2003), the Committee observed that only a minority of the prisoners were offered organised activities, and that 'the others spent most of their time in complete idleness' (CPT/Inf(2007)28: para 90). In its view, this state of affairs was particularly unacceptable in the establishments visited, as these held primarily sentenced prisoners. In 2007, the delegation focused solely on the regime in special departments (cf., infra). During the 2011 visit, the Committee noticed that prisoners falling under the authority of the Spanish government '...spent most of the day...outside their cells, either in the common areas of their respective modules or engaged in an organised activity' (CPT/Inf(2013)6: para 53). However, at two of the establishments visited, only a few inmates were involved in some of the organised activities. With respect to the regime for prisoners falling under the authority of the Catalan government, the CPT observed that an adequate offer of activities was available in two establishments. However, the situation was less positive in two other prisons: in one institution, the workshops were under-utilised and overburdened, and in the other, '...the opportunities to participate in purposeful activities were extremely limited' (CPT/Inf(2013)6: para 137).

How did the Spanish (and Catalan) authorities respond to these findings and recommendations of the CPT? After the 1994 visit, the Spanish authorities simply stated that the offer of activities in the prison criticised by the CPT was quite extensive and that the majority of the inmates could participate in these activities (CPT/Inf (96)10: 95–96). The Catalan authorities stressed that, in spite of the difficult situation caused by overcrowding, significant steps had been taken to improve the level of activities offered to the inmates detained in the establishment criticised by the CPT. But the Catalan authorities also added that the Spanish law did not stipulate '...the obligation to participate in treatment activities' (CPT/Inf 96)10: 106). However, the meaning of the last part of this reply is not entirely clear: does this mean that there is no obligation for prison management to organise activities for inmates, or merely that prisoners themselves are not obliged to participate in such activities? The Spanish authorities replied to the 1998 visit that efforts were being made to improve the factors restricting the provision of activities, and that the reorganisation of education in penitentiaries had had a positive effect on the activity level and the quality of organised activities in prisons (CPT/Inf(2000)6: 50–54). The Catalan authorities, however, simply stated that, as far as possible, efforts were being made '...to increase the volume of productive work to be carried out by the inmates' (CPT/Inf(2000)6: 54). After the 2003 visit, the Spanish authorities confirmed that not all prisoners participated in productive work but they added that this was complemented by the organisation of other educational, training, occupational, socio-cultural, sports and therapeutic activities (CPT/Inf(2007)29: 31). Finally, after the 2011 visit, the Spanish and Catalan authorities declared that the responsible administrations had already made and were still making considerable efforts to offer prisoners a wide range of purposeful activities (educational, vocational, cultural, therapeutic, etc.) geared towards their social reintegration. In this context, the Spanish authorities mentioned, in particular, the implementation of the so-called 'Intervention Specific Programmes' (which include inter alia a gender-related violence programme, a sexual aggression control programme and a foreigner inmates intervention programme; CPT/Inf(2013)7: 88–94), while the Catalan authorities made particular reference to the recently established 'Curricular Organisation Framework Programme'. This Framework Programme aimed to '...continue progressing in the field of intervention via activities geared towards rehabilitation' (CPT/Inf(2013)7: 156).

A particular concern of the Committee throughout its visits to Spain has been the regime offered to prisoners considered as dangerous or unadapted to an ordinary prison regime. During its inaugural 1991 visit, the delegation learned that the prison term for such inmates was divided into three phases. Notwithstanding individual differences, a common feature of the regime in the first two phases was a penury of regime activities. The Committee stressed that the strictest regimes in the first two phases were '... scarcely distinguishable from solitary confinement as punishment' and that holding prisoners for long periods under 'a regime of isolation and...under austere material conditions of detention with little or nothing by way of activity...constitutes inhuman treatment' (CPT/Inf(96)9[Part 1]: para 113). Also, the less stringent regimes in the first two phases were criticised by the Committee. The delegation highlighted that, also here, the notion of treatment was 'seriously undermined' (CPT/Inf (96)9[Part 1]: para 114). During its second periodic visit (in 1994), the delegation was informed that the three phases had been reduced to two. However, the regime in the first phase remained a matter of concern, as the delegation observed once more a penury of activities for prisoners placed in this phase, with limited out-of-cell time and a lack of programmes of organised activities (CPT/Inf(96)9[Part 2]: para 109). The Committee stated again that the situation of at least some of the prisoners placed in the first phase was comparable to solitary confinement as punishment and repeated that '...a combination of long periods of isolation, austere material conditions of detention and absence of activities amounts...to inhuman treatment' (CPT/Inf(96)9[Part 2]: para 109). However, the delegation was also informed about the drafting of a so-called 'Programme for the Recuperation of Conflictive Inmates', which would involve a reconsideration of the regime for prisoners considered as dangerous or unadapted to an ordinary prison regime (CPT/Inf(96)9[Part 2]: para 112). In 1998, the delegation was informed about certain noteworthy developments, such as the establishment of the Prison Rules. These rules stipulated that the regime for dangerous or unadapted to an ordinary regime prisoners may in no case involve restrictions equal to or larger than those of solitary confinement as disciplinary sanction. Furthermore, a distinction was introduced between dangerous prisoners, entitled to at least three hours of daily outdoor exercise, and prisoners unadapted to an ordinary prison regime, entitled to at least four hours of daily association. Both groups could be offered up to an additional three hours of organised activities. The exact content of the programme of activities offered to both categories of inmates was to be determined by the treatment board of a prison. It should include not only cultural, sports, recreational and educational activities but also work (CPT/Inf (2000)5: paras 65–66). In practice, however, dangerous prisoners could spend 10 hours per day out of their cells in one of the special departments visited by the CPT, while at the other special department out-of-cell time of dangerous prisoners, in addition to outdoor exercise, was limited to two-weekly sessions of two hours (CPT/Inf(2000)5: para 67). Prisoners unadapted to an ordinary prison regime held in closed units benefitted from more out-of-cell time than dangerous prisoners, but the CPT stressed that 'the range of activities offered to them during such time could usefully be developed' (CPT/Inf(2000)5: para 69). During the fourth periodic visit (in 2003), no improvements in the regime offered to dangerous or unadapted prisoners were observed. The CPT stressed that such prisoners '...should enjoy a relatively relaxed regime within their detention unit, by way of compensation for their severe custodial situation. In particular, they should be able to meet their fellow prisoners in the unit and be granted a good deal of choice about activities' (CPT/Inf(2007)28: para 81). In 2007, the Committee observed that dangerous or unadapted prisoners in the special departments of two Catalan establishments were offered few to no organised activities besides outdoor exercise (CPT/Inf(2011)11: para 95). It therefore reiterated that '...such prisoners should enjoy a relatively relaxed regime within their detention unit, by way of compensation for their severe custodial situation' (CPT/Inf(2011)11: para 96). As for the Spanish prisons, the Committee noted the adoption of the so-called 'Protocol on the Implementation of Treatment Programmes for Prisoners placed in Closed Regimes', 'the spirit and content of which do address some of the CPT's concerns' (CPT/Inf(2011)11: para 131), inter alia by prescribing a varied daily programme of activities. In practice, however, the CPT noticed that '...regime activities were, on the whole, very poor in all of the prisons visited. Inmates had little to no opportunity to spend the day constructively' (CPT/Inf(2011)11: para 132). Finally, in 2011, the so-called 'Closed System Intervention Programme', which was presented in the Spanish reply to the previous periodic visit as a multidisciplinary tool to progressively re-integrate dangerous and unadapted prisoners into an ordinary regime (cf., infra), did not seem to be operational in any of the prisons visited by the CPT (CPT/Inf(2013)6: para 65). The CPT repeated that the lack of activities and prolonged periods of isolation in special departments exacerbated the situation of prisoners '...who showed clear signs of mental health concerns' (CPT/Inf(2013)6: para 66). Based on its observations in the Catalan special departments, the CPT commented that more could be done to engage such inmates in the activity programmes (two establishments) or that few to no organised activities besides outdoor exercise were made available to them (two establishments; CPT/Inf (2014)21: para 134).

What were the Spanish and Catalan governments' responses to the issues raised with respect to the special regime offered to prisoners considered as dangerous or unadapted to an ordinary prison regime? In their reply to the 1994 visit report, the Spanish authorities announced that '...the Penitentiary Administration is making big effort to modify the rules of the closed regime' inter alia by introducing a bill which would '...establish expressly that in any case, the regime of life for the inmates in a closed regime can (sic) lay down equal or greater restrictions to the restrictions established for the punishment of isolation in cell'. But it was also argued that '…the CPT's remarks and recommendations are followed in the establishment of this unsurmountable limit' and that '…this limit has been accomplished scrupulously by the Penitentiary Administration on every occasion' (CPT/Inf(96)10: 93). So, probably, the word 'can' in the first quote is a typo and should have been 'cannot'. In any case, the Spanish authorities stressed that the 'Programme for the Recuperation of Conflictive Inmates' emphasised the treatment activities for such prisoners (CPT/Inf (96)10: 93). In its response to the CPT's queries listed in the 1998 visit report, the Spanish authorities indicated that '...a specific intervention program ...has achieved favourable results, on account of the increasing number of inmates who leave the special regime and integrate definitively into the ordinary regime' (CPT/Inf(2000)6: 48). However, it is not clear whether the Spanish authorities referred to the 'Programme for the Recuperation of Conflictive Inmates' or to another intervention programme for prisoners held in special departments. After the 2003 visit, however, the Spanish authorities responded that they were planning to re-orient the regime of the special departments, in such a way that it would include a model for intervention, as well as generic treatment programmes aimed at the progressive adaptation of inmates to the normal prison regime (CPT/Inf(2007)29: 29). After the 2007 visit, the Catalan authorities pointed at the circular on the 'Closed System Intervention Framework Programme', which aimed to introduce a new work and intervention model, and highlighted that in accordance with this programme individual assistance and group activities were being provided by a multidisciplinary team to dangerous and unadapted prisoners—this was also the case in the two prisons that were criticised by the CPT, so they argued (CPT/Inf(2011)12: 93–95). Also, the Spanish authorities stressed that quite some prisons had introduced this new 'Framework Programme' and that an ongoing assessment of special departments applying closed system programmes had demonstrated that all of them provided some activity in which inmates could participate. Prisons unable to be provided with closed system programmes did organise therapeutic, occupational and/or sports activities as compensation, according to the Spanish authorities (CPT/Inf (2011)12: 117–118). Finally, after the 2011 visit, the Spanish authorities highlighted the 'Protocol for Intervention and Rules in

Closed Regimes' and stated that this programme had, in the meantime, been established in every Spanish prison with a closed regime department. They also stressed that prisoners who did not want to participate in this programme or who were excluded from participation in the programme were in any event offered a varied range of activities (CPT/Inf(2013)7: 108–109). The Catalan authorities referred again (cf., their response to the previous periodic visit) to the 'Closed System Intervention Framework Programme', and repeated that in accordance with this programme individual assistance and group activities were provided to closed regime prisoners by a multidisciplinary team. They insisted that this was also true for the two prisons that were, in the CPT's view, not offering any organised activities besides outdoor exercise (CPT/Inf(2013)7: 157–159).

# 4 Monitoring the Implementation Gap

It is interesting to observe that over the years, the CPT has been critical about aspects of the regime in *all* three countries. Moreover, despite various repetitions of its recommendations, it seems as if state authorities in the three countries often fail to address the problems identified by the CPT in an adequate and efficient way. The implementation gap is therefore not only being observed for the 'usual suspects' (such as Poland which has attracted negative coverage by CPT, Ngo's and the ECtHR for a long time) but also for a country like Norway. To the outside observer, this may seem somewhat counterintuitive because Norwegian prisons are usually, like penitentiary institutions in other Scandinavian countries, characterised by low prison rates and decent and humane prison regimes. Indeed, the mild penal climate in the North of Europe has been discussed in the penological literature under headings like Nordic or Scandinavian exceptionalism (see, e.g. Pratt 2008; Pratt and Eriksson 2011). Interestingly, such welfare traditions (see also Horn and Ugelvik, this volume) have not made Scandinavian countries immune to critique from the CPT. For example, in October 2014, the CPT had the following to say about Finland:

> the principle of co-operation between State Parties and the CPT is not limited to steps taken to facilitate the task of a visiting delegation. It also requires that decisive action be taken to improve the situation in the light

> of the Committee's recommendations. In this respect, and despite ongoing efforts in a number of areas, the delegation is concerned by the lack of sufficient progress in the implementation of many of the CPT's longstanding recommendations (such as on the detention of remand prisoners in police prisons, on the practice of 'slopping out' in prisons, on the regime for prisoners segregated in closed units and on the judicial review of involuntary psychiatric hospitalisation measures). (CPT/Inf(2014)28: 3)

It is striking how the CPT seems to focus on specific issues depending on the country visited. For Norway, the CPT has exclusively pointed at the activities and opportunities for contact offered to prisoners subjected to solitary confinement. The extensive use of (pre-trial) solitary confinement seems to be a phenomenon that is also present in other Scandinavian countries (see Morgan 1999). Why are Scandinavian countries making so much use of pre-trial solitary confinement? The origins of this practice go back to the mid-nineteenth century, with the breakthrough of the Pennsylvania prison system which emphasised individual reform through isolation. By the end of the nineteenth century, pre-trial solitary confinement had become the rule rather than the exception in Scandinavian prisons, and this continued to be the case throughout the twentieth century, even though it was now justified in terms of reducing the risk of collusion rather than moral rehabilitation (Smith 2012). From the 1990s onwards, though, Scandinavian countries have been widely criticised for their extensive use of solitary confinement during pre-trial detention inter alia by academics and international monitoring bodies such as the Subcommittee for the Prevention of Torture of the United Nations (Smith 2012). Rod Morgan (1999) described the use of solitary confinement of Norwegian remand prisoners as a practice close to psychological torture, because of the severe pain it causes and the fact that prisoners are obliged to co-operate with the police in order to have it relieved.

The ongoing dialogue between the CPT and Norway (cf., supra) suggests that over the years the regime for remand prisoners placed under solitary confinement has improved significantly but also that, despite the fact that the CPT has repeatedly brought this theme to the attention of the authorities, Norway still fails to live up to the CPT's expectations (see Smith (2012) for Denmark and Sweden). The situation is different for other inmates: here, the CPT usually welcomes the various work, educational and leisure opportunities on offer. Liberal regimes have, indeed, been identified as a key feature of Norwegian and other Scandinavian prisons and indicative of the high level of normalisation of prison life in these countries (Pratt 2008; Pratt and Eriksson 2011).

The problems identified for Poland are different in nature. We have seen that the CPT has been particularly concerned about the limited work opportunities in the Polish prison system, next to other organised activities, such as training, education and sports. How can the unfavourable work situation in Poland be explained? Before the collapse of the Soviet Union, prison labour played a major role in the Polish prison system (Holda 1995, 1999). However, providing prisoners with work was dictated primarily by societal or economic interests; inmates were predominantly used as cheap labour force (Holda 1995; Platek 2013). Ninety % of convicted prisoners were provided with work (Holda 1999). However, work conditions were highly inadequate and remuneration was very low (Holda 1995, 1999; Holda and Rzeplinski 1991). Since the fall of the Soviet Union, the work conditions of employed prisoners have improved, but the role of prison labour was deeply affected by the transformation to a market economy. Because of a declining demand for inmates as labourers and poor economic performance of prison enterprises, the number of available work places decreased significantly which resulted in very high prisoner unemployment (up to 70 %; Holda 1999; Platek 2013). The negative impact of these developments on prison life was, moreover, more pronounced as also the number of inmates who were able to participate in other types of activities was drastically reduced after the fall of the Soviet empire. Here, serious problems of overcrowding in Polish prisons are the principal cause, as these have urged prisons to shift focus to ensuring security within the establishment rather than working with prisoners (Platek 2013).

The situation in Spain seems to be more mixed. The CPT has focused, in particular, on the insufficient offer of activities but with little specific attention for prison labour. However, Spanish academics have repeatedly pointed at the lack of paid work opportunities and the poor remuneration for prison labour as one of the major weaknesses of the Spanish prison regime (Cid 2005; de la Cuesta and Blanco 2001; Makin 2013). Notwithstanding its critical comments on the offer of activities, it is interesting to note, however, that the CPT has welcomed the extensive out-of-cell time for Spanish inmates which relieves at least to some extent the adverse consequences of prison overcrowding. But the repeated critical observations and related recommendations of the CPT are an unambiguous indication that the authorities' responses have not always been satisfactory. It is, moreover, striking to observe how progress at times can end abruptly: for example, during the third periodic visit, the CPT noted a considerable improvement in the provision of activities to prisoners, but during the next periodic visit, the delegation observed again that most prisoners spent their time in complete idleness without opportunities to take part in activities.

Next to describing and analysing the *content* of a state's reply to the CPT's observations and recommendations, students of the implementation gap may be advised to include aspects of *form* in their future reflections on the interactions between the CPT and state authorities. At times, a response may be difficult to grasp because it tends to get lost in translation. For example:

> The Polish prison system developed rules of organization and conditions of conduct of penitentiary impact against convicts, persons under detention on remand and punished persons who pose serious social danger or serious danger for security of the penitentiary institution or a detention on remand centre, kept in conditions ensuring increased security of the community and the security of the penitentiary institution. Such solutions are aimed at intensification and unification of impact against dangerous inmates. (CPT/Inf(2011)21: 50)

The same holds for what we could refer to as 'bulk responding', that is, a response strategy whereby state authorities group a large number of the CPT's observations and recommendations and suggest that these have been addressed jointly by pointing at a recent policy decision or simply by clarifying the law or the applicable rules (for examples related to Poland, see CPT/Inf(2002)10: 10–11; CPT/Inf(2011)21: 17–20).

Moreover, it is usually possible to identify different ways of responding to recommendations of the CPT (Daems 2017). The Norwegian authorities initially responded to the CPT's critical comments by stating that they would offer various activities 'as far as personnel and other resources permitted'. However, from the second visit onwards, its response strategy changed somewhat as it became less reserved: now Norway confirmed that efforts would be made to increase activities and/or contact opportunities for these prisoners. As noted above, in the meantime, certain improvements have indeed been observed by the CPT with respect to the regime for these inmates. Interestingly, the response strategy of the Spanish authorities towards the issues raised by the CPT with respect to the regime for dangerous or unadapted prisoners seems to have developed in the opposite direction. Whereas, initially, the authorities seemed to agree with the CPT's assessment and demonstrated their willingness to address the problems, this tended to change from the 2007 visit onwards: now it was suggested that dangerous or unadapted prisoners were already provided with such activities. An implicit contestation of the CPT's observations also seems to have informed the standard Polish response: the authorities often replied that dangerous prisoners were already offered an adequate regime. However, as we have discussed above, the CPT has observed little to no improvement in this respect in Polish prisons.

## Notes

1. Norway and Spain signed the Convention on 26 November 1986. Norway ratified it on 21 April 1989, Spain on 2 May 1989. Poland joined the Council of Europe in 1990. It signed the Convention on 11 June 1994 and ratified it on 10 October 1994. The reports as well as the responses for all three countries have been made public and are available on the CPT's website http://www.coe.int/en/web/cpt, with the exception of the Government response to the CPT's 1991 visit to Spain.

## Literature

Anagnostou, D., ed. 2013. *The European Court of Human Rights. Implementing Strasbourg's Judgments on Domestic Policy*. Edinburgh: Edinburgh University Press.

Cid, J. 2005. The Penitentiary System in Spain: The Use of Imprisonment, Living Conditions and Rehabilitation. *Punishment & Society* 7: 147–166.

Daems, T. 2017. Slaves and Statues: Torture Prevention in Contemporary Europe. *British Journal of Criminology* 57 (3): 627–643.

De la Cuesta, J.L., and I. Blanco. 2001. Spain. In *Imprisonment Today And tomorrow: International Perspectives on Prisoners' Rights and Prison Conditions*, ed. D. van Zyl Smit and F. Dünkel, 2nd ed. The Hague: Kluwer Law International.

Holda, Z. 1995. The Law of Corrections in Poland. In *Legal Reform in Post-Communist Europe: The View from Within*, ed. S. Frankowski and P.B. Stephan. Dordrecht: Nijhoff.

———. 1999. Poland. In *Prison Labour: Salvation or Slavery? International Perspectives*, ed. D. van Zyl Smit and F. Dünkel. Aldershot: Ashgate.

Holda, Z., and A. Rzeplinski. 1991. The Polish Prison System in Mid-course: Prisoners' Rights and Prison Conditions in Poland on the Verge of Becoming Civilized. In *Imprisonment Today and Tomorrow: International Perspectives on Prisoners' Rights and Prison Conditions*, ed. D. van Zyl Smit and F. Dünkel. Deventer: Kluwer.

Makin, A. 2013. Popular Punitivism and Cultural Mediation: The Case of Spain. *International Journal of Law, Crime and Justice* 41: 260–276.

Morgan, R. 1999. Moderate Psychological Pressure: The Scandinavian Way? *Kritisk Juss* 26: 201–204.

Platek, M. 2013. Poland: The Political Legacy and Penal Practice. In *Punishment in Europe: A Critical Anatomy of Penal Systems*, ed. V. Ruggiero and M. Ryan. Basingstoke: Palgrave Macmillan.

Pratt, J. 2008. Scandinavian Exceptionalism in an Era of Penal Excess: Part 1: The Nature and Roots of Scandinavian Exceptionalism. *British Journal of Criminology* 48: 119–137.

Pratt, J., and A. Eriksson. 2011. 'Mr. Larsson Is Walking Out Again'. The Origins and Development of Scandinavian Prison Systems. *Australian & New Zealand Journal of Criminology* 44: 7–23.

Smith, P.S. 2012. A Critical Look at Scandinavian Exceptionalism: Welfare State Theories, Penal Populism and Prison Conditions in Denmark and Scandinavia. In *Penal Exceptionalism? Nordic Prison Policy and Practice*, ed. T. Ugelvik and J. Dullum. London: Routledge.

**Jonas Visschers** is a Research Fellow at the Leuven Institute of Criminology (LINC), KU Leuven, Belgium.

**Tom Daems** is Associate Professor of Criminology at the Leuven Institute of Criminology (LINC), KU Leuven, Belgium.

# The Future of Europe in Prisons

Tom Daems and Luc Robert

## 1 Weighing in on Europe's Impact on Prisons

One key issue in this book concerns the influence or impact the European dimension has on domestic prison systems. In definitional terms, impact can be considered as a force exerted by European institutions such as the Committee for the Prevention of Torture (CPT), the European Court of Human Rights (ECtHR) and others on domestic prison systems. Impact can then range from no effect to full impact, with a large continuum between both extremes.

Furthermore, assessing the impact of European institutions on domestic prison systems is a very broad endeavour. On some topics, for some issues, in some domains, impact will be straightforward and direct,

T. Daems (✉)
Leuven Institute of Criminology (LINC), KU Leuven, Leuven, Belgium

L. Robert
National Institute of Forensic Sciences and Criminology (NICC), Brussels, Belgium



T. Daems, L. Robert (eds.), *Europe in Prisons*, Palgrave Studies in Prisons and Penology, DOI 10.1007/978-3-319-62250-7_12

while for others, there will be little or no impact, or an indirect or unclear impact of the European dimension per se. This further complicates the picture. Thus, when the focus is put on particular topics or domains, impact can be seen to be different according to the topic that is treated.

This is clearly shown in the chapters of this collection. In fact, most chapters illustrate strong variability within domestic systems along this continuum and dependent on the issues (e.g. Daems 2017). In all country-specific chapters and in the comparative chapter on Norway, Poland and Spain by Visschers and Daems, a nuanced take on impact is clearly present, as it is in the chapters by Anagnostou and Skleparis and by Vander Beken.

At the one end of the continuum, the impact of the European dimension is inexistent or very limited. For example, CPT recommendations can be vertically classified or neglected when they fly in the face of long-standing practices or collide with underlying assumptions or beliefs. In Austria, this is shown when the CPT recommends the prison system should revisit its policy about carrying firearms by staff in prison. The authorities rejected the CPT's recommendation. In Norway, in spite of CPT remarks that go against having metal bars meant for handcuffing detainees to the wall in police detention cells, police manuals still prescribe having these metal bars. Similar observations apply to other types of 'soft law', such as the Recommendations by the Council of Europe. Cid and Andreu point out that some Council of Europe Recommendations, such as the recommendation about conditional release, are not respected or followed up in Spain, which to them illustrates how gaps between European prison policies and Spanish prison policy continue to exist. Even for judgments by the ECtHR, which are higher on the ladder than the soft law sources, the impact can remain very limited and—temporarily—be kept off. Anagnostou and Skleparis show this in their analysis. Almost three quarters of the judgments in their database has not been implemented at the cut-off date for the study, and for the closed cases, they observe an average time to implementation of nearly 6 years. States can procrastinate in implementing the ECtHR judgments, and this lag risks hollowing out the credibility and thus also the effectiveness of the ECtHR as a guardian of European fundamental human rights.

The European dimension often does exert at least some influence on domestic prison systems, and this is where things become more complex. Impact can occur in a direct manner, with an arrow that points from the European dimension to the domestic system; the European dimension then is an important cause or driver of prison reform. A straightforward case is the situation in Albania, where the country's application for membership of the EU has been met with a number of human rights-related requirements that affect Albanian prisons. Albanian membership of the EU is dependent on fulfilling the priorities set out by the EU. In terms of its endemic problem with prison crowding, Pali and Vocaj interestingly mention that 'new institutions have been constructed with financial support mainly from the European Union'—which, in many ways, is quite curious, as some member states struggle with the endemic problem of prison crowding too, without many EU-related consequences, let alone that it is being met with financing new institutions within those member states. Another clear type of impact comes from the European Court of Human Rights' judgments (e.g. the chapters by Anagnostou and Skleparis and by Daems and Robert). In case of a violation, the direct impact might remain limited to the individual case and its resolution of the violation. In case of a pilot judgment, the impact of the ECtHR is likely to affect domestic practice and policies by forcing the country to at the very least address the structural issues identified by the ECtHR and discuss the judgment's implementation in the Council of Ministers.

Yet, when the European dimension is impacting upon a domestic prison system, this can also occur in a much less straightforward or indirect way. Analytically, it makes it harder to identify what the exact influence of the European dimension is. As shown by Bicknell and Evans in their excavation of the complexity in prison monitoring instances, the CPT has informed the setting-up of the UN Subcommittee for the Prevention of Torture (SPT). Furthermore, the SPT has adopted or borrowed in important ways from the CPT and has refrained from formal standard setting. This potentially reinforces the influence of the CPT, in that (so far) no competitive explicit standards are set and that some degree of alignment among international monitoring bodies pushes forward the standards and the agenda already developed by the CPT. This is but one example. Other examples show how the European dimension can serve as a springboard for change, without being the ultimate driver or cause of the change per se. Ireland's stance related to prisoner voting provides an excellent example. As Hamilton discusses, it was the ECtHR decision of Hirst v. UK that became a catalyst in bringing about change; prisoners were not formally disenfranchised, but their lack of practical means to be able to vote had the same end result. The ECtHR judgment of Hirst v. UK created a 'momentum for change through political rather than legal channels' in Ireland and eventually facilitated legislative reforms. Hamilton remarks how the 'desire amongst Irish political representatives to bring Ireland into line with European norms' may have helped push forward this legislation, alongside other sources. European institutions can thus conflate with leading ideas in a jurisdiction; they can serve as a catalyst or facilitator for change, as a source of authority, and so on.

A further consideration is the locus of the impact: European institutions can extend their influence beyond the remit of the Council of Europe or the European Union. Interestingly, countries that are not yet part of the EU and that are willing to join may go a long way towards adopting European standards, including human rights-related standards that affect prisons. The chapter on Albania shows how EU candidacy has pushed the authorities to tackle a series of well-known problems in Albanian prisons. Other candidate member states such as Turkey have received similar requirements in the past. Whether it means that this causes sudden shifts in the mores of a country, is doubtful, as is suggested by what happens in Turkey. Also, the example of Vander Beken's 'Eurovision Europrisons' in Azerbaijan goes some way to show how 'window-dressing' can also be a part of the aim of jurisdictions in convincing European institutions that European standards are being respected. Whether jurisdictions respect standards or whether they try to convince others that they do, without truly adhering to those standards, is a complicated matter that requires more than the standard monitoring approaches, and as Vander Beken shows, in this regard, prison tourism could bring in complementary data. The link between the CPT and the SPT is an example of another kind, in that the CPT has to some extent helped mould the SPT and that many of the CPT experts have later gone on to take up a position with the SPT, as Bicknell and Evans point out. This could also lead to a type of

'Europeanisation' of the SPT and its functioning, with potentially positive effects on prison systems beyond Europe but also with the risks for criticisms about Euro-centrism in its wake.

## 2 What Future for Europe in Prisons?

In the introduction to this volume, we highlighted that most chapters in this book focus on the ECtHR and the CPT. It seems plausible that both institutions will continue dominating the European scene for the foreseeable future but, at the same time, it would be unwise to restrict future reflections to these two key players. Indeed, some of the chapters in this book invite us to think more broadly about the meaning of 'Europe' in prisons. The chapter by Bicknell and Evans on the role of Optional Protocol to the Convention against Torture (OPCAT) in a European context is therefore tremendously important. Indeed, as they argue, OPCAT enriches but also complexifies the landscape of prison monitoring in Europe significantly. Moreover, the UN's renewed interest in prison issues following the 2015 revision of the Standard Minimum Rules for the Treatment of Prisoners (the so-called Mandela Rules) should give further impetus to think more imaginatively about the wider context of Europe in prisons. How do global influences impact on Europe and its prisons? Or, more fundamentally, what is the place of prisons—and how do prisons look like—in a truly cosmopolitan Europe?

But also within the borders of Europe, there is still considerable room for further research and reflection. One key actor that should definitely receive much more attention in future debate on Europe in prisons is the EU. The EU's role in this area goes much further than the question whether third countries (see the chapter on Albania) could become a member of the EU. In its 2011 green paper *Strengthening mutual trust in the European judicial area—A Green Paper on the application of EU criminal justice legislation in the field of detention*, the European Commission highlighted that detention conditions and prison management are the prime responsibility of member states, but that it is also interested in this issue '...because of the central importance of mutual recognition of judicial decisions for the area of freedom, security and justice' (European

Commission 2011: 2). Detention conditions are important in order to promote mutual trust and ensure the smooth functioning of mutual recognition instruments (such as the Council Framework Decisions on the European Arrest Warrant, the transfer of prisoners, mutual recognition of alternative sanctions and probation and the European Supervision Order). The EU, then, should become involved in prison matters in order to enhance mutual confidence and to avoid future cooperation in the judicial area being hampered by prison conditions that are below standard (Daems 2013).

However, this 2011 expression of interest in prisons by the European Commission was not followed by a concrete policy or legislative initiative to harmonize and improve detention conditions within the EU. Against this background, it is particularly interesting to observe how the EU Court of Justice recently stepped in. In an important judgment of 5 April 2016 which dealt with the European Arrest Warrant, the Court of Justice argues the following:

> …where the judicial authority of the executing Member State is in possession of evidence of a real risk of inhuman or degrading treatment of individuals detained in the issuing Member State…that judicial authority is bound to assess the existence of that risk when it is called upon to decide on the surrender to the authorities of the issuing Member State of the individual sought by a European arrest warrant. The consequence of the execution of such a warrant must not be that that individual suffers inhuman or degrading treatment.[1]

In other words, an (executing) EU member state cannot turn a blind eye on poor detention conditions in another (issuing) EU member state when the latter requests the surrender of an individual; mutual trust is therefore not blind trust. It would take us too far to discuss the details of this judgment here in-depth (see e.g. Bovend'Eerdt 2016; Fair Trials 2016; Gáspár-Szilágyi 2016), but the implications for the future of Europe in prisons seem to be obvious and potentially far-reaching: we may see the beginning of a European 'peer review'—system whereby (executing) EU member states are expected to assess the quality of prison conditions in (issuing) EU member states. Such a (horizontal) 'peer review' system (where the primary responsibility for determining whether prison conditions violate fundamental human rights is being transferred to domestic judicial authorities) is very different from the top-down (vertical) *modus operandus* that characterizes the CPT and the ECtHR.

Given the current political climate in Europe and the ongoing discussions on the future of Europe, it would undoubtedly feel strange to conclude this volume without briefly addressing the following question: does Europe in prisons *überhaupt* have a future? 2016 has been a bleak year for Europe. The UK has chosen to leave the EU. In Hungary, Poland and Russia, core European values and human rights have been deeply challenged. At the end of 2016, *The New York Times* published a remarkable article written by the European Commissioner for Human Rights. Thorbjorn Jagland expressed his concern about how the ECtHR and the European Convention '…have come under attack in a growing number of European countries' (Jagland 2016). And, indeed, as Jagland highlighted: 'In 2017, voters in a range of countries, including France, Germany, the Netherlands and now possibly Italy, will go to the polls'. It should be clear that the outcome of these elections, as well as further developments with respect to Brexit and human rights challenges in East and Central Europe, will determine the European debate and agenda for the months and years to come. Obviously, we do not have a crystal ball to predict the future. But, at the same time, it seems clear to us that dismantling this European human rights edifice, which has been so important for prisons in Europe, will not be as easy as some of its most fierce critics may hope. Penology in Europe is certainly entering uncertain times; but, at the same time, these will be interesting and challenging times for anyone with an interest in penology and Europe.

## Notes

1. EU Court of Justice (Grand Chamber) Judgment 5 April 2016 in Joined Cases Pál Aranyosi (C-404/15) and Robert Căldăraru (C-659/15 PPU), para 88.

# Literature

Bovend'Eerdt, K. 2016. The Joined Cases Aranyosi and Căldăraru: A New Limit to the Mutual Trust Presumption in the Area of Freedom, Security, and Justice? *Utrecht Journal of International and European Law* 32 (83): 112–120.

Daems, T. 2013. Punishment and the Question of Europe. In *European Penology?* ed. T. Daems, D. van Zyl Smit, and S. Snacken. Oxford: Hart Publishing.

———. 2017. Slaves and Statues: Torture Prevention in Contemporary Europe. *British Journal of Criminology* 57 (3): 627–643.

European Commission. 2011. *Strengthening Mutual Trust in the European Judicial Area—A Green Paper on the Application of EU Criminal Justice Legislation in the Field of Detention*. COM(2011) 327, June 14.

Fair Trials. 2016. Fair Trials Welcomes CJEU Judgement on European Arrest Warrant and Detention Conditions. April 6. https://www.fairtrials.org/fair-trials-welcomes-cjeu-judgement-eaw-detention-conditions/

Gáspár-Szilágyi, S. 2016. Joined Cases Aranyosi and Căldăraru: Converging Human Rights Standards, Mutual Trust and a New Ground for Postponing a European Arrest Warrant. *European Journal of Crime, Criminal Law and Criminal Justice* 24 (2/3): 197–219.

Jagland, T. 2016. Don't Caricature Europe's Court. *The New York Times*, December 12.

**Tom Daems** is an Associate Professor of Criminology at the Leuven Institute of Criminology (LINC), KU Leuven, Belgium.

**Luc Robert** is a Research Fellow at the National Institute of Forensic Sciences and Criminology (NICC), Brussels, Belgium.

# Index[1]



[1] Note: Page number followed by "n" denote footnotes.



T. Daems, L. Robert (eds.), *Europe in Prisons*, Palgrave Studies in Prisons and Penology, DOI 10.1007/978-3-319-62250-7

S



T



U

Kolibri 360 GmbH
Ferdinand-Jühlke-Straße 7
99095 Erfurt, Deutschland
produktsicherheit@kolibri360.de